Development in early childhood

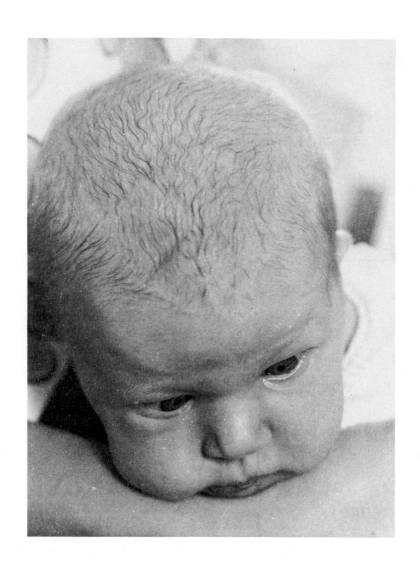

Development in early childhood

SECOND EDITION

D. Bruce Gardner
Colorado State University

HARPER & ROW, Publishers
New York, Evanston, San Francisco, London

Sponsoring Editor: Mary Lou Mosher
Project Editor: David Nickol
Designer: Frances Torbert Tilley
Production Supervisor: Bernice Krawczyk

Standard Book Number: 06–042231–9
Library of Congress Catalog Card Number: 73–11592

CONTENTS

Preface   xi

Part 1 How we study children 1

One   The field of child development   3

Two   Observation of children   32

Part II Foundations of development 61

Three   The nature and sources of development   63

Four   Development during infancy   95

Part III Aspects of development in the early years 135

Five   Physical growth   137

Six   Achieving body control   169

Seven   Communicating with others   193

Eight   The development of intelligence   228

Nine   Achieving selfhood: the personality of the young child   264

Part IV Agents of socialization 291

Ten   The child's cultural heritage   293

Eleven   The child and his family   320

Twelve   Schools for young children   349

Index   387

TABLES

1.1 Developmental schedules   12

2.1 Illustration of statistical data   56

3.1 Interaction of heredity and environment   81

4.1 Birth weight by maternal age and ethnic group   101

5.1 Effects of poverty on child height and weight   142

5.2 Comparative body sizes of groups of preschool children studied
in different parts of the world   144

10.1 Composition of households and courtyards in
six communities   304

11.1 Interactions in the consequences of warmth vs.
hostility and restrictiveness vs. permissiveness   336

12.1 Trends in enrollment of children in school programs   352

FIGURES

1.1 Child development in relation to other disciplines 22

3.1 Bodily proportions of infant and adult 65

3.2 Relation of prenatal dietary rating to the physical condition of the infant at birth 82

3.3 A diagrammatic representation of the directional tendency in physical and motor development 84

3.4 Major types of postnatal growth of the various parts and organs 87

4.1 Growth of a pair of identical twin boys 96

4.2 Motor sequence leading to upright locomotion 112–113

4.3 Developmental sequence in the achievement of prehension from 16 to 52 weeks 114

4.4 Diagrammatic representation of the development of emotion 125

5.1 Jackson-Kelly growth chart for boys, age 0 to 6 140

5.2 Jackson-Kelly growth chart for girls, age 0 to 6 141

5.3 Relation of mean height and weight among contemporary groups of children age 4 years 145

5.4 Height of boys related to maturation rate 146

5.5 Height of girls related to maturation rate 148

5.6 Standard x-ray photographs of wrists and hands 151

6.1 Increase in right-handedness with age 183

6.2 Percentages of each morning spent by a nursery child using a climbing frame 189

7.1 Chronological aspects of language growth 206

8.1 Changes in intelligence test scores of five male subjects 235

8.2 Schematic representation of intelligent behavior 245

8.3 Children's matrix problem 257

8.4 Results of children's performance on matrix problem 258

9.1 Relationships among early stages in the development of selfhood 272

12.1 Trends in enrollment of young children in school 353

PREFACE

When the First Edition of *Development in Early Childhood* was published in 1964, two main reasons were given for preparation of the book: (1) to provide a general introduction to the professional field of child development, and (2) to present a concise summary of development in the years before age 6.

These remain the primary purposes and the essential justification for preparation of a revised edition. It is my conviction, now as in 1964, that there is a need for a book that places the field of child development into perspective in the context of related disciplines and in the context of our current concerns for the welfare of children.

It is also my conviction that it is possible to write about significant aspects of developmental processes in early childhood in ways that are meaningful to students without extensive background in social or natural sciences or in research methods and statistics.

This is not presented primarily as a book on early childhood education per se, although a serious effort has been made to incorporate new material from this rapidly growing field. However, it is intended to provide a child development base for understanding and working with the young child at home; in school; in the child development center, the nursery, or day care center; or in whatever setting he or she may be found.

Similarly, the book is not intended primarily as a treatise on the exceptional child or on pathological processes in early development. Nevertheless, it is hoped that those who would aspire to work with exceptional children, while recognizing them as variations on the themes of normal development, would find useful support and encouragement here.

The explosive changes that have occurred during the past decade in the field of child development and in programming for young children necessitate extensive revision and updating. Much new material on infancy and early stimulation, social learning processes in childhood, cognitive development, early childhood education curriculum and teaching strategies, and new alternatives in child care arrangements as well as in family relationships have been brought into the revision. Newer insights into the effects of poverty on human development have also been incorporated. We have learned much and have yet much more to learn about relationships among people of varying ethnicity; some of these insights and issues are reflected in the revision.

No author of a textbook in child development should pretend to stand alone as the source of the ideas he has attempted to set forth. I am indebted to large numbers of students, teachers, colleagues, and especially children, who have served to test old ideas and to inspire new ones. More directly, I am indebted to Don Rapp and M. Kay Stickle, who gave helpful suggestions in preparation of the manuscript. Sincere appreciation is expressed also to the many authors and publishers who extended permission to use quoted material and results of their research.

This book is dedicated to the memory of my parents, Joseph and Martha Gardner. Their lives were the first to instruct me in the larger meanings of human development.

D. BRUCE GARDNER

PICTURE CREDITS

Cover   Jan Lukas, Rapho Guillumette

Frontispiece   Horst Schafer, Photo Trends

Part I   Photographic Laboratory, Public Information Service, Ball State University

Chapter 1   George Roos

Chapter 2   Inger McCabe, Rapho Guillumette

Part II   Jan Lukas, Rapho Guillumette

Chapter 3   George Roos

Chapter 4   Horst Schafer, Photo Trends

Part III   George Roos

Chapter 5   Sandra Turner

Chapter 6   George Roos

Chapter 7   George Roos

Chapter 8   William Simmons, Ford Foundation

Chapter 9   Board of Education, St. Louis, Mo.

Part IV   Don Connors

Chapter 10   George Roos

Chapter 11   Alice Kandell, Rapho Guillumette

Chapter 12   Carl Purcell, National Education Association

Tailpiece   The Bank Street College of Education

PART 1
How
we
study
children

Part I, consisting of the first two chapters, is a unit devoted to the professional and technical discipline of child development. There is some consideration of how the current approach to the study of the child has evolved—gradually—as an accompaniment to the general development of scientific thought and as a part of our total cultural evolution. The roots of child development in other disciplines and the theoretical foundations of the field are described.

Part I also stresses some differences between casual observation and scientific observation of children. One's competence as an observer, as well as one's enthusiasm for understanding the nature of childhood, can be enhanced greatly by some preliminary attention to strategies for observation of child behavior. Finally, Part I gives consideration to the fundamental professional concern for ethics in dealing with children and families, and the professional responsibilities of the child development specialist for safeguarding the privacy and personal integrity of the child and his family.

CHAPTER ONE
The field of child development

What is child development?

Where has this active young professional field come from?

What are the relationships between this and other disciplines and sciences?

What is the work of the modern child development specialist?

Society's concern—and lack of concern—for its children over the centuries makes a fascinating study in contrasts and contradictions. Man's interest in his own offspring, and his relationships with them, form a historical theme with infinite variation. Perhaps man's notion of the nature of childhood has always been a reflection of what he regards himself to be, as man. These notions have undergone dramatic changes over the years—no less revolutionary than those we have witnessed in science and technology.

Some notes from history

Certainly the well-being of children as individuals has not always been central in the thinking of adults. In some periods of history, for example, societies have accepted infanticide as a normal practice. In ancient Sparta any deformed child was killed, as the state itself forbade the raising of such children, whereas in Athens it was up to the parents to decide whether they would accept and raise a child or destroy it at birth. In ancient times in the Orient, the practice of infanticide was particularly common with female babies, while abandonment and exposure of infants to the elements was not uncommon in the Greek colonies. Coincidentally, as Payne (1916) has noted, the theme of the abandoned infant who was found and reared by someone, and who later became an outstanding figure in the society, was a popular one in the dramatic writings of the time.

Ariès (1962) writes that, in the Middle Ages, European civilization was marked by an unusual carelessness of its children. Ariès' account of the relationship between adult and child in medieval Europe provides a startling insight into the assumptions which that society must have made about the nature of the child. He notes, for example, that no attempts were made to shield children from sex, since no one assumed that children were innocent in the first place. That artists portrayed the child as a miniature adult is held by Ariès to reflect the attitude that generally permeated the medieval world. The child was apparently pretty much thrown into the adult world by the age of six or seven, at which time he was supposed to get along without his mother or mother-substitute.

The concept of individual differences among children—so central in our modern philosophy of child training and education—was, for all practical purposes, nonexistent during the Middle Ages. Yet, if we go back to philosophical writings from ancient Greek civilization, we can find evidences of an awareness of individual differences. Socrates had ideas for the organization of society based on differences among children, with some being fit for training along one line, and others being suited to quite different educational experiences. Plato also recognized basic differences among children with respect to aptitudes and talent. In his writings he encouraged the idea of discovering these individual talents at a child's early age and providing special training to develop them to the fullest.

Down through the ages, however, our ways of dealing with children have been influenced not only by philosophical considerations, but also by economic demands, military and political affairs, religious precepts, birth and death rates, and by famine and disease. Without doubt there were economic considerations in the heavy employment of children in the labor force prior to the middle of the nineteenth century. But, as Kessen (1965) has observed, it was the emergence of a new concept of the nature of the child, through the efforts of such men as Anthony Ashley Cooper in the British Parliament, which led to legislation to protect children from exploitation. Our notion of the fundamental nature of the child, then, has been a pervasive, underlying determinant of our treatment of him.

That this is still true is reflected in our modern concerns for children in poverty. At times and places the child of poverty has been treated as something less than human. It is not merely our modern awareness that the seeds of genius may be found in children of the poor as well as the rest of society; it is, rather, our sensitivity to the essential humanness of the child, whatever his social and economic circumstances may be, that forces our social conscience and demands humane treatment of all children.

Speculative, nonscientific approaches to the study of the child have been the rule throughout the bulk of recorded history, whenever man has concerned himself with the nature of children. Anything approaching a scientific outlook on the child is a very recent innovation. John Locke, the English philosopher, stressed in his writings the importance of experience and training in the child's life. When he wrote that the child's mind was, at birth, like a blank tablet upon which his experiences would write his personality, he had, unfortunately, no scientific evidence either to support or to refute his viewpoint.

Rousseau, almost a century later, still had little more to guide him than his own intellect and reasoning processes. He concluded that the newborn child is essentially unspoiled and natural, and that civilization has powerful distorting effects on his personality. These in turn prevent him from achieving his potential of goodness and nobility.

Early scientific approaches
to the study of the child

Probably the first significant efforts to get away from the speculative, philosophical approach and to turn more toward a child study based on direct observation were initiated by the early child biographers of the nineteenth century. Both Darwin and Preyer kept careful notes on the development and behavior of individual children over a period of months and years.

These early biographers did not, in themselves, provide much important information about children. They did, however, inaugurate a method of child study based on direct observation of behavior and characterized by repeated observations over a period of time. According to Dennis (1949), they served as a foundation for a science of child study and, in the process, raised important questions that were to be answered later through scientific investigations.

Anderson (1956) reports that it was in the late nineteenth and early twentieth centuries when the first truly scientific investigations of children were carried out. Two of the most important persons to stimulate the growth of a science of child development were G. Stanley Hall in America, and Alfred Binet in France. Each of these men was in his own way concerned with the central question of the *causes* of human behavior. Their achievements marked a turning point in our relationships with children, for their writings, and the writings of those who followed in their footsteps, called to our attention the need to understand the underlying causes of children's behavior.

Hall's contributions included the development of questionnaires to gain information about child behavior. In 1883 he published *The Content of Children's Minds* (cf. Dennis 1949), a study of concepts held by children upon their entrance in school. Binet's professional contributions were many, including the development of a method for testing the intelligence of children. His first intelligence scale, published in collaboration with Simon in 1905, underwent a series of revisions, which led to the development of the Stanford-Binet Scales in America. From Binet's work has been derived much of our American tradition of intelligence testing.

Perhaps more importantly, the work of such pioneer scientists led to the conviction that statements and generalizations about child behavior must be based on observable evidence. An outcome of this has been a heavy reliance, especially in America, on the use of standardized, controlled situations in which a child may be observed in order to detect his special reactions. From these beginnings, moreover, a revolutionary way of thinking of the child emerged, and has become a part of society itself as well as a part of scientific thought.

The dramatic change was from thinking of the child as a miniature adult, whose behavior was primarily a matter of his moral fiber and will, to thinking of him as having certain psychological resources at his disposal. These resources were limited both by his unique inheritance and his maturational level. Clearly, adult relationships with children become different when society ceases to hold the child morally responsible for his psychological condition and begins to think of him as an individual with unique properties to be understood.

This trend of thought was to undergo considerable modification with the addition of the notion of basic psychological needs on the part of a child, the satisfaction of which leads to enhanced development, and the frustration of which leads to faulty development. Thus the child's environment gradually emerged, in our thinking, as the setting that shaped the personality development of the child through satisfying, or failing to satisfy, the basic growth needs of the child. Such a conviction became a cornerstone in the thinking of many modern writers.

But we must remember how recently, historically speaking, these changes in thought have occurred. This should suggest to the thoughtful student that the current approaches to the study of the child, to which we now turn, represent emerging and evolving ideas subject to continuous revision and improvement.

Current approaches
to the study of the child

In this section we will examine the basic ways in which scholars and scientists have viewed the child during the present century. For convenience, five major streams of thought will be described: (1) the behavioristic approach, (2) the normative-descriptive approach, (3) the field-theory approach, (4) the psychoanalytic approach, and (5) the cognitive-developmental approach. For each of these major streams of thought, the work of one or two writers whose contributions have been central in shaping a modern conception of the child will be described briefly.

It should be understood that these, and other approaches which could be mentioned, were not historically independent of each other, nor do they operate in isolation from each other today. Historically, these developments were overlapping and concurrent rather than sequential. They should be considered as illustrations of the varying types of emphases that have been placed on the central question of the nature and causes of a child's behavior and development.

The behavioristic approach

This approach to child study can be traced to the Russian physiologist Ivan Pavlov and the American psychologist John B. Watson. Pavlov demonstrated that animals can learn—that is, acquire new habits—by forming new associations between a stimulus and a response. His experimental subjects were laboratory animals, especially dogs, who learned to salivate at the sound of a bell, thus illustrating the principle of classical conditioning.

Watson (1928) was extremely interested in such modes of learning. He saw in them the basis for much, if not all, human learning. He did not concern himself much with the basic nature of the child, apart from the influence of learning experiences. While he did recognize the importance of biological processes as a basis for human behavior, he felt that the higher level of organization was the psychological. The essential feature in the development of this higher level of human functioning was the conditioning, through experience, of new habits upon old ones. His major philosophy of child rearing is expressed by the term, "habit training."

The development of emotions serves as a good illustration of this point of view. Watson held that the complex and varied emotional behavior of growing children and adults could be accounted for by experiences that had associated a gradually increasing variety of stimuli with the primitive emotional responses of fear, rage, and love. Watson's view was that these three basic emotions were present at birth, and that they were gradually elaborated, through conditioning, into the complicated pattern of emotional responses of the adult. Indeed, for Watson, the child's total personality was essentially the outcome of his unique conditioning experiences.

Watson was a spokesman for objectivity, both in the laboratories of child psychology and in the practical, everyday care of children by parents. He was outspoken in his criticism of the sentimental, as this passage from one of his books makes clear:

> There is a sensible way of treating children. Treat them as though they were young adults. Dress them, bathe them with care and circumspection. Let your behavior always be objective and kindly firm. Never hug and kiss them, never let them sit in your lap. If you must, kiss them once on the forehead when they say good night. Shake hands with them in the morning. Give them a pat on the head if they have made an extraordinarily good job of a difficult task. Try it out. In a week's time you will find how easy it is to be perfectly objective with your child and at the same time kindly. You will be utterly ashamed of the mawkish, sentimental way you have been handling it. (1928, pp. 81–82)

Today's parents smile at such words of advice, for they have also been influenced by other lines of thought which stress the importance of close affectional ties between parent and child. At the same time, we should not underestimate the significance of Watson's contributions to our modern concepts of the child. He made us aware of the need to study children objectively, and of the vital role of learning processes in shaping the child's growth.

At present, however, relatively more emphasis in the behavioristic tradition is placed on *operant,* or *instrumental* conditioning, than on the classical conditioning studied by Pavlov and stressed by Watson. While *classical* conditioning deals with relatively passive associations formed between stimulus and response, operant conditioning is concerned with the organism's (child, adult, or animal) behaviors and the events that occur in the environment immediately following those behaviors.

Some events are *reinforcing,* that is, they have the effect of increasing the likelihood of the behavior being repeated. Thus, the emergence of complex behavior patterns which represent the personality of the child can be described primarily by a set of reinforcement contingencies—the events that shape and maintain the behaviors of the individual child. Rewards (both tangible and intangible) are regarded as reinforcing events, and when provided for a given class of behavior on a child's part, increase the likelihood that he will repeat that class of behaviors.

Extensive and elaborate descriptions of the ways in which the organism responds to the reinforcement contingencies of its environment have been outlined in careful, exhaustive, and scholarly detail by B. F. Skinner (1938, 1953), and these have been further elaborated and applied to a wide range of problems of child development by his students. It was Skinner, also, who devised the teaching machine and the educational strategy of programmed instruction. Far-reaching implications of his approach—not only for the development of individual children, but for the shaping of an ideal society—have also been outlined by Skinner (1971). In Chapter Twelve, we will review some ways in which his principles of operant learning are being employed in some programs for education of the young child.

The normative-descriptive approach

A second major source of our current knowledge of children has been those scientists who have painstakingly observed large numbers of children, individually as well as in groups, and who have carefully catalogued the behavior typical of each age level. Arnold Gesell and his colleagues and students have provided a wealth of information on development from conception to adolescence, concentrating on motor behavior, personal-social behavior, language, and adaptive or problem-solving behavior. In each of these areas, Gesell and his coworkers (1947, 1949) described the kinds of behavior that might reasonably be expected of normal children of each age level. These behavior descriptions, or "age norms," provided useful reference points by which the growth and development of a child can be described and understood more fully.

Table 1.1, taken from the work of Gesell, illustrates this kind of information. In this table, the brief statements under each major area of growth describe the typical responses, in clinical examinations, of children at the age of 24 months. The table also illustrates the patterning of behavior at ages immediately preceding and following the key age of 24 months, enabling the examiner to establish more clearly the developmental level of the child he is examining.

Comparable information was prepared by Gesell for other ages, beginning with early infancy. Thus it is possible to compare

TABLE 1.1. Developmental Schedules

21 Months	Key age: 24 Months	30 Months
	Motor	
Walks: squats in play (* . . .)	Walks: runs well, no falling	Walks: (dem.) on tiptoe
Stairs: walks down, 1 hand held (*24m)	Stairs: walks up & down alone	Jumps: with both feet
Stairs: walks up, holding rail (*24m)		Stards: tries stand on 1 foot
Large ball: (dem.) kicks (*24m)	Large ball: (no dem.) kicks	M. Cubes: tower of 8
M. Cubes: tower of 5–6	M. Cubes: tower of 6–7	Drawing: holds crayon by fingers
	Book: turn pages singly	
	Adaptive	
M. Cubes: tower of 5–6	M. Cubes: tower of 6–7	M. Cubes: tower of 8
M. Cubes: imitates pushing train (*24m)	M. Cubes: aligns 2 or more, train (*36m)	M. Cubes: adds chimney to train
Formbd: places 2–3 blocks	Drawing: imitates V stroke	Drawing: 2 or more strokes for cross (*36m)
Perf. box: inserts corner of sq. (*24m)	Drawing: imitates circular stroke	Drawing: imitates V and H strokes
Perf. box: retrieves ball	Formbd: places single blocks on (*30m)	Color forms: places 1
	Formbd: adapts after 4 trials (*30m)	Formbd: inserts 3 blocks on presenta.
	Perf. box: inserts sq.	Formbd: adapts repeatedly, error (*36m)
		Digits: repeats 2 (1 of 3 trials)

Language

Vocab: 20 words
Speech: combines 2–3 words spontan. (*24m)
Ball: 3 directions

Speech: jargon discarded
Speech: 3-word sentence

Speech: uses *I, me, you*
Picture cd: names 3 or more
Picture cd: identifies 5 or more
Test obj: names 2
Ball: 4 directions

Name: gives full name
Picture cd: names 5

Picture cd: identifies 7
Test obj: gives use

Personal-Social

Feeding: handles cup well
Commun: asks for food, toilet, drink

Commun: echoes 2 or more last words (*24m)
Commun: pulls person to show (*24m)

Feeding: inhibits turning spoon
Toilet: dry at night, taken up (*36m)
Toilet: verbal. needs fairly consist. (*42m)
Dressing: pulls on simple garment

Commun: verbalizes immed. experiences (*. . .)
Commun: refers to self by name (*30m)
Commun: compreh. & asks for "another"

Play: hands cup full of cubes
Play: domestic mimicry
Play: parallel play predom. (*42m)

Commun: refers to self by pronoun rather than name

Commun: repetit. in speech and other activ. (*36m)

Play: pushes toy with good steering

Play: helps put things away

Play: can carry breakable obj.

SOURCE: Gesell, A., and Amatruda, C. S. *Developmental Diagnosis*, 2nd ed. New York: Paul B. Hoeber, Inc., 1947, p. 79.

the growth of an individual child with a set of published norms, which are still used by some pediatricians and child development specialists. Being able to describe the growth of an individual child as normal, fast, or slow is only one of the features resulting from this normative-descriptive approach. Another feature has been the emphasis on stages of readiness of the child. Each stage was viewed by Gesell as having its characteristic pattern of mental and physical organization, of social and emotional behavior, and of play interests and activities. Each stage also has its characteristic degree of readiness to profit from new experience and from kinds of guidance and disciplinary measures used by adults. This sequential emergence of readiness on the part of a child was determined largely, in Gesell's view, by internal factors of heredity and maturation, and the child guidance implications of this view were that the child should be given experiences in keeping with his level of functioning.

The normative approach enabled us to set up reasonable levels of expectation for children. It also helped to overcome the lingering view of the child as a miniature adult, and fostered the contrasting view that children are individuals who require, at each stage of growth, experiences appropriate to their levels of functioning. Further, it helped us accept the normality of "problem behavior" at certain stages of a child's career. Recognition of the normality of the well-known negativism of children at age 2½, for example, has, if nothing else, allowed harried parents to commiserate and feel a touch of pride from the "obviously normal" behavior of their child, although that pride is mingled with the frustration inherent in living with a determinedly autonomous 2½-year-old!

Equally important to the contribution of providing for comparison of the development of a child with standards of normal progress was the comparison of rates of progress in different aspects of an individual child's growth. That is, his mental age may be greater than his social age, or vice versa, and his degree of emotional maturity may lag behind his physical maturation. While no two aspects of his development may be precisely even in their development, a child might be viewed as perfectly normal in the sense that his growth and behavior are adequate, healthy, and appropriate *for him.*

While the normative-descriptive approach has made marked contributions to our knowledge of children, it has certain limitations of which the student should be aware. Norms, as Gesell himself pointed out, are merely statistical averages and, as such, tell us nothing about the healthiness of the behavior. Knowing that by 12 months the average infant has two words in his vocabulary, for example, does not provide us with a reasonable goal to work toward in dealing with any particular infant. If we operated on that assumption, we might just as logically conclude that we should work toward making our child negative and uncooperative at age 2½, whether he wants to be or not, since that is the norm!

Another kind of limitation is that this approach by itself tells us little or nothing about the basic causes of child behavior. Its contribution in this respect is that it has raised many important questions about behavior and development. However, the assumption that behavior emerges largely as a function of age and the maturation process does not provide a satisfactory explanation for the modern student of child development. To say that a 3-year-old behaves the way she does because she is 3 should leave the student with an uncomfortable feeling that we have merely gone around in a circle without explaining anything. To gain a better appreciation of this limitation, we should consider other approaches to the study of the child, some of which have attempted deeper levels of explanation of child behavior.

The field theory approach

This stream of thought can be attributed largely to the brilliant work of the psychologist Kurt Lewin. Although others before and since his time were instrumental in organizing field theory, it was Lewin (1935) who was the leader in relating the theory to the development of the child.

Like Watson, Lewin was concerned with the environment. However, while Watson appeared to ignore the internal growth potentials within a child and stressed only the effects of external forces, Lewin argued that a child was more than a passive receiver of stimulation from the outside. In his view, the child's personality included numerous psychological systems that interacted with his environment in an increasingly complex manner. These psychological systems had their own sources of energy for initiating behavior; however, the form of the behavior was always affected by conditions in the environment.

Lewin believed that the environment included objects and persons having powers of attraction and repulsion for the child. He likened these forces of attraction and repulsion to the dynamic forces of the physical world, and attempted to explain human behavior in accordance with principles of mathematics and physics. His descriptions of conflict situations were of special interest in the understanding of the child. He described three basic kinds of conflict, all of them in terms of the interaction of the individual with his environment (1935, pp. 88–94).

1. The child is attracted, with about equal force, by two different objects. If he approaches one, it means going farther away from the other. It is comparable to the old story of the donkey that starved to death between two stacks of hay.

2. The child is caught between two forces both of which are negative and repelling and from which he would like to escape. However, to retreat from one of them means to get close to the other. An example would be a threat of punishment if he does not perform some chore that is distasteful to him. A mother tells her son that unless he "hits back" when a bigger child bullies him, she will spank him. Either prospect is unpleasant for the child.

3. The child experiences both positive forces of attraction and negative, repelling forces in interaction with a single object. A striking example most of us have observed is that of the very young child who encounters a strange animal—a rabbit, a puppy, or a cat—being held by another person. The child shows his wish to touch and stroke the animal and at the same time displays an anxious concern that it cause him no harm. So he stands perhaps a little distance away, not close enough really to touch it, and reaches his arms out as if to pet the animal.

The basic conflicts Lewin described have implications for a host of major and minor adjustment problems for children and adults of all ages. The third type of conflict, for example, has sometimes been described as ambivalence. It is illustrated whenever we have both positive and negative feelings about the same situation or about the same individual. We have come to recognize that such ambivalence is a very real and important part of the relationships between child and parent. Lewin also outlined the kinds of adjustments the individual child can make when he experiences conflicts. His theory, in short, has given us new insights into child behavior and has simultaneously enabled us to formulate a number of practical principles of child guidance.

The psychoanalytic approach

As the field of child study grew into a scientific effort to understand development and behavior of children, it was inevitable that more scholars and scientists would turn from the relatively simple problem of what children are like at different ages to the more complex "why?" questions. Lewin's approach offered one level of answer to the question of the causes of behavior. The work of Sigmund Freud, and that of his many followers, has offered another major stream of thought about the causes of behavior.

Although he was not a research scientist in the modern sense of the word, Freud's clinical studies of adult patients, using a pioneer method of recalling childhood experiences, resulted in a number of key insights into the complex role of early experience in shaping the personality. In addition, Freud (1933) developed an extensive and elaborate theory of the nature of human personality based on fundamental instincts and drives. These drives, he maintained, existed apart from the effects of experience. They were part of the natural equipment of the infant at birth, and they were the core of all human motivation. It was the effects of subsequent social experiences in the satisfaction or frustration of these drives, especially experiences with parents, that led to the formation of the adult personality. Some of these experiences satisfied the basic instincts; some led to their frustration; some had the effect of distorting instinctual strivings and resulted in the formation of faulty, neurotic behavior.

Freud made another contribution in outlining his view of the developing child. He helped us to see that human behavior, including that of children, is often motivated at an unconscious level. This was a revolutionary idea in Freud's day. Today we take it for granted that children are often unaware of the reasons for their own actions.

Freud saw human personality composed of three major divisions: (1) the *id*, the reservoir of basic energy giving rise to all forms of instinctual striving; (2) the *ego*, that part of the person concerned with, among other things, reality and the child's position in relation to the realistic elements of his world; and (3) the *super-ego*, concerned with moral values and the rightness or wrongness of behavior. Freud's concept of "psychosexual development" included the growing, increasingly complex set of relationships among these three basic elements of personality.

Some of the contributions of psychoanalytic thought to the understanding of the child have come largely through the persons who have modified the original Freudian concepts, whose impact on our current thinking about child personality is reflected in Chapter Nine. In general, it is fair to say that the thinking of the child development specialist, as well as of society at large, has been strongly influenced by the psychoanalytic approach. One of the difficulties with the approach, while it has afforded keen insights into the behavior of the child, is that it has proven exceedingly difficult to translate psychoanalytic concepts into hypotheses that can be tested in any objective, scientific manner.

The cognitive-developmental approach

Jean Piaget, a Swiss scholar whose brilliant insights into the mental activities of children have stirred the world of child development, has contributed strategies for observing perceptual and cognitive behavior, as well as a wealth of new research data in support of his far-reaching theory.

That theory is not intended to encompass all aspects of growth and development, but is best described as a theory of knowledge, since it concerns itself with the mental operations by which a child knows and understands his world. Thus it has not been regarded as a theory of personality development, in the sense of Freud's theory, nor has it focused primarily on personal-social behavior. However, Piaget's position is that cognitive, or mental, functions are not separate from the affective, or emotional; neither are these independent of biological and social interaction processes. This means that Piaget's theory of mental development does, in fact, extend its implications into aspects of child development that Americans have not traditionally regarded as "cognitive."

Piaget has delved deeply into fields other than psychology and possesses a keen knowledge of philosophy, biology, and mathematics, all of which have strongly influenced his writings about the mind of the child. Over a lifetime of experimenting, observing, questioning, and writing, he has evolved and is still revising his theory, which, as Piaget (1970) has pointed out, presupposes an initial understanding of its biological foundations before the theory itself can be fully understood.

Piaget's is a stage theory in that he sees mental organization undergoing significant changes at key points between infancy and adolescence. Each new stage brings distinctive qualities of thinking, which equip the child to deal with life tasks differently compared with previous stages.

Because Piaget's approach to the study of the child has differed radically from the American scientific tradition, his findings and theoretical insights were either discounted or ignored in this country for many years. The fact that many of his original observations were made on his own children contributed to the early skepticism with which his writings were received. In the 1950s and 1960s, however, many of his writings were translated from French into English, and American scientists have had easier access to his work.

While his methods have not utilized standard experimental procedures and he has not relied on statistical treatment of his data, Piaget's keen insights into mental processes, which have been derived from direct observation and questioning of children, have won him considerable acclaim in recent years. Since we will discuss this approach more carefully in a later chapter on intellectual development, no attempt is made here to describe the details of his theory.

Although their approaches were quite different, Watson, Gesell, Freud, Lewin, and Piaget all made significant contributions to the field of modern child study. All placed great stress on the importance of the early years in the child's life. All raised basic questions about the ways in which behavior develops, and all offered tentative answers to at least some of the questions. Many of their answers still provide fruitful insights today; other aspects of their theories have served their primary purpose in stimulating further research by students.

A modern concept
of the child

The efforts of such figures as Watson, Gesell, Lewin, Freud, and Piaget laid the groundwork for a totally new concept of the nature of the child. Through their work other scholars have gradually organized a point of view which places the growth tasks of the child in a central position. The child himself is seen as an active, dynamic agent in perceiving and making use of those elements of his world that support his growth needs, rather than as a passive or inert organism who merely becomes imprinted with the experiences he undergoes. This does not mean that there is consensus among present-day child development scientists. Indeed, there is much disagreement on many of the details of human growth and development. As Baldwin (1967) has observed, however, it is not so much that the major theories of child development are in distinct disagreement with each other as it is that they have focused their attention on somewhat different questions and aspects of the total complexity of the child.

From the rich accumulation of facts and ideas derived from these theorists, however, it is possible to discern additional themes where there is general agreement beyond the view of the child as an active, dynamic, determiner of his own world. We no longer raise serious questions as to which is more important, heredity or environment, but rather, ask more precise questions as to the ways in which hereditary and environmental forces interact to produce characteristics, qualities, and the emergence of new stages of development in a child.

We tend to perceive the child as an *open system,* as described by the biologist Bertalanffy (1967). This open system is characterized by (1) *equifinality,* that is, the same state or goal of development may be reached from different initial conditions or through different avenues; (2) *differentiation,* that is, the system becomes increasingly complex and varied and the process is directed by both inner and outer forces; (3) *self-maintenance,* that is, the capacity for generating and maintaining a continuing and more or less consistent self persists in spite of the millions of chemical and biological changes that occur constantly in the growing system; and (4) *symbolism,* which includes the idea that the human child has the capacity for generating symbolic activity and rules governing the relations among symbols. These are abstract and difficult ideas, but they represent key aspects of the view of the child, which seems to be emerging in the latter half of the twentieth century. Perhaps the most fundamental notion of all is that child development is viewed as a construction process, where all aspects of the child's personality are viewed as being constructed, largely by the child himself, out of his internal and environmental resources.

Meeting the growth needs of children, in this modern conceptualization, is not a matter of coddling the child or catering to his whims at the expense of others, but rather is a matter of providing those external supports most appropriate to the internal organization present at any given moment. Although various writers differ over the usefulness perceived in the notion of "self-development," it is fair to say that the key to the modern concept of the child is the enhancement of the child's self. The differences found in philosophy and strategy may or may not be resolved, but the notion that the ultimate objective of the field of child development is to provide an understanding of the ways and means by which a child may become all that he is capable of being appears implicit in this modern view.

Child development in relation to other professional fields

Child development as a professional field and as a specialized area of study is relatively new on the scene. As we have noted, only during the present century have we had available a reliable body of knowledge about the child; also, it has been only in the present century that society has perceived the need for the emergence of a new professional specialist who is competent in the interpretation and application of that body of knowledge. In one sense, child development is more complex because of our dependence on a variety of other basic disciplines as the source of our knowledge. One of the tasks of the field is the integration of the findings from these other disciplines—biology, genetics, nutrition, psychology, sociology, and anthropology—into a useful body of knowledge focused on the growing child. This foundation of child development in other disciplines is illustrated in Figure 1.1.

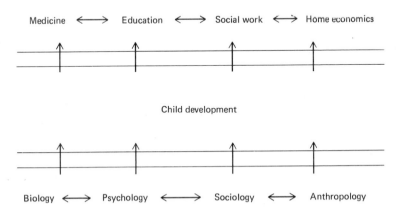

FIGURE 1.1 The relationship between child development and other disciplines.

Child development also has the function of making its integrated body of information available to a variety of practitioners, or specialists in applied services for children, including psychiatrists, educators, social welfare workers, and home economists. This section will attempt to describe very briefly each of several sources of child development in related disciplines and each of several areas of specialized application of knowledge about the child.

Sources in the biological sciences

Historically, child development has grown up from roots that lie, in part, in several biological sciences, including physiology and genetics. The biologist and natural scientist have shown us man's position in the animal kingdom, have organized the facts of human reproduction, and have shed light on the inheritance of characteristics through genetic laws. Physiologists have provided us with information on the growth and functioning of tissues, organs, and systems of the body. Without access to these basic biological facts, the field of child development as we know it could not exist.

Sources in psychology

Psychology is an extremely broad, inclusive discipline concerned with behavior in general. Developmental psychology, in particular, concerns itself with the progressive organization of behavior in the growing organism. Other specialized aspects of psychology are concerned with particular aspects of sensing, perceiving, knowing, and coping with the world of objects and people. Still others are concerned primarily with learning processes, or with the interpersonal behavior of individuals. All of these and other aspects of psychology have relevance for child development, which is concerned with such processes in the growing child. The two basic psychological questions for the child development specialist are (1) what are the laws and principles that govern the behavior of all children, and (2) how can we account for the unique development of the behavior pattern of an individual child?

Sources in sociology

Sociology can be defined in many different ways, but it is generally concerned with man's behavior in relation to other human beings. It brings its tools and insights to bear on the organization of groups, social institutions, and society itself. It has shed much light, for example, on the groups that have a primary role in the socialization of the child, particularly the family. But in addition to describing the nature of the family and other groups that participate in the development of the child, sociology has provided a basic understanding of the nature of social organization and the various institutions of society that lend shape to thoughts, feelings, and actions of the individual.

The powerful role of the community in shaping the life of the child is one aspect of this. Sociologists have provided insight into the formation of attitudes and value systems through their analyses of social class structure. They have helped us to understand that the basic nature of the child is almost impossible to separate from the societal environment—the milieu wherein the child constructs his personality.

Sources in anthropology

Anthropology, broadly defined as the study of man, is concerned with large questions about the nature of man and how he has come to be what he is. The two major divisions within the field are *physical anthropology* and *cultural anthropology*. The first of these is concerned with man as a physical being, whereby his physical status and characteristics, his origin and evolution, are central problems. Some physical anthropologists compare the physical characteristics of man with those of the other primates (apes and monkeys); others compare the so-called races of man with each other. Still others specialize in physical growth and development processes. Through their careful measurements of the human body and its parts at different periods of development, they have provided us with much useful information on the nature of the growth process.

Cultural anthropology seeks to answer the question of man's

nature in relation to his inventions, including his social behavior since this, too, is a part of what he has devised. In this connection, certain anthropologists have become vitally interested in the socialization processes of society; that is, with the systems devised by societies for inducting children into membership and for fostering the kinds of development that allow them to participate fully in a given society. In this area, the anthropologist and the child development specialist work together in producing and utilizing knowledge about children.

Contributions to other disciplines

As was illustrated in Figure 1.1, child development may be viewed as a specialized field which integrates the findings of other disciplines and focuses these on an understanding of the growing child. It organizes these findings into a coherent body of knowledge, which it makes available to a variety of fields of application. Among these fields are medicine, education, social work, and home economics.

Medicine

Today's physician is acutely aware that the health of the growing child involves far more than freedom from disease. Healthy growth is a progressive series of orderly changes working toward higher levels of physiological, mental, and social functioning. The physician charged with the treatment of children, whether a general practitioner, a pediatric specialist, or one of the emerging specialists in family practice, is concerned with far more than keeping height and weight charts, giving inoculations, prescribing diets and vitamins, and treating the usual childhood diseases. Beyond these functions, which may be more or less important in the practice of medicine, the physician is concerned with the total well-being of his patient—child or adult. In his practice, the physician relies heavily on a thorough knowledge of the basic facts of child development.

Psychiatry, as a specialized branch of medicine, is concerned primarily with the treatment and prevention of mental and emotional illness. In his work with children and adults, the psychiatrist must also be familiar with normal human development if he is to discriminate between the normal variations found in all individuals and any signs of illness or pathology. The modern psychiatrist is highly specialized, well trained, and has a wide variety of tools and techniques at his disposal, but none of his competencies is more essential than his understanding of human development.

Education

Over the years, the professional field of education has benefited from an ever-increasing knowledge of the characteristics of the growing child. The child development point of view has permeated the schools to a marked degree. Schools attempt to design and organize their programs in keeping with the readiness of the child to profit from education. There has been increasing emphasis in school programs on understanding the causes of child behavior, and on seeking the mutual understanding by parents and teachers alike of the individual child and his educational progress.

Individualization of the curriculum and of teaching strategies has been one of the major contributions of the child development point of view. It is based on our understanding that the child brings with him into the classroom all his special attributes—talents, attitudes, values, skills, emotional organization, and so on—and that the child and the subject matter cannot reasonably be separated from each other in the classroom. Today's school is more than a series of courses; it is a set of experiences based on a sound knowledge of the nature of child growth.

In Chapter Twelve we will discuss in greater detail the educational provisions and practices with young children. For the moment, however, we should note that society's provisions for the education of its children have been profoundly influenced by our increasing awareness of the nature of child development processes.

Social work

Child development's emphasis on the importance of satisfying the basic needs of children, which dominated much of our thinking in earlier parts of this century, created a new atmosphere and philosophy for the care of all children. In particular, it led to the formulation of practices, some of them codified into law, that regulate the treatment of dependent, neglected, delinquent, and economically disadvantaged children. There has emerged a treatment philosophy, for example, in work with delinquent children that is based in part on increasingly sophisticated understandings of the bases for socially adequate and inadequate behavior.

An essential aspect of this treatment approach has been its focus on the sources of distortion in human development, and the education of the society toward the removal or correction of these sources. One example of the effects of this change in philosophy has been the striking trend away from the placing of dependent and neglected children under institutional care and toward placing them in private homes, either for temporary foster care or for legal adoption. The insights of the child development specialist have contributed significantly to this and other trends in services to children and families.

Home economics

Home economics has had a long and illustrious career in America and has made countless contributions to the well-being of individuals and families, the extent of which would be difficult to measure. In home economics, as in other professional fields, there have been important trends and developments in philosophy, technical knowledge, and practice.

There may have been a time when the professional home economist was known primarily as an expert in food preparation, clothing construction, or housekeeping efficiency. Today's home economist, however, is more likely to have had special education in understanding the family as a unit of interacting personalities and as a setting within which child socialization occurs. While a knowledge of nutrition and food preparation, and family resources and principles of management are as important to the homemaker and professional home economist as ever before, the latter has found it essential to develop competencies in understanding processes of individual and family development through every stage of the family's life cycle.

Even such basic and vital concerns as diet, clothing, housing, and family finance tend to be conceptualized as means to the greater end of the healthy development of the individual human person. To achieve this end, the home economist relies more than ever before on our knowledge of the ways in which children grow and achieve maturity in their relationships with others.

The child development specialist

The relationships between child development and other disciplines make it natural for the child development specialist to be found in any of a variety of settings and employed in a range of vocational and professional activities. At the level of the college graduate, large numbers of specialists work in the various types of programs for the education of young children. While the majority of these programs are geared to children between the ages of 3 and 6, there are also emerging programs for infants and toddlers, which employ child development personnel. With the advent of large-scale programs of early stimulation during the late 1960s and early 1970s, particularly for disadvantaged children, it is reasonable to assume that the demand for qualified workers will continue to increase.

In the early years of intervention programs such as Head Start, we reached only about 10 percent of the eligible children. Zigler (1971) has also noted a serious disparity between the demand and supply of well-prepared child development personnel, citing the United States Labor Department's estimate that we will need 23,000 new teachers of young children each year until 1980. Zigler proposes, through the Office of Child Development, the establishment of a new professional in the field: the

"Child Development Associate," prepared in a thorough 2-year course combining some formal academic work with supervised experience with children. Such a plan would give national recognition to the large numbers of people it is anticipated will be needed, particularly as demands for developmental day care programs increase.

Some child development specialists have been in demand in children's hospitals, particularly as directors of educational play programs for hospitalized children. Such programs have been recognized as valuable adjuncts to the total therapy program. In the hospital setting, the child development specialist may work directly with physician, nurse, and other members of the treatment team in outlining and carrying out a planned therapy program for the individual child.

Other specialists work in a variety of social welfare agencies, in camps and treatment centers for handicapped children, or in recreational programs sponsored by civic or religious organizations. Some work in various state extension-service programs, conducting activities for children and participating in educational programs for parents. Some work directly in public or private schools as teachers or counselors, while others obtain graduate degrees and enter highly specialized careers as research workers and teachers at the college level, or as practitioners in specialized programs for treatment of normal or exceptional children.

In general, the outlook is for an expanding field of work with children, which will afford many varied career opportunities that give personal satisfaction while at the same time provide a useful service our society is now beginning to recognize more than ever before.

One of the encouraging trends is the increasing number of young men who are choosing careers in working with children. This is desirable in part because of a recognized need for male "models" in the lives of young children, particularly those whose contact with adult males is limited or nonexistent because of a fatherless home.

Finally, it should be mentioned that one of the fringe benefits in preparing oneself to work with young children—somewhat apart from the excellent professional opportunities for a career of service—is that one must, in the process, achieve a reasonable level of insight into his or her own personality. Living and working with children requires a kind of self-understanding which may be far less critical in some other careers!

Summary

Child development as a scientific field of endeavor had its beginnings in the late nineteenth and early twentieth centuries. It began with isolated studies of individual children, which aroused questions about the nature of children in general. These beginnings led to large-scale investigations of child development processes and yielded a wealth of information for parents and professional workers. Five major streams of thought that have influenced our current thinking in child development were briefly described: (1) the behavioristic approach, which emphasized what is visible in child behavior and the role of experiences in producing these visible behaviors; (2) the normative-descriptive approach, which stressed that growth comes from inside the child and appears in a successive sequence of orderly stages that have been described by detailed age norms; (3) the field theory approach, which viewed the growing child in relation to the dynamic forces of his environment; (4) the psychoanalytic approach, which brought forth a new concept of personality development based on instinctual needs and unconscious motivation; and (5) the cognitive-developmental approach, which is concerned with the child's mental operations in the process becoming familiar with his world.

Child development has roots in other disciplines: biology, psychology, sociology, and anthropology. A major function of child development as a professional discipline is the organization of the body of knowledge derived from these related fields and focusing that body of knowledge specifically on the growing child. In turn, still other disciplines—medicine, education, social work, and home economics, for example—rely heavily on the field of child development.

Today the child development specialist is recognized as a professional person with unique competencies, whose qualifications to work directly with children places him or her in demand in a variety of careers. In addition, there are significant benefits to be derived from training in child development, such as personal satisfaction, self-understanding, and preparation for competent and enlightened parenthood.

References

Anderson, J. E. "Child Development: An Historical Perspective." *Child Development* 27 (1956) 181–196.

Ariès, P. *Centuries of Childhood.* Translated from the French by R. Baldick. New York: Knopf, 1962.

Baldwin, A. *Theories of Child Development.* New York: Wiley, 1967.

Bertalanffy, L. von. *Robots, Men and Minds.* New York: George Brazilier, 1967.

Dennis, W. "Historical Beginnings of Child Psychology." *Psychological Bulletin* 46 (1949) 224–235.

Freud, S. *New Introductory Lectures in Psychoanalysis.* New York: Norton, 1933.

Gesell, A., and Amatruda, C. S. *Developmental Diagnosis.* 2nd ed. New York: Hoeber-Harper, 1947.

Gesell, A., and Ilg, F. L. *Child Development, an Introduction to the Study of Human Growth.* New York: Harper, 1949.

Kessen, W. *The Child.* New York: Wiley, 1965.

Lewin, K. *A Dynamic Theory of Personality* (selected papers). New York: McGraw-Hill, 1935.

Payne, G. H. *The Child in Human Progress.* New York: Putnam, 1916.

Piaget, J. "Piaget's Theory." In Mussen, P. H., ed. *Carmichael's Manual of Child Psychology.* 3rd ed., vol. 1. New York: Wiley, 1970, pp. 703–732.

Skinner, B. F. *The Behavior of Organisms.* New York: Appleton-Century-Crofts, 1938.

———. *Science and Human Behavior.* New York: Macmillan, 1953.

———. *Beyond Freedom and Dignity.* New York: Knopf, 1971.

Watson, J. B. *Psychological Care of Infant and Child.* New York: Norton, 1928.

Zigler, E. "A New Child Care Profession: The Child Development Associate." *Young Children* 27 (1971) 71–74.

CHAPTER TWO

Observation of children

How can we come to understand children through observation?

How can we make our observations more useful and reliable?

How does the child development scientist make use of observation procedures?

What methods are used to report the results of observations?

What are the ethical considerations in observing and working with children?

There are two levels of information about children, and the student of child development makes use of both: first, the level of personal insight and understanding based on one's own observations of children, and, second, the level of information about children in general, based on careful observations by trained scientific workers.

One level is neither superior nor inferior to the other; they are both essential to the student. Neither are they independent of one another, since in the final analysis the generalizations of the scientist must become personal insights in order to be meaningful and useful to us individually. At the same time, in order to be useful, personal insights must have validity and authenticity just as the scientist's findings do.

There are some close similarities—and also some fundamental differences—in scientific and informal observation procedures. It is the purpose of this chapter to outline observation procedures as they apply to both levels of understanding. The first part of the chapter deals with the informal observation procedures—those we can all use to further our understanding of the children with whom we have contact. This is followed by a discussion of the techniques used by the child development scientist in providing us with valid generalizations.

Informal observation

It's an unusual adult who has no opportunities to observe children—at home, on the playground, in school, at church, at the supermarket, in front of a television set, or perhaps in the role of goblins at the front door on Halloween. Our observations under such informal, "natural" conditions are probably not very scientific. The ideas we form from these may or may not be accurate as far as they go, but they are certain to be incomplete.

Casual observation of a neighbor's child suggests that the boy is slow in talking and seems less alert mentally than some other children, but that he is well coordinated, physically strong, and a fast runner who likes to throw and catch a ball. If our "observations" somehow seem to support a belief we may already have, that "athletic children are likely to be slow mentally and academically," then we are not really engaging in observation so much as we are engaging in the process of finding "evidence" to support a belief (in this case, a false belief!) we already hold. But informal observation can be much more useful than this. A brief episode in a supermarket, in which we observe a child and a woman who is probably his mother, provides an illustration:

> Child, a black male about 2½ years of age, dressed neatly in brightly colored shirt, short trousers, shiny shoes . . . lags behind mother who pushes grocery cart along otherwise vacant aisle . . . body movement is combination of walk-dance-jump-glide-bounce as his eyes rest fleetingly on can of peaches, then a box of pancake flour, then a low bin filled with assorted candy bars, at which point all movement stops. Squats, eyes riveted, body motionless as if held by a magnet. Right hand moves slowly toward large, red and white wrapped candy bar, grasps it firmly in right hand, then both hands, squeezes, seems to listen to wrapper noise and feel texture of candy inside. Moves from squat to erect position in one smooth effortless motion without using hands for support. Mother, far down the aisle, looks his way and shouts, "Joey! Put it back!" Boy's body seems to shrink slightly, shoulders hunch, head down, stands very still, holding candy in both hands, facing bin, not looking at mother. She leaves cart and approaches child, deliberately and with no indication of anger or upset. About five feet away from child she stops, says "Joey!" in firm, even voice. As if propelled by a sling-shot, candy bar is in the bin and Joey runs, dodging past his mother and bouncingly toward her grocery cart. Before he gets there, he stops momentarily in front of a box of powdered sugar, sticks tongue out as if to lick the box but doesn't touch it, dances away and grasps side of grocery cart, looks up at mother and grins as she approaches.

This episode is worth examining, not because it presents anything unusual and not because it is necessarily typical, but simply because it describes a child's actions in a common setting, in relation to the physical objects and important people in that setting. The report focuses on *behavior* rather than on *evaluation*. An important point is that it does not attempt to classify the behavior as "good" or "bad," for if the observer is preoccupied with the moral issues—the goodness or badness of the behavior—he may miss important features of the behavior itself.

One learns to see behavior more clearly, in greater detail, and with greater insight, by focusing on its sequence and pattern, and by delaying judgment about the child who is being observed. Note, for example, there is nothing in the preceding anecdote that "judges" either the child or his mother. Did she do the right thing? Should she have let him have the candy? If she hadn't wanted him to have things like that, should she have allowed him to lag behind her in the store?

But we don't really have information for answers to such "Should she . . . ?" questions. What we do have is an interesting account of one small slice of a boy's behavior in a grocery store one day. The account raises more questions than it answers: What were the physical properties of the setting for this episode? How did the long aisle filled with brightly colored objects stacked high above his head influence Joey's behavior? What was the significance of the fact that at no time did Joey's mother control him through direct physical actions, but rather by approaching and using words? How frequently does Joey visit the supermarket with his mother? How typical for him was his behavior on this occasion? How typical would it be for other children his age, older, or younger? How typical for girls? Was his behavior influenced by his bodily state (for instance, hunger, fatigue, need to go to bathroom)? His behavior could well be influenced by any such factors, plus the whole history of his interaction with his mother.

Such things become background questions which we might need to know about in order to make more sense of a child's behavior on any given occasion. But our first big step in the direction of becoming a competent observer of children is to learn to see and describe the sequence of events—the child's actions: *what* he does, and *how* he does it, in relation to *which* objects and people in his setting. *Why* he does whatever he does—the matter of motives and regulating forces that arouse, direct, and shape the pattern and sequence of his actions—are usually matters of interpretation. Motives are not directly observable, but can only be inferred from behavior.

Since we can't know the motives operating in any given episode, it is especially important to remember the same actions could stem from different combinations of motives. Furthermore, distinctly different actions could arise from the same sets of motives for different children or even for the same child at different times and in different settings.

Even though the motives may be obscure to the observer, who learns to be properly cautious about attributing behavior to any single cause, it is possible to learn a lot from such informal observations. The episode provides insight into the child's degree of body control, his style of movement, his responsiveness to visual, tactual, and auditory stimulation, the kinds of objects likely to capture his attention, his responsiveness to parental control, and so on. Would we expect a 6-year-old to move through a supermarket aisle in the same manner as Joey did? Would an older child be as drawn to each new object his eyes met, or would he be relatively more guided by an internal "plan" that organizes longer segments of body action? Is Joey relatively more "episodic" in being pushed and pulled by smaller fragments of external objects and events, thus giving his behavior an appearance of discontinuity?

Some of the genuine values of keen observation are in the questions and answers that are raised through discussion, reading, and further observation of children. But one learns to be tentative in forming hypotheses and to avoid premature conclusions about causes of behavior. Perhaps it is always true that thorough observation raises more questions than answers, but it is equally true that the questioning attitude is one of the central attributes—perhaps the chief prerequisite—for the student of child development. This attitude requires not merely curiosity, but a willingness to hold one's mind open and to refuse to accept the first easy answer that might close out further consideration of the issues involved.

Again, in the supermarket episode, the observer might have

dealt with the events by noting merely "There was this boy in the store; he wanted some candy and his mother wouldn't let him have it." Of course, we don't *know* that he "wanted" some candy, any more than we *know* that Joey wanted to test his mother to see if she would control his behavior when he couldn't control it by himself. Either of these two ideas is an interpretation of motives rather than an observation. But more important, such a report closes out further questioning about what the boy did, what the mother did, and the possible sources of control over the actions that occurred.

There is a powerful tendency for an observer to see those things that fit in with his beliefs, and fail to see those things that are contrary to them. This selective perception appears to be at the root of much of what we call prejudice, and suggests another aspect of the problem of becoming a competent observer. As we have already implied, one must learn to see without prejudging. But beyond this, one must learn to weigh all kinds of behaviors equally, regardless of whether they support or refute one's favorite belief.

One way an observer gradually becomes more objective and avoids the pitfalls of selective perception is by careful analysis of his own beliefs, and open recognition of their existence. This suggests then that the child development student needs not only to learn the factual information of the discipline, but to examine continuously his own assumptions, partly in order to question their validity, and partly to assist him in recognizing their potential role in the selective perception of child behaviors.

Another problem is that it is all too easy to assume that our informal analysis of a specific child's behavior on a given occasion is somehow applicable to children in general or, perhaps, to some broad category of children who have something in common with the one observed. We note that an 18-month-old runs, arms outstretched, toward a stranger; we see a 2-year-old walking easily up and down stairs, alternating his feet; we hear a 4-year-old telling her father she doesn't like her tricycle any more because she knows how to ride a real bicycle and wants one of her own. All of these things might happen, and might be observed and reported, and in each case we might conclude that the child involved is like other children of the same age and the behavior is somehow typical of all children. It is not.

The tendency to associate some obvious characteristic of a child with a particular behavior we see him engage in is also very powerful. Skin color and body build are two examples of characteristics readily visible, and the task of the observer is to avoid drawing inferences of association between such characteristics and the behavior of a child. Imagine, for example, an American Indian child, age 5, living with an Anglo family in a Midwestern community, who is being observed in a kindergarten classroom. The observer has never closely observed an American Indian child. He notes that the child has not smiled during a full hour of observation, nor has he expressed any form of emotion; he has said very few words, and when he has moved about the kindergarten room he has done so very quietly and unobtrusively.

Perhaps it should seem obvious that the observer has no business generalizing the behavior of this child—on this occasion, in this setting—to the Indian child in America. It should also be evident that we could not safely generalize to the particular Indian tribe of which his parents are members, nor can his behavior in this instance be accounted for by his dark reddish-brown skin or black hair. All these things *should* be obvious, yet there is always a powerful tendency to generalize some behavior to a broad class of individuals having some basic characteristic in common. To avoid it requires a type of mental maturity that allows the observer to perceive and record the behaviors of a child independent of the fact he also happens to be a member of an identifiable ethnic, socioeconomic, religious, or national group. Not only may a child's behavior be atypical of any broad group in which he is a member, but the behavior may not be typical of this child or other children in the same family unless it is observed frequently in a variety of settings. What we see on a given occasion *may* come to our attention precisely *because* it is unusual—even for that child.

For these and other reasons it is not safe to generalize about children on the strength of informal observations. Yet, in studying child development, we can never completely negate our personal experiences and the effects they have on our attitudes, opinions, and understanding. We cannot suddenly become completely objective about and impervious to attitudes and information—and misinformation—we may have lived with for years. It is better to begin with the clear recognition that our present reactions to children *are* very much influenced by our past experiences, and by recognizing our own limitations, we are taking an important step toward improving our observations and making them more reliable and useful.

Improving informal observations

The usefulness of our observations will depend, in large measure, on the questions we ask ourselves before, during, and after the incident was observed. For example, we may have watched a child in the act of picking up some small object from the floor. How did he go about it? Did he bend from the waist and reach for it with one hand? Did he flex his knees and assume a squatting position to reach the floor? Did he reach with one hand or with both? Did he make contact with the object first with the tip of one finger, or two fingers, or thumb and forefinger in opposition to each other? Or did he palm the object with the flat surface of what the poet called the ". . . baby's starfish of a hand"? And when he obtained the object, what happened? Did he examine it with his eyes? With his mouth? While he was examining it, was the rest of his body active or still? How did he react to the color, the size, the weight, the shape and the texture of the object? How long did it hold his attention? Did he perform only one action with the object or a variety of actions? What senses did he employ? What muscle systems? How long did it hold his attention? Did he seem to be enjoying it?

There are countless questions that could be raised about an action as brief and simple as picking up and examining a small object. Without scientific attention to such detailed and specific questions, we would never have the volumes of information currently available about the facts of child development. But such questions also serve a useful purpose for the observer in the sense that they alert us to behavior that would otherwise go unnoticed.

The keenest observers are those who refuse to take behavior for granted; they are observing for a purpose, and the purpose is to answer questions. The refusal to take behavior for granted allows many questions to be raised—and answered, at least tentatively—that might otherwise escape us completely.

The usefulness of our observations depends also on the kinds of records we make of whatever we see and hear. Keeping some kind of observational record serves the dual purpose of forcing us to organize our observations into meaningful statements in order to put them down on paper (or in some instances on a tape recorder) and, at the same time, of providing a permanent record which can be referred to at a later time, compared with other records and so on, without having to rely solely on memory.

In making observation records, it is helpful to distinguish clearly between *behavior,* on the one hand, and *interpretation,* on the other, as suggested by Pease (1958). There may be occasion when it is appropriate to record our personal interpretations of the meaning of a bit of behavior, along with our task of keeping an objective account of events as they occur, but differentiating clearly which class of material we are recording.

Guides for observation records

An adequate observation record begins with the necessary descriptive information on the setting: date, time, and place. The child's name and age, if known, should be recorded along with the sex and a brief description of physical characteristics such as physique, complexion, eye and hair color, and facial characteristics—all of which are particularly useful if the child is unfamiliar to the observer.

Wearing apparel, although not ordinarily very useful in helping to identify a child later, may be important in the child's behavior, and therefore should be recorded. An example would be a child in a day care center, wearing a spotless, frilly dress, who is watching the other children playing with messy materials such as clay and finger paints. She does not participate herself. The observer notes the wearing apparel, the lack of participation, and in his observation notebook writes the interpretation that these two things may be related. When he observes this child again, he is alert to note again the kind of wearing apparel and the degree of participation in messy activities. A cumulative series of records of the child's behavior may help to establish the nature of her attitude toward such materials and possible clues as to the sources of these attitudes.

Observations of children are frequently based on a particular topic, or aspect of behavior. Such topics might include physical or motor characteristics, emotional behavior, language, problem-solving, or social behavior. An observation guide or outline can be helpful for such a procedure. Examples of detailed and comprehensive outlines are provided by Suchman (1959). Additional insights and information on the problems of observation of children are given by Almy (1959), Carbonara (1961), Cohen (1958), Pease and Pattison (1956), and Hutt and Hutt (1970).

For some observation sessions, however, the primary objective may be to gain a better understanding of a particular child, including all aspects of behavior suggested above. An observation guide will still be useful, although perhaps more inclusive and less detailed in any one of the categories of child characteristics and behavior. The following is a suggested set of items, which might be included in an observation guide for this general purpose:

I. Physical characteristics and body build.
II. Body control.
    A. How did he move about? What was the tempo of his movements? Did he walk? Run? Skip? Dance? Was bodily activity smoothly flowing? Awkward and uncoordinated?
    B. Did he use climbing equipment? Did he play daringly? Cautiously? Did he appear to have good balance?
    C. How did he hold objects (blocks, crayons, tools, paintbrush, and so on)?
    D. Note situations calling for coordination of hands with eyes, and describe his behavior.

III. Social behavior.
   A. In what kinds of social situations did he participate? Did he initiate these, or was he responding to suggestions of others? Did he change the nature or direction of a social action after it was in process?
   B. Did he use oral speech to participate socially? Any other forms of communication?
   C. Was his social behavior exclusively with one other person? Was it exclusively with other children? With adults? Did he participate freely within a group social activity?
   D. Did he show leadership behavior? In what ways? How did other children respond to him?

IV. Language and intellectual behavior.
   A. Did he use oral speech to make a request or state a need?
   B. Was his speech clearly intelligible? Did he use complete sentences? Were the words of his sentences distinctly articulated, or did they tend to be blurred together?
   C. What behavior on his part revealed evidence of a concept, or that he understands a rule of some kind?
   D. Did he classify or organize materials or objects in any manner? If so, what was the basis for this classification (for example, color, form, function, and so on)?
   E. Describe ways the child met and coped with any problem or task that arose. How did he resolve or fail to resolve it?
   F. Was there any behavior on his part that could be called creative? Describe it.

V. Self-evaluation.
   A. Did he give any clues in his behavior as to his evaluation of himself? If so, describe.
   B. How would you describe his level of self-confidence? Why?
   C. Did the child seem to feel comfortable and at home in

the situation where you observed him? Was there any evidence that he felt uncomfortable or that he didn't belong?

D. Did he attempt any activities that he failed to carry through?

E. How did he respond to any frustrating event that occurred (for example, by attacking the problem directly, attempting some kind of compromise, or retreating to a safe place)?

F. Did you observe the child regarding himself in a mirror? In what manner? Was there evidence of satisfaction or dissatisfaction?

G. Did the child make any verbal statements about himself? What kind? Did he compare himself with others in any way?

It should be clear that any such list we might prepare is incomplete. Students should ask themselves what additional items or questions might be included for such a general set of observation guidelines.

Still another approach to gaining a better understanding of a particular child is through the use of the *diary record*. This is a running account of the behavior of a child for a stated period of time. With practice, an observer learns to record the most significant events that relate to a child's use of objects and materials, and the nature of his interaction with people.

It is possible to record a straightforward, objective account of a child's behavior for, say, 5 minutes at a time, followed by a period of about the same length in which the observer goes back over the record to clarify hastily written notes while the events are still fresh in his memory, and to make additional notes, comments, questions, and interpretive statements. This leads to the development of an attitude of objectivity on the part of the observer, but at the same time encourages him to try to understand the behavior and the possible reasons for it. An example of this approach to observation is provided by the following excerpt from the notebook of a student:

Child: Carol G————, girl, 4–4

Behavior	Interpretation
10:47 Carol is playing on the big boxes and boards (outdoor area, nursery school) with Laura and Anita. She slides, feet first in a sitting position, down a board propped against a big box. She is wearing a parka and mittens.	Laura and Anita seem to form a pair, with Carol being accepted in the play at their discretion. Carol seems pleased with this role, but says very little and seems to be in doubt about how much to assert herself.
10:48 Anita asks Carol if she is trying to get in their house (boxes) and Carol says "Yes" and smiles. Now Carol runs over to the sandbox and says she is going to play. She fills up a pan with sand and takes it over to the boxes for their party. She pats the sand carefully in the pan and gives it to Laura.	Her enthusiasm has increased now that the party is under way.
10:52 Laura and Anita go after more sand and Carol yells for them to hurry. Miss Avis comes out on the porch and Carol yells, "Hi, teacher! We're having a party—you can come to our party!"	Carol's relationship with the other children is easily disrupted by the teacher's presence.
10:54 Carol now crawls in one of the boxes and rapidly out again, telling the teacher about their house. Now she pushes a tricycle out of her way and runs over to the sandbox again, quickly filling some more pans.	
10:57 She runs back to the house, sits down in one corner and is very still for a long time (about 1½ minutes). She	I wonder if Carol's behavior here means that she doesn't care much about continuing

	watches the other children playing around her.	to play with the others, or if she would really like to but
10:59	Some of the other children are starting to go inside now, and Carol jumps up suddenly, runs to the door of the nursery school, yelling, "Let me in! Let me in!"	isn't sure enough of herself and finds it safer to withdraw for a time.

The foregoing excerpt was not selected because of any unusual incident or any special significance to the interpretive material, but because it illustrates the separation of behavioral from interpretive material. It also includes enough of the child's language and physical actions as well as the setting, objects, and other people present to enable the reader to follow the main patterning of Carol's behavior during the period of observation. It further illustrates one of the roles of observation: the raising of questions in the observer's mind, which can lead to further attempts to understand a child. The process of formulating a significant question is a key step in the direction of understanding.

Anecdotal records, in contrast with diary records illustrated above, are not based on a unit of time, but rather on an event or incident in the child's interaction with his environment. The earlier account of the child in the supermarket illustrates anecdotal reporting. It begins as a child enters a setting (in that case, the aisle of the supermarket) and lasts as long as it takes for the event to be completed.

In addition to the child, who is the main subject of the observation, the record should include data on any other principal participants—children and adults—and the nature of the child's interaction with each. A given event may be long or short, routine or unusual, and pleasant or unpleasant for the persons involved. It may include many people as it progresses, or it may be carried out in isolation. The following is an example of an anecdote taken from the records of a child development student observing in a nursery school:

Child: Linda B————, girl, 3–9

Behavior	Interpretation
Linda has been playing by herself at a table, working a picture puzzle. Two other girls had tried to get involved in the play but she had ignored them. At this point a teacher sits down at the piano nearby and starts to sing a song, encouraging the children close to her to join in the singing. It is a song about "Miss Polly," whose dolly was sick.	Linda is a child who talks well at home, but does not speak at all in nursery school. This incident shows how she has learned to get along in the nursery school without having to use words.
Linda stops playing with the puzzle and joins the other children near the piano. She acts out the story of Miss Polly with body movements but does not join in the singing with the other children and the teacher. When that song ends, they sing another; this time Linda does not participate at all, except to watch the other children.	

Some laboratory schools and child development centers have special facilities which make it possible for large numbers of students to observe children simultaneously. Observation booths —adjacent to a classroom and equipped with two-way mirrors and sound systems—can even make it possible for an instructor to work with a group of observers as part of their training to teach children. Closed-circuit television equipment also can be used profitably to provide indirect observation experience, and has the added feature of providing video-tape recordings of children's behavior, which can be used repeatedly, and in settings where it may not be possible to make direct observations. Such features are aids to observation, but do not change the fundamental task of the child development student, which is to become a keen observer of behavior.

Scientific
child study

The second level of information is based on careful observations made by the child development scientist. Such observations become the basis for research findings, some of which can be translated into practice by teachers, parents, and others who work with children.

The child development research worker is a scientist, just as a chemist or biologist is a scientist, to the extent that he makes careful use of the scientific method. In order to make accurate and useful generalizations about his subjects, the scientist normally proceeds methodically through the following steps:

1. Defining a problem.
2. Stating a hypothesis—a possible solution for the problem.
3. Collecting data that bear directly on the problem.
4. Organizing and analyzing the data.
5. Drawing conclusions.

The child development scientist's data (step 3) are the material he has collected through observation. In the section to follow, we will examine two types of observational material and the ways in which such material is used in research. We should keep in mind, however, that a particular research project might involve both of these approaches—or it might be a variation on one or both of them—and still follow the basic strategies of scientific child study.

Direct observation

As an approach to child study, direct observation incorporates many of the features of informal observation already discussed. It might, for example, employ either the diary or the anecdotal record. In such cases, however, the research worker is obligated to determine the degree of reliability of his observation material, and reduce as much as possible the sources of error or bias in the material. One way to establish the reliability of such data is to have two independent observers record the same events, then compare the two records to ascertain the degree of agreement. Many research projects require extensive training of observers to develop the degree of reliability essential to enable them to draw correct conclusions.

The essential feature of this direct approach to observation is that it attempts to achieve a clear picture of child behavior without influencing or modifying that behavior. Such strategies are employed in natural settings—homes, schools, playgrounds, and camps—and do not depend on a controlled laboratory environment.

In addition to the use of diary and anecdotal records, research workers using direct observation have employed a variety of refined strategies, including *time sampling, event sampling,* and *trait rating.* Such methods have been described in detail by Wright (1960).

TIME SAMPLING This is a procedure that focuses the observer's attention on a child (or in some instances, on a group of children) for a specified time interval. In a typical study, the observer might seek to establish the frequency of a given class of behavior, such as instances of aggression. He devotes a period of time, such as 6 minutes, to a given child, and records (usually employing a coded observation sheet prepared in advance) each instance of aggressive behavior occurring during that period on the part of the child. He may then devote the same length of time to the next child, proceeding through the number of subjects he plans to observe.

The procedure may be repeated each day for a week, or once each week for 10 weeks, or some other variation, to allow the observer to establish the frequency with which his subjects exhibit aggressive behavior. Such a procedure is generally used with children in a school or some other institutional setting. According to Wright (1960), the method is a relatively reliable one, and economical to use, but has limited ability to reveal anything beyond the frequency with which certain types of behavior occur, such as the appearance of the behavior (for example, what does aggressive behavior *look* like in a child?) or the probable causes of the behavior. Furthermore, unless the behavior under consideration occurs very frequently, this method is inappropriate; hence it probably would not be used in the study of aggressive behavior if by such behavior the researcher meant only actual physical aggression of one child upon another.

EVENT SAMPLING This procedure is related to time sampling in that it is also used to study a certain class or type of behavior. An investigator may wish to know more, for example, about the ways in which children use a certain type of equipment or materials. He may station himself in close proximity to where such behavior is likely to occur, await its occurrence, then describe it in careful detail. In an example given by Wright (1960), an investigator made a careful study of children's quarrels, using an event-sampling procedure. From that study, it was possible to determine duration of quarrels; the content (what the children quarreled about); the manner in which each child participated, including verbal and motor accompaniments; and the outcome of each quarrel. Such a procedure can be rich indeed in the amount and kind of material it makes available.

TRAIT RATING This is different from the other direct observation procedures in that the observer uses a scale or a battery of scales that describe one or more dimensions of behavior. The rating scale is used by the observer to summarize a child's behavior after he has devoted some period of time in observing that child. A wide range of such rating scales have been used by researchers in the history of child study, and dimensions on which children have been rated include cheerfulness, conformity, friendliness, respect for authority, sense of humor, and adjustment to new situations.

In general, the direct observation methods of the child study research worker provide kinds of information that cannot be obtained in any other way. Their unique contribution is that they provide a basis for examining child behavior without interfering with that behavior, or subjecting the child to artificial laboratory controls.

Controlled laboratory experimentation

There are some kinds of research questions where it is essential to take measures to control the child's environment for the purpose of determining exactly what effect a given variable has on a child. The need for such procedures is described in the following statement by Bijou and Baer (1960, p. 140):

> The essential concept involved in the definition of experimental technique is that of control. In experimental logic, phenomena do not change without cause. A statement of cause and effect can be made only when a variation in the supposed effect is coincidental to a preceding variation in the supposed cause, if no other factor has changed. The best guarantee that no other factors have changed is to gain control of them and keep them at fixed values.

These authorities go on to explain that a laboratory is merely a place where essential controls can be conveniently applied and where objective measurements may be taken. The child study experimentalist frequently employs mechanical instruments to aid in objective measurements and to increase reliability of his procedures. As Bijou and Baer point out, ". . . experimentation, well executed, generates relatively precise statements of cause and effect which are remarkably unambiguous" (1960, p. 141).

Two broad classes of experimental procedures may be defined. In the first, which is the more or less traditional approach to experimenting with children, it is typical to compare an *experimental,* or *treatment,* group with a *control,* or *nontreatment,* group. Individual children are assigned to experimental or control groups at random. The experimental children are then exposed to the treatment, which represents the experimental variable the researcher wishes to investigate. The control children are given either no treatment or control treatment of a nature that will insure the two groups are comparable in all respects except for the experimental variable being investigated. Finally, the two groups are compared through the use of statistical procedures to determine whether or not the treatment has brought about some observable change in the behavior of the experimental children that is not observable in the control group. There are many complex variations on this procedure, but the essence of it is to bring as many as possible of the important factors that could affect the behavior under experimental control, and in such a way that if a difference is found between the two groups, it is most probably the experimental treatment that has produced this difference.

In important experimental studies with children, new findings frequently need to be replicated by research workers before they can become accepted generalizations about child behavior. Replication of a result, with a different group of children, increases the weight of evidence as to the validity and generality of a finding.

An example of an aspect of behavior in early childhood, which has been investigated through the use of experimental procedures, is that of the sensory discrimination and learning processes. Terrell and Kennedy (1957) performed such an experiment whereby 4-year-old children were divided into two groups and given a simple learning task. The task required that the children discriminate between the larger and smaller of two objects, presented systematically, by pushing a button representing the larger in each case. Both groups had the same task, but the experimental group received candy as a reinforcement for learning, while the control group received only a flash of light to indicate the correctness of their response on each trial. The "candy" group not only learned the task in fewer trials, but were better able to generalize their learning to a new situation based on the same principle. In that study, additional comparisons were made among other groups and other experimental treatments were employed besides the use of candy reinforcers, but the comparison discussed here illustrates the use of the more or less standard experimental procedure.

A variation on the experimental approach is currently being employed widely by researchers who describe their procedures as *behavior analysis*. This strategy is designed to reveal the precise effects on a child's behavior, which result when one or more kinds of reinforcement are manipulated experimentally. Reinforcement may be regarded as any event that increases the probability that a given bit of behavior will occur again. Praising a child when he behaves in a certain manner is an obvious example of reinforcement if it leads to the child's repeating the behavior. Rewarding his behavior with a privilege or with attention are other examples. It is generally assumed that whatever behavior the child was engaged in at the time of or just prior to reinforcement is the behavior he will repeat.

The behavior analysis strategy does not depend on the use of experimental and control groups, but uses the child's own behavior as a reference point, or *baseline*. It brings systematic reinforcement to bear on the behavior under consideration, and employs one or another kind of observation procedures to discover whether the reinforcement strategy brings about significant change in the behavior. Thus at one point the child is a "control," and at another point, an "experimental" subject.

Often it is the *rate* of a certain class of behavior that one may wish to change, for example, the frequency with which a child makes use of a certain class of equipment, such as climbing frames and other large-muscle development equipment. A child who rarely or never uses such equipment might be given social reinforcement (adult attention and praise) as he moves into the vicinity of such apparatus. Subsequently, he may be praised if he comes very close and touches the equipment. In successive stages, he might be reinforced for supporting part of his body weight on the apparatus, then for getting both feet off the surface and onto the equipment, until eventually his behavior has been modified to the extent that he plays, with evident satisfaction, in a kind of activity which previously he did not engage in.

Through the use of this strategy, dramatic changes in the behavior of individual children with respect to the rate, or frequency, of the occurrence of certain classes of behavior have been reported by Harris, Wolf, and Baer (1967). A large number of experimental studies of this general type have been carried out in recent years, and by using various types of tangible and social reinforcers, they have shown considerable promise as a method of investigation and as a method for guiding the behavior of individual children, even during infancy. Some of these studies are discussed in subsequent chapters.

Mixed strategies

An intriguing research approach, which has some of the features of direct observation and experimentation, has been the primary method employed by Piaget and Inhelder (1969). Piaget has called his strategy the "concentric clinical" method. It relies on presentation of tasks to children, sometimes in a highly standardized and carefully controlled manner. However, Piaget has deliberately chosen to "follow up" the responses to these tasks by using the child's leads. Thus the course of an experiment will vary in this strategy depending upon the directions taken by the child. In Piaget's view, this procedure is necessary to allow the investigator to go beyond merely assessing whether the child knows the right answer or can or cannot solve a problem accurately. If one wishes to know, additionally, the quality of a child's mental operations, he may also need to consider the way a child thinks *even while getting a wrong answer*. This technique provides a kind of flexibility which has allowed exploration of dimensions of mental operations which might not reveal themselves under more highly controlled situations which stress the judgment of a child's response as being correct or incorrect.

Use of tests and measurements

Those who work with young children frequently make use of information obtained from individual children through the administration of one or more kinds of tests, or measuring instruments. Scales to determine intelligence; individual differences among children in a variety of personal and social attributes; perceptual, motor, and physical characteristics; and motivational tendencies may be considered aids to observation. Some of these are highly developed instruments that require special training to administer. Nevertheless, they remain aids to observation because they bring into focus certain aspects of the behavior of a child and allow the observer to determine with greater confidence the limits of a child's capabilities or the strength of his behavior tendencies.

A test of intelligence, for example, requires that the child perform certain more or less standardized tasks in such a way that a highly trained observer, qualified to administer such examinations, may record his performance and compare it with norms, or standards of intellectual behavior. Even though a child's performance might be scored, and the scores converted to figures such as mental age, or IQ units, the process involved in collecting such information is still one of observation. The same statement may be made with respect to personality ratings, sociometric instruments, and other measuring devices.

A comprehensive source of detailed information on specific types of measuring devices used with both children and adults is found in Buros (1965).

Interpreting scientific research

Students of child development—teachers, parents, physicians, psychologists, social workers, and home economists—are continually relying on generalizations about children that have been developed through observation of one kind or another. It is important for the student to have a clear understanding of the nature of these research reports and of basic statistical concepts which are employed in the reports.

It is important, for example, to know *how many* children were observed as a basis for some generalization. A study of the social behavior of 4-year-old children which does not reveal how many children were studied would be difficult to interpret, at best. It is customary to include a report of "N," or number of children observed. However, it is equally important for the student to note the description of the children, which the researcher will generally provide, including such information as ages and sex of the children, and any peculiar conditions in their lives that might affect the study.

If the study of children's social behavior were made with children reared in an orphanage, it may still be useful information—but with application only to children of such a background rather than to children in general. Similarly, generalizations about children reared in large cities may not apply to children growing up in small communities or in rural areas, research reports on observations of boys may not apply to girls, and so on. It is the responsibility of the reader, as well as the writer of scientific reports, to be clear on the degree to which the findings of a particular study may be safely generalized to larger groups of children.

Use of statistical tools

Statistics are used frequently to provide a meaningful description of a group of children because the description of a given child does not adequately characterize the entire group. Three main types of statistical tools are most widely used in research reports, and the student's ability to interpret research will depend, in part, on his understanding of these three kinds of tools.

MEASURES OF CENTRAL TENDENCY   The average figure is often the most useful one for describing some characteristic or tendency of a total group. If we wish to describe the height of 4-year-old boys, for example, we could do so by stating that they are, on the average, 40.9 inches tall (Watson and Lowrey 1962). An average of this kind is called the *mean,* and might be designated as "M," or sometimes as $\overline{X}$. A mean score is simply an average obtained by adding all the scores in a group and dividing the sum by "N" (the number of individuals).

Another measure of central tendency, which provides a somewhat different kind of information, is the *median.* Like the mean, the median is a way of characterizing the total group, but it differs from the mean in that it tells us that point in the total set of scores that divides the group exactly in half. That is, if we measured the height of 20 4-year-old boys and then ranked them in order from tallest to shortest, the median would be the score that fell exactly in the middle of our set of scores, dividing the tallest ten from the shortest ten.

MEASURES OF VARIABILITY   In addition to the figures that tell us average central tendencies of a group, it is frequently helpful to have information on the amount of variation in the group. We may want to know how big a *range* there is between the highest and lowest score in a group, for example. We may want to know what percent of the total group score is above a given point. Or we may wish to know how much, on the average, each score in the group differed from the mean for the total group.

The most widely used measure of variation is the *standard deviation*. As an index of the amount of variability in scoring, it provides valuable information which is useful in many ways, but is especially useful in the comparison of two or more groups. If we wished to know whether there are important sex differences in language behavior, for example, we would want to know not only the mean score for boys and girls with respect to some measure of language development, but also the standard deviation score for each sex. This would inform us as to whether or not the two sexes are equal with respect to the amount of variability in language development.

Table 2.1 provides data taken from a study illustrating basic procedures frequently used in reporting data. The first column identifies the group of children, and the second column indicates the number of children in each group. The third column, $\bar{X}$, shows the mean number of trials required by children in each of the three groups to learn to push the correct button on a box. When the correct button was pushed, a marble was delivered to the child through an opening in the box. The table tells us that Group I required relatively few trials. The fourth column, "Standard Deviation," gives information on the degree of variability of performance within each of the three groups. It tells us that there was much more variation in performance on the part of children in Groups II and III than in Group I. The final column tells us the range of scores for each of the three groups,

TABLE 2.1. Tabular Presentation of Basic Statistical Data

Group	N	$\bar{X}$	SD	Range
I	24	18.62	15.60	18–87
II	15	53.93	28.98	24–124
III	19	50.95	28.02	21–135

and indicates that the range was relatively small for Group I in comparison with the other two groups.

MEASURES OF RELATIONSHIP   Another form in which data are frequently reported is in terms of the degree of relationship between two different sets of scores. For example, we may be interested in knowing whether there is any relationship between the height of children and their intelligence. In order to find out, we could measure both height and intelligence with the same group of children and determine whether the tallest ones were also the brightest and the shortest ones also the dullest. But obviously there would be a lot of cases where this would not be true, so we should have to check ourselves mathematically to see whether, on the average, there is any tendency for brighter children to be taller and duller children to be shorter. We would do this by computing a correlation coefficient, which would tell us whether any such relationship between the two variables actually exists.

The limits of the correlation coefficient are +1.00 and −1.00, both of which represent perfect relationships. In the case of positive correlations, there is some degree of the tendency for the two sets of scores to vary *directly*, that is, for high scores in one to be associated with high scores in the other. In the case of negative correlations, there is a tendency (becoming stronger as the correlation coefficient approaches −1.00) for the two sets of scores to vary *inversely*, that is, for high scores in one to be associated with low scores in the other.

Correlation coefficients of zero or very close to zero, either positive or negative, indicate that no relationship has been found to exist between the two sets of scores. In general, the nearer a correlation coefficient is to either +1.00 or −1.00, the greater is our assurance that there is a real relationship between the two variables under consideration.

In the field of child development, it is important to know which of certain characteristics of growing children tend to be associated with each other. For this reason, data are often reported in terms of correlation coefficients. However, the student should keep in mind the fact that variables that are associated with each other do not necessarily bear any *causal* relationship. In the case of height and intelligence, for example, where some studies have found a slight tendency for these two variables to be positively correlated, it would be just as absurd to think that the physical characteristic height is the *cause* of intelligence as it would be to think intelligence is the cause of height. Two variables may be correlated without one of them being the cause of the other.

Ethical considerations in child study

Observations of a child through any of the methods described can reveal much about his personal and even intimate nature. Some of the information that might be obtained may be only incidental to the initial objectives of the observer. The child may reveal much in his language behavior, for example, about his relationship with his parents and about family religious matters or other practices and beliefs, even though the observer's concerns are primarily with the language behavior of the child. A cardinal principle of the professional child development specialist is that neither the child nor his family become objects for discussion among friends and acquaintances. This applies also to such information as a child's scores on tests. Persons having access to a child's test information are assumed to have accepted the principle of protecting the privacy of the child, and to be personally and professionally mature enough to safeguard such information. In situations where it is appropriate to discuss the behavior or characteristics of children, such as in research reports, the identity of the individual child is concealed. Material discussed in staff meetings or classrooms on individual children is obviously not appropriate for discussion among friends outside those situations.

Another general principle is that a child is not coerced into being the subject of observation, whether for informal or research purposes. The right of a child to refuse to participate, and of his parents, guardians, or caretakers to refuse to allow him to participate, is respected in the study of children.

Additionally, being an observer or student of child development does not qualify one to make diagnoses or to prescribe courses of action (for example, child guidance procedures) to parents, even though parents might seek such diagnoses or prescriptions.

The student of child development, by becoming involved in the observation of children, also becomes committed to a standard of professional ethics which is premised on the fundamental rights of privacy and dignity of all people in our society, regardless of their age.

Summary

We all make informal observations of children and, to a greater or lesser degree, make judgments and form attitudes and opinions on the basis of those observations. We can improve the quality of those informal observations, however, by being aware of the element of personal bias and by taking steps to control that bias. While laboratory settings provide unique opportunities for observation, particularly in connection with controlled research investigations, there are additionally many opportunities to gain a keener insight into the behavior of young children in playgrounds, parks, schools and child development centers, camps, churches, supermarkets, on public transportation, and in private homes. Material from such informal observations ordinarily cannot be generalized to apply to all children, or even to the same children at different times; nevertheless it can sharpen our insights and raise questions in our minds for further investigation.

The scientist, as well as the student, makes use of observation procedures. In some cases, the scientist observes behavior in a natural setting without attempting to control it; in others he attempts to bring it under very precise experimental control. The data derived from these observations are often reported in statistical terms; hence, the student who is generally familiar with such terms will be in a stronger position to read and discuss child development research findings.

The student of child development has the ethical responsibility for safeguarding the rights and protecting the dignity and welfare of any children who are subjects of observation.

References

Almy, M. *Ways of Studying Children*. New York: Bureau of Publications, Teachers College, Columbia University, 1959.

Bijou, S., and Baer, D. "The Laboratory-Experimental Study of Child Behavior." In Mussen, P., ed. *Handbook of Research Methods in Child Development*. New York: Wiley, 1960, pp. 140–197.

Buros, O. K., ed. *The Sixth Mental Measurements Yearbook*. Highland Park, N.J.: Gryphon Press, 1965.

Carbonara, N. T. *Techniques for Observing Normal Child Behavior*. Pittsburgh: University of Pittsburgh Press, 1961.

Cohen, D. H. *Observing and Recording the Behavior of Young Children*. New York: Bureau of Publications, Teachers College, Columbia University, 1958.

Harris, F., Wolf, M. M., and Baer, D. M. "Effects of Adult Social Reinforcement on Child Behavior." In Hartup, W., and Smothergill, N., eds. *The Young Child*. Washington, D.C.: National Association for the Education of Young Children, 1967, pp. 13–26.

Hutt, S. J., and Hutt, C. *Direct Observation and Measurement of Behavior*. Springfield, Ill.: Charles C. Thomas, 1970.

Pease, D. *Child Development Laboratory Notebook*. Dubuque, Iowa: Brown, 1958.

Pease, D., and Pattison, M. "Observation: A Method of Learning About Children." *Journal of Home Economics* 48 (1956) 755–757.

Piaget, J., and Inhelder, B. *The Psychology of the Child*. Translated by H. Weaver. New York: Basic Books, 1969.

Suchman, J. R. *Observation and Analysis in Child Development: A Laboratory Manual*. New York: Harcourt, 1959.

Terrell, G., Jr., and Kennedy, W. A. "Discrimination Learning and Transposition in Children as a Function of the Nature of the Reward." *Journal of Experimental Psychology* 53 (1957) 257–260.

Watson, E. H., and Lowrey, G. H. *Growth and Development of Children*. 4th ed. Chicago: Year Book Medical Publishers, 1962.

Wright, H. F. "Observational Child Study." In Mussen, P., ed. *Handbook of Research Methods in Child Development*. New York: Wiley, 1960.

PART 11
Foundations of development

Human development is not exempted from the natural laws underlying the orderliness of the universe. Understanding the growing child calls for understanding basic principles that govern his development. If all of human growth may be characterized by major themes arising out of these basic principles, then every individual child may be seen as a complex and unique variation on these great themes.

Since the main sections of the book that follow Part II will be devoted to the child from 2 to 6, we should also turn our attention to a preliminary consideration of the infancy period. Our insights into the nature of infancy, and the significance of this stage of human growth, are keener and more meaningful in the 1970s than has been true in any previous period of man's history. This concentration on the infant, in Chapter Four, will serve to set the stage for a more detailed examination of the processes of development in early childhood, in the remainder of the book.

CHAPTER THREE

The nature and sources of development

What kinds of changes occur in the growing person that can be
 included in the term "development?"

What general principles apply in describing each of these kinds of
 changes?

What are the major sources and causes of developmental change?

What is meant by "interaction" as the basis for all human
 development?

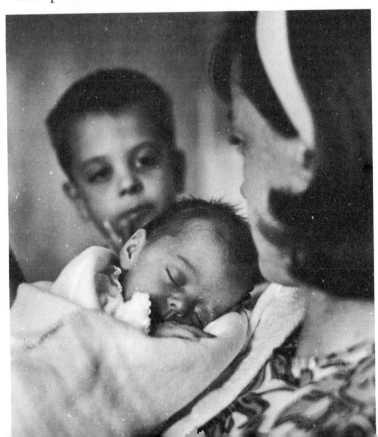

The processes
of development

The processes by which a fertilized egg cell, or *zygote*, microscopic in size, becomes a human adult with billions of cells having markedly specialized functions, weighing perhaps 150 pounds, are little short of incredible. We can understand and appreciate these processes more fully if we examine the kinds of changes that occur in the growing individual. *These changes, taken together, constitute development.*

Growth in size

We might think it strange if, upon being introduced to a stranger, he inquired as to our body weight. Most likely we would not regard it as any of his business. But the fact that we do not think it strange to inquire about the weight of a newborn infant suggests that we hold assumptions of a relationship between birth weight and physical well-being. While bigger, heavier babies are not invariably healthier babies, there is a natural concern for both parents and scientists regarding body size, since it is one index of normal growth. The consistent, regular, and more or less steady increase in weight and length during the early months is one evidence of healthy development.

In general, there is a positive relationship between physical growth and physiological functioning. However, sheer increase in the amount of body tissue is not the most important aspect of human development. In infants and young children its importance rests primarily in (1) what it signifies about underlying developmental processes, and (2) its social significance. The latter pertains to our tendency, often unjustified, to regard body size as a legitimate basis for judging maturity level and for deriving social expectations. Aspects of development other than sheer body size provide better indices of maturity level and of the expectations we can reasonably hold for the emergence of new behavior patterns.

Changes in body proportions

Consider a normal, healthy infant, of less than a month in age. Make a mental note of the fact that his length, approximately 21–

22 inches, will be multiplied roughly by three before he reaches maturity. Now visualize that infant increasing in size and becoming a 5-foot 8-inch adult, while maintaining the same body proportions he has right now. The picture this creates, while ludicrous, helps us envision the changes in body proportion which occur between infancy and maturity. Figure 3.1 provides a graphic contrast in body proportions between infant and adult. It is obvious, then, that different parts of the body must have different rates of growth and must undergo differing amounts of growth before reaching maturity:

The head will about *double* in size.
The trunk will about *triple* in length.
The arms will increase about *fourfold* in length.
The legs will increase about *fivefold* in length.

Differences among children with respect to stature and body proportions are associated with such variables as sex, race, nutritional status, and general physical condition, in addition to the fundamental genetic controls over individual body size and build. However, the summary of changes in body proportions

FIGURE 3.1 The bodily proportions of the newborn infant and the adult. (From K. Buhler, *The Mental Development of the Child*, London: Routledge & Kegan Paul.)

given above is a fair rough estimate of changes in proportions which the average infant will undergo.

Changes in complexity

Increases in size and weight, and changes in body proportion are, of course, occurring simultaneously. At the same time, there are basic increases in complexity of the total system. While it would not be accurate to characterize the human organism as "simple" at any stage, even prior to birth, we are referring here to relative degrees of complexity, from which standpoint there are marked differences from one period to another. Growth may be characterized as progressing from the simple and undifferentiated toward the complex and differentiated. This trend applies to anatomic, physiological, psychological, and social organization. Both in *structure,* or organization of parts and subsystems in relation to each other, and in *function,* or action of these parts and subsystems in relation to the whole growing system that is the child, he becomes increasingly complex with age.

The notion of *differentiation* as a growth process is the key idea here. We are referring to a process by which elements or components of a total system become specialized in structure and function, as for example the differentiation of cells in the embryonic stage of prenatal life, with some cells achieving specialized capability for sensory action—the visual and auditory systems, for example—some achieving structural and functional capacities for a digestive tract, others for bone tissue, and so on.

The fascinating question of differentiation of parts and subsystems during human growth ultimately must be traced back to what is present in the original zygote, which represents a sort of blueprint for the manufacture of increasingly specialized, that is, differentiated cells, tissues, organs and subsystems of the body. It will help to envision the individual child as a total system in the process of becoming elaborated. With each new elaboration come new possibilities for relating of parts to each other within the system and for relating of parts to the total system.

We will see in the following chapter that the newborn infant has an impressive repertoire of behavior, yet it is clear that he is not capable of interacting with his world in the complex manner of, say, the 5-year-old. The energies and resources of the infant system are relatively more preoccupied with the intake of food and oxygen, reflexive responses to sensory stimulation, the establishment and maintenance of physiological equilibrium, elimination of body wastes, and tissue growth and differentiation. By contrast, the child of 5 is capable of maintaining a remarkably complex set of relationships with his world of objects, over which he has achieved considerable mastery, and with his world of people, with whom he interacts in subtle ways using complex cues, codes, and language processes.

Acquisition of new functional capacities

Increasing complexity of the system is related to the emergence of new kinds of behavior and capabilities which were not present at earlier levels. The newborn's capacity for reflex action is far more elaborate than his capabilities in the embryonic or fetal stages of prenatal life. The 6-month-old, sitting erect in his crib, has far greater body control than he did at birth. The 12-month-old, who has several words in his speaking vocabulary, was not articulating words at 9 months. The examples could be endlessly multiplied.

Most such new functional capacities represent some mix, or combination, of biological and psychological processes; few may be attributed simply to the operation of heredity or to the simple effect of experience. We are coming to view the acquisition of new capacities as the product of interaction between the presently existing capabilities of the system and the environmental resources available to that system. It cannot be doubted that there are powerful internal growth forces that regulate the emergence of new capacities, as evidenced in the orderly growth of structure and function. A striking example is the regular sequence of stages in the development of upright locomotion during infancy. Nevertheless, the impact of environmental resources and constraints is real and powerful at every stage of growth.

The environmental impact is thought to be of special significance in the achievement of given capacities at key points during development when these capacities are undergoing rapid differentiation. This is the notion of "critical periods," which holds that certain environmental resources are essential for the emergence of a given capacity at critical stages in the differentiation process. One kind of illustration of this critical periods hypothesis comes from the first trimester of the prenatal period when, if the mother should contract rubella, the biological environment of the fetus is such that some tissues and subsystems might fail to differentiate properly. The fact that the neurological and sensory birth defects that can result from maternal rubella are associated with the *timing* of the disease in relation to pregnancy is what illustrates the critical periods hypothesis. Rubella late in pregnancy, following the early, rapid differentiation of the vulnerable neurological and sensory systems, does not lead to the same defects.

Analogous arguments have been presented for the emergence of psychological and social processes following birth, and at subsequent stages of growth, as for example the crucial role of early mothering experiences, which are thought to provide an essential foundation for the development of healthy personality.

Some of the evidence supporting this critical periods hypothesis has been drawn from studies of lower animals—laboratory rats, dogs, and monkeys especially—suggesting that a given kind of environmental event and its impact on the emergence of new capacities may be relatively slight at one stage of growth and of crucial significance at another. In general, this line of evidence supports the notion that heredity and environment do not operate independently in the construction of new capacities, but rather that these forces interact with each other in their combined effect on growth.

Disappearance of parts and functional capacities

In the course of development it is as natural and normal, although perhaps less apparent, for certain parts and functions to decline and even disappear as it is for parts and functions to make their appearance with new stages of growth. Perhaps this is most clearly seen in relation to aging processes, in which physical capabilities—sensory capacities such as vision, hearing, taste and smell—may diminish or be completely lost. What is equally important to our concept of development, however, is that there may be loss of function as an integral part of the childhood processes of growth.

Simple examples occur in the motor capacities of children who find it gradually more difficult to insert the toe in the mouth, or to walk on all fours with the knees straight in a bear-like fashion. Other examples are seen in the loss of certain infantile reflexes, such as the grasp reflex. But of greater significance are examples from children's intellectual development. A thorough understanding of mental growth, for example, requires that we comprehend not only a child's newly organized capacity for engaging in certain types of thought processes, but also his *inability* to function in the more primitive fashion of his earlier days.

Some scientists (for example, Bruner, et al. 1966) have linked this to the childhood amnesia we all experience—our inability to recall events from our early lives. Their interpretation is that possibly we "forgot" the events that were formulated in mental processes which were replaced by or absorbed into more advanced kinds of mental processes in the early years.

Years earlier, Gesell and Ilg (1949) noted that the average 4-year-old, in his uninhibited freedom of fantasy and self-expression, can portray what he wishes on paper, be it a horse, a tiger, a car, or his mother; and regardless of what it looks like to the adult, it serves the child's purposes well enough. But the 6-year-old may be unable to do it at all; he may be unable to get started in drawing a horse, for example, because he "doesn't know how!"

Biologically, too, there are changes that illustrate the loss of parts and functions. The newborn infant has, typically, immunity to certain diseases, provided his mother established immunity through the development of the appropriate antibodies. But this immunity is only temporary, and in most cases will disappear during the first few months of postnatal life.

Other examples include that of the thymus gland, located in the upper thorax, which is present at birth and grows rapidly during early childhood, then more slowly until puberty. It then begins to decrease in size, until in the adult it is relatively small and is composed of fibrous, nonfunctioning tissue (Nossal 1969). In a similar way, the pineal body at the base of the brain is a "disappearing gland" because, in the normal processes of development, it shrinks in size and appears to lose any functional capacity.

The biologist can point to other, perhaps more basic, processes under the heading of metabolic changes associated with development. Along with the anabolic changes that represent growth, there are continuous catabolic changes that represent disorganization and destruction. Blood cells, for example, have a relatively short life span; new blood cells are continually being manufactured in the bone marrow to replace dying cells.

Truly, life and growth are dynamic processes which can be understood only in terms of positive, building, and organizing forces operating in a favorable balance with negative, destructive, and disorganizing forces from the moment of conception until death.

All of these kinds of changes are important aspects of human development: increase in size, changes in body proportions, increases in complexity, acquisition of new parts and functional capacities, and disappearance of old parts and capacities.

It is apparent that the concept of development is a complicated one and cannot be given a simple definition. From the discussion so far, however, we may summarize with a definition in terms of the kinds of changes it includes: *development is the total complex of processes resulting from internal and external forces, leading to revisions of the form, structure, and functioning of the individual.*

In the next section we will examine these internal and external forces in greater detail and attempt to illustrate their reciprocal, interacting roles in bringing about the changes that constitute development.

Sources
of development

As defined above, development is a long-range process made up of many parts, rather than of a single, narrow feature of a child, or of merely one aspect of his personality. Some of the sources of the overall process lie within the child himself; others are to be found outside him. The latter are the elements of the environment that participate actively in stimulating his growth. They play essential roles in the overall drama of development. (For convenience we will give emphasis first to internal growth factors, then to environmental factors, and finally attempt to understand the complicated interaction of these forces.) Beth

Factors within the child

Chromosomes are tiny bodies within the nucleus of the cell and are believed to carry the genes that constitute the basic determiners of heredity. The genes are thought to be transmitted from parent to offspring, with half of the genetic effect derived from the father through the sperm cell and half from the mother through the egg cell. In the immature germ cells these genes exist in pairs, and there are estimated to be about 10,000 pairs for each human chromosome. In the cell maturation process, the pairs separate so that only one gene of each pair remains in the mature sperm or egg cell, to be passed along to the zygote, which is the initial cell of the new individual. In this process, any given father or mother each has over 8 million different combinations of characteristics to pass on to their offspring. This helps account for the uniqueness of each individual, since the likelihood of a given combination of genetic effects repeating itself, except in the case of identical twins, is indeed remote (Sanford 1965).

At the time of conception, the heredity of the child is permanently established. The egg cell, which contained 23 chromosomes, has become a zygote with 46 chromosomes and with no further possibilities for exchanging any one of the chromosomes in that complete set for any other. One of the chromosomes from the sperm cell determines the sex of the child. Other genetic effects determined by the unique combination of genes include the color of hair and eyes, skin pigmentation, physique and body proportions, many aspects of mental and psychological capacities, and to some extent even emotionality. Vandenberg (1967) has concluded that such personality traits as extroversion-introversion, emotionality, and activity level are strongly influenced by hereditary factors.

About 2 weeks following conception, after the zygote has undergone many consecutive cell divisions and has implanted itself in the lining of the uterus to establish a source of continued sustenance, it enters the *embryonic* period. During the embryonic stage the new individual changes from a diffuse and apparently unorganized ball of cells to a remarkably structured, patterned state in which major parts can be identified. The limbs, fingers and toes, head and face, sense organs, brain and spinal cord, heart and lungs, and other vital organs and subsystems emerge through the process of cell differentiation. At about the end of the ninth week of prenatal life, the end of the embryonic stage and the beginning of the *fetal* period is marked. During the remaining portion of the prenatal period the parts and subsystems of the body, which are essential to maintenance of life outside the mother's body, must mature and become functional if the baby is to survive.

This patterning of prenatal development is accomplished through the operation of a genetic "ground plan"—the "blueprint" referred to earlier. Since the initial state of the zygote is that of a single cell with 46 chromosomes, the question of how sets of cells and tissues for each of the specialized subsystems occurs is indeed a large question in the mystery of human growth.

Some aspects of this question appear to be answered through the operation of the chemical substances, DNA and RNA (deoxyribonucleic acid and ribonucleic acid, respectively). The DNA molecule is thought to be the fundamental component of the hereditary material of the cell (McClearn 1970). This DNA molecule is described as a spiral shaped ribbon, in two strands, held a fixed distance apart, in a ladder-like structure. The genetic material, or coded "blueprint," exists in a doubled state, such that when cell division occurs, half of each "ribbon" goes to each new cell where complementary strands are formed. Thus the ribbon reproduces itself, using the chemical building materials available in the nucleus of the cell, and using itself as a "template" or model for construction of its counterpart in the complementary strand of the ribbon.

The chromosomes containing DNA are located in the nucleus of the cell, but much of the work of the cell occurs outside the nucleus, in the cytoplasm. For this work to occur, the coded genetic "information" contained in a single strand of the ribbon must be transmitted to the cytoplasm. It is thought that this takes place by the transcription of the DNA information onto an RNA molecule, which enters the cytoplasm as a "messenger" and becomes involved in protein synthesis.

It appears that the chemical code in the DNA molecule contains all the essential information for the construction of all body parts and systems. A rather novel approach to determining whether or not heredity plays a role in the development and organization of abilities and personality was undertaken by Freedman and Keller (1963), who based their research on the principle that identical twins are alike in heredity, while fraternal twins are not. While fraternal twins *might* be of the same sex, identical twins *must* be of the same sex.

These researchers examined 20 pairs of same-sex twins each month during the first year of life. Neither the researchers nor the parents of the twins were sure whether any given set of twins were identical or fraternal until after the study was completed, at which time a series of blood tests established that nine of the sets were identical and eleven were fraternal. The ratings of these twin pairs on both mental and motor capacities revealed a higher degree of similarity for the twins that were discovered to be identical, and a lower degree of similarity for the twin pairs found to be fraternal. Hereditary factors, apparently, revealed their effects in the mental and motor development of these infants.

For ages, philosophers and scholars have discussed and argued the determinants of man's characteristics and the relative role of "nature" vs. "nurture" in his development. We no longer question which is the more important, heredity *or* environment, because we recognize the absolute importance of both of these general factors. However, we do continue to ask *how* each of the general forces operates in order to understand the unique individuality of each child. It is the "how" question to which we now turn, in the case of the environmental forces in the development of the child.

Environmental factors

Even during the 280 days, more or less, of the prenatal period, there is a very active physical and chemical environment operating in the life of the embryo and fetus. That environment must provide nutrients for building the new system and must also make provisions for the elimination of the waste products of this building process. It has been well said that birth is not really the beginning, but a milestone along the way; this would seem to apply to the role of environment in development, as well as to the role of heredity.

Nevertheless, birth is a most significant milestone not only because it signifies physiological independence, but also because it means confronting for the first time an infinite array of stimuli, possibilities for the satisfaction and frustration of needs, and social definitions of appropriate and inappropriate behavior.

It is the child's sensory processes that bring the environment to him and enable him to derive meaning from it, while at the same time, his muscular system enables him to influence and modify that environment. Piaget and Inhelder (1969), and Bruner, et al. (1966) have proposed that the infant's incessant practice in coordinating the sensory with the motor processes participates actively in the structuring of his mental life. There is evidence that environmental stimulation is a factor in the achievement of readiness for a wide range of intellectual, social, and motor behaviors, including the academic behavior expected of the school child. There is a circular relationship implied in this. The child's experiences with things seem to enhance his motivation for further involvement, as well as to take a more direct role in the construction of readiness.

A few minutes' observation of a normal 18-month-old child should convince one of the significance of his environment, which he will proceed to explore and manipulate. If given reasonable opportunity, he will poke, pinch, grasp, bite, suck, hit, step on, pick up, and generally maul a wide assortment of objects accessible to him, including other children, who seem to fit in the same category as objects. One achieves a revised perspective on child behavior if he recognizes the primary role of the mouth in this sensory-motor exploration of the world, for much of the action of the infant and toddler involves bringing objects to the mouth, which seems to be an essential "link" in the sensory-motor process of coming to know his world.

The environment, through its social elements, also participates actively in structuring the personality of the infant and child. It is generally assumed, for example, that the emergence of language in the early years is based heavily on social interchange between parent and child. Although there are differences among scientists as to the degree of emphasis placed on the role of experience in language development, there can be little disagreement that the role is a vital one. Typical of the research that has led to this conclusion is the work of Rheingold, Gewirtz, and Ross (1959), which concluded that social reinforcement, in the form of adult attention given when an infant vocalized, led to increased amounts of vocalizing. The social responsiveness of adults also participates in other aspects of early development. Rheingold (1956) observed that the number and kind of "caretaking contacts" by an adult had a significant effect on the social responsiveness of 6-month-old babies.

The infant is obviously dependent on others, and his resistance to being separated from the important adults in his life affords an understanding of their role in his social environment. One definition of dependency is provided by Hartup (1963), as follows: "Whenever the individual gives evidence that people, as people, are satisfying and rewarding, it may be said that the individual is behaving dependently." Much of the behavior of the infant and the young child fits this definition. One view of the impact of the social environment on the child is that his initial dependency becomes the basis for the entire process of socialization.

Data reported by Gardner, Hawkes, and Burchinal (1961) indicate that it is not critical whether infants are reared by their own biological mothers or by foster or adoptive mothers. There is every reason to assume that what counts is the mother's interest in the child, her desire to provide adequate care and nurturance, and her resources for doing it. These resources include her knowledge of the facts of child development as well as her personal competencies for engaging in maternal behavior.

We should not overlook the reciprocal nature of the social interaction between infant and mother in the early social environment. The infant may be seen to play an active part in the "construction" of his mother's maternal behavior. That is, individual infants have their own special qualities of temperament, excitability, tempo, and responsiveness, which tend to elicit some aspects of the mother's repertoire of maternal behaviors more than others. The infant's "personality" also gives different degrees of satisfaction, which might be thought of as reinforcers of different forms of maternal behavior, thus actively shaping the way a mother comes to respond socially to her own child. As Schaffer and Emerson (1964) observed, mothers alter their behaviors over time. These researchers described some infants as "cuddlers" and some as "noncuddlers," and observed changes in maternal behavior which appeared to be a function of which kind of infant the mother had.

One critical aspect of the early social environment of the child may be the degree to which it defines for him an appropriate set of attitudes and response tendencies in relation to segments of the larger society. Generalized attitudes toward groups may be developed prior to any direct experience with those groups, on the basis of imitation of parent behavior. Attitudes toward same-sex persons, and opposite-sex persons, may also be a function of the role models provided by parents. Attitudes toward religion, education, persons in positions of authority, dependent persons, the aged, crippled or sick persons, death, illness, or accidents, personal hygiene, foods, achievement, and so on, may all be seen as variables in a child probably affected to some unknown degree by the process of identification, or imitation of significant adults, particularly parents. Needless to say, the role of such identification with parents in the formation of attitudes toward minority groups may be a major one.

Clearly, then, the social environment of a child is crucial in the formation of his personality. The entire notion of personality, in fact, becomes meaningless apart from the socializing experiences of childhood. However, we have yet to discuss the central process by which the environment, and the objects and people of that environment, become a part of the child's personality. One very important way is through the learning process.

The role of learning

Briefly, learning may be thought of as the acquisition of any new behavior, or the modification of any existing behavior, that results from a child's experience. It applies to new or revised skills, knowledge and information, and attitudes and values, since all of these have behavioral manifestations, even though some are not directly observable.

One most basic form of the learning process is that of *classical conditioning*, which is the formation or strengthening of an association between a stimulus and a response. The process is illustrated whenever a child associates one of his responses with a new stimulus.

A clear example is afforded from the early literature of child psychology, in which Watson and Rayner (1920) introduced a furry white rat to an infant boy named Albert. The moment Albert reached toward the animal, the experimenters made a loud sound, sufficient to startle the boy. The same procedure was repeated several times, and with each successive trial Albert became less and less willing to reach toward the animal. Soon he withdrew and attempted to get away from the animal each time it was presented to him, whether or not the loud sound occurred.

This withdrawal behavior persisted, and even generalized to a number of other stimuli which had some features in common with the furry animal—a piece of cotton wool, a fur coat, and a Santa Claus mask. In this example, Albert already had the response capability of "startling," becoming afraid, and withdrawing. What was learned, however, was the association between this response capability and the stimulus of the furry animal, as well as a generalized class of stimuli having things in common with the animal.

Stimulus generalization in classical conditioning has a number of implications for understanding child behavior, which might otherwise be hard to understand. A child who has experienced pain and fear in connection with a visit to a doctor's office may readily generalize to a wide range of stimulus events having perhaps even remote (at least, to adults) elements in common with the medical setting. The generalization could readily extend, for example, to settings where there are people waiting (a bus terminal, for example), to settings where there are shiny instruments (barber shop or restaurant), to settings where there are small rooms (employment office, welfare agency), and many others.

Classical conditioning and stimulus generalization may account for kinds of learning other than that of emotional behavior, of course. It may play a significant role in the child's learning of the names of objects, for example. In this case the name, which may be thought of as a new stimulus, becomes associated with an object or class of objects through repeated use of the name by others in the child's presence.

That stimulus generalization occurs is evidenced by the fact that children typically use a name for a thing, for example, "doggie," to refer to a broader class of things than was intended by the adults and, in this example, cows, cats, horses, and a miscellaneous assortment of specimens in the zoo may, for a time, all be "doggies" so far as a toddler is concerned.

A further learning process in relation to this tendency to over-generalize is that of *discrimination learning*, which seems to be helped by learning new names for the items or events which, in this case, are not really "doggies." A child continually refines the broad categories of things experienced into smaller units, with increasing precision and specificity of meaning, through learning to distinguish more subtle cues. Where one category existed, "doggie," several categories emerge—"doggie," "kitty," "horsie," and so on—through this process of discrimination learning. It is a matter of learning "to tell the difference" at levels of increasing refinement, and is a process closely related to the *differentiation* process we discussed earlier.

Instrumental learning, which also involves an association between stimulus and response, is given its name because the learner's behavior is instrumental in bringing about a reinforcement of some kind. A baby may be said to engage in instrumental learning, for example, if his crying consistently brings the attention of a nurturant adult, and this relationship between events leads to more frequent crying episodes. In this case the attentive behavior of the adult is reinforcing to the baby's crying behavior, and thereby increases the probability of the baby's use of crying behavior in the future. We might note in passing that the learning, in this instance, can be affected by a number of other conditions. It is more likely to occur if the adult is attentive *only* when the baby cries, and it will probably lead to louder and more prolonged crying if the adult is attentive to it and not to soft cries early in a crying episode.

But infant crying behavior is only one small example of the way instrumental learning might operate in a child's life. Much of the rich learning in which children engage might be viewed as complex sequences, or chains of instrumental associations, parts of which may have been learned separately, later to become integrated into higher order learnings.

If we watch a 3-year-old carefully for, say, an hour of free play, we will probably see many instances of small segments of learned behavior that have become integrated into larger sequences of action. A simple example might be a sequence like this: Grandma comes to the house, and sits in the big living room chair. The boy turns away from his blocks, immediately runs to her and climbs in her lap, then looks expectantly at her big handbag at the side of her chair. She reaches into it and extracts a piece of candy. He reaches for it, grasps it between the forefinger and thumb of his right hand, and puts it in his mouth. After he slides himself off Grandma's lap while his mother approaches from the other room, he manages to come up with a muffled "Thank you, Gra-muh!" spoken in the general direction of his blocks, which he now approaches.

The example is intended to remind us of the child's capacity to incorporate small units of learned behavior, many of which might be instrumental learnings, into complex sequences of actions. In this case, the child had already learned that climbing on his grandmother's lap could be instrumental in obtaining a piece of candy. Much earlier, he had learned the motor co-ordinations necessary to grasp small objects and put them in his mouth. He had also learned, perhaps, that prolonged sitting on his grandmother's lap never brought a second piece of candy while his mother was in the house, and he had learned that saying "Thank you, Gra-muh!" is instrumental in avoiding a certain strain in his relationship with his mother when Grandmother is present.

Later, we will have occasion to examine some implications of instrumental learning processes in children in relation to other aspects of their socialization and education. For now, we should keep in mind that the entire learning process is a complex one about which we have many unanswered questions.

We are fairly certain, however, that there may be important discrepancies between what a child *learns* at times and what the adults in his life *intend* that he learn. One mother taught her toddler to stay in bed after being put there by telling the child "There is a mean, black, dirty old man under your bed, and he will grab you if you try to get out!" Unfortunately, it was not possible to continue to observe that child since the family moved away shortly after the mother reported success in getting the girl to stay in bed. But it serves as a reminder for us to inquire, when a "technique" for teaching something to a child is reported to be effective, "What else is the child learning, besides the behavior we want him to learn?" In the case of the girl who learned to stay in her bed, there are a number of additional kinds of learning about which we could speculate!

The interaction of heredity and environment

We have described genetic and learning factors as the two fundamental processes in development. We can never know precisely just what proportion of a given kind of growth is hereditary and what proportion is the result of environmental forces. We can, however, cite examples of characteristics that seem to be relatively more a function of one than the other of these two forces. Table 3.1 provides a very crude comparison,

TABLE 3.1. Relative Significance of Heredity and Environment for Basic Human Characteristics

Quality	Role of heredity	Role of environment
Eye color, complexion, body build	very high	very low
Intelligence, aptitudes, talents	high	low
Skills and abilities based on training	low	high
Attitudes, values, beliefs, prejudices	very low	very high

and suggests that most any kind of development is best accounted for in terms of the interaction between the two processes.

Even during the prenatal period, very significant environmental forces have already begun to interact with genetic factors in producing growth. Certain kinds of infections in the mother's body can be transmitted to the fetus and influence development, for example. There is evidence that the mother's nutritional status before and during pregnancy affects the size, weight, and health status of the baby at delivery. In the study reported by Burke, et al. (1949), summarized in Figure 3.2, marked differences in the percentages of newborn infants whose physical condition was described as excellent, good, fair, or poorest were found for groups of mothers whose dietary ratings were described as excellent, fair, poor, or very poor. In addition, fetal development may be affected by maternal use of drugs, alcohol, and tobacco.

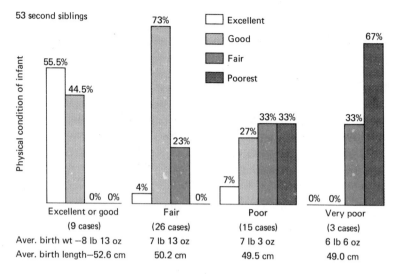

FIGURE 3.2 The relation of prenatal dietary rating to the physical condition of the infant at birth. (From B. S. Burke, et. al., "Nutritional Studies During Pregnancy, Relation of Maternal Nutrition to Condition of Infant at Birth: Study of Siblings," *Journal of Nutrition*, 1949, *38*: 462.)

We have already noted the serious effects on the development of the fetus that can result if a mother contracts rubella during the first 3 months of pregnancy. Another line of evidence on the interaction effects comes from the many accumulated reports of progressive retardation of intellectual development, which has been found to be associated with conditions of extreme poverty. Children from some such populations, who, at the age of 1 year, are more or less within the normal range of mental development, and who have been found to become progressively more retarded with increasing age (Klaus and Gray 1968), serve to illustrate that intelligence, long assumed to be a function of genetic endowment, is better characterized as a continuing process of the construction of a set of mental operations through the inter-action of genetic potentials with environmental resources.

Piaget's theory of intellectual development recognizes the existence of maturational processes as well as environmental forces, but places the main emphasis on the interaction of the two. According to Flavell (1963), an American interpreter of Piaget, a key idea in the theory is that development occurs through the process of *equilibration,* which involves the constant interchange between the child and his world.

Equilibration is, in fact, regarded as the "propellant" that brings about transition to higher stages of functioning. In essence, equilibration refers to the process of striving for balance, or stability. It is this striving in the face of discrepancies, incongruities, conflicts, and ambiguities that results in the achievement of higher levels of mental organization. According to Piaget and Inhelder (1969), ". . . An equilibration is necessary to reconcile the roles of maturation, experience with objects, and social experience" (p. 159).

From the evidence available on a variety of kinds of development we may then conclude that hereditary and environmental forces are very real, and that they function in interaction with each other in producing significant changes in the child's structure, the organization of his total system, and behavioral possibilities.

Some generalizations about development

With the accumulation of much scientific data, it has become possible to formulate some general principles that apply to the processes of development. There is an orderliness to human growth. It gives evidence of lawfulness and coherence. That lawfulness can be described under a few major headings, which we will list and discuss briefly in this final section of the chapter.

1. Development proceeds in an orderly fashion.
2. The rate of development is not constant.

3. Different parts and subsystems have their own individual patterns and sequences of development.
4. Development includes the processes of differentiation, integration, and hierarchization.

Development as an orderly process

From conception to maturity, development is a continuing sequence of stages that are more or less regular and predictable. Each stage is an outgrowth of the one preceding it; each, in turn, provides a foundation for the stages to follow. One way in which the orderliness and lawful continuity of development are illustrated is in the *directions of growth,* dramatically demonstrated in the prenatal period and throughout infancy. Two major directions of development are discernible: first, development proceeds in a *cephalocaudal* direction, that is, from upper portions of the body toward the lower portions; and second, development proceeds in a *proximo-distal* direction, that is, from the centerline of the body outward toward the peripheral, or distant parts. Figure 3.3 represents these two directions of development.

The orderly, systematic nature of development from head to toe and from midline to periphery of the body has important im-

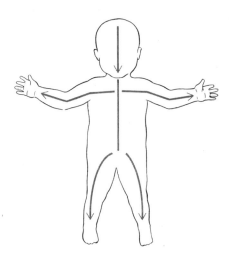

FIGURE 3.3 A diagrammatic representation of the directional tendency in physical and motor development. (From *Developmental Psychology,* 3rd. Ed., Florence L. Goodenough and Leona E. Tyler. Copyright © 1959. By permission of Appleton-Century-Crofts, Educational Division, Meredith Corporation.)

plications for understanding a child's readiness to engage in new activities. For example, we expect a child, during the latter half of his first year, to be able to sit up without support, balancing the head and trunk well, long before he stands up and walks on his feet. This is not just because to sit up is easier than to stand; it is also because the nerves and muscles that control the sitting behavior are relatively more mature at 7 months than the nerves and muscles that control standing and walking.

Similarly, we expect a child, from infancy through the early years, to be relatively more adept at controlling the large muscles involved in moving whole limbs or total body action, than he is in controlling the fine muscles involved in manipulation of tiny objects with the fingers. From such examples we may draw the general inference that there is a basic pattern and sequence underlying human development, and progress in the growth of the individual child is normally achieved by moving through, rather than bypassing, the stages of this sequence. The major stages of the early years appear to be heavily influenced by the genetic code.

Inconstancy of developmental rate

This principle is most easily illustrated in physical growth, but has application to other aspects of development as well. In measurements of the same child, taken at different periods of his life, it will normally be found that he is growing very rapidly at some stages and very slowly at others. Physical growth proceeds unevenly, with the rapid spurt of infant development followed by much slower growth during the years from 3 to 6. While the rate of visible physical growth becomes slower, however, some very important changes may be taking place in motor development; the emergence of language; and mental, social, or emotional development. In each of these areas, too, the rate of growth differs from one stage to another.

Rapid changes in mental development do not necessarily coincide with similar increases in other areas (Bayley 1956). There is some evidence that motor and language development may have complementary spurts of growth during the second year.

During the period that a child is making rapid progress in standing, walking, and running about there may, for a time, be a period of "motor specialization" during which language, for example, improves very slowly. Later, when the motor skills necessary to walking and running become well practiced, other aspects of growth, including language, progress more rapidly. This suggests that different aspects or subsystems of the child have their own timetables of development, which do not necessarily coincide with each other.

Patterns of individual aspects of development

Closely related to the previous one, this principle is illustrated in some of the same phenomena as have just been cited. Another way to illustrate its operation is to compare different organs and subsystems of the body with respect to their rate of maturation, during the prenatal as well as the postnatal periods. Gesell and Ilg (1949) observed that by the early part of the fetal period the nervous system is structurally complete. By contrast, the skeletal, muscular, circulatory, and respiratory systems are relatively much further from completion. Many centers of ossification in the skeletal system do not make their appearance until the child is well along the road to physical maturity. Similar examples may be drawn from later childhood. Sexual maturity, for example, is reached only when the other basic physiological processes are well established. Yet, emotional and social maturity are not necessarily achieved even at this stage, as parents of adolescents will testify.

Figure 3.4 provides a graphic illustration of the marked differences in the rate of development of different body subsystems. It also shows an interesting feature of development in the tendency of some parts and subsystems to decline in their functional capacity much more rapidly—once they have reached their highest level—than others.

Processes of differentiation, integration, and hierarchization

These three processes are discussed together because of their integral operation in the development of the individual child. At the same time as his body cells, tissues, organs, and subsystems

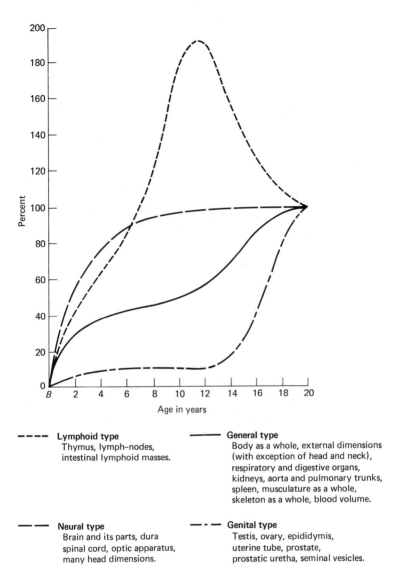

FIGURE 3.4 This graph shows the major types of postnatal growth of the various parts and organs of the body. The several curves are drawn to a common scale by computing their values at successive ages in terms of their postnatal increments (to 20 years). (From Richard E. Scammon, "The Measurement of the Body in Childhood," in J. A. Harris, C. M. Jackson, D. G. Peterson, and R. E. Scammon, *The Measurement of Man*. University of Minnesota Press. Copyright 1930, University of Minnesota.)

are becoming more differentiated and specialized in their functions, a child is achieving greater capability for using each part or subsystem in relation to other parts and subsystems. And while these two processes are occurring, there is simultaneously the development of higher order and lower order operations in the structure and functioning of the total system.

A homely analogy, which might make these three processes more meaningful, would be the mental operations an adult might go through if he had never learned anything about the mechanics of an automobile and had, in fact, never looked under the hood of a car to see what was there. If this person, for some reason, now has occasion to look under the hood, and is confronted by a mass of wires, cables, tubes, and assorted mechanical features of strange design, his perception of this is undoubtedly a global, diffuse, and *undifferentiated* one. With further experience and help in learning to identify the names and functions of each particular part, his perception of the things under the hood becomes differentiated in the sense that the distinct parts emerge more clearly from the mass of unorganized machinery, and each part takes on a differentiated meaning for him.

A still higher level of functioning for this man, however, would be that of learning the interrelationship of parts by achieving an understanding of how the ignition system works in relation to, or *integrated* with, the fuel system, and how these two are tied in with the drive train, which is, among other things, supported by a frame and suspension system.

Finally, at the same time as this integration process is occurring in the mind of our adult learner, it is quite likely that he will achieve a *hierarchical ordering* in his overall view of the automobile, in which higher level subsystems of the machine are seen to be organizations of lower order subsystems. Thus, the operation of the electrical system is more clearly understood, and its role in integration with other systems becomes more understandable when this man recognizes the subroles within the electrical system played by battery, alternator, distributor, spark plugs, and so on.

At first, such a mechanical example may appear to be far

removed from the processes of human development. It becomes less distant, however, if we remind ourselves that it is the structuring in the mental operations of the human being that we are illustrating, and not that in the car. The general "message" in this example is that many, if not all, aspects of human growth can be characterized as undergoing this interacting combination of processes of differentiation, integration, and hierarchization.

Probably in no sphere of human functioning is this more evident than in the achievement of complex skills such as in instrumental music. Differentiation occurs at several levels, beginning with (in the case of the pianist) such elemental learnings as what "Middle C" looks like and where it is located on the keyboard, in contrast with other keys, which at first may have all looked alike, or undifferentiated.

Another kind of differentiation, usually occurring much later, has to do with making one's right hand perform in a manner somewhat independent of what one's left hand is doing, possibly even using different temporal as well as spatial cues for the organization of behavior. It is obvious, though, that a listenable performance calls for some degree of integration of what one hand is doing with the performance of the other!

Finally, we could also illustrate hierarchization at different levels, but perhaps it is most clearly seen in the sensitive subordination of some aspects of a musical performance to others, on the part of a very proficient artist. His performance, far from being merely mechanically or technically accurate, is characterized by a weaving together of dominant and secondary themes, with awareness of the overriding progression of the total composition and the contribution of the subsystems, each in turn with its still smaller components. A single note is not merely the equivalent of every other single note, but makes its contribution then through its organic involvement in successively larger subsystems, hierarchically organized.

To summarize the processes of this fourth general principle of development, we may say that development proceeds as the total system—the child—(1) achieves clearer, more identifiable structure and function in its separate parts and subsystems, (2) achieves greater capacity to bring the subparts into meaningful relation with one another, and (3) achieves an increasingly functional organization of the parts of the total system into superordinate and subordinate components.

The goal of development

The preceding section, which outlines some general features of the growth process, says little about the objective, or goal, toward which these developmental processes are reaching. From the scientist's standpoint, this is a philosophical question, more teleological than scientific in its implications. That is, the question implies that there must be some ultimate purpose in natural law, representing the goal toward which the individual human child strives. In this view, the developmental changes represent a striving to fulfill the natural law.

Admittedly, such concepts neither lend themselves readily to experimental investigation, nor to direct observation. In spite of this difficulty, some students of human development and personality growth have taken the position that growth has, as its central theme and objective, the achievement of a state of *self-realization.*

It is the position of Erikson (1963), for example, that the mature personality is characterized by *ego-integrity.* This implies that the individual has achieved the essential fullness of his childhood potentials, and has integrated those earlier potentials into a concept of himself, which he finds satisfying. The earlier stages in personality formation, in this view, are essential steps—prerequisite to, and leading in the direction of—this ultimate state of human maturity.

Another approach to this issue has been outlined by Maslow (1943), who is concerned with man's basic motives. He envisions these motives as operating in a hierarchical system, with need satisfaction at each level being prerequisite to the individual's freedom to function at the next higher level. Thus *physiological needs,* such as hunger and thirst, must be satisfied for the person to be free to operate at the next level, which is that of *safety needs*, such as freedom from threats. Satisfaction of safety needs provides the essential prerequisite for functioning at the level of *love needs*, including the needs for affection, acceptance, and belonging. *Esteem needs*, at the next level in Maslow's hierarchy, include the notion of self-esteem from mastery of elements of the environment, and also assurance of one's fundamental worth as a unique being. Finally, Maslow describes the *need for self-actualization*, which only comes into operation if needs at the more primitive levels are satisfied. This ultimate motivational level implies a readiness to involve oneself in creative self-expression in personal and social achievements; it implies a need to act freely, to satisfy one's curiosity, and to understand one's world.

While Maslow is not describing a historical sequence of events in individual development—needs at all levels persist throughout one's life and are not to be identified with a stage in development—his classification of human motives may nevertheless be interpreted as a continuous striving for higher levels of functioning. In this view, man is forever seeking to function at the higher levels, and needs only to be freed from the constraints of the more primitive needs to enable him to do so. Self-actualization (or self-realization, as we have chosen to term it here) may be construed as the ultimate objective and goal of human behavior.

Regardless of the scientific merit of these descriptive statements about human development and functioning, they may be turned to useful guidelines by the person who chooses to work with children. The teacher, for example, who perceives the child's efforts to satisfy primitive needs as requiring support, even when the child's behavior is unattractive, can develop a constructive philosophy of child guidance, which views the child *in process*, and which incorporates an understanding of the child's immediate needs with a long-range view of his growth tasks. We should note that this statement does not provide any specific formula for behavior to employ in order to satisfy a child's growth needs. It is, rather, a philosophical frame of reference, which can afford greater insight into the complexities of child growth. Implicit in this frame of reference is the assumption that the motivation for achievement of higher levels of functioning exists within the child, and that the role of the adults is essentially a supportive one.

Perhaps the most obvious illustration of what we are describing here is to be found in the behavior of the infant who has just achieved upright locomotion. He may be so delighted with his new achievement, that he gives the impression he has personally just *invented* walking behavior! But the striking thing about his new mode of getting around, especially since it can lead him into all sorts of trouble as well as give him certain advantages over the creeping mode, is that he does not need to be encouraged to do it, or taught how to do it. The motive for walking appears to be "built in," and in its earliest stages, walking brings its own rewards of satisfaction quite apart from the fact that it gets the infant from point A to point B!

The position we have taken here is that walking is merely one of many achievements of the human child toward fulfilling, to a greater or lesser degree, the fundamental urgency to become what one's tissues promise.

Summary

In this chapter, development has been defined as the total complex of processes arising from internal and external forces, which result in changes in the form, structure, and functioning of the individual. The internal, genetic forces and the external, environmental forces interact with each other to produce developmental changes at all levels and stages of growth. Major environmental contributions to development occur through processes of conditioning, discrimination learning, and instrumental learning.

Development proceeds in an orderly, systematic fashion; it is not haphazard or capricious. Its rate varies from one stage to another, and is different for various parts of the total child system and for different aspects of his development. It includes subprocesses of differentiation, integration, and hierarchization. It is possible to conceptualize the overall goal of human development as that of self-realization—the achievement of the potential levels of structure and function given in the genetic material inherited by the child.

References

Bayley, N. "Individual Patterns of Development." *Child Development* 27 (1956) 45–74.

Bruner, J., Olver, R. R., and Greenfield, P. M., eds. *Studies in Cognitive Growth*. New York: Wiley, 1966.

Burke, B. S., et al. "Nutrition Studies During Pregnancy, Relation of Maternal Nutrition to Condition of Infant at Birth: Study of Siblings." *Journal of Nutrition* 38 (1949) 453–467.

Erikson, E. H. *Childhood and Society*. 2nd ed. New York: Norton, 1963.

Flavell, J. *The Developmental Psychology of Jean Piaget*. Princeton, N.J.: Van Nostrand, 1963.

Freedman, D. G., and Keller, B. "Inheritance of Behavior in Infants." *Science* 140 (12 April 1963) 196–198.

Gardner, D. B., Hawkes, G. R., and Burchinal, L. "Noncontinuous Mothering in Infancy and Development in Later Childhood." *Child Development* 32 (1961) 225–234.

Gesell, A., and Ilg, F. L. *Child Development: An Introduction to the Study of Human Growth*. New York: Harper, 1949.

Hartup, W. W. "Dependence and Independence." In Stevenson, H. W., ed. *Child Psychology*. National Society for the Study of Education Yearbook, Part 1. Chicago: University of Chicago Press, 1963, pp. 333–363.

Klaus, R., and Gray, S. W. "The Early Training Project for Disadvantaged Children: A Report After Five Years." *Monographs of the Society for Research in Child Development* 33 (1968).

Maslow, A. H. "A Theory of Human Motivation." *Psychological Review* 50 (1943) 370–396.

McClearn, G. "Genetic Influences on Behavior and Development." In Mussen, P. H., ed. *Carmichael's Manual of Child Psychology*. 3rd ed., vol. 1. New York: Wiley, 1970, pp. 39–76.

Nossal, G. J. V. *Antibodies and Immunity*. New York: Basic Books, 1969.

Piaget, J., and Inhelder, B. *The Psychology of the Child*. Translated by H. Weaver. New York: Basic Books, 1969.

Rheingold, H. "The Modification of Social Responsiveness in Institutional Babies." *Monographs of the Society for Research in Child Development* 21 (1956).

Rheingold, H., Gewirtz, J. L., and Ross, H. W. "Social Conditioning of Vocalizations in the Infant." *Journal of Comparative and Physiological Psychology* 52 (1959) 68–73.

Sanford, F. H. *Psychology: A Scientific Study of Man.* 2nd ed. Belmont, Calif.: Wadsworth, 1965.

Schaffer, H. R., and Emerson, P. E. "The Development of Social Attachments in Infancy." *Monographs of the Society for Research in Child Development* 29 (1964).

Vandenberg, S. G. "Hereditary Factors in Normal Personality Traits." In Wortis, J., ed. *Recent Advances in Biological Psychiatry.* Vol. 9. New York: Plenum Press, 1967, pp. 65–104.

Watson, J. B., and Rayner, R. "Conditioned Emotional Reactions." *Journal of Experimental Psychology* 3 (1920) 1–14.

CHAPTER FOUR
Development during infancy

In what respects is the neonatal period a continuation of prenatal development?

What are the physical and psychological characteristics of the neonate?

What are the major accomplishments of the child during the period of infancy?

To what extent are long-term personality characteristics formed during infancy?

What is the importance of early stimulation in the environment of the infant?

Birth
as a milestone

At the time of delivery, a baby has completed 9 months, more or less, of the most rapid growth in size and complexity that a human being ever undergoes. Each newborn brings with him his own special characteristics and idiosyncrasies, both physical and psychological. Babies differ, one from another, in size, weight, skin texture and complexion, amount and thickness of hair, and other obvious features, but they also differ in degree of responsiveness to the environment, in activity level, in "tempo," in readiness for vigorous grasping of the environment, and many other ways—some quite clearly observable and others much more subtle. These individual differences had their beginnings at the time of conception, in the uniquely coded "information" in the zygote, which represented the genetic inheritance from both mother and father. The unique combination of genetic information interacted, throughout the three major stages of prenatal development, with the biochemical environment of the mother's body.

Individual differences in development, which had their beginnings in the genetic material and the prenatal environment, are then continued into the postnatal stages of development. We are accustomed to thinking of identical twins as having the same genetic endowment; therefore differences between such twins present illustrations of the complex factors involved in producing the unique individual each child is.

Such differences are well portrayed (see Figure 4.1) by a pair of male twins carefully described by Falkner (1966). At birth, Twin B weighed 2806 grams, while Twin A weighed 1460 grams, was classified as "premature," and remained in the hospital for premature infant care for 37 days following delivery. These twins showed close similarities in dental and skeletal development, and hair and eye color. However, Twin B was consistently taller and heavier than Twin A from birth through 48 months. No data were reported by Falkner with respect to intellectual development, but he did cite differences in behavior patterns, based primarily

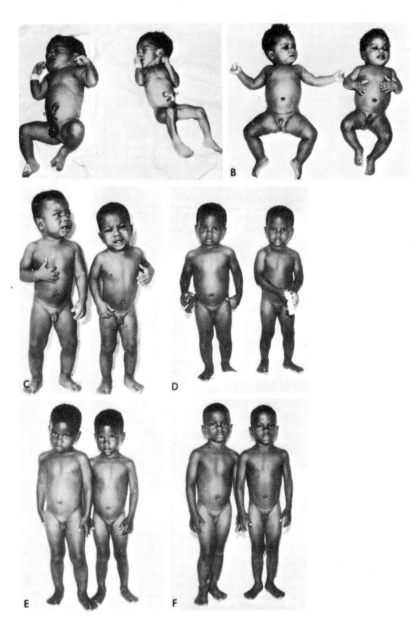

FIGURE 4.1 Growth of a pair of identical twin boys. (From
F. Falkner, ed., *Human Development*, Philadelphia: Saunders,
1966.)

on the mother's reports, indicating that Twin A was touchy, irritable, and bad tempered while Twin B was placid and more affectionate.

Following birth, it is normal for infants to continue the growth rates characteristic of the later fetal period and then, near the end of infancy, to enter the period of stable gain in height and weight that will characterize their development until the spurt of adolescence. However, this does not explain the wide individual differences observable among newborns, which remains one of the intriguing questions in the field of child development.

Brazelton (1969), writing from the perspective of the practicing pediatrician, presents a warm, understanding, and useful description of the variations in behavior patterns of infants at birth and through the first year. This authority illustrates and describes active babies, quiet babies, and "average" babies through the device of case materials, well presented, to highlight the individuality of infant development.

The neonatal period

The term *neonate* has been given a variety of definitions. Some writers have included only the first week or 10 days following birth as the neonatal period. Others have included the first 2 weeks, or the first 4 weeks, and some have even equated the neonatal period with the entire period of infancy. But the critical thing about the neonatal period is that during it a satisfactory level of physiological stability is established with respect to such functions as circulation, respiration, ingestion and digestion of food, elimination of wastes, and body temperature regulation. While the infant may be ready at birth to engage in these processes, the establishment of physiological stability in the processes themselves takes longer. A fair degree of stabilization is reached, typically, by the end of the fourth week following birth. For our purposes, then, we may think of this early physiological adjustment period as the period of the neonate, which lasts about 4 weeks following birth.

Physical appearance and characteristics

In our society it is customary for new parents to announce not only the birth of a child, but his name, sex, and birth weight. The matter of birth weight is of greater significance medically than socially, however. Much of the birth weight is achieved during the last 2 months prior to delivery, and is one indicator of maturity. The weight gain during the final weeks of prenatal growth is primarily an increase in fatty tissue under the skin. That tissue has some insulation properties during the neonatal period, while body temperature regulation is not yet well established.

The neonate may lose up to 10 percent of his birth weight during the first 3 or 4 days following birth, but the typical weight loss is mostly a matter of losing excess body fluid rather than a loss of solid tissue. By the fifth day, the neonate is typically starting to regain weight, and many will have reached their birth weight by about 10 days. Most will do so by 14 days. Ordinarily, breast-fed infants do not gain weight quite as rapidly as those on a cow's milk formula.

Healthy, full-term, neonates vary in length from 18 to 22 inches, averaging 20 inches for males and 19¾ for females. In weight, male babies are only very slightly heavier, on the average, than female babies, but a good rough average birth weight for American infants of both sexes is 7¼ to 7½ pounds. There is little or no relationship between birth weight and adult body size, and only a slight relationship between birth length and adult height. By age 2, however, when the infancy period has ended and the childhood growth rate has been established, there is a much more reliable relationship between childhood height and adult height.

Because of the differential growth rates for different parts of the body, during the prenatal as well as postnatal years, the body proportions of the neonate are markedly different from those of the older child or adult. The head appears very large in comparison with the rest of the body and is approximately the same circumference as the chest. The feet, by comparison, look tiny and have an "unfinished" appearance. The upper part of the head and face are more developed than the chin and lower jaw. The head may be covered with a heavy growth of long, dark hair and may even extend down over the temples; there is typically a wide distribution of very fine hair, or *lanugo*, over the neonate's body.

At birth the neonate's skin is covered with a greasy protective coating, the *vernix caseosa*. The skin color of white babies is ruddy and prone to bluish tinges at the extremities. The skin is thin and tender. Since temperature control and circulation are not yet well established immediately after birth, it is not uncommon for the hands and feet to feel cool to the touch. Nails are firm and well formed in the full-term infant. The new baby's eyes are typically blue except in nonwhite infants, but it is difficult to predict later eye color from this. The eyes are functionally ready for gross vision, although they may not focus or coordinate well. It is doubtful that the neonate has good color vision, however, since the cones of the retina are not yet developed.

Birth weight is affected by plurality (that is, twins and triplets weigh less than singletons). It is also affected by geography. (Babies born in the Mountain States, for example, weigh slightly less than Pacific Coast babies!) It is obviously influenced by length of gestation. (In 1966, for example, live births after 28–31 weeks averaged 1500 grams, while those for 40 weeks averaged 3340 grams.) It is affected by birth order (first babies weigh less, on the average, than second, third, or later-born babies). From Table 4.1 it is clear that birth weight is also affected by age of mother, and by racial or ethnic group. Since the interaction of these factors with genetic and nutritional effects is so complex, the traditional practice of classifying neonates of less than 5½ pounds as "prematures" is questionable. Falkner (1966) argues that we should refer to such infants as "ILBs" (infants of low birth weight), and that we should treat them as "prematures" depending on the *reasons* for the low birth weight in a particular case. Tanner (1970) agrees that for scientific purposes it is more appropriate to speak of them as ILBs.

TABLE 4.1. Median Birth Weight for United States Babies, 1966, by Color and Age of Mother

	Birth weight in grams*		
Age of mother	White	Nonwhite	Total
less than 15	3200	2960	3040
15–19	3270	3040	3210
20–24	3300	3120	3270
25–29	3330	3170	3300
30–34	3350	3190	3320
35–39	3360	3210	3330
40–44	3360	3230	3340
45–49	3380	3280	3360
Total, all ages	3310	3120	3280

* There are 453.59 grams per pound; thus 5 pounds = approximately 2268 grams, 6 pounds = approximately 2722 grams, 7 pounds = approximately 3175 grams, and 8 pounds = approximately 3629 grams.

SOURCE: *Vital Statistics in the United States,* 1967, Washington, D.C.: National Center for Health Statistics, U.S. Public Health Service.

Physiological processes and motor behavior of the neonate

All of growth and, for that matter, all of life, require continual adjustment of vital body processes. At no stage of development, however, are the changes in physiological functioning more critical than at the time of birth. During the prenatal period the mother's body played the major role in such basic processes as respiration, ingestion and digestion of food, and excretion of body wastes. Even blood circulation, although carried on independently by the fetus, was markedly different prior to birth because the lungs were not functioning and oxygen had been provided for the baby's bloodstream through the placental membranes.

At birth, or very shortly following birth, significant changes in such processes must occur if the infant is to survive. He must get air into his lungs to provide oxygen and to provide for elimination of excess carbon dioxide. He must also redirect the flow of blood to send venous blood to the lungs for oxygenation.

Other anatomic and physiological changes also occur when the umbilical cord is cut. The initiation of pulmonary breathing requires the beginning of expansion of the lungs. More complete expansion usually occurs within the next few days.

Stitt (1960) reports that gastrointestinal function does not proceed as rapidly, but that the healthy infant has its own supply of nutrients that will meet the needs of the first few days. The neonate is, however, capable of sucking, swallowing, and ingesting liquid food, and of reflex action leading to evacuation of the large bowel. Functioning of the kidneys also begins shortly after birth. However, the efficiency of this function in removing waste products and in maintaining water balance in the body tissues improves gradually throughout the neonatal period.

The neonate's resources for intelligent behavior

It is not uncommon for adults to ponder, when inspecting a new baby, "What is going on in his little head?" Since we have no personal memories of our own experience as neonates, and since the baby cannot describe his "thinking" to us, we can only speculate on the mental life of the neonate. William James, famous psychologist and philosopher of the late nineteenth and early twentieth centuries, described the infant's mental life as a "blooming, buzzing confusion" (1890, p. 488). Gesell questioned this, and suggested that the baby probably ". . . senses the visible world at first in fugitive and fluctuating blotches against a neutral background" (Gesell and Ilg 1949, p. 22).

Gesell argues further that the mental life of the baby includes sounds, the pressure of his body weight, feelings of his own movements of mouth and limbs, feelings of satisfaction associated with feeding, and distress from hunger or cold. It is highly unlikely, however, that the newborn infant can find much "meaning" in the world outside his own skin. It is the biological development of the central nervous system, combined with the accumulating effects of experience, that results in the organization of coherent, connected mental action.

Thus, to understand the neonate's potential for intelligent behavior, we must take into account the biological equipment with which he is endowed and his resources for receiving stimulation from the outside world. These latter resources are his sensory capacities—his equipment for seeing, hearing, feeling, tasting, and smelling.

At birth, the brain has already accomplished a great deal of growth and maturation, and has already reached approximately one-fourth the size it will be at full maturity. It has grown much faster, relatively, than the rest of the body, and it continues to do so following birth. Watson and Lowrey (1962) report that about half of all the growing the brain will do between birth and maturity will be done during the first year.

With respect to functioning, it appears that certain parts of the brain and spinal cord are more mature at birth than others. The outer portion of the cerebrum, or cerebral cortex, is the part that is most directly involved in the higher mental processes of learning, thinking, remembering, and reasoning. This part of the brain is what enables us to engage in the rich and complex varieties of behavior of which we are capable, and to pursue complicated and indirect courses of action in order to solve problems and reach goals.

The lower portions of the brain, by contrast, are more directly involved in controlling vital physiological processes and the more or less stereotyped, automatic, and reflexive behavior in response to specific stimulation. These lower-brain centers are relatively more developed and functional at birth than are the higher-brain centers. The evidence for their functioning is found in the operation of the reflexes, some of which are well established before the child is born.

One example of this is the *moro reflex*, typical of the neonate in response to sudden change of position, jarring, or sudden loud sounds. When stimulated in such a manner, the neonate tenses his muscles, extends his arms widely, and then brings them toward each other as if to embrace or seize. A similar reflex action has been observed in infant monkeys, leading some students to speculate that the reflex, which disappears after the first few weeks of life, served as a protective and survival mechanism in human evolution.

Another example of a reflex behavior pattern characteristic of the neonate, which also disappears later, is the *tonic neck reflex,* involving a natural coordination of the position of head, arms, and legs. The neonate, when lying on his back, may automatically assume a position with his head turned to one side—typically to the right. The arm and leg on the side he is facing are extended, while the arm and leg of the other side are flexed. This is sometimes referred to as the "fencing position." If the infant's head is turned by an attendant to face in the opposite direction, there may be a corresponding shift in arm and leg positions. This reflex coordination of head and limbs is much more pronounced in some infants than others, and may persist for the first 3 to 6 months.

Some of the more significant and interesting reflexes from the standpoint of survival and healthy development have to do with feeding. The neonate is equipped with a fairly complicated set of reflex-response mechanisms, which enable him to take in food. One of these is the *rooting reflex* described by numerous infant observers. In response to stimulation on the side of the face, the infant turns his head in the direction of the stimulus, simultaneously opening his mouth. Such a pattern obviously increases the likelihood of making and maintaining contact with the mother's breast.

Along with the rooting reflex, sucking reflexes play an important role in the ingestion of milk. A very light stimulation of lips, cheeks, or chin may result in vigorous sucking movements, including coordination of tongue and lower jaw. These movements, in turn, are coordinated with swallowing reflexes and respiration. An interesting observation of the special characteristics of newborn infants is that they are able to coordinate vigorous sucking, swallowing, and breathing in a manner difficult, if not impossible, for the adult.

These and the many other reflex patterns which have been observed (see Kessen, et al. 1970, pp. 311–315), while not directly or immediately involved in the higher mental processes, represent one major resource for intelligent behavior, and at the same time give one line of evidence of the functioning of an intact nervous system.

The neonate's sensory capacities represent another major resource for intelligent behavior. Research on this question has stressed vision, but has also examined senses of touch, hearing, taste, and smell. It is important to make a distinction here between sensitivity, on the one hand, and meaningful perception, on the other. Visual sensitivity, for example, is readily demonstrated by the neonate's reflex reactions to light, including pupillary contraction as well as blinking of the eyelids. But the ability to make visual distinctions, as between light and dark or between figure and background, does not imply the ability to make sharp visual discriminations of *objects*.

There is a great deal of learning involved, as well as maturation, in the development of visual processes. This includes learning to bring images into clear focus on the retina, and learning to follow moving objects with precision. For the neonate, the size, shape, and rapid growth of the eyeball itself make it unlikely that a sharp image could readily be brought into focus.

The research on neonatal reactions to color is not entirely conclusive. Color perception is mediated by the cones of the retina, and some authorities hold that these are not functionally present during the neonatal period. There is some evidence of clear-cut visual response to color by the third or fourth month following birth.

The sense of touch exists even before birth and is quite evident in the neonate, especially on the face, and particularly around the mouth.

The auditory mechanism is present and functional at birth, although there may be little or no hearing until the eustachian tube is well opened and any amniotic fluid or debris cleared out of the middle ear. However, as Watson and Lowrey remark, "The middle ear, concerned with the collecting and transmitting of sound waves to the internal ear, is practically of adult size at birth, although the drum membrane may be smaller and more oblique" (1962, p. 192). Acute hearing sensitivity is shown by the neonate's startle response to sounds within a few days.

Gustatory (taste) and olfactory (smell) senses are also present at birth, although the neonate does not appear to make fine distinctions between sour, salty, and bitter substances. He does respond vigorously to the smell of such substances as ammonia and acetic acid, although it is difficult to determine whether this is truly an olfactory response independent of pain.

In general, it is clear that the neonate is equipped with an active, functioning sensory system. In their extensive review of the literature, Kessen, et al. (1970) report that the neonate is "competent," in that he responds to stimulation in all sensory modalities. Thus we might conclude that in both sensory and intellectual functioning, the neonate is born with the essential biological resources for the emergence of these functions.

Resources for personal, emotional, and social behavior

The neonate's resources for personal, emotional, and social behavior—those qualities that are commonly thought of as the "personality" aspects of the child—are more difficult to establish among his characteristics and responses. However, it is clear that there are individual differences in babies from the very beginning.

We are no longer likely to make the error of assuming that differences in personality among older children and adults are exclusively a matter of learning. Personality development is an interaction process from its beginning—interaction of internal, inherited biological forces with environmental, experiential forces. Because the environmental forces were limited and restricted in the prenatal period, the effects of genetic endowment are more clearly evident in the neonate, and these differences are indeed significant.

Some neonates, as we have noted, are more reactive to stimulation than others. There are marked differences in amount and depth of sleep. Some spend a much larger proportion of each 24-hour period in quiet wakefulness, others in crying. There are wide variations in tempo and speed of growth, in interest in the external environment, in vigorousness of feeding behavior, and so on. The significance of such differences lies not only in illustrating the primary effects of genetics in establishing "personality" characteristics, but also in the subtle interplay of these early differences with the social environment. For example, we believe that these differences play a role in eliciting and shaping the attitudes and responses of the baby's mother toward the baby. It is as if the baby participates in structuring the maternal behavior, which in turn plays a vital role in shaping his own personality.

It is not possible to specify any precise relationship between neonatal characteristics and later personality development, given our present state of understanding and the many factors that will intervene in the constant reshaping of the personality of the infant and child. Much of that personality shaping is essentially a social process, achieved in the interaction of infant and child with others. At first, the infant is essentially asocial; he has no distinct notion of "self" as an entity in a relationship with others. With social behavior, as with intellectual behavior, it is more accurate to say that the neonate has resources and potentials for its development, rather than that he engages in such behavior.

The newborn's equipment for emotional behavior is similarly immature, and will undergo much modification as he learns new ways to respond to new things. Nevertheless, he is quite capable at birth of reacting to his bodily states and to his environment with responses which could be called emotional.

Modern students of infant behavior are more inclined to speak of affective states—noting degrees of arousal—and studying these in relation to psychological and physiological conditions such as heart rate, respiration, and responsiveness to external stimulation. Specific emotions, such as fear, anger, joy, and affection, probably do not exist at first, but the "raw materials"—in the form of variations in affective state, out of which these emotions will be constructed in interaction with stimulus events in the environment—are present from the beginning.

Emotion is aroused by internal stimulation as well as by external conditions such as hunger and temperature change, respectively. The general capacity to respond with emotion to such conditions stands the neonate in good stead, of course, since he has no other way of informing the world of his needs or of correcting situations calling for attention. At first, however, a mother is not able to tell on the basis of the sounds he makes whether he is crying from hunger, colic, or a wet diaper. Later, as he responds somewhat differently to each of these situations, mothers report that they can detect differences in the kind of crying the infant engages in. A part of this may relate to the mothers' ability to predict what is likely to be a source of discomfort; but in the development of emotional behavior it is safe to assume there is a strong social involvement, with interaction between baby and adults in influencing the manner of construction of the emotions.

It is natural to think the neonate has a long way to go to achieve the characteristics that mark him as a responsive, purposeful human being. From our discussion thus far, however, it should be clear that some of the most vital and important steps along this road have already been taken by the time of his birth. If we are inclined to think of the infant as helpless, we might keep in mind the truly remarkable range of capacities with which he is equipped at birth—capacities without which he could not survive—and which provide the essential foundation for the next steps in infant development.

Development during infancy

Some writers define infancy as the first postnatal year; others suggest that the first 18 months is a more meaningful period from the standpoint of developmental change. The derivation of the word itself is from the Latin *infans*, formed from the combination of *in* (not) and *fari* (to speak). Thus one definition of infancy might be given as the period of development that precedes speaking. Some writers make a distinction between infancy and toddlerhood, suggesting a motor development basis for defining the period.

For our purposes, however, we will consider the first 2 postnatal years to be representative of the period of infancy. This is a meaningful age span, since it includes a number of most significant accomplishments, such as the achievement of upright locomotion and speech. It is also the span of the sensory-motor stage of intellectual development described by some developmental theorists, and a period representing the formation of important social attachments. Our discussion of infancy, then, will be organized under the headings of the most significant achievements following the neonatal period up to the age of 2 years.

Physical growth achievements during infancy

Increases in size and weight are important in their own right, as well as having implications for other aspects of development. They also serve as a rough indicator of the health status of the infant. Tanner (1970) reports that the *rate* of growth decreases rapidly and steadily during infancy, and becomes relatively stable during the years from 3 through preadolescence. Boys are longer and heavier than girls, on the average, although differences are small throughout infancy. The rapidity of the early growth of the postnatal months is really a continuation of the rapid growth of the prenatal period. At no time in the child's life, even during the adolescent growth spurt, will physical development again proceed as rapidly.

Different parts of the body grow at their own rates, resulting in gradual but definite changes in body proportion. The infant changes from a relatively slender newborn to a more plump or "chunky" 1-year-old. The change is accounted for largely by an increase in subcutaneous fatty tissue. Growth of bone and muscle tissue continues at a relatively steady pace from the first year on through early childhood. Internal organs such as liver, spleen, and kidneys also seem to follow the general growth curve of rapid early development followed by slower, steady development during the years of childhood.

Over a period of years, scientists have worked out a variety of means by which to evaluate the physical growth of the individual infant, in comparison with statistical averages and with himself at different points in time. One example of such a technique is the Baby Grid, developed by Wetzel (1946), based on average figures for a large number of infants. This is a chart that provides "growth channels" on the assumption that an infant, if developing normally, will follow his own channel based on his individual physique. Marked changes, or departures from the infant's own channel, may indicate the need for careful medical examination to determine possible causes for growth irregularity.

One general point pertaining to all such growth charts is that no single index of physical growth can be properly interpreted apart from others. Height, weight, skin condition, subcutaneous fatty tissue, and development of the basic bodily systems (circulatory, alimentary, skeletal, nervous, muscular, respiratory, and glandular) must be considered in relation to each other by the physician in order to appraise the overall progress of the infant.

Achievement of upright locomotion

Walking behavior, which for most of us becomes an easy, "automatic" behavior, is in reality a highly complex activity. It requires the coordination not only of a number of different muscle groups, but of muscles acting in well-organized, systematic relationship with sensory processes of vision, touch, kinesthetic sense, and body-balance or static sense mediated in the inner ear. The sensory processes provide essential feedback for maintaining a standing position, or locomotion, and give guidance for the direction of muscular action. Upright locomotion is not merely a matter of muscular development; yet muscle action and its changes with age represent the most visible aspect of the child's achievement of walking.

We have already noted that the neonate has a variety of reflex behavior patterns. When held in a standing position with his weight supported and his feet in contact with a flat surface, the baby will often make primitive stepping movements. These are rudimentary and have no immediate usefulness except to indicate that the basic human pattern for walking is genetically determined and is present at birth. The initial neural control is reflexive and independent of the higher, conscious brain centers.

Walking, like other forms of body control, follows the basic principle of development from general to specific behavior. At first body movements are random, vague, diffuse, and involve relatively larger body segments. With increased maturation, movements become more controlled, direct, and specific, and involve the portions of the body most immediately concerned with carrying out the appropriate action. This principle can be seen rather clearly in the sequence of stages leading to walking—a sequence that has been well described by Shirley (1931), Bayley (1935), McGraw (1935), and other early students of child development. While there are minor variations among the accounts provided by these authorities, they clearly agree on the major stages of development of upright locomotion.

Figure 4.2 summarizes the sequence of stages and the typical ages of their occurrence, as described by Shirley (1931). From this, walking may be seen as the culmination of a long, involved sequence that began, in an important sense, in the prenatal period. Neither is the sequence complete when the infant takes his first independent steps, for there are important changes still to follow. These include changes in walking posture (becoming more upright); improvement of body balance; learning to avoid obstacles; coordinating walking with other activities such as reaching, grasping, carrying, throwing, catching; and so on. Thus, while the achievement of independent walking at a little over 1 year of age is a dramatic moment in the lives of babies and their parents, it is neither the beginning nor the end of a sequence of stages in the development of upright locomotion; rather, it is one important milestone along the way.

There are wide variations among healthy babies with respect to the rate of movement through this sequence. Not only do different babies reach each stage in their own good time, but it is not uncommon for an infant to pass up a certain stage, going directly to another, more advanced one. Some infants, for example, do little or no true creeping, while for others, creeping is a "way of life" for many weeks. Some creep, after a fashion, in ways markedly different from others. Some prefer a kind of stiff-legged "bear-walk" on all fours. Some engage in a smoothly efficient hitching along in a sitting position with one leg flexed

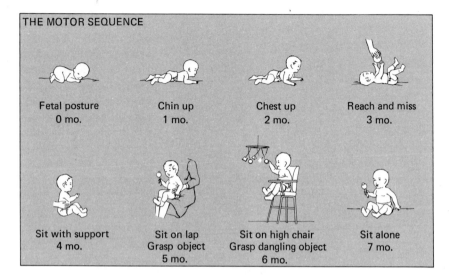

FIGURE 4.2 The motor sequence, leading to upright locomotion. (From Mary M. Shirley, *The First Two Years, Vol. II*, Minneapolis: University of Minnesota Press. Copyright 1933 and 1961, University of Minnesota.)

and the other extended. Some learn to scoot backwards so well that it is easier for them to get where they want to go by turning around and backing up to it! There seems to be no one right way to go through the creeping stage, although some students of early development have argued that it is a crucial stage in the development of neuromotor integration.

The prewalking sequence described in the early work of Shirley (Figure 4.2) also illustrates a second basic principle of motor development in that it occurs in a *cephalocaudal* direction. This principle, sometimes referred to as the "law of developmental direction," means that development of both structure and function occurs first in the upper portions of the body and later in progressively lower portions. Thus the control of head, neck,

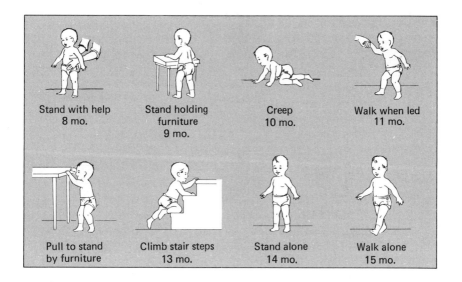

Stand with help	Stand holding	Creep	Walk when led
8 mo.	furniture	10 mo.	11 mo.
	9 mo.		

| Pull to stand | Climb stair steps | Stand alone | Walk alone |
| by furniture | 13 mo. | 14 mo. | 15 mo. |

and arms appears before the infant can control foot movements. This principle can be seen in the progressive stages of Figure 4.2.

Development of prehension

Along with walking behavior, an important aspect of body control in infancy is the development of the ability to use the hands for seizing, grasping, manipulating, and releasing objects. An early student of this process was Halverson (1931), who made use of motion picture photography to investigate development of prehension in babies between the ages of 16 and 52 weeks.

Halverson's subjects were supported in a specially designed chair which allowed them freedom to reach for and grasp objects presented to them on a table. A small cube was presented to each infant in a standardized manner, and the reactions recorded on film. Careful analysis of the records revealed four main steps in the act of prehension: (1) the visual location of the object, (2)

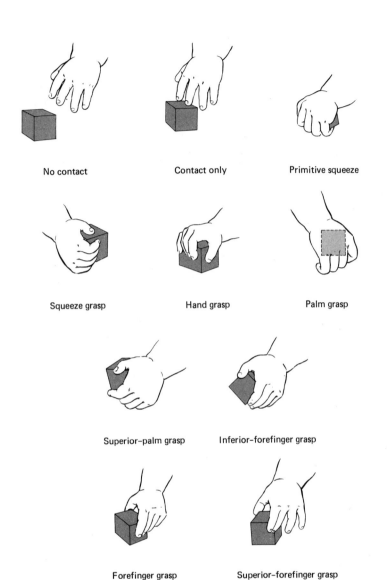

No contact Contact only Primitive squeeze

Squeeze grasp Hand grasp Palm grasp

Superior-palm grasp Inferior-forefinger grasp

Forefinger grasp Superior-forefinger grasp

FIGURE 4.3 The developmental sequence in the achievement of prehension from 16 to 52 weeks. (Adapted from H. M. Halverson, "An Experimental Study of Prehension in Infants by Means of Systematic Cinema Records," *Genetic Psychology Monographs*, 1931, *10*:107–286.)

the approach by the hand, (3) the grasp, and (4) the disposal of the object. Each of these phases showed its special course of development during the first year, with many evidences for regularity and orderliness in its progression. Figure 4.3 charts the major sequences in the achievement of prehension as described by Halverson. He summarized a portion of his findings in this manner:

The more characteristic reactions to the cube by the infants of different ages are as follows: at 16 weeks, infants follow the examiner's hand after she presents the cube, slide their hands about on the table, and often keep one or both hands on the table during the entire situation. At 20 weeks, infants scratch the table, and attempt to get both hands about the cube after reaching with both hands simultaneously. If they succeed in touching the cube, they either push it out of reach or simply hold it. At 24 and 28 weeks, they approach the cube in a scooping manner, sometimes using both hands, and then corral and surround the cube or push it out of reach. After grasping the cube, they hold it, take it to mouth, inspect the cube, and release it and regain it. At 32 weeks, the infants use the scooping approach to surround the cube, inspect it, take it to the mouth, release and pick up the cube again, and exchange it from one hand to the other. They often disregard the cube when there are other cubes present. At 36 weeks and at 40 weeks, the infants execute a number of bilateral approaches and shift the cube from one hand to the other. They also bring the cube to the mouth, simply hold the cube, inspect it, hold it with both hands, release and regain it, bang the table with it, exchange hands on it, execute a number of bilateral approaches, and hold it in both hands. The 52-week infants often put the cube down and pick it up again, bang the table, exchange hands on the cube, simply hold it with one hand or both hands and inspect it, but do not bring it to the mouth. The 16-weeks infants do not, as a rule, reach the cube. (1931, pp. 277–278)

The Halverson study of a small sequence in the overall motor development of infants provides us with additional evidence of the patterning of behavior resulting primarily from maturation processes, although it is in interaction with environmental stimulation that these patterns emerge. The study also reveals the trend of progress from the coarser, large-muscle control toward the finer, small-muscle control, which has been noted by many observers. The earliest approach to the cube involves mainly the large shoulder and arm action, which is relatively crude and lacking in precision. With further development there is greater involvement of hand, wrist, and fingers, with finer control of the smaller muscles leading to greatly improved performance.

Beginnings of intellectual development

There is a wealth of data from which we can conclude that the infant is an active learner, which is one aspect of his intellectual growth. He learns both through classical and instrumental conditioning processes; it is also clear that his learning abilities improve rapidly with age. Learning is interwoven with the development of sensory and perceptual processes, out of which the child actively constructs an internal, or mental representation, of the objects and events in the world around him.

Piaget (1952) has provided one account, in considerable depth and detail, of intellectual development during infancy. In his view, intelligence is a matter of adaptation, and intellectual development is a process of continuously creating increasingly complex mental structures through the adaptation process. But adaptation, for Piaget, is not merely a process of adjusting passively to environmental stimulation. Instead, he views adaptation as arising from basic biological realities which exist within the infant, but which progress through a continuous series of transactions with the environment.

These transactions include the two subprocesses of *assimilation,* which is the incorporation of environmental realities into the presently existing mental structures, and of *accommodation,* which is the revision or modification of presently existing structures resulting from pressures exerted by the environment. These are complementary processes that work in relationship to each other in the constant interchange between the infant and his environment. Intellectual development (throughout life, as well as during infancy) is viewed by Piaget as a very active process of constructing an internal world, that is, learning to know the environment through progressively higher and more complex forms of equilibrium between the processes of assimilation and accommodation.

A simple example of these two subprocesses from adult experience may help to make their function clearer. If a person has learned to drive a modern automobile, using an automatic transmission, it is ordinarily not difficult to drive a different car that also has an automatic transmission. The new car, even though the person has never been in it before, is operated with a set of behaviors that are readily *assimilated* to the previous structures. However, if this person attempts to drive a car with a manual transmission, the structures (previous driving behaviors) are inadequate, and the person must either *accommodate* his structures by learning to operate a clutch and manual shift lever, or give up in frustration and fail to operate the car.

Similarly, the infant experiences many events that are "like" previous events, for which he has a set of mental structures, and therefore assimilates the new events readily. Repetitive behaviors are of this sort, and much of infantile play is viewed as assimilative in nature. A reliable response of an infant to a given stimulus is the simplest example of the existence of a structure that can assimilate the stimulus readily.

Piaget shows, through his detailed and painstaking observations of the development of sucking behavior in infancy, that while the primary "structures," in the form of reflex mechanisms for sucking, exist at birth, the form of the behavior undergoes considerable modification as the infant adapts himself over time to variations in the nursing situation. That adaptation consists of assimilating the external events (nipple and tactile stimulation on or near lips) and accommodating (including searching behavior when the nipple is not readily available, and discrimination of that which yields milk from that which does not).

Progressively higher levels of adaptation are described and illustrated by Piaget throughout the first 2 years of life, which he characterizes as the *sensorimotor period* of intellectual development. He subdivides this period into six major stages. These stages describe the rapid elaboration of behavior patterns, which incorporate objects and aspects of the environment, especially through the circular relationships between motor actions, which produce effects on the environment, and sensory processes, which are stimulated by those effects. These circular reactions produce what Piaget calls *intentional* behavior, which has to do with recognizing relationships between means and ends. This is the infant's discovery of the effects of his own behavior on the environment—a central aspect of intellectual development that we will consider more fully in Chapter Eight.

Close observation of infant behavior gives the distinct impression that a baby finds much satisfaction in making things "happen" in his world, suggesting that there is a kind of built-in motivation which serves as the impetus for mental growth. The baby—lying on his back in a crib, eyes focused on a brightly colored mobile suspended above him, hitting it erratically at first and observing its movement, then repeating the act with greater precision and laughing delightedly each time he produces the movement—is perhaps illustrating a most central principle in mental development.

Toward the end of the second year there is active experimentation to discover new means-end relationships, and the beginnings of invention, which is the development of new, internalized ways of representing the world. As these internalized structures become less dependent on the immediate sensorimotor events, the child becomes capable of greater fluidity and flexibility of intelligent behavior, for he is beginning to manipulate images and symbols internally, which is the beginning of reflective intelligence.

The foregoing is a very brief and sketchy account of Piaget's description of early intellectual development, intended merely to give the general flavor of his approach. The student who wishes to pursue this topic will find many helpful references readily available, including Piaget (1952), Flavell (1963), Baldwin (1967), and Phillips (1969).

Some American writers have also presented extensive descriptions of early intellectual development, although none in such comprehensive fashion as those of Piaget. However, Bruner, et al. (1966) have described the infancy period of intellectual development as the *enactive* period, a term that has much in common with Piaget's sensorimotor period. For Bruner also, early intelligence is a matter of performing motor acts on the environment and sensing and perceiving the effects of those actions.

Achievement of language

The ability to use language in a meaningful way to communicate ideas, emotions, and questions to others is a remarkable achievement. True language is a uniquely human behavior and a far more complex process than that carried on by parrots and other "talking" birds.

Spoken language—oral speech—is only one form of language, and we shall later have occasion to examine other aspects of communication in children. However, the period of infancy is critical in that during this time we expect a child to achieve the ability to pronounce words. Furthermore, we expect him to articulate words well enough that others than his parents know what he is saying, and we expect him to use the words appropriately, with commonly accepted meanings.

We surely don't expect him to do all these things at once, and he will still have a long way to go in language development after he has left infancy behind. Nevertheless, his language progress during the first 2 years is generally measured by these criteria: (1) understanding the meaning of words spoken to him, (2) pronouncing words with clear articulation, and (3) using words with meaningful association, accepted by others.

Understanding the words of others develops earlier, and more rapidly, than does the ability to form word sounds clearly and to use them meaningfully. Before the end of the first year the infant shows in many ways—long before he can reproduce the sounds himself—that he can respond appropriately to the speech of others. The process by which this learning comes about is not at all simple. It probably does not begin with words at all, but with gestures, facial expressions, tone of voice, and other aspects of the *context* within which words are used in his presence.

The meaning of the total situation to him may be essentially affective: it represents comfort or discomfort, satisfaction or unpleasantness. As particular situations repeat themselves in the daily cycle and routines of the infant, and as the same sounds ("words") are used consistently in given situations, the words come to stand for the rest of the elements that make up the total situation that bring forth the feeling associated with it for the baby. Lewis (1959) has described this process as follows:

We have seen that the beginning of a child's responses to speech emerges in his development as a result of a number of varied factors. As always, there is a convergence between what the child does and what others do. First, he has long been responding with expressions of feeling to the sound of the human voice. Then through babbling and rudimentary imitation, he has begun to pay attention to particular words—or, rather, particular phonetic patterns. Now he hears one of these phonetic patterns, a word or phrase, spoken by his mother in a certain intonation to which he has already been responding in ways that are expressive of the feelings that the intonation arouses in him. The word comes to him regularly in a particular situation which has emotional significance for him. As he hears the word he sees the play of expression on his mother's face, her gestures, and her movements; and all this happens in a situation in which distress or contentment, sight, sound, smell, touch, and much else are richly mingled. As the word recurs for him with varying intonations, its phonetic pattern takes over for him much of the expressiveness that hitherto has been held in the intonational patterns. Added to all this, the very form of the word as a typical fragment of baby-language will have a special place in the child's own speech-behaviour and his experiences. (Lewis 1959, pp. 77–78)

Lewis places particular emphasis on the importance of talking to infants. While the assumption that they "can't understand words" may largely be true at first, there is evidence of the value of being stimulated with a language environment from the very beginning. One of these advantages seems to be that the infant begins to associate words with the emotional experiences of his life, and thereby to develop a powerful motivation to participate, himself, in the use of language to convey significant feelings.

Needless to say, a baby's ability to differentiate words and understand meanings is no guarantee that he will always abide by them! Such expectations would be quite unrealistic. Long after he "understands" the meaning of "No, no!" he may be quite inconsistent and irregular in his response to it. And of course, any mother can recount instances in which the infant is asked to perform some remarkable feat of intelligence to impress the visitors ("pat-a-cake, darling," "wave bye-bye, sweetheart") only to have him stare blankly at the strangers in his most uncomprehending manner. This lack of consistent performance is not at all difficult to account for in the strangeness of the surroundings and people present, and is certainly not evidence of lack of understanding.

As he progresses, the baby's understanding of words is greatly facilitated and broadened by his own efforts to make word sounds. The meaning of the sound "Mama," which is found, incidentally, in infant speech in most all languages, is revised for a baby as he uses it and as significant people in his life respond to his use of it. The other criteria of language development in infancy—pronouncing words clearly enough for others to understand them, and with appropriate meaning—have been studied a great deal by researchers. Progress toward forming clear speech sounds is very gradual, beginning with the almost formless sounds of the neonatal period, and the vocal crying that was initiated after delivery.

During the second and third months small, throaty, gurgling noises while the infant is asleep or awake and the beginnings of cooing and primitive babbling form the vocal exercises of most babies. By the fourth month, cooing may be observed in response to another person's presence or attention, or to music or other sounds. Babbling may begin in earnest about this time, although there is considerable room for individual variation not only at the age it begins but in the amount of babbling. For some infants, babbling is an active, enthusiastic enterprise, and it may be observed to occur regularly at certain times of the day in keeping with the daily routine of eating, sleeping, and wakefulness.

One infant of 4 months had established a consistent routine of being "burped" after his breakfast, then lying contentedly on his back in the crib for a period of from 15 minutes to a half hour, during which he would babble vigorously and with apparent delight. His parents observed that the babbling increased when they hovered over the crib and talked back to him. The experience of these parents is not unusual. Babbling, sometimes thought of as useless and meaningless vocalizing, should be recognized as a significant step, valuable in its own right as well as paving the way for the next higher stages of speech. The infant is stimulated and reinforced by his own speech sounds, is encouraged to continue them, and engages in the exercise of the entire vocal apparatus at the same time. Furthermore, his babbling has a natural appeal to most adults, and the response from them results in increased social stimulation.

By 6 or 7 months the typical infant is vocalizing several well-defined syllables, according to Gesell and Amatruda (1947). Sometime during the 6- to 9-month period there may be beginnings of imitation, of efforts to duplicate the sounds he hears others make. At 11 or 12 months he may be successful in imitating such repetitive syllables as "Dada" or "Mama."

A number of infant intelligence scales are based on the assumption that the year-old infant will typically have one or two words in his vocabulary. There is, however, great variability among normal infants with respect to age of speaking first words. There are many reasons, some of which have nothing to do with intelligence, why a particular child may not say words until well after his first birthday.

The second year is marked by considerable growth in the ability to form words clearly and distinctly. This is a time of learning to approximate the sounds of the mother tongue, and it involves learning not only how to combine sounds, but also to eliminate speech sounds that are not part of the language. As Lewis points out:

> . . . an English child does not normally hear the sound *ch* that occurs in the Scottish word *loch*. But careful observations assure us that every English child, like every other child, says *ch* during his earliest months as one of his comfort noises and in his babbling. Yet because this sound is not heard by him in the baby-language spoken to him, his use of it is not reinforced; it ceases to occur in his babbling. The time will come when he will be "unable to make it," as those who try to teach English schoolchildren the German word *doch* know only too well. Asked to imitate *doch*, an English child of twelve will usually say *dock*, giving the nearest sound from his own repertory. With toil and trouble he may at last succeed in saying *ch;* yet at the age of six months he said it spontaneously. (Lewis 1959, p. 92)

The second year is also the time when the infant will be observed to use a single word to express a complete thought. This is sometimes referred to as the "one-word-sentence," or holophrastic speech, as described by McNeill (1970). When an 18-

month-old says "ball," for example, he may mean "There is the ball," or he may mean "Where is the ball?" or "I want the ball," and so on. However, these first words are more the expression of "feelings about objects" than they are primarily concerned with the names of the objects. Wishes and feelings of the infant seem to be the primary motivating force behind this early talking; it is understandable that the words themselves have a heavy affective component.

The vocabulary increases rapidly during the second year, although there may be periods of plateaus with no apparent improvement intermixed with periods of rapid gains for individual children. It is not uncommon for a child to slow down his rate of speech development during the period he begins to walk, for example. It is as if he is using his available energy to become accomplished at the thing that counts most at the moment. When the walking behavior becomes relatively well established and "automatic," as it usually does by 18 months, then language development may spurt ahead again.

Not only is there rapid progress in acquiring new words, but in the last 3 months of the second year there is combining of words to form larger segments of thought. By 24 months, according to Gesell and Amatruda (1947), the child uses simple phrases and sentences. This more complex kind of language behavior calls for mastery not only of word meanings but of key relationships among words, and their appropriate use for the expression of ideas. The use of pronouns and prepositions, which are useful in the clear expression of ideas, also has its beginning about this time.

Accuracy of usage, like accuracy of pronunciation, is still lacking in precision, but the period of infancy brings a truly remarkable human achievement of true language in accordance with all three major criteria: comprehension, pronunciation, and meaningful usage. As we shall see in Chapter Seven, the achievement of language is more a matter of learning *principles* than merely *words*. Even during infancy, the human child is learning principles of the classification of things, for example, and these principles involve themselves in the structuring of his language.

Finally, we should take note of the fact that the urge to become a language user is a powerful one in the infant. As Lenneberg (1964) points out, it is so deeply rooted in man that children learn it even in the face of dramatic handicaps such as congenital blindness, deafness, criminal parental neglect, or congenitally deaf parents. There is indeed much evidence that language, and the learning of one's mother tongue in infancy, is not so much a matter of teaching by adults as it is a matter of construction by a baby.

Elaboration of emotions and the personality

The earliest emotional responses are probably best understood as general, rather than specific, behavior. An early research investigation of the ability of adults to judge emotional reactions of infants (Sherman, 1927) revealed that judgments were made on the basis of the situation and events leading to the emotional behavior, and not on the behavior itself. When the adults did not know the causes of the emotional arousal, they could not identify the emotion. Thus hunger, loss of bodily support, restraint of bodily movement, and being pricked with a needle all resulted in behavior that looked the same, so it might be concluded that the infant has a general emotional response capability, which might be aroused by any of a variety of circumstances, but which appears to take the same general form regardless of the stimulus events.

Bridges (1932), another early investigator of emotional development, also concluded that the first emotions are vague and poorly defined, but that they become more specific and differentiated with increased age. Figure 4.4 illustrates the gradual differentiation of emotional responses over the first 2 years, as outlined by Bridges. Distress is differentiated from the general state of excitement by about 1 month of age, and delight appears somewhat later, around 2 months of age, in response to being nursed, petted, or cared for. Delight is more clearly defined by 3 months, and by 4 months more active signs are apparent in the form of laughter, smiling in response to another's smile, and efforts to raise the body in approach to an attentive person.

(The exact age at which any specific emotion becomes reliably

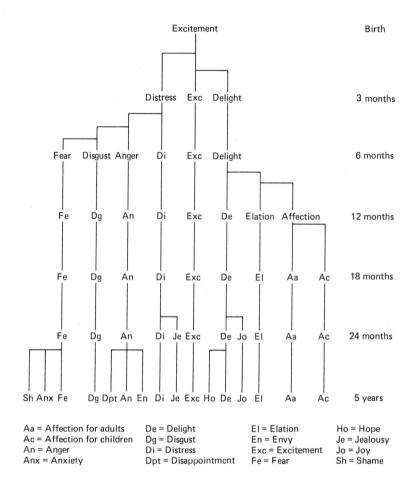

FIGURE 4.4 A diagrammatic representation of the development of emotion. (From H. F. English, *Dynamics of Child Development*, New York: Holt, Rinehart and Winston, 1961, p. 114, as combined from two diagrams by K. M. B. Bridges, *Journal of Genetic Psychology*, 1930, 37:524, and *Child Development*, 1932, 3:340.)

differentiated from a more general emotional reaction is less important than the implications of this general-to-specific trend of development.) As the more specific behavior patterns emerge, it becomes possible for them to be attached, through conditioning, to a variety of events and circumstances. Such learning represents one major source of individuality—the unique personality of the baby.

Emotional behavior is unstable throughout infancy; that is, the infant can move suddenly from one emotional state to another with little evidence of carry-over from one moment to the next. Infantile emotional behavior also tends to be "all-or-none," in that there is, compared with older children and adults, less of a gradation from mild to extreme reactions. The infant tends to respond to an emotion-arousing condition with his whole being and with all his available energy.

The significance of infancy for the establishment of a healthy foundation for personality development has long been recognized. Erikson (1953), for example, portrays infancy as the critical period for the development of a sense of basic trust. In this view, the notion of trust has far-reaching implications for later personality growth and the achievement of a mature sense of self. Erikson says of trust:

> . . . the firm establishment of enduring patterns for the balance of basic trust over basic mistrust is the first task of the budding personality and therefore first of all a task for maternal care. But it must be said that the amount of trust derived from earliest infantile experience does not seem to depend on absolute quantities of food or demonstrations of love but rather on the quality of the maternal relationship. Mothers create a sense of trust in their children by that kind of administration which in its firm quality combines sensitive care of the baby's individual needs and a firm sense of personal trustworthiness within the trusted framework of their community's life style. (This forms the basis in a child for a sense of identity which will later combine a sense of being "all right," of being oneself, and of becoming what other people trust one will become.) Parents must not only have certain ways of guiding by prohibition and permission; they must also be able to represent to the child a deep, an almost somatic conviction that there is meaning to what they are doing. (Erikson 1953, p. 195)

It is apparently through the repetition of experiences that trust has its foundations. In the daily cycle of stimulation and response, of need arousal and need satisfaction, of discomfort and recovery from discomfort, of excitement and calm, there emerges a basis for a kind of anticipation, or "prediction," on the infant's part that things will work out, that his world is essentially supportive, and that he will not be overwhelmed by conditions inside or outside his body.

One aspect of the importance of early experience for personality development is suggested by the interesting work of Harlow (1960) with infant monkeys. A central question in this research was the role of early sensory experiences of the infant animals in the development of love and affectional relationships. Harlow devised surrogate mechanical "mothers" for the infant monkeys, constructed of either wire-mesh or with a soft terry cloth cover. In either case there was a nipple and a constant milk supply available from the body of the surrogate mother. Some of the infants were fed from the terry cloth device, and others from the wire-mesh device.

The assumption was that if the nursing situation, per se, was the primary factor in the development of affectional relationships, then the infants would form attachments to whichever mother was the source of the nursing comfort. But this was not borne out. By recording the time spent in contact with the devices while not actually nursing, it was possible to estimate the relative strength of attachment. Regardless of whether the infants were fed from the wire-mesh or the terry cloth devices, they spent a much greater amount of time in contact with, or clinging to, the terry cloth figures.

These experiments strongly suggest an important role for touch and texture as sensory experiences which make an early contribution to the development of the affectional system. Furthermore, it was the terry cloth figures that the infants turned to when frightened, for these figures appeared to become a source of "security"—a sort of base of operations from which they extended their explorations, and then returned to when threatened.

The implications of these experiments are that the earliest love attachments, which Harlow points out are related to the later ability to form adult attachments, are based to a great extent on early experiences with touch and texture, and that the psychological benefits of nursing are mainly to ensure close body contact between baby and mother. To the extent that such a suggestion is meaningful for the human infant, it seems clear that this aspect of early development of the healthy personality could be provided regardless of whether the child is breast- or bottle-fed.

It is not easy to determine just what features of the mother-infant relationship are most essential to a good foundation for personality development. Ribble (1943), Spitz (1946), Bowlby (1951), and others placed great stress on the need of an infant for an intimate, one-to-one relationship in which a great deal of attention and "tender loving care" is consistently provided. Such an emphasis, along with its implications that any lack of such consistency in loving care would impair development, led to considerable concern among parents as well as in professional circles for infants who cannot receive the consistent care of one mother.

As one example of this concern, infants who had been placed in college home management houses to provide an educational experience in infant care for home economics students were said to be deprived, thereby, of normal mothering. In at least one institution the infants were removed from this arrangement on the grounds that such "multiple mothering" was harmful to their development.

Subsequent findings by Gardner, Hawkes, and Burchinal (1961) indicate that fears of this kind are largely without foundation. Not only is the human infant remarkably sturdy physically and psychologically, but it appears that there are many different ways in which his fundamental needs can be satisfied. Warmth and consistency of mothering are, of course, important considerations. However, during even the first weeks and months of life there seems no inherent reason why the infant will be harmed by a variety of caretakers. In the Gardner, et al. research, it was also found that infants who live in foster homes or who are adopted do not necessarily suffer from the experience.

Nevertheless, these early months are of vital importance. For our purposes, we may divide the infancy period into two major phases and note that there are critical aspects to each: (1) the early dependency period, in which need gratification is essentially provided from the outside upon the infant's demand, with no effort on his part other than to make the demand known; and (2) the later infancy period, particularly the second year, in which his own behavior becomes instrumental in the direct satisfaction of his needs. The distinction between these two phases is important; it emphasizes a vital learning process that normally occurs during this period. In brief, it is learning to use one's own resources in the never-ending struggle to cope with the environment and to satisfy one's needs.

Complete failure in such learning is rare, fortunately, but there are degrees of success. The infant who is overly controlled, inhibited, prevented from exploring his world, and frustrated in his efforts to develop his own resources is, to that degree, destined to find the later tasks of personality development more difficult, frightening, and disturbing. On the other hand, the infant who is allowed and encouraged to explore his world; to meet obstacles and to cope with them; to make use of his body in relating himself at ever-higher levels to the objects, persons, and situations he finds there is indeed fortunate. He has an excellent beginning for the tasks of growth which lie ahead.

Programs of infant stimulation

There is a current increase of interest in the development of programs—both home-based and institutional—for planned stimulation of infants, for the purpose of providing an optimal environment for mental and personality development. This interest can be traced to a number of factors, including our awareness of the significance of the environment for development, and our accumulated findings and conclusions especially from intervention programs such as Head Start, which points out that environmental enrichment, to be effective, must begin very early in a child's life.

A related factor in this increased interest is probably our

awareness that many parents of young children do not have access to—or resources to implement—much of what is known about early child care. Thus programs of early stimulation have been emerging which are designed to support parents by giving them tangible guidance in child care practices.

It would be premature to judge the merits of many such programs on the basis of child development outcomes, since we do not yet know exactly what kinds of early stimulation produce what patterns of behavior and personality in later childhood and the adult years. However, it is likely that social and economic conditions will continue to foster the development of a variety of alternatives, including such experimental programs as day nurseries for infants and toddlers.

One such type of program has been well described by Keister (1970), where babies spend from 6 to 9 hours daily in a group care center. It is an unhurried, relaxed situation, where feeding, sleeping, and toileting routines are attended to by warm and supportive caretakers. There is a rich environment conducive to the emergence of sensorimotor skills, language, and personal-social development. However, there is little or no effort to "program" an infant, or to push him to achieve specific skills. The philosophy of this particular program is expressed in the following statement:

> We believe that when children are very young, normally healthy and active, they may be left alone to accomplish their own learning. When supported by a natural curiosity, busyness and a pleasurable give-and-take between themselves, a vivid, varied environment *inevitably* produces learning, cognitive development. We leave our babies free to "take it or leave it," to make a choice at any one point in time. This is not to say that talking, showing, explaining, naming, reading, demonstrating how things work, have no place in our scheme of things. They are central to an environment that produces relevant learning and continuing growth. (Keister 1970, p. 32)

While there is no such thing as one "right" pattern for the operation of such a center, and there are wide variations in the kinds of facilities, staff personnel, equipment, and routines, as well as in the objectives and strategies of caretakers in different centers, it seems safe to say that no harm to infants has been demonstrated to result from the type of program described by Keister.

As we discover more of the essential features of desirable care and stimulation of infants, and gradually succeed in separating fact from myth pertaining to their needs, presumably we will discover at the same time ways to make such care and stimulation available to a larger proportion of the infants in our society. In all likelihood, that will include agencies and institutions designed to provide group care in support of home and family functions, and will not be, as some have supposed, intended to replace family functions.

Summary

The neonatal period is critical in that the baby must establish physiological stability for basic body functions. There are wide individual differences in newborn babies, but the neonate is "competent" in that he is an active learner with many capabilities and resources for further development. His early behavior is largely reflexive.

The period of infancy, extending to the end of the second year, is a time of major accomplishments: rapid physical growth, the achievement of upright locomotion, the accomplishment of much learning based on sensorimotor functioning, the achievement of true language, the elaboration of emotional behavior, and very significant beginnings of personality formation.

Recognition of the importance of the infancy period for subsequent development has led to research on the effects of early stimulation, and to experimentation with a variety of types of programs of infant care, both home-based and in group-care settings.

References

Baldwin, A. *Theories of Child Development.* New York: Wiley, 1967.
Bayley, N. "The Development of Motor Abilities During the First Three

Years." *Monographs of the Society for Research in Child Development* 1 (1935) 1–26.

Bowlby, J. *Maternal Care and Mental Health.* Monographs Series, no. 2. Geneva: World Health Organization, 1951.

Brazelton, T. B. *Infants and Mothers: Differences in Development.* New York: Delacorte Press, 1969.

Bridges, K. M. B. "Emotional Development in Early Infancy." *Child Development* 3 (1932) 324–334.

Bruner, J. S., Olver, R. R., and Greenfield, P. M. *Studies in Cognitive Growth.* New York: Wiley, 1966.

Erikson, E. H. "Growth and Crises of the Healthy Personality." In Kluckhohn, C., Murray, H. A., and Schneider, D. M., eds. *Personality in Nature, Society, and Culture.* 2nd ed. New York: Knopf, 1953, pp. 185–225.

Falkner, F., ed. *Human Development.* Philadelphia: Saunders, 1966.

Flavell, J. *The Developmental Psychology of Jean Piaget.* Princeton, N.J.: Van Nostrand, 1963.

Gardner, D. B., Hawkes, G. R., and Burchinal, L. "Noncontinuous Mothering in Infancy and Development in Later Childhood." *Child Development* 32 (1961) 225–234.

Gesell, A., and Amatruda, C. S. *Developmental Diagnosis.* 2nd ed. New York: Hoeber-Harper, 1947.

Gesell, A., and Ilg, F. *Child Development.* New York: Harper, 1949.

Halverson, H. M. "An Experimental Study of Prehension in Infants by Means of Systematic Cinema Records." *Genetic Psychology Monographs* 10 (1931) 107–286.

Harlow, H. F. "Primary Affectional Patterns in Primates." *American Journal of Orthopsychiatry* 30 (1960) 676–684.

James, W. *Principles of Psychology* (2 vols.). New York: Holt, 1890.

Keister, M. E. *The Good Life for Infants and Toddlers.* Washington, D.C.: National Association for the Education of Young Children, 1970.

Kessen, W., Haith, M. M., and Salapatek, P. H. "Infancy." In Kessen, W., ed. *Carmichael's Manual of Child Psychology.* 3rd ed., vol. 1. New York: Wiley, 1970, pp. 287–445.

Lenneberg, E. H. "A Biological Perspective of Language." In Lenneberg, E. H., ed. *New Directions in the Study of Language.* Cambridge, Mass.: Massachusetts Institute of Technology Press, 1964.

Lewis, M. M. *How Children Learn to Speak.* New York: Basic Books, 1959.

McGraw, M. *Growth: A Study of Johnny and Jimmy.* New York: Appleton-Century-Crofts, 1935.

McNeill, D. "The Development of Language." In Mussen, P. H., ed. *Carmichael's Manual of Child Psychology.* 3rd ed., vol. 1. New York: Wiley, 1970, pp. 1061–1161.

Phillips, J. L., Jr. *The Origins of Intellect: Piaget's Theory.* San Francisco: W. H. Freeman, 1969.

Piaget, J. *The Origins of Intelligence in Children.* Translated by M. Cook. New York: International Universities Press, 1952.

Ribble, M. *The Rights of Infants.* New York: Columbia University Press, 1943.

Sherman, M. "The Differentiation of Emotional Responses in Infants: II. The Ability of Observers to Judge the Emotional Characteristics of the Crying of Infants, and of the Voice of an Adult." *Journal of Comparative Psychology* 7 (1927) 335–351.

Shirley, M. M. *The First Two Years: A Study of Twenty-five Babies.* Minneapolis: University of Minnesota Press, 1931.

Spitz, R. A. "Anaclitic Depression." *Psychoanalytic Studies of the Child* 2 (1946) 313–342.

Stitt, P. G. "Progress During Infancy." In Stuart, H. C., and Prugh, D. G., eds. *The Healthy Child.* Cambridge, Mass.: Harvard University Press, 1960.

Tanner, J. M. "Physical Growth." In Mussen, P. H., ed. *Carmichael's Manual of Child Psychology.* 3rd ed. New York: Wiley, 1970, pp. 77–155.

Watson, E. H., and Lowrey, G. H. *Growth and Development of Children.* 4th ed. Chicago: Year Book Medical, 1962.

Wetzel, N. C. "Baby Grid: An Application of the Grid Technique to Growth and Development in Infants." *Journal of Pediatrics* 29 (1946) 439.

PART III
Aspects
of development
in
the early years

The chapters that form Part III attempt to portray certain dominating themes in the behavior and development of children from about 2 through 6 years of age. These major themes—physical and motor development, language and communication, intellectual growth, and the emergence of the personality— are inextricably interwoven in the growth of the whole child. Their separation into chapters is justified only as a means to give proper attention and emphasis to each aspect.

Observation of individual children while studying Part III will assist the student immeasurably in maintaining a realistic sense of the relationship of each aspect of growth to the total, functioning child. Perhaps most of all, the student should note the heavy involvement of the child's personality and sense of self (Chapter Nine) with the aspects of development described in Chapters Five through Eight.

CHAPTER FIVE
Physical growth

What are the important changes in body size and proportion between
  ages 2 and 6?

What methods of measurement have helped us to understand the
  nature of physical growth?

What are the major growth needs and health requirements of the
  young child?

How does the child develop immunity to infectious diseases?

What are reasonable goals in the prevention of childhood accidents?

$\mathcal{S}$ometimes people tend, unfortunately, to separate the child's "mind" from his "body," and think of these as if they were independent aspects of the child. The physical body and its development have been regarded, too often, as a subject for discussion quite apart from such psychological attributes as thinking, perceiving, feeling, and valuing.

Today's child development specialist recognizes the complex interrelatedness of physical development with psychological and social processes. Indeed, we cannot understand the growth of personality apart from the physical status of the child. Students wishing to investigate physical growth in greater detail would do well to study the excellent technical summary presented by Tanner (1970).

Significance
of physical development

The term *growth* is often used in a limited way to refer to increases in size and weight. *Development* is sometimes contrasted with it as a term that implies increasing complexity of functioning or of behavior. However, Meredith, an authority on physical growth, has argued that there is really no useful distinction between these terms and that they may be used interchangeably. He has defined growth as "the entire series of anatomic and physiologic changes taking place between the beginning of prenatal life and the close of senility" (1945, p. 445).

Our focus in this chapter will be on those changes in body size, proportions, and functioning, which occur during early childhood. It matters little whether we refer to these changes as "growth" or "development," so long as we understand that more is involved than mere increase in body tissue.

Understanding of physical growth is important for a number of reasons. It provides a rough index of nutritional status and general health. Extremes of rapid or slow growth give early warning of potential abnormalities of development. Knowledge of normal changes in stature can be of help in indicating revised requirements for food intake, exercise, and rest routines.

A further justification for understanding the physical growth of the child is to be found in the complex relationship between physical development and personality. A child's height may be an important factor in his "point of view," speaking both figuratively and literally!

Changes
in body size

During early childhood, growth is relatively slower and steadier than during infancy. Average weight gain is about 4 or 5 pounds each year. The typical 2-year-old American child weighs about 27 pounds. By age 3 he has gone up to 32 pounds. At age 4 he is about 36½, and at age 5 around 41½ pounds. There is not a large difference between boys and girls during these years, although boys are just slightly heavier, on the average (Watson and Lowrey 1962). It must be remembered, of course, that there are wide variations around these average figures, and that variation is not the same as abnormality. Changes in body length—or height—follow the same general rule: growth is slower and steadier than during infancy.

The 2-year-old is about 34 inches tall; by age 3 he is nearly 38 inches; by 4 he is 40.5 inches; and by 5 he is about 43 inches. There is variation among normal children in height, of course, just as there is in weight; however, fewer than 3 percent of American children will be less than 40 inches tall at age 5, and fewer than 3 percent will be taller than 47 inches. Thus, the variation is within a fairly narrow range.

For weight, by comparison, the average figure for 5-year-olds is 41 pounds. However, as many as 10 percent of normal children may weigh less than 35 or 36 pounds, and another 10 percent may weigh 48 pounds or more. It is evident that weight is a more variable quality than height.

Figures 5.1 and 5.2 illustrate the shape of the growth curve in height and weight for boys and girls, respectively, from birth through age 6. These curves also show the decreasing rate of growth that occurs as the child moves from infancy into the years

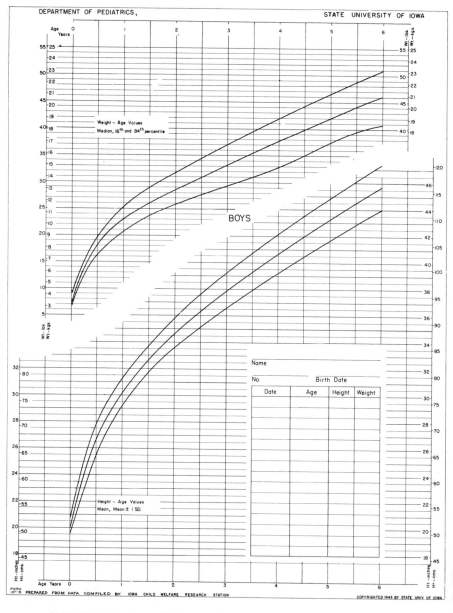

FIGURE 5.1 Jackson-Kelly growth chart for boys, aged 0 to 6 years. (Copyright 1943 by The University of Iowa. Reproduced by permission.)

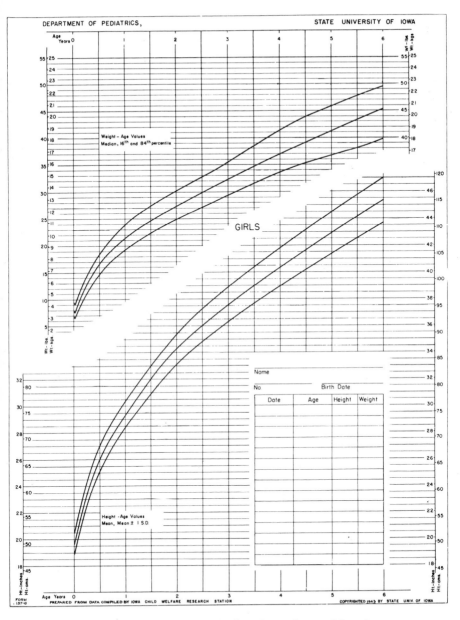

FIGURE 5.2 Jackson-Kelly growth chart for girls, aged 0 to 6 years. (Copyright 1943 by The University of Iowa. Reproduced by permission.)

of early childhood. The range of variation around the average tends to increase, for both sexes, with age.

Standards, or norms for height and weight, vary depending on the sample population on which they are based, the geographical region from which the sample was drawn, and the date of the sample, among other possible factors. As Meredith (1963) has observed, there has been a significant increase in physical size of children, age for age, since the latter part of last century. Nebraska children at the turn of the century were shorter in stature than children in Iowa in the 1920s and 1940s. Colorado boys and girls were taller in 1952 than the children in the earlier samples, particularly in the later stages of growth. The precise reasons for these variations with time and geographical conditions are not clear, but probably relate to nutritional status as well as genetic variation with time and location.

Growth studies summarized by Hathaway (1957) revealed height differences of 1.2 to 1.9 inches, favoring boys from economically advanced areas as compared with economically poor

TABLE 5.1. Comparison of Heights and Weights of 6-year-old* Children from Favored and Underprivileged Areas (1932–1934)

Condition and area	Boys		Girls	
	Heights	Weights	Heights	Weights
	Inches	Pounds	Inches	Pounds
Favored:				
Philadelphia	45.8	47.8	45.6	46.9
Minneapolis	47.7	48.7	47.0	48.0
Underprivileged:				
Philadelphia	44.6	45.5	44.3	44.0
Minneapolis	45.8	46.4	46.4	44.8

* Heights and weights of Philadelphia children were adjusted to age 76 months; data on Minneapolis children are unadjusted.

SOURCE: Data from M. L. Hathaway, "Heights and Weights of Children and Youth in the United States," Washington, D.C.: Home Economics Research Reports, No. 2, U.S. Department of Agriculture, 1957.

areas, at age 6. Somewhat less striking differences were noted for girls, and for both sexes, differences were noted for weight between the privileged and underprivileged samples. These data are shown in Table 5.1.

Differences in physical growth patterns from one country to another also probably reflect both nutritional and genetic factors. Such geographical and ethnic group variations are remarkable, as shown in the wide range of average heights and weights for different samples of 4-year-old children shown in Table 5.2. These data are a portion of the information compiled by Meredith (1968), who summarized over 90 research reports on the physical growth of children, done mostly between 1950 and 1960. Meredith's data included a variety of additional body measurements, in addition to those shown in Table 5.2, such as sitting height, head size, trunk size, and limb size.

One index of physique, of course, is the relationship between height and weight. Such a relationship is shown for a number of the groups compared by Meredith in Figure 5.3. That figure becomes more meaningful if one mentally draws a line, diagonally, from the lower left-hand corner of the figure to the upper right-hand corner. Groups falling above that line tend toward the "slender" physique (relatively light for their height), and groups falling below the line tend toward the "stockier" physique, being relatively heavy for their height.

The wide range, from the relatively tall and heavy Dutch, Swiss, Latvian, and Austrian children to the relatively shorter, lighter children of India and Vietnam, is most impressive. As Table 5.2 indicates, the mean height measurements for 4-year-olds ranged from 85 centimeters for a group of children in the "poorest strata" of Bombay to 104 centimeters for a group of 4-year-olds in Prague, Czechoslovakia. This range of nearly 20 centimeters is equal to about 8 inches! For weight, the range between the lightest and heaviest group means was 6.2 kilograms, or about 13.5 pounds.

The use of height-weight-age norms has been properly criticized as giving insufficient attention to individual differences, which should be considered along with these three variables. It

TABLE 5.2. Comparative Body Sizes of Groups of Preschool Children Studied in Different Parts of the World

Group	Place	Time	Height		Weight	
			Cm	N	Kg	N
Indian	Bihar State	Ca 1955	85.8	3,441	11.8	3,441
Thai	Thailand	1957–1960	90.9	206	12.3	202
Chinese	Shanghai, Peiping, Hong Kong	1954–1964	98.0	744	14.9	744
Slovak	Czechoslovakia	1951	99.7	Ca 4,000	16.2	Ca 4,000
Russian	USSR	1953–1963	100.5	Ca 5,700	16.2	Ca 5,700
Italian	Northern and Central Italy	1949–1963	100.6	Ca 1,450	16.2	Ca 1,450
E. German	Deutschen Demokratischen Republic and Berlin	1957–1958	101.0	1,949	16.3	1,949
British	United Kingdom	1947–1960	101.1	Ca 5,500	16.5	Ca 5,700
U.S. White	United States	1947–1961	102.9	457	16.7	478
Czech	Czechoslovakia	1949–1960	103.8	Ca 9,000	17.1	Ca 9,000

SOURCE: Adapted from Howard V. Meredith, "Body Size of Contemporary Groups of Preschool Children Studied in Different Parts of the World," *Child Development*, 1968, 39:335–377. Copyright 1968 by The Society for Research in Child Development, Inc. Reprinted by permission.

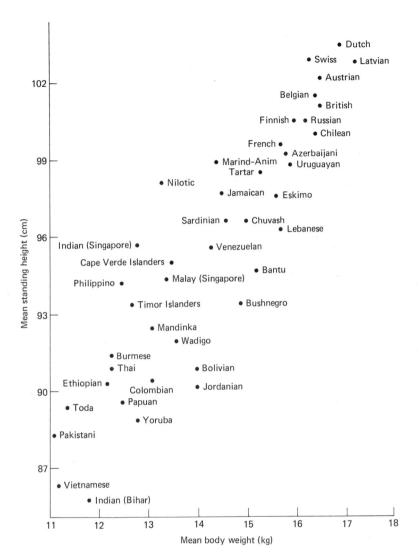

FIGURE 5.3 The relation of mean height and mean weight among contemporary groups of children age 4 years. (From Howard V. Meredith, "Body Size of Contemporary Groups of Preschool Children Studied in Different Parts of the World," *Child Development,* 1968, *39:*335–377. Copyright 1968 by The Society for Research in Child Development, Inc. Reprinted by permission.)

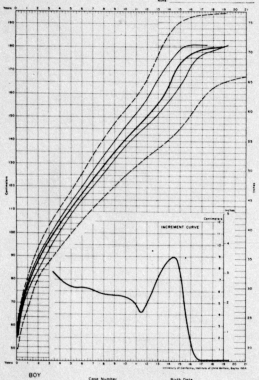

GROWTH CURVES OF HEIGHT BY AGE BOYS MATURING AT AVERAGE, ACCELERATED AND RETARDED RATES

INCREMENT CURVE

BOY

University of California, Institute of Child Welfare, Berkeley 1934

Case Number _____   Birth Date _____

PERCENTS OF
MATURE HEIGHT

Age Years	Average	Accelerated	Retarded
Birth	28.6		
1.0	42.2	44.5	40.4
2.0	49.5	51.3	47.0
3.0	53.8	55.6	51.6
4.0	58.0	60.0	58.0
5.0	61.8	64.0	59.7
6.0	65.2	67.8	63.8
7.0	69.0	70.5	66.8
8.0	72.0	73.5	69.8
9.0	75.0	76.5	73.2
10.0	78.0	79.7	76.4
11.0	81.1	83.4	79.5
12.0	84.2	87.2	82.2
13.0	87.3	91.3	84.6
14.0	91.5	95.8	87.6
15.0	94.1	98.3	91.6
16.0	98.3	99.4	95.7
17.0	99.3	99.9	98.2
17.5		100.0	
18.0	99.8		99.2
18.5	100.0		
19.0			99.8
20.0			100.0

RECORD OF MEASURES

Date	Age Year	Month	Stature Inches	Cent	Annual Gain	Skeletal Rating Age Eq	Predict of Adult Height

is easy to make the mistake of assuming that what is "average" or "above average" means the same thing as what is "good" or "better." Actually, what is good for one 4-year-old boy may not be the same as what is good for another, depending on complex variables of physique and rate of maturation.

Bayley (1956) has provided a meaningful analysis of growth in height and weight, which takes into account maturation rate of the individual child. Figures 5.4 and 5.5 illustrate this approach for boys and girls, respectively. In these figures, data have been grouped in such a way that for each curve, the measure at any point represents an average for children who were at equivalent levels of physical maturity.

The lower segments of each of these figures also provides another useful index of growth, which is the rate of increase (in this case, of height) at each age during the entire growth period. As was pointed out earlier, the rate of growth in height is decreasing during infancy and early childhood, as is clearly shown by these increment curves. It reaches its lowest childhood rate for boys between 11 and 12 years of age, and for girls at about age 8. But the growth spurt for boys, associated with puberty, lasts longer and continues until age 14 or 15, while for girls the period of high growth velocity is brief, ending sharply before age 12 on the average.

Changes
in proportions

Changes in body proportions are of as much significance as increases in size and weight. The typical change is a "lengthening out" process as the child emerges from babyhood into true childhood. This includes a considerable loss of the baby fat

←————————————————————————————

FIGURE 5.4 Bayley's data relating heights of boys to rate of physical maturing. (From Nancy Bayley, "Growth Curves of Height and Weight by Age for Boys and Girls, Scaled According to Physical Maturity," *Journal of Pediatrics*, 1956, 48:187–194.)

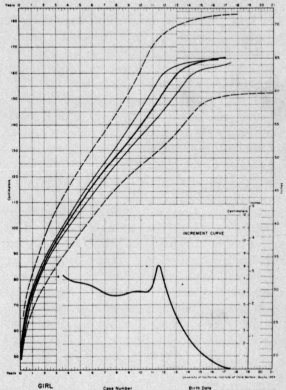

GROWTH CURVES OF HEIGHT BY AGE: **GIRLS** MATURING AT AVERAGE, ACCELERATED AND RETARDED RATES

Name _____

INCREMENT CURVE

University of California, Institute of Child Welfare, Berkeley, 1954

GIRL

Case Number _____   Birth Date _____

PERCENTS OF MATURE HEIGHT

Age Years	Average	Accel-erated	Retarded
Birth	30.9		
1.0	44.7	48.0	42.2
2.0	52.8	54.7	50.0
3.0	57.0	60.0	55.0
4.0	61.8	64.9	59.8
5.0	66.2	69.3	63.9
6.0	79.3	73.4	67.8
7.0	74.0	76.0	71.5
8.0	77.5	79.5	74.5
9.0	80.7	83.5	77.7
10.0	84.4	87.9	81.0
11.0	88.4	92.9	84.9
12.0	92.9	96.6	88.2
13.0	96.5	98.2	91.1
14.0	98.3	99.1	95.2
15.0	99.1	99.5	97.8
16.0	99.6	99.9	98.9
16.5		100.0	
17.0	100.0		99.6
18.0			100.0

RECORD OF MEASURES

Date	Age Year	Month	Stature Inches	Cent	Annual Gain	Skeletal Age Eq	Rating	Predict. of Adult Height

associated with infancy, as well as actual lengthening of the long bones of the arms and legs. Thus the child takes on a leaner, "harder" appearance. This is accounted for partly by the incessant activity and natural exercise of the healthy child. There is a heavy demand on energy for the sake of activity during this time.

Changes in body proportion are the result of differing rates of growth for different parts of the body. Analysis of the total process of physical growth from conception to maturity would reveal that different parts and systems of the body approach their own level of maturity and functional capacity at quite different rates, thereby achieving maturity at different points in the life of the individual.

The science of body measurements, known as *anthropometry,* is a highly developed and complex field of study by itself. Standard measurements of height and weight, used for years to form a crude estimate of physical development, are merely two indices of growth. When combined with measurements of chest and head circumference, hip width, arm and leg length, sitting height, calf circumference, and the thickness of subcutaneous tissue on the back or the calf of the leg, such measures can provide a much more precise index of the physical and nutritional status of the child.

Skeletal development

Much of the change in body proportions that occurs during the growing period is attributable to the manner in which the skeleton develops. Since different parts of the skeleton grow at different rates, and some bones are growing very rapidly while others are not, it is understandable that body proportions change as a result. The most obvious change in body build during the early years is the lengthening out process, since the long bones

←——————————————————————

FIGURE 5.5 Bayley's data relating heights of girls to rate of physical maturing. (From Nancy Bayley, "Growth Curves of Height and Weight by Age for Boys and Girls, Scaled According to Physical Maturity," *Journal of Pediatrics,* 1956, 48:187–194.)

are growing more rapidly in comparison with the rest of the body than was true during infancy.

The growth of the skeleton is an interesting phenomenon in its own right, and some of the implications of skeletal development are still not completely understood. It is far more complex than mere increases in the size of bones already present. During the total growth period there are changes in the number of bones in the body (both increases and decreases) and in the quality or composition of bone tissue, as well as in shape and size.

Most bones have their beginnings in the form of cartilage, which is a fairly soft, plastic material (the cartilage in the tip of one's nose gives a good example of the texture and flexibility of this material). Cartilage, which is present in the general shape of the bones that are yet to come, provides a kind of model of bone formation. Within the cartilage, ossification centers appear. These are points at which calcium and other mineral salts are deposited, resulting in the hardening of mature bone tissue. Thompson (1954) reports over 800 such ossification centers in the human body. Half of them do not make their appearance until after birth, and some do not appear until adolescence.

In the long bones of the arms and legs, growth takes place as follows: the cartilage increases in length and at the same time ossification (hardening, with depositing of calcium) occurs, beginning with ossification centers within the cartilage and proceeding toward the extremities. These central ossification centers form the *diaphyses,* or main portion of the long bone. Additional ossification centers appear at the ends of the cartilage, which form the *epiphyses.* Growth of the bone continues so long as the cartilage between the epiphyses and the diaphyses continues to grow. When the cartilage reaches adult length, it ceases to grow and the diaphysis and epiphysis merge and unite to form a continuous and solid bone structure.

The development of bone tissue occurs in a remarkably regular, predictable manner. Much of what we know about bone development has been learned through the use of X-ray photography. The bones of the hand and wrist, especially, have been given in-

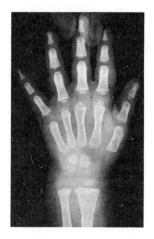

A

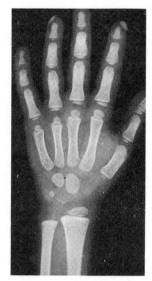

B

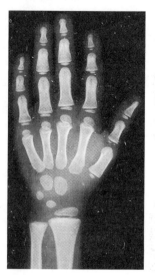

C

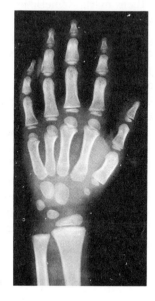

D

FIGURE 5.6 Standard X-ray photographs of the wrists and hands of preschool children: A, at 2 years; B, at 3 years C, at 4 years; and D, at 5 years. (Reprinted from *Radiographic Atlas of Skeletal Development of the Hand and Wrist,* second edition, by William Walter Greulich and S. Idell Pyle, with the permission of the publishers, Stanford University Press. Copyright © 1950, 1959 by the Board of Trustees of the Leland Stanford Junior University.)

tensive study, because they provide an accessible and reliable index of overall skeletal development.

While this X-ray procedure is not necessary for ordinary purposes with most children, it is an extremely important source of information about the course of normal physical growth. Properly taken, hand-wrist X-ray photographs are not harmful to the child and, according to Garn (1958), they provide information not available from any other source, while exposing a child to no more radiation than would occur naturally from normal background radiation in a few minutes of ordinary living.

X-ray photographs of the wrist and hand bones of young children illustrate clearly the progress of skeletal development from ages 2 through 5. Figure 5.6 shows how the ossification process is occurring during this time.

One reason for the use of X-ray photography in assessing physical development is that skeletal development is closely related to overall physical growth. Conditions that affect the overall growth leave their mark, sometimes permanently, on bone tissue. Greulich and Pyle (1950) noted that the development of individual bones can be impaired by illness, especially if the illness occurs at critical stages of bone development. These authorities also suggest that bone "scars," or transverse lines across the long bones, readily visible in X-ray films, may be the result of a period of serious illness and thus represent periods during which growth in the length of these bones was interrupted.

These authors studied groups of Japanese children who lived in Hiroshima and Nagasaki when those cities were destroyed by atomic bombs during World War II. The studies were made about 2 years after the children had been exposed to atomic radiation. A large percentage of the children of comparable ages showed bone scarring, located at about the same distance from the ends of the bones. Such scarring was considered to be the result of the radiation and other injuries suffered at the time of exposure.

Through the use of X-ray procedures, the impact of dietary deficiencies and severe illnesses on the growth of the young child has been better understood.

Development
of the teeth

Growth and eruption of the teeth also provide an index of the overall physical development of the child. There is an orderly timetable and sequence in tooth eruption. The deciduous, or "baby" teeth, begin to calcify during the fifth month of prenatal life. The process of calcification, or hardening, is not complete until about 3 years of age. The appearance of the first tooth usually occurs at about 6 months of age, although it may be as late as 12 months, and there are numerous cases on record of infants who displayed their first tooth along with their birth cry.

These first teeth are shed between the ages of 6 and 12, usually, as the permanent teeth replace them. The fact that they will be lost has led some adults to assume that care of the baby teeth is unimportant. For a number of reasons, however, it is vitally important that these first teeth have the best possible care. One reason is that the temporary teeth play an important role in the positioning of the permanent teeth. A second reason is simply that proper chewing of food is important for nutrition in the early years, just as in later years, and the teeth need to be in good condition for effective mastication.

Muscular
development

Body movement is produced and controlled by the action of the skeletal muscles. The alternating contraction and relaxation of these muscles, in interrelated systems under the stimulation of the nervous system, provide the power, strength, and speed of body movements. Since these body movements are essential to a host of other aspects of development—motor skills, intellectual growth and problem-solving, and even social and personality development—a basic understanding of the action of the muscular system is important.

The voluntary muscles, those over which the child achieves more or less conscious control, are distributed generally over the body, mechanically attached to the skeleton by ligaments. They generally operate in pairs, with one muscle contracting while its opposing muscle relaxes, thus providing for a kind of reciprocal action which makes movement possible. The strength and size of muscles for a given age vary considerably from one child to another, depending heavily on genetic factors. However, nutrition, exercise, and general bodily health also have important effects on muscular development.

Muscle fibers are present in the child's body prior to birth. They are relatively undeveloped during infancy, however, which helps account for the infant's lack of strength and absence of body control. During the early years the growth of muscle tissue is nearly proportional to the total increase in body weight. Muscle tissue makes up a significant part of body weight. Although it is a smaller proportion in early childhood than later, muscles constitute between one-fourth and one-third of body weight during the early years.

The processes of muscle growth include not only increases in gross size, but also important changes in structure. In early childhood the muscle system is composed of water (about 72 percent) and solids (about 28 percent). Zubek and Solberg (1954) report that it is only much later, during puberty, that these percentages change significantly, and the proportion of solids increases. Because of the high water content in the child's muscles, and also because the muscles are not yet as firmly attached structurally to the skeletal system, muscle fatigue is a very significant feature of the life and routines of the young child. He tires easily, and adequate rest periods during the day as well as sufficient sleep at night should be a consistent feature of his daily routine.

Even in early childhood there are important differences not only in the amount and size of muscle tissue, but in strength and endurance, from one child to another. There are also variations from time to time in the same child, depending on physical and nutritional status. During the early years there are only slight differences to be accounted for by the sex of the child. Hurlock (1956) reported that children with broad, thick muscles are stronger, while those with smaller muscles are more agile and better coordinated.

Physical growth needs and health requirements of the young child

The early years are of special significance in the establishment of physical health for a number of reasons. First, growth is still progressing rapidly—although less rapidly than in infancy—and, at the same time, energy demands are high as the child's activity increases and as he explores his world through a wider range and variety of activities. Furthermore, he is not yet mature or experienced enough to be aware of the nature of his own bodily needs, nor to take responsibility for his own health routines without continuous adult guidance.

For these reasons we should turn our attention briefly to a consideration of health requirements—adequate nutrition, exercise, rest and sleep, and freedom from infection. In addition, we will consider in this section the problems of safety and of accident prevention, as these are vital factors in the health and physical well-being of the young child.

Nutrition

Since growth is relatively slower from 2 to 6 years than during infancy, there is typically a lessened appetite and an accompanying decreased interest in food. But a *smaller* appetite is not necessarily a *poor* appetite. The body is lengthened out and thinner than previously, but this thinness by itself is not evidence of poor nutrition or poor health. Nevertheless, there are reasons to be alert to the possibilities of malnutrition during these years, since it is more common than at any other time during the entire growth period (Burke 1960).

Nutritional needs during this time are also complicated by the fact that the child is becoming more independent and likes to express his growing autonomy by refusing to cooperate in various ways with the wishes of his parents. It is understandable that the parent who fails to take this special combination of conditions into account may produce stubbornness and negativism in relation to eating routines. This in turn may have a bearing on nutritional status.

By age 2, a child can learn to know and like most of the common foods that will be available to him on a regular basis throughout his entire life. During the early years the diet should supply sufficient nutrients to perform the following functions: (1) maintenance and replacement of tissue, (2) increase of body tissue commensurate with physical growth, and (3) provision of energy for normal activity. A suitable diet for the young child does not require drastic changes during the period from 2 through 6 years, but remains remarkably stable. In most cases, an adequate diet can be obtained from the regular family meals, assuming these are varied and well balanced.

An important learning for young children is the enjoyment of new food experiences. This learning is enhanced if new foods are introduced in small amounts, at a time when the child is hungry, and without adult pressure. As Martin (1971) observes, the same meats, vegetables, fruits, and cereals as those for the rest of the family are usually suitable for the young child; only the amounts and at times the form of the food should be adjusted to meet his capabilities. Children generally like simple foods, and learn to enjoy individual foods for their own distinct flavor (Martin 1971, p. 267).

The eating habits of a child are, of course, significant. Attitudes toward food, formed during the early years, play a vital role in nutritional status and development throughout later childhood and the adult years as well. Burke (1960) argues that a child should not be allowed to eat too many foods that interfere with normal appetite because of their excessive sugar or fat content, since the appetite may be satisfied and the caloric requirements met without necessarily meeting the structural needs for tissue maintenance, replacement, and growth. Thus, such foods as cakes, cookies, crackers, pies, doughnuts, fried food, gravies, soft drinks, and candy should be avoided in the planned diet for young children. With reference to these and similar foods, Burke comments: "The child between one and three should not have these foods, except occasionally simple desserts at regular meals. Between three and six years of age, if these foods are used to any extent, they still will replace essential foods. Parents should realize that the child does not miss what he never has had and does not need" (Burke 1960, p. 173).

In the formation of sound eating habits, the child's hunger should be taken into account. That is, he should not be allowed to "nibble" between meals so that he comes to the table without hunger. The presence of hunger at mealtimes leads to the pleasant association of food with the relief of hunger, and thus food likes are established. Food dislikes may sometimes be traced to the opposite. Being expected or forced to eat despite the absence of hunger may lead to an eating problem in the child, or to specific dislikes for foods the child is forced to eat.

It is also true, however, that excessive hunger can interfere with normal appetite, which suggests that the time span between meals should not be too long. Factors that interfere with appetite include between-meal snacks, hurry and emotional upset at mealtimes, fatigue, excessive hunger, and illness and convalescence. Burke presents the following suggestions as aids in avoiding the development of feeding problems:

> Supply the child with a pleasant, quiet place in which to eat, with furniture and utensils adapted to his size and abilities.
> Prepare and serve his food so that it is appetizing and attractive. Serve it in small portions to stimulate appetite and interest in self-feeding. Be sure the food is not too hot.
> Avoid forcing him to eat; avoid any comment on his eating; avoid "rewards" for eating.
> Set a well-balanced meal before him for a definite time—twenty minutes should be sufficient. At the end of this time excuse the child without comment.
> If he shows a particular dislike for certain foods, avoid serving these for a time. Do not discuss or demonstrate food aversions in front of him.
> Preferably have only one person supervise the child's feeding, one who maintains an attitude free of overconcern or oversolicitude.
> Do not let him nibble between meals. If he becomes hungry at

such times, he may be offered a small glass of milk or some fruit if it will not interfere with his appetite at the subsequent meal.

Prior to and during meals the atmosphere should be peaceful and tranquil. (Burke 1960, pp. 175–176)

Exercise

Brief observation of the child should readily convince us of the vital role played by physical activity in his daily routine. There is an almost continuous flow of activity. There is a primitive urge to make use of the muscle systems, which are gradually being brought under control. It appears to be fundamentally satisfying to a child to make use of his body and its possibilities for movement, manipulation, and use of energy.

Through the early years there is increasing emphasis on the use of muscle action as a means to other ends—in the creation of projects, in artistic pursuits, in more highly controlled games and motor skills, and so on. But such activities find their origins in the more primitive action of the child that is initiated as an objective in its own right. That is, muscular action is satisfying and necessary for its own sake before it is used as a basis for organized activities.

This continuous physical activity, which naturally tends to emphasize the large muscle action involved in gross body activity, contributes to muscular development and coordination. At the same time there are many other benefits. The respiratory and circulatory systems are benefited by normal muscular action; their healthy growth is stimulated by the increasing demands resulting from activity. Further, in the normal course of physical activities, the child's sensory processes are continually stimulated and much learning results.

The child is motivated to correlate the sensory images—what he is seeing; hearing; touching; tasting; smelling; and feeling in his muscles, tendons, and body joints; and so on—with the muscle action, which gradually becomes more controlled and purposeful. The physical activity also contributes to psychological and social stabilization: The child experiences feedback from his own muscle action, which yields information that certain kinds of activities bring personal, social, and physical satisfaction, while others lead to pain or discomfort or social unpleasantness. Thus his muscular activity plays a direct role in the establishment of knowledge about himself and his world.

In the normal course of events it seems unnecessary to impose any planned exercise program for the sake of body conditioning, since his own internal motivation leads to ample amounts and forms of activity if his play is uninhibited. An adult who attempts to duplicate the precise physical movements of a normally active 4-year-old for, say a 1-hour period will probably testify to the truth of this statement! Not only is there much vigorous action, but there is involvement of a large number of muscle systems, some of which the adult may have forgotten. It may be desirable, however, to evaluate the child's exercise routine from time to time, making certain that there are sufficient play opportunities in safe settings. Adequate, but not excessive, social stimulation also contributes to a healthful activity routine. Excessive and prolonged expenditure of energy can lead to undue fatigue, which might reveal itself in the form of irritability, lack of emotional control, difficulty in relaxing for rest or sleep, or—in extreme cases—failure to gain weight normally.

Control of this general condition, provided it is not symptomatic of a physical condition requiring medical attention, normally consists of some reduction in the amount and variety of stimulations given a child, and provision of a consistent and pleasant rest and sleep routine. In unusual cases, over- or underactivity can be symptomatic of neural or glandular disorders, and suspicion of unusual activity levels in young children, or marked departure from previous activity levels, should be brought to the attention of a physician.

Finally, we should note that in cases of perceptual-motor problems, a planned program of activities designed to improve perceptual-motor functioning may be inaugurated, making use of equipment under the direction of child development specialists trained in these processes.

Rest and sleep

The child's natural demands for rest and sleep are the best guides for providing satisfaction for these needs. Since there are wide variations in the amount of rest and sleep required by individual children, it is not possible to state a precise number of hours of sleep that all children of a given age should have, or to give a precise age at which children should discontinue an afternoon nap or rest time.

Such rigid prescriptions, which at one time were given rather freely, violate our understanding of individual differences. We do know, however, that young children benefit from some planned quiet periods during the course of the day, long after they have discontinued a formal nap time. If these are not actually planned by parents or teachers, the child might be expected to show his need for such quiet periods in his behavior, sometimes in what appears to be hyperactivity and overstimulation.

A child is very much geared to the present—he does not succeed well in planning ahead for delayed satisfactions and cannot be expected, on his own, to plan to rest "now" for the sake of feeling better "later." He needs adult help in carrying out this kind of routine, and the constructiveness of his activities later will give evidence of the validity of his body's need for occasional rest.

Infectious diseases and the development of immunity

The incidence of illnesses of all kinds during childhood varies with the age of the child, his sex, and his individual ability to cope with infectious agents. However, childhood illnesses are such a normal part of the process of growing up that they must be considered a predictable and inevitable feature of childhood.

In the Harvard Longitudinal Studies, in which detailed health and illness records were maintained for 134 children from birth to maturity, the illness records ranged from a minimum of 17 to a maximum of 104 illnesses during the first 18 years of life. These included any and all illnesses in all degrees of severity.

The following description by Valadian is revealing not only of the normality of childhood illnesses, but also of some ways in which illness records were associated with age and sex of child:

> The majority of boys experienced from 36 to 70 illnesses while the majority of girls had 20 to 36 illnesses. The median number for

boys was 52 whereas for girls it was 42. This greater frequency of illness among the boys than the girls is characteristic of all age periods except from 10 to 14 years, but most striking for the age periods 2 to 6 and 6 to 10 and least so during the first 2 years. It was found in this study that the median number of illnesses for each age period were as follows: in infancy, boys, 6.7, girls, 5.8; in the preschool period, boys, 16.6, girls, 12.7; in the school period, boys, 12.2, girls, 9.4; in early adolescence, boys, 6.1, girls, 6.2; and in late adolescence, boys, 5.6, girls, 4.0. The illnesses experienced by the group tended to be mild to moderate on the average throughout total childhood. In both infancy and in the preschool period the great majority of boys and girls had about equally mild and moderate illnesses. In the school period there were considerably more girls in the mild category than in the moderate but boys were still more nearly equal in each. The highest values for both the numbers and severities of illnesses were in the preschool period with relatively high values in infancy and the school period and a definite increase after 10 years. They reached their lowest levels in late adolescence. (Valadian 1960, p. 28)

Elsewhere in this same study some light was shed on the general types of illnesses. It was noted that at all ages throughout the 18-year span, by far the largest proportion of cases (over 75 percent) were of a respiratory nature. However, the proportion of respiratory to total illnesses did vary considerably by age level. It was lowest during the early years and highest during adolescence as other illnesses became more rare. These respiratory illnesses were mostly mild to moderate infections of the common cold variety, although allergies constituted a significant number as well. Such respiratory illnesses predominated to such a degree that not a single child escaped them during their 18 years (Valadian 1960).

A major consideration in evaluating the development of the normal child is his history of mild and acute infections. Exposure to infectious agents is inevitable, but the ability to resist infections is a quality that varies greatly from one child to another.

Healthy growth is not fostered by either extreme of attempting to protect a child against every source of infection (such as not allowing him to play with other children, since they "might have germs") or deliberately exposing a child needlessly to any and all sources of infection (on the assumption that "it builds up his immunity"). In the ordinary household and in the normal associations of a child with other people there is ample exposure to a variety of infectious agents, which can stimulate the development of degrees of immunity to a large number of diseases.

This same general principle is used in the planned medical programs of immunization, beginning in infancy and continuing throughout childhood and the adult years—the principle of exposure to mild and controlled dosages of the infectious agent, which stimulates the body's defense mechanisms, usually in the form of antibodies in the bloodstream, thereby enabling it to ward off subsequent attacks of the same or similar types of agents. A planned program of artificial immunization, beginning in infancy, plays an essential role in the healthy development of children.

Nossal (1969) reports that immunization has been remarkably effective in the prevention of virus diseases such as smallpox, yellow fever, poliomyelitis, measles, and mumps. "Vaccination against these is safe and practically 100% effective" (p. 165). Immunization is also effective in diseases caused by a poisoning effect of an invading microbe, such as tetanus (lockjaw) and diphtheria. In the latter examples, immunity is achieved through the injection of toxoids several times in the early years, and at intervals thereafter to maintain the immune state. While this procedure does not guarantee absolute immunity, it is rare for an immunized person to develop the disease, and in those rare cases, the disease is usually very mild.

Immunization against diseases such as whooping cough, typhoid, paratyphoid, cholera, and plague makes use of whole, killed bacteria as immunogens (Nossal, p. 166). While somewhat less reliable than the procedures mentioned earlier, these are nevertheless considered desirable when conditions warrant their use.

Some public health authorities strongly recommend that children should be exposed to certain diseases in order to acquire immunity and thus prevent the disease from occurring at a later age when the symptoms may be more serious, or when there may be more complications. Mumps, for example, can mean acute involvement of reproductive organs if it occurs during adolescence.

An even more critical consideration arises in the case of rubella which, if contracted by a woman in the early stages of pregnancy, can produce serious congenital defects in the fetus. According to Eichorn (1971), this can lead to malformations of the heart, cataracts, mental retardation, deafness, and other serious abnormalities. Some states now vaccinate school children against rubella, but we need additional experience with the vaccine in order to assess accurately its effectiveness in preventing the occurrence of congenital defects.

An interesting and far from insignificant example of a modern environmental health hazard for children is the common "lead" pencil. The "lead" inside the pencil is not really lead at all, but graphite, and is not in itself a serious problem. However, some pencils contain, in the exterior paint, a sufficient quantity of real lead to be toxic to a child who chews on pencils.

The Department of Health, Education, and Welfare's Bureau of Community Environmental Management reported in 1971 that all pencils that agency had tested had lead contents which could be hazardous. In one group of pencils tested the paint contained approximately 12 percent lead, compared with a maximum "safe" amount considered to be 1 percent.

Ingesting even small amounts of such paint constitutes a serious health hazard, and while many pencil paints do not contain such large quantities of lead, no pencil containing *any* lead in the paint should be regarded as safe for a child who habitually chews on pencils. Reputable pencil manufacturers in the United States have developed a formal certification program which provides for yearly testing of each manufacturer's product to ensure minimum lead content. However, this does not eliminate the production of pencils by nonparticipating companies, nor does it eliminate hazards from pencils manufactured prior to discovery of this existing hazard. As Picharello (1971) has noted, this is an example of an environmental health hazard that is correctible, both at the manufacturing level and at the child supervision level.

Childhood accidents

More young children lose their lives as a result of accidents than from any other cause. In addition to the startlingly high rate of fatal accidents, large numbers of children are temporarily or permanently incapacitated or crippled as a result of mishaps. Many of these accidents could be avoided, and it is likely that sound knowledge of the nature and characteristics of the growing child could contribute materially to accident reduction.

Mortality statistics available up to 1971 in the United States showed that for the total population, accidents were the fourth leading cause of death, outranked only by heart disease, malignancies, and vascular lesions affecting the central nervous system, as reported in *Accident Facts* (1971), published by the National Safety Council. With the exception of the early infancy period, however, accidents were the *leading* cause of death for children of all ages; for ages 1 to 14, accidents claimed more lives than the six leading diseases combined. Among neonates and very young infants, the largest number of deaths result from such causes as congenital defects, asphyxia, and "immaturity." In the age range 1 to 4 years, the largest number of fatal accidents during 1968 involved motor vehicles (1668 fatalities). Fires and burns caused 895 fatalities in this age range, while 780 deaths resulted from drowning. Another 246 children died that year from poisoning, and 1154 died as a result of miscellaneous or unclassified accidents.

Many of these accidents occur in and around the home, and leading causes of fatalities include poisoning; falls; blows from falling or projected objects; accidents caused by machinery (in addition to automobiles); electric shock; exposure to fire and explosions, hot substances, corrosive liquid or steam; accidents with firearms; suffocation from inhalation of food; accidents caused by bites and stings of animals and insects; drownings; and exposure.

Poisoning ranks particularly high in fatalities for young children, and also represents preventable incidents in many cases. Negligence on the part of adults, in making poisonous substances available to young children, may be based on the adult's ignorance of the child's inability to discriminate between edible and poisonous substances on the basis of taste, texture, smell, or the label on the container.*

This inability, combined with the young child's natural propensity for sampling the interesting substances he encounters, represents a kind of entrapment which can only be avoided through the alertness of adults and their sensitivity to the nature of the "trap" before a child becomes a victim. Poisonous substances simply should not be accessible. This includes aspirin tablets and other home medicines, which can be poisonous in quantity, and kerosene or other petroleum distillates commonly stored around houses, garages, farmyards, or sheds.

Stuart (1960) reports a sharply higher accident rate for boys than for girls. This is probably accounted for, in part, by differences in kinds of physical activities engaged in, and differences in amount and type of supervision provided for the two sexes. In addition, it is possible that boys, as they get older, are more inclined to take physical risks as they imitate the behavior of adult males, than are girls, who are taught to imitate their mothers.

The solution to the problem of accident prevention is not a simple one, nor is it entirely reasonable to strive for the complete elimination of all hazards in a child's life. Normal progress toward independence and self-protection demands that a child gradually acquire competence in meeting and handling an increasing variety of hazards he will inevitably encounter. To protect him against any and all small hazards throughout early childhood is not only unrealistic, but would defeat his own efforts to become self-reliant and realistic in coping with larger hazards later.

There is a reasonable balance between the extremes of overprotection and lack of supervision. This balance allows the child to experience the normal bumps, scrapes, and bruises of the early

---

* Some children are more attracted than repelled by the traditional skull-and-crossbones caution symbol. A new design, known as "Mr. Yuk," was reported in *Time Magazine* November 27, 1972. Developed by Dr. Richard Moriarty of the Poison Information Center at the Children's Hospital of Pittsburgh, it consists of a face with a protruding tongue and agonized expression.

years without making too much of an issue of them. At the same time, it avoids the too-early introduction of hazards with which the child is simply not prepared to cope. Just as we would not let a child go swimming without supervision, neither should we prevent him from having early, satisfying experiences in the water.

Accidents are the result of multiple causation, with factors in the child himself (age, sex, agility, personality), in the physical environment, in his relations with his parents, in geographical location, and even in time of day (accidents seem to increase between 3:00 and 6:00 p.m.). In spite of the complexity of the causes involved, it is likely that a thorough understanding of child development can enable adults to be more perceptive of the potential hazards presented to a young child by his world.

A problem related to accidental injury or death, which is becoming more visibly recognized, is that of child abuse by parents. Every year, according to Helfer and Kempe (1968), tens of thousands of children in the United States are severely battered, mutilated, or killed. It is a tragic phenomenon which occurs in most civilized countries, and which is not limited to any specific age of children.

Recent efforts to understand the psychology of abusive parents have not yielded a clear-cut picture of any single "type" of parent who physically mistreats children. Melnick and Hurley (1969) compared ten abusive with ten control mothers and found that the abusive mothers were not necessarily more chronically hostile or domineering, but that they were less able to empathize with their children, that they appeared to have severely frustrated dependency needs, and that they had a probable history of emotional deprivation. Not only do we need more understanding about the capacity of normal parents to provide nurturance without being abusive, but we also need further research in the pathological behavior of those parents who mistreat their children.

Summary

In this chapter we have examined the general trends in physical growth during the early years. The major change in physical appearance is a lengthening out process, attributable to growth of the trunk and long bones of the body and a loss of baby fat. Gross changes in size and weight occur much more slowly between 2 and 6 than in the preceding period of infancy. The young child's skeleton is still immature both in size and quality; some ossification centers have not yet made their appearance. The use of X-ray photography has enabled specialists to learn much about the regularities of human development. Care of the deciduous teeth has been stressed, in part because of the role they play in the alignment of the permanent teeth. Muscular development has been seen to play a significant role in the child's expanding efforts to control body action and in relation to all aspects of cognitive and personality development.

The primary physical growth needs include adequate nutrition, exercise, rest, and sleep. Childhood diseases are normal, but the importance of a comprehensive program of immunization was also stressed. The frequency of accidents—the leading cause of mortality among young children—could be significantly decreased by careful attention to and understanding of the nature of the young child, and through attention to his physical environment and its hazards. Aside from automobile accidents, most serious and fatal injuries to young children occur in the home. The home, regarded by most as a haven of protection and security, represents a severe threat to the physical well-being of thousands of children whose parents mistreat or abuse them.

References

Bayley, N. "Growth Curves of Height and Weight by Age for Boys and Girls, Scaled According to Physical Maturity." *Journal of Pediatrics* 48 (1956) 187–194.

Burke, B. S. "The Nutrition of the Preschool Child." In Stuart, H. C., and Prugh, D. G., eds. *The Healthy Child.* Cambridge, Mass.: Harvard University Press, 1960, pp. 169–176.

Eichorn, M. M. "Rubella: Will Vaccination Prevent Birth Defects?" *Science* 73 (20 August 1971) 710–711.

Garn, S. M., and Shamir, Z. *Methods for Research in Human Growth.* Springfield, Ill.: Charles C Thomas, 1958.

Greulich, W. W., and Pyle, S. I. *Radiographic Atlas of Skeletal Develop-*

ment of the Hand and Wrist. Stanford, Calif.: Stanford University Press, 1950.

Hathaway, M. L. "Heights and Weights of Children and Youth in the United States." Washington, D.C.: Home Economics Research Reports, No. 2, U.S. Department of Agriculture, 1957.

Helfer, R. E., and Kempe, C. H., eds. *The Battered Child.* Chicago: University of Chicago Press, 1968.

Hurlock, E. B. *Child Development.* 3rd ed. New York: McGraw-Hill, 1956.

Martin, E. A. *Nutrition in Action.* 3rd ed. New York: Holt, Rinehart and Winston, 1971.

Melnick, B., and Hurley, J. R. "Distinctive Personality Attributes of Child-Abusing Mothers." *Journal of Consulting and Clinical Psychology* 33 (1969) 746–749.

Meredith, H. V. "Toward a Working Concept of Growth." *American Journal of Orthodontics and Oral Surgery* 31 (1945) 440–448.

———. "Changes in the Stature and Body Weight of North American Boys During the Last 80 Years." In Lipsitt, L., and Spiker, C., eds. *Advances in Child Development and Behavior.* Vol. 1. New York: Academic Press, 1963, pp. 69–114.

———. "Body Size of Contemporary Groups of Preschool Children Studied in Different Parts of the World." *Child Development* 39 (1968) 335–377.

National Safety Council. *Accident Facts.* 1971 ed. Chicago: National Safety Council, 1971.

Nossal, G. J. V. *Antibodies and Immunity.* New York: Basic Books, 1969.

Picharello, J. "Lead Poisoning: Risks for Pencil Chewers?" *Science* 173 (6 August 1971) 509–510.

Stuart, H. C. "The Principles of Growth and Development." In Stuart, H. C., and Prugh, D. G., eds. *The Healthy Child.* Cambridge, Mass.: Harvard University Press, The Commonwealth Fund, 1960, pp. 3–21.

Tanner, J. M. "Physical Growth." In Mussen, P. H., ed. *Carmichael's Manual of Child Psychology.* 3rd ed., vol. 1. New York: Wiley, 1970, pp. 77–155.

Thompson, H. "Physical Growth." In Carmichael, L., ed. *Manual of Child Psychology.* 2nd ed. New York: Wiley, 1954, pp. 292–334.

Valadian, I. "General Features of Illness by Age." In Stuart, H. C., and Prugh, D. G., eds. *The Healthy Child.* Cambridge, Mass.: Harvard University Press, The Commonwealth Fund, 1960, pp. 22–32.

Watson, E. H., and Lowrey, G. H. *Growth and Development of Children.* 4th ed. Chicago: Yearbook Medical, 1962.

Zubek, J. P., and Solberg, P. A. *Human Development.* New York: McGraw-Hill, 1954.

CHAPTER SIX

Achieving body control

What are the three major components of motor action?

Why is motor development of special significance in a child's life?

How does motor behavior relate to mental, social, and personality development?

What are the most important trends of development in the patterning of motor control?

How can we apply reasonable principles of guidance in facilitating motor development?

Man's unique position in the animal kingdom and his remarkable history of technological progress are in no small measure a reflection of his special abilities with respect to body control. Two important illustrations are (1) his uniquely precise coordination of thumb against forefinger, which allows him to engage in infinitely varied manipulatory action; and (2) his special capacity for control of a complex speech mechanism, which enables him to communicate freely his rich culture, with its expanding technology, from one person to another as it is accumulated. Both of these are examples of motor behavior. And both undergo essential developmental processes in early childhood.

By motor *behavior* we mean essentially the use of the voluntary muscles in bringing about movement and control of body action. Motor *development*, then, is the gradual process of bringing the skeletal (voluntary) muscles under volitional control. It is a long-term process leading toward improved coordination of the *sensory receptors* (eyes, ears, and so on), with the *central nervous system*, and in turn with the *muscles* themselves. All three of these are essential components of motor action, and the development of all three components—*sensory, neural,* and *muscular*—is essential to the achievement of body control.

Achieving one's potentials as a human being is, in part, a matter of achieving control of body action. It includes the accomplishment of a vast number of skills, many of which we take for granted since they are well learned without specific instruction at such an early age. Since motor behavior and development is so easily taken for granted, and since its importance is so easily underestimated, it will be well worth the effort to give careful consideration to the importance of motor development in the life of the growing child.

Significance of motor development

Motor behavior and body control play major roles in the child's life and in his overall development, not only because motor action is important in its own right, but because it makes possible a wide variety of activities that are not ordinarily thought of as being motor behavior.

From another point of view, the failure of a child to achieve a reasonable level of body control as compared with others of his age can have a significant impact on the kind of personal adjustment he makes, for the kinds of interests and attitudes he develops, for the feelings of achievement and competence he holds toward himself and, in general, for the self-concept that he gradually organizes. In this section we will examine some of these implications more closely.

From the very beginning of life, motor behavior plays a part in the child's perception and awareness of his world. Motor activity brings his eyes, hands, and total body into varied and changing relationships with his world of objects and people. Through sensory coordination of his environment in this continuously changing set of relationships, he gradually builds up concepts about the nature of his environment. His own motor activity contributes to the process of concept building, and is thus fundamental to cognitive growth.

Motor activity is also essential for development of speech. Vocal activity itself is motor behavior. The fine control of the vocal apparatus required for articulation of sounds is well developed during the early years. In speech there is simultaneous action of certain sets of muscles and inhibition of other sets, in rapidly shifting sequences, which makes it possible to move the jaw, tongue, and lips to form essential sounds, and to move rapidly but with clarity from one sound position to another. Indeed, the complexity of the motor action required for speech deserves the sincere respect of the student of child development, for the wonder is that so many children learn to talk so well in such a short time.

Motor behavior is, of course, essential to the performance of any and all activities associated with athletics. While we do not ordinarily associate athletics with early childhood, it is a significant period in laying a foundation for the smooth performance of body action that will later be put to use in organized athletics. Already during the early years great differences in body control and smoothness of activities such as running, jumping, climbing, and swinging are observable from one child to another.

The role of motor behavior in aesthetic activities is also a central one. Coordination of body action is essential to dancing, which is engaged in spontaneously by most young children. In part, the degree of satisfaction and the motivation to develop such activities further is dependent on the degree of body control that the child acquires in these early years. Another aesthetic activity that is highly dependent on motor proficiency is musical performance. Both singing and instrumental music depend upon body control; indeed some instruments are exceptionally demanding of fine muscle coordination. The child's aptitude for piano playing, for example, is dependent to a great extent on sensory-motor coordination. And art in its many forms has a basis in motor activity also. Freedom or inhibition in the expression of feelings and concepts through creative media is in some respects a direct reflection of the level of mastery of body movements. Similarly, many of the crafts, hobbies, skills, and even the beginnings of vocational competencies that are being organized in the early years have an important basis in motor activity and body control. Obviously, much of the world's work requires high levels of mastery of one's body, and the significance of the early period in its development should not be overlooked.

But equally important to all of these considerations is the role of motor development in the achievement of self-confidence and acceptance among one's peers. The well-coordinated child has certain advantages, other things being equal, in that he may be more accepted and admired, more sought after, more ready to assume leadership roles, and more likely to think well of himself as he moves through childhood and into the adult years.

One critical aspect of personality development has to do with the degree of autonomy, or self-directedness of behavior, that a child achieves. The child who is prevented from engaging in the normal amount of exploration of his world, who is not allowed to do things for himself in routines of eating, sleeping, toileting, dressing and undressing, and so on, and who does not acquire the the skills needed for such independence of action can be handicapped not only in respect to the skills themselves, but in his general attitude toward himself. It is essential to achieve attitudes toward oneself that make one feel capable of mastering and controlling various elements of the environment.

Failure in this aspect of development leads to an attitude of helplessness, or powerlessness, and inability to take care of one's own needs. The resulting overdependence on others is neither pleasant for a child nor for those who live with him. Neither does it allow him to make the best uses of whatever intellectual and physical resources he may have inherited.

In summary, then, we may think of body control as an aspect of the child's development, which will be reflected in his total relationship with his world of people and things, and which becomes a cornerstone of his personality development.

Some general trends in the patterning of motor behavior

There is a systematic orderliness to the achievement of body control; general sequences of motor development may be found in all normal children, and in the same order of appearance. As in other aspects of human development, wide latitude is present within the normal range, yet there is solid evidence of the operation of genetic laws that determine the sequence of steps in the motor behavior of childhood, and it is possible to describe the process in terms of general principles, or trends.

Reflexive control, cortical control, and unconscious control

Some motor activity occurs even during the prenatal period and, as noted earlier, there is a wide variety of motor behavior in the repertoire of the neonate. He blinks, sneezes, hiccups, grasps with his hands, flexes arms and legs, turns his head, and in general engages in a wide range of actions calling for use of the skeletal muscles.

The action in which the newborn engages is essentially reflexive in that it is under the control of neural structures that operate in the brain stem and spinal cord but are not controlled by the higher brain centers associated with conscious thought. It is not necessary for the infant to be consciously aware of the bright light which, when it strikes his eyes, leads to blinking. Nor is it necessary for him to think about the process of grasping the adult finger to which his hand may cling, automatically.

These reflex behaviors occur with no conscious thought on his part, and represent the first major stage of body control. Some of the more specific reflex patterns of behavior have been described earlier, in connection with infancy, but the significance for the present discussion is that the beginnings of motor behavior are to be found in the reflexive patterns of infancy, which represent an intact linkage of sensory, neural, and muscular components—the essential ingredients of motor action.

The second general stage of motor development involves gradually increasing participation of the higher brain centers. Both the cerebrum, which includes a region of the brain that directs body movement, and the cerebellum, which is essential in the control of body balance and coordination, become more involved as the child matures. With this increased involvement of the brain in motor behavior that is no longer automatic, it becomes necessary for the child to control body action to a much greater extent by "thinking about" that action. He consciously directs his hands and feet to a much greater degree than in earlier stages.

But with continued maturation and practice in the development of particular skills comes the final and highest stage of motor control, which releases the child once again from the need to give continuous conscious direction to the operation of the skeletal muscles. This is the stage of the highly developed motor habit, in which a smooth and polished action seems to occur spontaneously with no conscious effort required. Actually, the polished performance is the result of continued practice, in which one phase of the action has consistently followed another phase so that each action serves as a cue, or stimulus to the performance of the next. The result is the smoothly flowing pattern of behavior that does not require conscious direction. Walking, which involves a repetitive sequence of flexion and extension of each leg, is an illustration.

As a matter of interest, we might note that the interruption of such a smoothly patterned sequence by conscious analysis of the process itself may be enough to destroy the pattern of the motor action. This could be observed in the case of a child who has developed a complex skill to the point of habit, who, right in the middle of the performance begins to question whether or not he can move his hands or his feet in the appropriate manner and, as a result of the questioning, loses the smooth continuity of the action sequence.

The movement from the first to the second and third stages of body control cannot be equated directly with the child's age level. Even as adults, we may have to move through all three stages in the acquisition of a new motor skill. That is, our general pattern of reflexive behavior, and the intact linkage of sensory, neural, and muscular components, provide the basic resources for learning a new skill, such as driving an automobile; but in learning to control a car there is initially a great deal of conscious effort necessary to perform the basic actions of operating the controls. With consistent practice, however, the movements become "automatic," and the performance simultaneously becomes smoother, as the experienced driver no longer needs to "tell himself" what to do with the controls in each situation.

This movement through the three key stages then, instead of being a matter of age, is a central pattern of development of motor control at any age. Many examples could be given. The fact that adults do not have to think about how to shape each letter of their name in order to write it; the skilled typist does not look at the typewriter keyboard or ask herself where her fingers are going at any particular moment; an accomplished pianist moves hands and fingers in exceeding complex sequences of shifting patterns without consciously directing each specific movement; the aesthetically pleasing body movements of the professional athlete or dancer whose graceful body action is freed from the constraints of thinking about each set of muscles involved; and so on—all represent progress to the highest stages of body control. The 5-year-old who has learned to "pump" in the swing can do it gracefully and efficiently without having to tell himself consciously how to go about it. And if that same child has learned to skip, he can do that also without any conscious questioning of "which foot goes next."

One is not in the same stage for all kinds of motor activities at the same time, of course. The 4-year-old who is in the second stage with respect to buttoning his favorite jacket may reveal it in his studied intentness in coordinating buttons with holes, and making his fingers get the job done—sometimes with much trial and error. That same child may still be in the first stage when it comes to tying shoelaces, and in the third stage when it comes to walking up and down stairs, or riding a tricycle.

Other trends in the patterning of motor action

The lawfulness and orderliness of the process by which a child achieves body control is illustrated further in the operation of two additional principles: (1) there is development from bilateral to unilateral control of body action, and (2) there is development from maximum to minimum muscular involvement.

BILATERAL TO UNILATERAL CONTROL "Bilateral" refers to both sides of the body. The neonate is essentially symmetrical, tending to use both sides of the body to about the same extent and about the same degree of efficiency. While this generalization has an exception (the tonic neck reflex is an early manifestation of one-sided behavior), it still may be stated that the early infancy period involves largely a two-sided, or bilateral, approach to the world.

Observations of a large number of infants by Gardner and Pease (1961) supported the general hypothesis that the approach of an infant to objects presented to him while he is supported at a table is essentially a two-sided approach at first. That is, when cubes, pellets, spoons, and other objects were presented to infants during the course of psychological examinations, in the midline of the baby's vision and from the opposite side of the table, the tendency during the first half year was for the baby to approach the object in a surrounding motion, with both arms and both hands involved in an attempt to corral the object.

Later in the second half of the first year a pronounced shift was observed, with the infants making much more use of one or the other hand while inhibiting the action of the opposite one. The implications of this shift for the development of handedness during the early years will be discussed later. At this point we should note that the older child has established a relatively clear-cut unilateral approach, with not only a strong preference for the use of one side of his body, but a significantly greater accuracy and level of efficiency for the preferred side in many kinds of motor activities.

MAXIMUM TOWARD MINIMUM MUSCULAR INVOLVEMENT Early motor behavior typically involves excessive muscle action, with large segments and components of the body entering into even fairly simple motor activities. The well-known example of the child who, at about age 5, may want to tie his own shoelaces, serves to illustrate this point. In his first attempts to tie his own shoelaces, he calls into action many large and small muscles that are not essential to the act of shoelace tying. He may even involve head and neck muscles, facial and tongue muscles, and so on, in grimacing and posturing, all of which indicates the excessive muscular involvement. With practice and increasing skill, he will gradually eliminate this excess action of unneeded muscle systems, and the essential action of the relevant muscles will perform the action smoothly and without interference. As a new motor skill is being learned, however, it is natural for excess tension and muscle action to occur in parts of the body not relevant to the skill.

The development of motor control then is not merely a matter of learning to use the appropriate muscles for a given action. It is also a matter of learning to inhibit the action of nonessential muscle groups. One of the reasons it is aesthetically pleasing to observe the performance of a skilled dancer or an accomplished athlete is that such a person has learned well how to eliminate nonessential movement and body tension. The result is the avoidance of clumsy or stilted movements and waste motion. We describe it as a "polished" performance.

Development of gross motor control

The achievement of independent walking early in the second year is neither the beginning nor the final step in the development of upright locomotion. With increased practice, muscular and neural development, and changes in body proportion there are important changes also in the manner of walking and in the variations and additions to the basic walking pattern. The first tottering steps are taken on short legs, balancing a body that has a high center of gravity because of the proportionately large head. The body position in this first walking period is not yet completely vertical; the knees are bent and the stepping movement is high and exaggerated. The feet are placed far apart to improve balance.

Often a child will walk better and with more self-assurance at first if he has something in his hand. Apparently this relates to the fact that he was holding on to something such as a rail, a piece of furniture, or an adult finger much of the time just prior to independent walking, during which he was practicing stepping movements and gaining balance. An example of this was Don B., who for the first few days while taking independent steps consistently held his right earlobe securely between thumb and forefinger!

Not only does the body position gradually become more vertical and at the same time more relaxed; the walking child rapidly increases the smoothness and efficiency of his stepping and balancing. Incidental skills that are related but not central to walking may be developed so rapidly as to be almost overlooked by parents. For example, the ability to go from a sitting position to a standing position without support, in the center of the floor, and move about unaided, then to sit down gracefully and easily as only the toddler can, is really quite a remarkable achievement. But in the typical parental excitement over walking itself, this skill may not be observed. It does not usually occur until some time after independent walking has been established.

Extensive investigation of the motor behavior of infants and young children has been carried out by Bayley (1935, 1965). She observed that by about 24 or 25 months, children will walk up and downstairs, advancing the preferred foot each time and then bringing the other foot to the same level. Alternating the feet to walk upstairs will probably not occur until about 35 or 36 months, and alternating the feet while going downstairs will usually come much later, around 50 months.

A similar progression in jumping and hopping was observed. At about 24 or 25 months children were observed to jump off the floor with both feet, and at a little over 25 months to stand on the right foot alone, but not until 49 months could they hop on one foot alone. By around 42 months the children could jump over a string held less than 20 cm off the floor, and they could make a distance jump of 14 inches by 39.7 months and of 24 inches by 48.4 months. The regularity of these progressions in motor capabilities are consistent with the findings of other investigators, such as Gesell and Amatruda (1947).

One of the most significant aspects of motor development is the fact that behavior, which is at first motivated by the child's own need to do that which his body is prepared to do, becomes a means to some greater end or objective. Walking and running are good illustrations. These are activities in which the child participates, at first, by concentrating all his energy, strength, and coordination on the process itself, for the sake of the process itself. The reward for the activity is inherent in the satisfaction of engaging in it. But as the activity becomes an established habit so that balancing, stepping, starting, and stopping and all the component parts of the walking act become routine and do not call for his complete and undivided attention, the act becomes a means to the larger end of getting the child where he wants to go.

The importance of this point lies partly in our understanding that the motivation for beginning walking—and many other kinds of motor activity—is not the same for a child as for an adult, but arises largely from the satisfaction of using the bodily capabilities that are emerging through maturation. It is nicely illustrated when a 14-month-old suddenly wants to get somewhere in a hurry. Although he has been walking for over a month, he may now resort to fast creeping—a very reliable behavior—to fulfill the immediate interest. A few months later, when walking has become a reliable behavior, it will be the preferred "means to the end" of getting him where he wants to go.

The development of handedness

The question of what causes some children to be left-handed has been an interesting and, to some parents, disturbing question. To the child development specialist, however, there is a far more basic question to be understood: what causes a child to develop *handedness*, whether it be right- or left-handedness? Furthermore, what causes a child to develop dominance of one leg over the other? What causes us to develop unilaterality with respect to use of the eyes? For most of us there are definite preferences in these matters and, if we had a mouth on each side of our face to correspond with each eye, chances are most of us would use the right one for talking! Kimura (1963) found the right ear to be dominant over the left in children as young as 4 years.

Much has been written on the subject of handedness over the years, with conflicting theories being advanced as to the cause and proper treatment of left-handedness even from the time of the early Greek philosophers. Clearly, it can be a problem for the individual who is strongly left-handed, since society is in many respects geared to the right-handed majority. At the same time, there are circumstances under which the strongly right-handed person is at a disadvantage if he has never trained his left hand to do routine tasks.

An example of this occurred in the life of one active young girl who suffered an arm injury, which necessitated the wearing of a cast on her right arm for a period of several weeks. This girl, age 3, had already established a considerable degree of right-hand dominance. However, it was interesting to observe the relative ease with which she reorganized such routine habits as eating, dressing, manipulating puzzle pieces, and so on. Chances are that at a later age it would be somewhat more difficult for her to shift habits from one hand to the other as readily as she did at age 3.

In general the theories of handedness have stressed the relative effects of heredity and learning as the basic determinant of preferences. However, there is no simple explanation for hand dominance, and any theory that is put forward is probably, at best, only a partial explanation. One of the aspects of the problem derives from the fact that the control of body movements by the brain is governed by the opposite side of the brain from the limb or body part involved. The left hemisphere of the brain controls motor activities of the right side of the body, and vice versa. Orton (1934) argued that hand dominance is primarily a matter of which side of the brain develops dominance over the other, and that it is normally the left side of the brain that becomes dominant. This theory fails to explain, however, why one side of the brain becomes dominant and why, for most people, it is the left side.

The other major theoretical argument, that handedness is primarily a matter of social learning in a world where we expect and assume right-handedness, rests on assumptions that the infant is at first bilateral and develops handedness as he acquires experience in his social world, especially with adult models who are predominantly right-handed. Other evidence has been cited to indicate that lower animals—the great apes, chimpanzees, and monkeys—are able to use both hands with about equal facility. This suggests that human beings, by virtue of their intelligence, culture, and language, all of which provide each new infant with a complex cultural environment and many rich learning experiences, force the majority of children into the pattern of right-handedness at an early age with no observable ill effects. This would illustrate the adaptability of children, which is supported by the fact that most young children can adapt to use of either hand as the need arises.

The percentage of right-handedness is higher for girls than it is for boys, and there are few of either sex who could be called truly ambidextrous—having equal facility with either hand. The question of why more boys than girls develop left-handedness is somewhat unsettled, although it has been argued that this reflects a greater susceptibility of girls to social learning influences.

Most students of the problem agree that handedness remains indefinite and changeable during most of the first year. It begins to be well established in most children by the end of the second year. Even here, however, the findings should be interpreted with caution, since it is possible for a child to be right-handed for some activities and left-handed for others. Again, this has been explained partly in terms of the types of activities that are most likely to be observed, and in which there is most likely to be social pressure applied to make a child right-handed.

Figure 6.1 shows the percentage of cases in which handedness is established by age level, as described by Hildreth (1949b). It would appear from this that in the majority of cases it is well established prior to the kindergarten year.

Guidance of the development of handedness

Because of the conflicting ideas about handedness that have been expressed by different writers, parents are often left with feelings of doubt and anxiety about the proper course of action to follow in cases where a child shows some early signs of left-handedness. The advice sometimes given is that he should be trained from the start to use his right hand in order to avoid the problem in later years. But other writers have stressed leaving the child alone to develop his own hand preference, since interference with handedness has been thought to lead to other problems, such as speech difficulties.

Since speech too is a motor activity that is controlled to a great extent by specific areas of the left cerebral hemisphere of the brain, it has been held that interference with handedness can involve the neural control centers for speech. The evidence that changing handedness will cause stuttering is not entirely conclusive. One reason it is difficult to evaluate such evidence is that stuttering is also correlated with excess muscular tension.

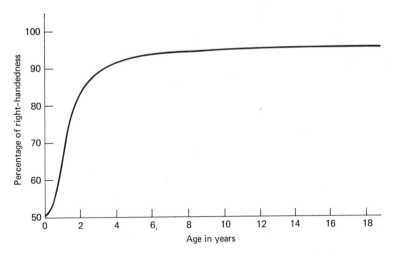

FIGURE 6.1 The curve showing the increase in right-handedness that occurs with age. (From G. Hildreth, "The Development and Training of Hand Dominance: III. Developmental Tendencies in Handedness," *Journal of Genetic Psychology,* 1949, 75:221–254.)

Tension, in turn, may be related to parental pressure and coercion. The same parents who enforce a change of handedness may be the ones who are coercive and tension producing in other respects. Hence, if stuttering does result, we cannot be certain of the exact cause.

Nevertheless, there may be some general guidelines that can help in determining whether or not it is appropriate to attempt to change the handedness of a particular child. Hildreth (1950) presented the following criteria, not with the idea that it is either absolutely right or wrong to change a child's handedness, but as a guide to knowing under what circumstances it might be advisable:

The child is under 6 years.
The child uses both hands interchangeably.
The handedness index is bilateral.
A trial period shows no permanent damage.

The child is agreeable to the change.
The child is above average in intelligence.

It is Hildreth's conclusion, after careful investigation of the problem, that not all children who show signs of left-handedness should be forced to change. In fact, it might be concluded that if much force is required to bring about the change, it is rarely justified and may result in more problems than it will solve. For the student who may wish to explore the interesting problems of handedness further, the discussions by Eyre and Schmeekle (1933), Hildreth (1949a), Thompson (1962), and Landreth (1967) are recommended.

Guidance of motor development

The importance of motor development makes it justifiable to consider carefully a sound program of guidance to facilitate that development. In general, such a program consists of three major elements: (1) the equipment available to a child with which he can exercise his growing capacity for body control, (2) the experiences and instruction provided a child that allow for the development of skills, and (3) the attitudes of the adults in a child's life, which play a vital role in determining his own feelings about motor activity. All three are vital aspects of the guidance program.

Equipment for motor activities

The motivation for motor behavior comes, as we have stressed, from inside the child as he achieves the capacity to engage in each new level of action. The manner of using his energies and the channeling of his motor impulses will depend to a marked degree on the kinds of play equipment available. The need for good equipment is illustrated most clearly by the child himself: if there are no other things available to climb on, jump from, swing on, or hang from, he will probably try to make use of the living room furniture for such natural activities.

But providing good equipment is justified by far better reasons than that of protecting the furniture. An examination of the play area of a well-equipped children's center will give an idea of the variety of play equipment and materials that stimulate healthy motor activity. Climbing, a natural and appealing activity, is stimulated by the jungle gym and similar climbing frames in both indoor and outdoor play. Swings and slides are useful in developing general body coordination. Boxes and barrels are particularly versatile items: they can be moved, piled, climbed in or on, and so on for development of strength and skill. Sturdy tricycles are always appropriate for 2- to 5-year-olds, since the skillful handling of a tricycle calls for considerable coordination and timing. The circular motion of the legs is difficult to achieve before the age of about 24 months but, once achieved, opens up an avenue of motor development that leads to other accomplishments as well.

Excellent illustrations of a wide range of outdoor play equipment—some of which is the natural environment, does not represent great expense, and shows the creative uses of such equipment by children—are to be found in the profusely illustrated book by Stone and Rudolph (1970), published by the National Association for the Education of Young Children. That organization also has available a variety of kinds of inexpensive literature regarding play activities and equipment.

While the emphasis during the early years is on the achievement of large muscle control, and the aforementioned equipment is intended for gross body involvement, the idea that young children should not be allowed to engage in fine motor activities is a false and misleading one. The young child gets considerable satisfaction from a variety of activities that stimulate eye-hand coordination—painting and coloring, block building, manipulation of clay and other soft materials, cutting and pasting, and picture-puzzle play. With such materials there is natural stimulation, which leads to healthy coordination of motor and mental activity without any necessity for imposing a particular pattern of hand or limb movements by adults.

This is especially desirable since the child's focus of attention is on the process of the activity and the satisfaction to be derived from it rather than on the making of specific movements. Motor development seems to make better progress in the absence of undue attention to or inhibition of such specific movements.

Experiences and instruction provided by adults

Much of healthy motor development occurs as incidental activity or as an accompaniment to other normal activities of children. In addition to providing a safe environment with some basic equipment and materials, much can be accomplished by judicious planning and guiding the child's experiences. The motivation for the activities comes from within the child; therefore a major consideration in guidance is providing a sufficiently stimulating setting, combined with sufficient adult control and supervision, where potential hazards are kept to a minimum.

Specific instruction in body skills in the early years is not ordinarily needed. An early research worker in this area was McGraw (1935), who studied a pair of twins, one trained and the other untrained in specific motor tasks, and found that maturational readiness was essential in order for the child to profit from training experiences. The exception is the child who requires a particular kind of therapy, such as physical therapy or speech therapy under the direction of a qualified specialist. In certain cases therapy may be indicated in the early years.

In recent years, however, much has been accomplished in the area of movement education, as described by Sweeney (1970). Such skills as dancing and swimming can be taught with considerable success to young children by an experienced teacher, and many adults are surprised at the ability of 4-year-olds to control such body movements.

Even in these activities, however, it is inadvisable for most adults to attempt direct instruction, particularly the kind that stresses specific body movements, unless they are competent both in the activities and in child development. Emphasis on specific movements may prove in the long run to be more disruptive—frustrating adult and child alike—than helpful in achieving body control.

The key to healthy guidance of motor development, then, would seem to be in providing safe and age-appropriate equipment, adequate supervision for its use, and maintenance of positive and constructive attitudes on the part of adults. The planned activities of the modern child development center, including movement education activities for groups and individual children, do not place a premium on absolute standards of performance, but on the satisfaction to be derived through increasing body control.

The role of adult attitudes
in the guidance of motor development

Much of the child's task in achieving motor development requires the maintenance of healthy attitudes toward himself. It is essential that he have a generally competent feeling about his ability to handle himself and the objects and situations that confront him. Such an attitude is based on having had satisfactory experiences, over a long period of time, which lead him to feel confident that he can handle himself appropriately in whatever situations arise.

The role of parent and teacher attitudes in fostering feelings of confidence in the child is paramount. Attitudes of fear and doubt, reflected in excessive protection and sheltering of a child from the normal bumps and bruises, tend to result in an overly cautious, anxious approach in the child. Essentially this is an approach characterized by conflict. The child's conflict, rooted in his own doubts and fears about his ability to handle himself in climbing, tumbling, jumping, and such activities, is expressed in his inhibition of the smooth flow of muscular activity. The resulting "jerkiness" and unevenness in his behavior reflects a "start and stop" attitude on the child's part.

This inhibition of the smooth flow of action interferes with its effectiveness, and reinforces the feeling that he cannot do things well. Thus, a vicious circle of uncoordinated, inhibited action leading to attitudes of incompetence can result. On the other hand, if, from the beginning of infancy, parents can maintain attitudes of acceptance of the naturalness of bumps and bruises and the inevitable risk involved if the child is to achieve normal motor control, these attitudes will carry over in significant ways to the child also. For one thing, parents with such atttitudes are not as likely to make big issues of small bumps, and thus the child is less likely to develop a distorted notion of the significance of such events in his life.

It is possible, however, to go to extremes in allowing the child motor freedom in an unsupervised setting. Obviously there must be concern for the child's safety and well-being. It helps to remember, though, that the child himself adapts very rapidly, given sufficient freedom and adequate equipment and stimulation, to the limits of his own ability to keep himself out of serious trouble.

In a properly equipped child development center, within the limits of the play-yard fence, the children are not much restricted as to what equipment they can use and what they cannot, since it is there for their use. If a child wishes to climb on a jungle gym, his motivation to do so is typically consistent with his ability to handle himself in such a situation. The teacher does not place him on top of the apparatus and leave him to his own devices, but instead allows him to climb it himself when he is ready to do so. Normally, the child does not get himself into situations he does not handle, but it must be remembered that any equipment can be hazardous under some circumstances, and calls for adult supervision.

On occasion, an inhibited child who is reluctant to engage in vigorous large-muscle activities even though he is physically capable of doing so can be helped by the use of positive social reinforcement. This does not require the child to perform in any way that he does not choose, but merely provides an additional source of support for his own wishes to engage in such activities. One such child has been described in detail by Johnston, et al. (1966). He did not make use of the climbing equipment or engage in other vigorous forms of play in the nursery school. Teachers had expressed concern over his apparent lack of strength and motor skills, and the fact that he consistently stood quietly about the play area while other children ran about, rode tricycles, and climbed on a variety of kinds of equipment.

In this study, a particular piece of apparatus was selected (a climbing frame), and the child was first given social reinforcement (attention) whenever he moved close to this equipment. By successively reinforcing the child for moving closer, for touching the frame, for climbing it a little, and finally for extensive climbing, the teachers were able to observe a dramatic change in the amount of climbing behavior of this child, as shown in Figure 6.2. In that figure, the baseline period is a 9-day period of observation during which the amount of time the child normally spent on the apparatus was carefully observed.

The reinforcement period, days 10–18, was a time when the child was given adult attention as he approached and engaged in climbing. During the extinction period, no reinforcement was given, and the child returned to his previous level of climbing

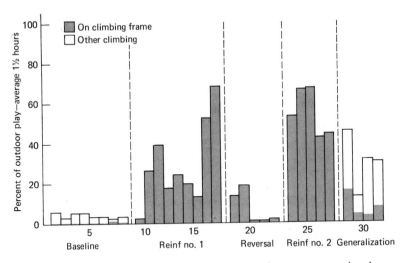

FIGURE 6.2 Percentage of each morning spent by a nursery school boy in using a climbing-frame apparatus. (From Margaret K. Johnston, C. Susan Kelley, Florence R. Harris, and Montrose M. Wolf, "An Application of Reinforcement Principles to Development of Motor Skills of a Young Child," *Child Development*, 1966, *37*, 379–387. Copyright 1966 by The Society for Research in Child Development, Inc. Reprinted by permission.)

activity. When reinforced again (days 24–28) he played more consistently than ever on the climbing apparatus. Finally, it was shown that the child generalized his behavior on the climbing frame to other forms of vigorous motor activity, again with the help of the teachers through their positive reinforcement of this type of activity.

Such an investigation provides dramatic evidence that the attitudes and behavior of adults in relation to a child's motor behavior can make a profound difference in the amount of motor action of a child. While we cannot accurately assess the attitudes of the child toward himself, it seems reasonable to assume that he found such vigorous action satisfying, and supportive of a positive view of himself.

Summary

Motor development may be defined as the gradual achievement of control over body action involving the voluntary muscles. It is based on steadily improving coordination of sensory, neural, and muscular action. The importance of motor development is seen not only in improved muscular coordination per se, but in major contributions to aesthetic, intellectual, social, and personality development. The child's self-concept is dependent in no small measure on his feelings about his ability to control his own body movement and to control the objects and tools of his environment. General trends in the achievement of body control include (1) the sequence from reflexive to cortical to unconscious control, (2) the movement from bilateral to unilateral control, and (3) the trend from maximum toward minimum muscular involvement.

The early years are a time of incessant gross motor activity, during which there is continual practice and improvement in locomotor action with all its variations, manipulation of objects, and increased skill in coordinating body action with sensory stimulation. The prevalence of large-muscle activity among young children does not mean that the child is uninterested in small objects, or that he should not be allowed to exercise fine muscle coordination.

Positive guidance of motor development includes attention to three major considerations: (1) equipment for motor activities, (2) experiences and instruction provided by adults, including movement education activities of child development centers, and (3) adult attitudes toward the child's motor action.

References

Bayley, N. "The Development of Motor Abilities During the First Three Years." *Monographs of the Society for Research in Child Development* 1 (1935).

————. "Comparisons of Mental and Motor Test Scores for Ages 1–15 Months by Sex, Birth Order, Race, Geographical Location, and Education of Parents." *Child Development* 36 (1965) 379–411.

Eyre, M. B., and Schmeekle, M. M. "A Study of Handedness, Eyedness, and Footedness." *Child Development* 4 (1933) 73–78.

Gardner, D. B., and Pease, D. "Performance of Infants on Three Standardized Scales." Unpublished research report. Ames, Iowa: Iowa State University, Agricultural and Home Economics Experiment Station, 1961.

Gesell, A., and Amatruda, C. S. *Developmental Diagnosis.* 2nd ed. New York: Hoeber-Harper, 1947.

Hildreth, G. "The Development and Training of Hand Dominance: I. Characteristics of Handedness." *Journal of Genetic Psychology* 75 (1949a) 177–220.

————. "The Development and Training of Hand Dominance: III. Developmental Tendencies in Handedness." *Journal of Genetic Psychology* 75 (1949b) 221–254.

————. "The Development and Training of Hand Dominance: V. Training of Handedness." *Journal of Genetic Psychology* 76 (1950) 101–144.

Johnston, M. K., Kelley, C. S., Harris, F. R., and Wolf, M. M. "An Application of Reinforcement Principles to Development of Motor Skills of a Young Child." *Child Development* 37 (1966) 379–383.

Kimura, D. "Speech Lateralization in Young Children as Determined by an Auditory Test." *Journal of Comparative and Physiological Psychology* 56 (1963) 899–902.

Landreth, C. *Early Childhood: Behavior and Learning.* 2nd ed. New York: Knopf, 1967.

McGraw, M. B. *Growth: A Study of Johnny and Jimmy.* New York: Appleton-Century-Crofts, 1935.

Orton, S. T. "Some Studies in the Language Function." *Proceedings of the Association for Research in Nervous and Mental Diseases* 13 (1934) 614–633.

Stone, J. G., and Rudolph, N. *Play and Playgrounds.* Washington, D.C.: National Association for the Education of Young Children, 1970.

Sweeney, R. T., ed. *Selected Readings in Movement Education.* Cambridge, Mass.: Addison-Wesley, 1970.

Thompson, G. G. *Child Psychology.* 2nd ed. Boston: Houghton-Mifflin, 1962.

CHAPTER SEVEN

Communicating
with
others

What differences are there between learning to speak and learning to communicate?

How does language contribute to personality development?

What are the main functions of language in a child's life?

In what sense is language a tool for thinking?

What specific tasks must the child accomplish in order to communicate well?

What factors influence the development of a child's language behavior?

True language is a distinctively human accomplishment. It is probably the most tangible and overwhelming bit of evidence of the superior place of man in the animal kingdom. At the same time, it is through language that much of his development occurs in intellectual and social areas, and in the achievement of a mature personality structure. For these reasons it is essential that we understand the processes of language development in the young child. In addition to understanding language as a basis for the child's intellectual, social, and personal development, we may discover that it can be a fascinating subject in its own right.

Language encompasses much more than just oral speech and hearing. It includes all forms of human interaction in which a person is made aware of a thought, feeling, or question experienced by another person. In its broader sense, then, language is the vehicle for all human communication, including speech, writing and printing, gesture and pantomime, code signals, musical notations, mathematical symbols, and many other devices for conveying thoughts, feelings, and questions.

In this larger sense, it is the task of every child to become acquainted with, and competent in the use of, a seemingly endless array of techniques of communication. To become a competent member of his society, he must become familiar with an assortment of languages, some of them formal and rather well defined, such as the English language; some subtle, fluid, and poorly defined, such as the languages of body and posture and facial expression. In the latter, as in many other languages, the child eventually learns to convey whole systems of messages, quite apart from the specific meanings of spoken words.

Speech, in contrast to language, constitutes a much narrower range of human experience. Speech occurs whenever distinct vocal sounds are articulated by a person and understood by a listener. This definition may help us to recognize the difficulty of pinpointing the age at which a child is truly speaking. The first "words" of an infant may not be easy to recognize, except perhaps by his parents. However, if his vocal efforts represent a consistent attempt to convey particular thoughts or feelings, and if those efforts are understood by a listener, then the child may be said to be speaking. His first word for his bottle may be, for example, a single syllable, such as "ba," or a single syllable repeated, such as "baba"; but if he uses the word consistently in the appropriate context and is understood by his mother, the word is serving the purpose of communication rather well.

When we speak of the communication process we are speaking of the basic elements of human interaction—a process fundamental to the development of human qualities of thought and action. Personality does not develop in a social vacuum; it is only through interaction with others that it can come to fruition. Language, in a sense, defines the limits and possibilities of personality development for every individual. It becomes the child's primary device for translating raw experience into meaningful units that can be dealt with coherently and his technique for the solution of myriad problems. As such, it serves as a tool for his thinking. It also becomes part of his repertoire of responses to frustration. It is, in short, the organizing essence of his personality structure.

Speech development, then, is only a specific illustration of the larger problem that confronts the child—the problem of communicating with his world in an effort to make sense out of that world. Yet speech development, while a relatively smaller matter than this total problem, can certainly become a *big* problem when something goes wrong, or when, for example, the child does not speak when his parents think he should, or as well as they think he should. Slow progress in the achievement of clear speech creates anxiety in many parents. Sometimes, it is helpful for the student of child development to reverse the question most often asked under such circumstances: "Why doesn't he talk well?" and ask, instead *"Why does any child talk well?"* An understanding of that question can take us a long way in understanding both the talking child and the child with limited or delayed speech development.

The functions of language for the child

In addition to understanding that the child is rewarded for his speech efforts, and therefore tends to speak more, we can also understand his normal progress better by understanding the functions that language serves in his life. For convenience, we can group the purposes served by language under the following five major headings: (1) language as a means to make wants and needs known, (2) language as a means for the expression of emotion, (3) language as a tool for thinking, (4) language as a means of initiating and maintaining social interaction, and (5) language as an aid to the achievement of personal identification. These are not mutually exclusive functions; they are overlapping and related, and are listed here in a somewhat arbitrary fashion in order to highlight the vital role of language in the life of a child.

Language as a means to make wants and needs known

Occasionally, a child may be observed to make slower than normal progress in speaking, or failing to use anything more complicated than grunting and pointing, primarily because he has no need to engage in more complex language. If the "grunting and pointing" routine is being reinforced by attentive parents who run through a series of guesses each time as to what the child wants, then the child need not increase the range and complexity of his own speaking vocabulary; he is counting on his parents to provide the flexibility, which more elaborate speech could provide, but which is not necessary so long as his parents are totally responsive to his more primitive, undifferentiated language behavior.

This point should not be construed as a recommendation for parents to be unresponsive! Nevertheless, it illustrates a prime source of motivation for the child to move to more advanced and versatile speech patterns through his own recognition of an increasingly elaborate array of interesting things and possibilities in his world. The child learns, in other words, that he can make a wider range of wants and needs known through the use of varied speech behavior. Thus, the need-meeting function of language becomes part of the explanation of why children talk and why they improve their language skills.

Language as a means for expression of emotion

During infancy, laughing, cooing, and crying are the chief vocal means by which the child expresses pleasure and displeasure. In early childhood, however, the world broadens into an exciting, stimulating, and often frustrating set of events, to which a child learns to respond with increasingly subtle and diversified vocalizing.

It is true that there is much "wordless action" on the part of the toddler and young child, including such direct physical responses to the world as hitting, running away, biting, hugging, clinging, and so on. But there is a clear trend, in the early years, toward the use of words to represent the circumstances that lead to emotional responses. Thus, words come to stand for the emotional components of experiences and events, and gradually tend to replace many of the directly physical modes of response, such as biting, hitting, and running away.

In some cases, it seems fairly obvious that a child is substituting specific words for actions, as in the case of a child who learns to substitute "hitting" words for hitting behavior. Subsequently, we hope, he may be able to learn more helpful and constructive words to deal with his frustrations or to express his anger. Language may also serve to clarify and interpret emotional experience and to contribute to a child's appreciation of the naturalness of feelings in his own life and in the lives of others.

Language as a tool for thinking

Relationships between language and thinking have been a source of speculation for philosophers and psychologists for many generations. Man has the capacity for observing his own thought processes to a degree. He is able to think introspectively and monitor some of the events occurring in his brain. One can become more or less aware of his mental imagery, and discover that some portions of that imagery are primarily visual in quality (imagine a sunset, for example), some portions are primarily auditory (imagine sitting in a darkened room while a violent thunderstorm rages outside), and still others may involve senses of smell, taste, touch, kinesthesis, temperature, or interesting mixtures of these. But man's thinking processes are clearly not limited to imagery.

If one attempts to solve any complicated problem, he will probably discover that his thinking processes include some language components which may, depending on the nature of the problem, completely overshadow the visual, auditory, or other sensory imagery. Even in the case of imagining the sunset, the powerful visual imaging becomes mixed with language components very quickly if one sets for himself the task of describing the sunset to a blind person.

Such relationships have led us to speculate that mature thinking may be largely verbal. Indeed, some scholars have argued that thinking can be described essentially as "inner speech" (Vygotsky 1962). Further, some students of the problem have suggested that the verbal categories available to a person more or less define the limits of his ability to think about his world (Whorf 1956). This hypothesis has been supported, it is argued, through our observations that different cultures have differing degrees of refinement in their verbal categories, which allow persons in different cultural settings to think with varying degrees of complexity about various apsects of their experiences.

Thus, for example, the middle class American child experiences a highly differentiated set of verbal categories with respect to the automobile. We can classify the automobile by body style (sedan, 2-door or 4-door; coupe; convertible; station wagon; pickup truck; and so on), by engine type (8 or 6 cylinders, in-line or V-type), by engine location (front or rear), by transmission type (automatic or "stick" shift), by location of transmission controls (steering column or floor); we could go on at great length and in vast detail before exhausting all the other possibilities and resorting to such aspects as simple size, style, color, and year model! The Australian aborigine, we might speculate, may be less sensitive to fine differences in body style than is the American adolescent!

The hypothesis we are talking about proposes that there is a crucial relationship between a person's ability to see and understand such fine distinctions, and the degree of differentiation of the language available to him. It is not merely that the Australian aborigine has not had a great deal of experience with cars; it is also that he does not have a language that makes a distinction between a "6" and a "V-8" or a "hardtop sedan" vs. a "station wagon."

The implications of this line of argument are indeed very important for the student who would understand child development. If a child's thinking is essentially shaped and constrained by the verbal categories available to him, then "thinking," especially in its higher, more complex problem-solving forms, becomes a matter of achieving language competence, and the guidance of the intellectual development of the child becomes a matter of the guidance of his language development.

We have learned, however, that the relationship between language and thinking is not as simple as may be implied by the preceding argument. In the past, we have tended to approach the question in a sort of "chicken and egg" fashion, by asking which comes first, the child's thinking, or the child's language, on the implicit assumption that whichever came first probably served as a foundation for the other.

If language comes first, then it provides a tool of gradually increasing scope and complexity which allows the child to think to the level of complexity afforded by the language to which he has access. If thinking comes first, then it allows the child to develop verbal categories, names of things, and so on up to the limits of his thinking ability.

Our current approaches to the problem lead us to believe that neither of these views is satisfactory, but rather that "language" and "thinking" have somewhat independent origins in the child (Lenneberg 1970), and that in the course of growing up the child becomes increasingly adept at integrating the two processes. Piaget (1926) has maintained that language, while vitally important to the child, does not serve as the primary basis for his thinking, even though it has been shown (for example, Bruner, et al. 1966) that the ability to handle Piaget's conservation problems depends upon the child's having some internalized verbal formula which shields him from the overpowering appearance of the visual displays.

We will consider this intricate relationship between language and intellectual behavior from a somewhat different point of view in the following chapter, after we have had a chance to consider some of the aspects of intellectual development in greater detail. Meanwhile, we should be alert to the child's task of developing a language system with specific competencies which relate to his ability to engage in thinking and problem solving. It is a fundamental task of the child.

Language as a means to social interaction

Language behavior and social motivation of the young child are inevitably involved with each other. Since the child is initially dependent on the cooperation of others for the satisfaction of his needs, much of his language emerges in a social context. Indeed, language is the basic adhesive that binds any society together. Even the most primitive groups of which we have any record have relied on language as a means of organizing for group action and cooperation. Through language it is possible to assign roles: "You will do this and I will do that, and together we can do something which neither could accomplish separately."

The language behavior of the young child has been described by Piaget (1926) as essentially egocentric, meaning that the child regards his own point of view as the only possible point of view, and this is reflected in his speech. He is incapable of putting himself into the position of someone else, according to Piaget's view, because he is unaware that another person *has* a position, which can differ from his own. Thus it is not surprising to discover that the young child engages in a variety of kinds of monologues in which a listener, if there is one, need not participate in order to keep the speech going.

A vitally important task of development, then, is the gradually increasing use of language to recognize and take into account the position of persons other than self. Language is both expressive of this increasing ability to take the position of others into account, and also may serve as a tool to facilitate its development.

Perhaps most of all, it is only through language that one can truly reach agreements with others—not agreements in the sense of liking and disliking the same things as others, but agreements about the fundamental nature of things experienced. Language is the only device by which human beings can avoid being overwhelmed by the psychological threat of isolation. Man needs others of his kind if he is to fulfill his potentials as a human being. It is through the medium of language that the child learns to give and receive in interaction with others of his kind.

Language as an aid to personal identification

The gradual emergence of a definition of oneself as a person, unique and separate from others but related to others, is regarded by some child development specialists as the most fundamental theme in the organization of human personality. The beginnings of such a process of self definition are obscure, difficult to locate precisely at a given chronological age, and probably very vague initially. But language spoken to the infant and, later, language used by the child, appear to serve a clarifying function in establishing his identity and marking off the separation of self from not-self.

The child's name, for example, seems to be one of the clarifiers of self. It is difficult to imagine what it might mean to a child to grow up without any name in a world in which all other people have names. But the answer to the very basic question "Who am I?" implies more than merely having a name. While the name supplies a verbal label, which becomes invested with much personal meaning, the total self-definition that emerges and is revised during childhood must somehow incorporate the roles one plays, the relationships one sustains to others, the competencies one achieves, one's reputation, and a host of attitudes and values.

While language may not be the only basis for the formation of such personal qualities, it appears to be an important one, perhaps because it allows the child to establish meaningful perceptual categories, or classes to which verbal labels may be attached (for example, "Daddies are big; I am little." "Sister is a girl; I am a boy.").

Through language, the child reaches out to make tentative

assertions about what he is and what he might be. The responses offered him by his environment serve to validate or refute those assertions. In addition, many of the expectations held by others as goals for a child are transmitted to him through the medium of language. His degree of conformity or failure to meet those expectations become part of his definition of himself as acceptable, worthy, competent, and so on, or the counterparts of such self-appraisals in lack of acceptability, unworthiness, and incompetence.

The tasks
of language development

Jersild (1954) recounts an interesting anecdote of a conversation between a mother and her two small daughters, Peggy (age 2) and Marian (age 3):

MOTHER: *Oh, look, there's a monkey wearing a red coat!*
PEGGY: *Oh, yook!*
MARIAN: *Don't say yook, say wook!*

The anecdote implies that even errors in articulation seem to proceed through a more or less regular sequence, gradually approximating standard English. But it also illustrates one of the major tasks of language development—that of achieving clear expression. The clear articulation of speech sounds (phonemes) is a complex motor task, which can only be appreciated by a person who has struggled to make the appropriate sounds of a second language (for example, German), which calls for establishing a new set of motor habits to make sounds which, at first, seem quite unnatural.

A second major task of language development is that of gradually expanding one's comprehension of the speech of others. It is more, of course, than merely increasing the vocabulary. It includes understanding of inflection, prosody (stress and intonation), variable meanings of words in different contexts, increased ability to understand and engage in verbal reasoning, and the ability to understand language in its more symbolic or abstract forms when the referent for specific words may be very intangible. The referents for such words as *dog, ball, bottle, block, coat,* and so on are very tangible and observable, and the child has many opportunities to associate the word with the thing for which it stands. However, the referents for such words as *democracy, love,* and *freedom* are not directly observable; yet these also become challenges to the child's verbal understanding.

But the tasks of clear expression and of useful comprehension still do not fully account for the complexities of language development. Consider the following rule, which governs one aspect of the English language: "A word ending in either a vowel or a voiced consonant forms its plural with the voiced sibilant /-z/ as in *dogs, crows,* and *ribs;* a word ending in the singular with either /s/ or /z/ forms its plural with /-z/ plus an interpolated neutral vowel as in *classes* and *poses*" (Brown and Fraser 1964, p. 46).

These writers go on to point out that we all "know" these rules, as adults, and follow them readily by forming the correct plurals for words according to the classes named in the rule. Thus, for example, if an adult learned a new noun word, *tazz,* and were then asked to name two of the items having that word label, he would surely say *tazzes*. It is unlikely, however, that he would be able to state the rule governing his decision to pluralize with the /-s/ ending. Instead, it is likely that he would regard his decision as "just natural" and not requiring any rule at all! Indeed, unless one studies the above rule very carefully and ponders its implications at some length, he may find that merely reading the rule creates more confusion than help in understanding the use of English!

Recent research in the investigation of language behavior strongly suggests that children do not learn language merely by imitating the language of those around them. It appears that the child is a very active builder of his own language system and that he engages in this building process by forming rules that govern the use of language. The forming, refining, and modifying of the rules of language, then, may be seen as a third major task closely related to the first two.

The task of clear expression

The enormity of this task will be better appreciated by the student who ponders the implications of the following statement by Lenneberg:

> Held in the lungs as in a bagpipe, (air) must be released at precisely controlled rates and divided into precisely measured packets to produce the unique kind of "music" known as speech. Such behavior is based on the workings of elaborate neuromotor mechanisms, the coordinated activity of more than a hundred muscles in the tongue, lips, larynx, thoracic and abdominal walls, and so on. The production of a single phoneme (elemental speech sound) requires that the brain send an appropriate message to each one of these muscles, specifying its state of relaxation or tension, and we are capable of talking at a rate of some 840 phonemes or 120 words per minute—for hours on end if the occasion arises. (Lenneberg 1970, p. 167)

Articulation, the clear and accurate pronunciation of speech sounds, has its beginnings in infancy by employing the native equipment with which the infant is endowed. In the normal course of events the infant's more or less random babbling and cooing, consisting of most of the vowel sounds and many of the consonants, goes through a refining process in the latter part of the first year. Part of this process includes the forming of distinct syllables, meaningless at first to the infant himself, which are easily repeated. The *ma* sound (pronounced with a vowel sound similar to that in *cat*) is a common example. His repetition of such a syllable in vocal play illustrates a circular reaction in which he experiences the effects of his own vocalizing effort, and that experience reinforces the effort.

It is common for infants to go through a late babbling stage called "echolalia," and it is of more than passing interest to most young parents that two of the frequently repeated syllables are *ma-ma-ma-* and *da-da-da-*. These sounds, easily formed by the speech apparatus, are typically reinforced by parents' enthusiastic social response, which may account in part for the fact that these sounds often become the basis for the "first word."

It is during the second year when a dramatic spurt, or "flowering," of speech development occurs in the form of rapid acquisition of new words. Lenneberg describes this stage as the "naming explosion":

> An astonishing spurt in the ability to name things occurs at a definite stage in language development. It represents the culmination of a process that unfolds very slowly until the child reaches the age of about 18 months, when he has learned to utter between three and 50 words. Then, suddenly and spontaneously, the process begins to gather momentum (Figure 7.1). There is a burst of activity at 24 to 30 months, so that by the time the child completes his third year, give or take a few months, he has built up a speaking vocabulary of (approximately) a thousand words and probably understands another 2,000 to 3,000 words that he has not yet learned to use. (Lenneberg 1970, p. 165)

Imitation appears to play a powerful role in the naming of things, and in other aspects of early language acquisition. We might speculate that the child, by reproducing speech sounds of those around him who care for him, can ensure the repetition of that nurturant care, or can bring it about. It is as if he were taking upon himself the power to minister to his own needs through reproducing the sounds made by others as accompaniments to their ministrations. But, regardless of the validity of these speculations, the process of imitation alone cannot explain all of the fascinating details of language behavior.

Soon after the vocabulary begins to expand in the second year, another kind of expansion is also found: the child uses words not only as names of individual objects, persons, or ideas (bottle, dada, mama, bed, or night), but suddenly he seems to be using a single word to express a complete thought. It is not simply that the child associates *bottle* with his own feeding; he may be using the word in a very imperative manner to mean *"Get me my bottle—now!"* Some students of child language have used the term *holophrastic* to describe this form of speech in which one word represents a more complex idea (Werner 1961). As a stage in the development of speech, it has also been characterized as the "one-word sentence."

The combining of two words to form a more complete thought is now not far away. Gesell and Amatruda (1947) indicate that children combine two words in ordinary speech by the age of 21

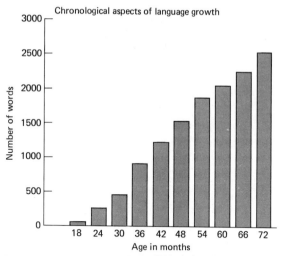

Data from 10 sample groups of children show sudden jump in vocabulary that consistently occurs around the third birthday.

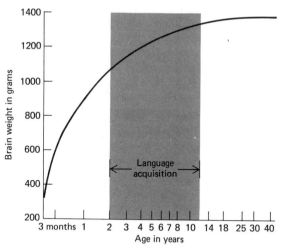

Period of maximum ability to aquire language appears to end at about the time the normal brain acquires its full weight.

FIGURE 7.1 Chronological aspects of language growth. (From E. H. Lenneberg, "The Biological Foundations of Language," *Hospital Practice*, December 1967, pp. 59–67.)

months. Other researchers place it variously at between 18 and 24 months. In any case, it is clear that late in the second year the idea of putting words together, and the ability to do so in order to express a complete thought, is much in evidence. In part, the child's task in this connection is one of phonology, that is, learning to mark off (articulate) the separation between words, as well as one of learning the pronunciation of individual words.

In this task, the interaction of speaking and thinking is of interest, because the child must *mean* two words in order to articulate their separateness. The achievement of this meaning, that is, the formulating of a thought, which requires the articulation of two words in a meaningful sequence, is an impressive feat! Among other things, it signifies a primitive grasp of parts of speech and of the relationship between nouns and verbs, which we will examine more closely under the heading of the third task, that of rule making.

The combining of single words into two-word utterances is not just a random, haphazard affair. Students of language development have observed that these early two-word sentences employ a consistent use of two classes, or categories, of words. A *pivot* word is typically combined with an *open class* word (Braine 1963). Thus the toddler who grasps the significance of such a useful pivot word as *allgone* may be observed to apply it appropriately in combination with a fairly wide range of open class words: "Allgone Daddy"; "Allgone milk"; "Allgone doggie"; and so on.

Analysis of the speech of toddlers has shown that pivot words comprise a small class in which words are added very slowly to the vocabulary. However, it is a very significant and flexible class of words, since they may be combined with great fluidity with the much larger and rapidly expanding open class. Two pivot words are not combined in a two-word sentence, although two open class words may be.

However, the important implication of this distinction of classes of words in the emergence of the child's vocabulary is that in his expression of ideas with words, he is not limited to the notion that all words have the same function. Instead, he achieves remarkable flexibility, very early, by separating words into classes with each class performing a different kind of function. Words of one class operate in fluid combination with words of another class, enabling him to produce a much richer and more flexible set of statements about his world.

The order of occurrence of the parts of speech is of some interest in this connection. The first words of most children are predominantly nouns. This seems to accompany the rapid growth in naming objects in the middle of the second year. About that time the child seems suddenly aware of the fact that everything has a name, and his job is to know it.

However, it should be kept in mind that the overwhelming predominance of nouns noted in the research studies of young children's speech may be due in part to the fact that nouns predominate in the language, and research methods commonly employed base their estimates on the proportion of words spoken to the number of words in the language itself. McCarthy (1954) points out, however, that when a young child uses a noun, he may not *mean* it as a noun, as in the case of the 18-month-old using a one-word sentence. Such holophrastic speech may function as a combination pronoun, verb, and noun so far as the apparent intent of the child is concerned.

Pronouns typically begin to appear about the end of the second year. However, the understanding of the concepts underlying their use may still be very limited, and many errors in pronoun use will persist throughout the early years. From 2 through 5 years of age the use of nouns does not decrease, but the relative proportion of modifying and clarifying words—adjectives, adverbs, interjections—all increase along with size of vocabulary and length of sentence.

Researchers have also noted the "telegraphic" quality of the speech of the young child (Brown and Bellugi 1964). In their early combinations of words into complex thoughts, children omit connecting words and modifiers, but do so in an orderly and systematic manner. That is, it is the "content" words that are retained (those essential to communication) and the "function" words that are omitted. This latter class of words are useful guides, which provide a sort of "map" to interpret the speech of others and to clarify one's meaning, but which may not be absolutely essential in expressing fundamental meanings. In imitation of the speech of adult models, for example, young children were observed to condense speech samples in such characteristic ways as follows:

Adult model	Child's imitation
I'll make a cup for her to drink.	Cup drink.
Mr. Miller will try.	Miller try.
Put the strap under her chin.	Strap chin.

In this study, children's speech imitations of adult models had three essential characteristics: (1) they selected the most *recent* words (that is, the words toward the end of the model's speech sample), (2) they selected the most *emphasized* words, and (3) they preserved the word order used by the adults. Note, in all three examples given above, that while many words are omitted by the children, in no case has the child revised the order of words (Ervin 1964). Brown and Bellugi (1964) have observed further that the telegraphic properties of the young child's speech are systematic in the kinds of words omitted, not only in direct imitation of adult speech, but in the child's spontaneously produced speech as well.

Sentence length as a measure of language development has been given considerable attention by research investigators. It provides one useful index of the level of language maturity of the child and is a relatively easy one to measure. Data reported by McCarthy (1954), from several investigations, revealed a consistent trend in the increase in length of sentences of young children from ages 2 through 5, which may be very roughly summarized as follows:

Age:	2	2½	3	3½	4	4½	5
Sentence length:	1.8	2.9	3.5	4.3	4.5	4.8	5.0

(average number of words)

The above figures do not represent norms or standards and should not be construed as expectations. These figures are a crude average of data from several investigations using different samples of children at different points in time. They are shown here merely to illustrate a general trend and to provide some "feel" for the length of sentences constructed by children at different ages.

We should note also that as a child's language facility increases, he becomes more adept at making *transformations*—reordering and recombining of words, changing sentences from active to passive form, and so on—and that one of the potential effects of such transformations may be to *reduce* sentence length. Thus a child's increasing competence includes both the ability to construct *longer* sentences and the ability to organize more effective *short* sentences.

As we noted earlier, the articulation errors of speech are gradually corrected, and the pattern of this correction process is somewhat orderly and systematic. A major factor in the child's correction of his articulation errors, assuming there is no defect in the speech apparatus itself, is the speech model available to him. It is not necessary to call the child's attention to his errors; in fact it is ordinarily inadvisable. A child's motive to correct his mispronunciations is not supplied by a concerned adult! The motive, rather, appears to reside in the child as a function of his *relationship* with adults, and that relationship is complicated, rather than facilitated, by overly concerned attention to the details of speech errors when a child is very young.

Most articulation errors will have disappeared, without special attention, by 5 or 6 years of age. However, there are many children who, for any number of reasons, still make consistent errors (substituting the /w/ sound for the very difficult /l/ sound, for example). A qualified speech therapist can facilitate the child's clear articulation of correct speech sounds, and is trained to do so without inducing undue pressures on a 5- or 6-year-old child.

The reasons that speech correction efforts should be left to the specialists, however, go beyond the fact that these persons have unique and highly specialized training; they also pertain to the fact that these people are *not* the child's parents, and therefore there is less likelihood that the child's relationship with his parents becomes complicated by their concerns over his speech "defects." Conversely, it is less likely that his speech misarticulations become compounded by tension or anxiety about parental pressures to perform in a more mature way.

Expanding comprehension

At all ages from infancy on, we understand and respond appropriately to a larger number and variety of words than the ones we speak to others. The infant reacts appropriately to verbal commands and prohibitions for some time before he is able to articulate words himself. Throughout the early stages of single words, one-word sentences, short phrases, and on to the development of mature speech patterns, the child continues to progress more rapidly in the understanding of words and phrases than he does in the ability to express words clearly and correctly.

Perhaps one reason for this apparent discrepancy is that, while both types of task (expression and understanding) require a basic understanding of meanings, the expressive task requires two additional competencies: (1) the selection and ordering of words in meaningful sequences, and (2) the psychomotor coordination for translating thoughts into audible, articulated speech sounds. According to one student of language development (Ervin 1964), we know that recognition precedes production, and that people can understand many more words than they can produce, which may be accounted for in part by the fact that the number of cues for recognition is less than the information needed for accurate production, as well as the fact that in recognition we can profit from redundancy.

In spite of this, other authorities have raised questions about the validity of this generalization on the superiority of "understanding" over "expression" in child speech. The argument has been made, for example, that while most of us can understand a play by George Bernard Shaw, none of us can write one. But if we ask the question "How many of us can understand the play *as Shaw understood it,* then the answer is far from clear" (Bellugi and Brown 1964, p. 41).

The point is that evidence for a child's understanding of words, phrases, sentences, and so on has been accepted even when it is little more than a child's "correct" performance in response to adult language. Unfortunately, so far as research validity is concerned, this criterion is not always valid. If one says, for example, "Would you like some ice cream?" and the child walks to the refrigerator, it *may* be that the child understands the words, or it *may* be that we have asked other questions, using similar intonation and rising inflection before, which pertained to a food treat of some kind, and that the child has no real comprehension of the words per se. Carefully controlled studies of such questions would regulate prosody, among other variables, and would provide for clear indications of the understanding of words apart from body posture, facial expression, familiar context, gestures, and so on. At present, the "well-known" fact of comprehension being much larger at every age than expressive speech must be interpreted with a degree of caution.

Understanding of the speech of others requires a very active participation on the part of a child. It is a dynamic process which must be learned, for a given language is a completely arbitrary code system based on social agreement and convention rather than on "natural law." It is a long and difficult learning process, fraught with many hazards and sources of frustration and potentialities for misunderstanding. The wonder is not so much that childen and adults often misunderstand each other, but rather that there are so many occasions when they come so close, apparently, to genuine understanding!

Measurement of children's comprehension has been accomplished through the use of a variety of tests, some of which require only that the child be able to point to the one picture in a set of pictures, depicting the word spoken by the examiner. Estimates of the total understanding vocabularies of normal children are impressive in the number of terms and concepts understood at relatively early ages.

However, a set of "norms" or standards for the number of words understood by normal children at each age level would be misleading, at best, because it would tell us little about the child's ability to comprehend words in combination, to distinguish declarative from interrogative sentences, to grasp the meaning of prosody, to comprehend the significance of negation in the context of sentences (for example, he may understand the meaning of *no* and *not,* yet fail to grasp the distinction between *does* and *doesn't,* when the two are used in sentences), and to recognize various shifts in word meanings when the context changes. In the latter instance, for example, two children might both have a working understanding of the word *run* but be far different from each other in their relative ability to recognize the variety of meanings of that word as it is used in various contexts.

There is no real line between verbal understanding, on the one hand, and intelligence (as it has commonly been understood), on the other. Tests of verbal comprehension and performance on intelligence tests are strongly influenced by a multitude of factors in a child's life.

The complexity of a child's emerging understanding of language is nicely illustrated in the research studies referred to earlier, which show a consistent use of pivot words and open-class words by very young children. Many other instances could also be cited to illustrate the child's comprehension, not only of individual word meanings, but of *principles* that govern the use of language. A few of these will be described in the following section, which deals with the child's task of constructing language rules.

The task of constructing language rules

As we have noted, not all of the child's language can be accounted for by the simple process of imitation of the language of others. One of the lines of evidence that a child is a "rule-maker" in his language development is the common observation that children make systematic errors in speaking. That is, their "mistakes" are not merely accidental, random errors, but often stem from the application of a principle.

The English language, having many arbitrary exceptions to principles, affords a child many opportunities to reveal his understanding of given principles by generalizing them to situations in which they do not fit, by the arbitrary rules of English grammar. The way in which our language represents the shift from present to past tense serves as an example: there are "regular" verbs, which change to past tense by adding the suffix /ed/ as in "Will it *rain?*" "It already *rained,*" and "I *hate* him" becomes "I *hated* him," or "I *love* him" changes to "I *loved* him," and so on. The child's generalization of the underlying principle is revealed through systematic errors, which take the form of "regularizing" verbs, which in English are irregular: go—goed; run—runned; throw—throwed.

The formation of plurals in English also has some regular and highly irregular features, and therefore can trap a child into systematic errors if he generalizes a limited principle. Many nouns, of course, are pluralized by adding /s/ to the singular form, so it is not uncommon to hear a child referring to *mans,* or *foots.* The significance of these errors lies in their illustration of the child's rule-forming capacity, for without grasping the principles underlying tense inflection, or pluralization, the child's speech would not contain these systematic errors.

Also, as Brown and Fraser (1964) observe, such errors indicate that a child's speech development cannot be accounted for merely by imitation, since it is highly unlikely that he will have heard adults use such expressions as "I digged in the yard" or "I saw some sheeps"! Again, the fact that his errors are not only systematic, but that they reveal themselves in speech patterns he may never have heard from others, argues strongly that the child engages in an active process of rule-making.

If this is true—and there is much evidence to support this view—then it has vastly important implications for our understanding of the nature of the child. One rather apparent implication is that it is not necessary for a child to be exposed to every instance of language in order to understand and use it. By dealing with language as a set of principles, or rules, a child can "manufacture" sentences, for instance, which he has never heard used by anyone else. Therefore, he is not limited either in his language or his thinking by the boundaries of the language and thinking to which he has been exposed.

This suggests a practical consideration in the matter of how adults respond to a child's language. If a child can think and say things in combinations he has never heard, then it is possible he will think and say things adults will fail to recognize as valid, important, or worth noting; hence adults may not feel inclined to reinforce the child's verbal inventions, but will pay attention primarily to those verbalizations that somehow conform to their preconceptions of what is important to say.

But if adults only reinforce their own standard ways of thinking and speaking, they may be engaging actively in a process of gradually extinguishing creativity in a child. If rule-making can be considered an act of creativity, then every child who learns the English language is creative! Perhaps there is a hint, then, in the responses adults make to child language efforts, as to why creativity appears to decline and wither for some children!

Factors in the development of language behavior

A variety of theories of language development have been proposed by different students of the problem. Some (for example, Skinner 1957) have viewed language acquisition as another instance of the development of increasingly complex habits from simpler ones, through the process of learning. Some (Mowrer 1952) combine principles of learning with the notion that the child's initial exposure to language is in the context of his mother's satisfaction of his needs; hence language takes on reward value, or emotional significance for him, which motivates his own language efforts.

Some current attempts to understand language development are based on the assumption that language arises out of the basic biological organization of the child. Lenneberg is one of the leading proponents of this point of view. He argues compellingly that

. . . the capacities for speech production and related aspects of language acquisition develop according to built-in biological schedules . . . they appear when the time is ripe and not until then, when a state of what I have called "resonance" exists. The child somehow becomes "excited" in phase with the environment, so that

> sounds he hears and has been hearing all along suddenly acquire
> a peculiar prominence. The change is like the establishment of new
> sensitivities. He becomes aware in a new way, selecting certain
> parts of the total auditory input for attention, ignoring others.
> (Lenneberg 1970, p. 167)

No single theory seems to account well for all aspects of the
acquisition of language. It remains a most challenging question
for the scientist. A satisfactory theory must, among other things,
provide us with a reasonable explanation not only of the regularities, the trends and stages which can be found in all children
regardless of the specific language they learn, but must also give
satisfactory understanding of the wide range of individual differences from one child to another and from one group to
another.

As we shall see in this section, there are indeed many sources
of differences, which make each child's language a variation on
the general theme of language acquisition shared by all children
by virtue of being members of the same species.

Intelligence

Without question, intellectual factors play a role in the
achievement of language and in the degree of fluency and comprehension on the part of a child at every age. However, the
relationship between language and intelligence is far from simple.
Most of what we know about the relationship is based on studies
using the correlation coefficient as an index of the extent to which
two or more things are related to each other. McCarthy (1954),
for example, cites studies reporting a correlation coefficient of
.79 between mental age and "length of unit," which is one index
of language maturity. This is a very substantial relationship,
which may be interpreted to mean that the child's performance
on an intelligence test and his language behavior tend to go
together, and the child who tends to be advanced in one will
likely be advanced in the other. The conclusion is not startling,
of course, when one considers that most tests of mental ability
are heavily verbal in their content!

It is true, also, that correlational measures do not give us any information on "cause and effect" relationships. The fact that language behavior and intelligence, even when the latter is measured with nonverbal tests, are highly correlated with each other cannot be taken as evidence that intelligence is the *cause* of language behavior any more than language behavior is the cause of intelligence!

Nevertheless, the persistent observation by researchers, concerned parents, teachers, and others of the relationship between intelligence and language gives rise to fears that the child with no language, or with delayed language, may be mentally retarded. The mentally retarded child will have varying degrees of language deficit; however, the reverse of this may not be inferred. It is not correct to reason that the child with language deficits must, therefore, be mentally retarded, since there are many other factors, in addition to intelligence, that play a part in language behavior.

The relationship between intelligence and language behavior seems to be clearer and stronger for children of below average intelligence than for children with high intelligence. Perhaps one reason for this is that some children who are very bright have the capacity to devise alternate forms of communications systems, including nonverbal techniques, which may serve them very well in the early stages, yet give them the appearance of being retarded in speech.

Linda, for example, was a nursery school child who never spoke a single word during almost 2 years of school. She was unusually adept, however, at communicating with teachers through a complicated set of hand signals, facial expressions, tugging on teachers' hands or clothing, and so on. In fact, it turned out that Linda (who scored in the genius range on certain tests of intelligence) was successful in teaching her nonverbal communication system to each generation of teachers who came and went each school term in the university laboratory school she attended! Obviously, her nontalking behavior could not be attributed to lack of intelligence. Indeed, it may have persisted, in part, because she was bright enough to develop the alternate forms of communication to a very elaborate degree.

Sex

There is considerable agreement in research literature that girl talk at an earlier age than boys, and that their vocabularies are consistently larger at each age level. In most studies the differences are not great, and could not be used for reliable predictions about differences between a given boy and girl. However, the consistency with which the finding of *average* differences has been made, in favor of girls, leaves little doubt about it being a reliable one.

The reasons for it are not entirely clear; they may relate to biological differences in rate of maturation, or in the tendency of mothers to have closer and more consistent verbal contact with daughters than with sons, or (more likely) some combination of biological and social factors.

Order of birth

Whether a child is an oldest, middle, youngest, or only child also seems to bear some relationship to his language behavior. McCarthy (1954) found that children who associated chiefly with adults were accelerated in language development, apparently because they get more practice in the use of mature language forms in the presence of an adult model. Similarly, McCarthy reports a number of research investigations showing that twins and triplets are slower in their speech development than singletons, with triplets seemingly more affected than twins.

It is reasonable to speculate that this difference also might reflect the relative proportion of time spent by a given child in verbal interaction with adults, compared to that spent in verbal interaction with peers who do not provide adult speech models. One researcher (Day 1932) came to the interesting conclusion that the average length of response for 5-year-old twins in her sample was slightly below that of 3-year-old singletons! Day interpreted this as a reflection of the reduced need of the twins to form broader social relationships beyond the relationship with the other twin. According to Davis (1937), twins with retarded language behavior in the early years tend to catch up as they enter school and are stimulated by a broader range of experiences.

Mothering experiences

Consistent with Mowrer's theory of language acquisition, researchers have found that in cases of severe emotional deprivation in infancy and early childhood, the language process suffers and fails to thrive. The subjects studied by Goldfarb (1945, 1955) were institutionalized children who received very little active stimulation and only minimal care in the early years. The retarding effects on their language development persisted on into adolescence. Spitz (1948), Rheingold and Bayley (1959), and others have demonstrated that when children suffer from inadequate maternal care, their language development is likely to be an area in which the effects are most marked.

After reviewing the research on this subject, McCarthy (1954) concluded that even in ordinary homes the quality of the mother-child relationship has an important bearing on the acquisition of language. The kind of quality most helpful to the child is difficult to describe or to measure scientifically, but appears to be made up of such things as how much the mother wanted the child, the extent to which she feels she is competent to take care of him, the amount of tension and anxiety she feels while caring for him, the extent to which she talks with him or, conversely, is silent while giving physical care, and the extent to which she develops a close relationship with him.

This variable of maternal styles, or mothering experiences, relates to the process of identification of a child with his parent figures. Identification, the powerful process of incorporating the behaviors of "models" into one's own repertoire of behaviors, has been cited as one vital basis for the emergence of language. The child talks, in this view, to the degree that he can identify with important people who talk. In circumstances where the identification process is made difficult, as with the emotionally deprived child, it is argued that there is little motivation for acquiring language, especially since language serves no important psychological need system on the child's part.

Sensory factors

Vision, hearing, touch, and probably kinesthetic and other sensory processes participate in the child's acquisition of language. Their roles become most obvious in the case of a child who is handicapped in one or more sensory capacity. The deaf child is at an extreme disadvantage in learning to speak because he does not have the normal experiences of feedback from his own language efforts to guide the process of gradual approximations of adult speech. This affects all aspects of his language, both on the expressive and the comprehension sides. The deaf child who, with special training, has been taught to achieve a high degree of articulation skill, may nevertheless have difficulty with prosody because of his lack of direct experience with the stress and intonation of others, and inadequate feedback on his own prosody.

The importance of this sensory feedback is illustrated even in the case of some adults who have lost their hearing, whose speaking patterns become a monotone. This suggests that even the maintenance of speech habits once acquired depends upon sensory feedback. However, the degree to which deafness influences language development is a function of the age at which it occurs as well as the degree of hearing loss. Much has been learned about specialized techniques for the teaching of speech to children with hearing loss, with very encouraging results.

Loss of vision has a less direct influence on language development, and in some cases (Maxfield 1936) it has been reported that blind children may show accelerated verbal behavior, such as asking more questions and resorting less to nonverbal communication. Any effects of blindness may operate indirectly, through the experiences the blind child is provided with and the attitudes of the important people in his life. If a blind child is given different amounts and kinds of attention, compared with the sighted child, then his language behavior may not be entirely a function of his blindness so much as a side effect of these variations on relationships with other people. Blindness, per se, whether congenital or occurring during childhood as a result of illness or accident, need not necessarily result in retarded language development, even though it may complicate the child's efforts to use language symbolically.

Poverty

There is also much evidence that economic poverty is associated with impaired language development. Economically disadvantaged children have language deficits, which are observable at a very early age and which tend to persist or even intensify with increased age, according to Minuchin and Biber (1968). While it is true that these children may have positive language strengths, along with a certain richness of functional language fluency, which is adaptive to their special environments, nevertheless their overall language performance appears to be less articulate and less effective as a tool for thought and communication as compared with middle class children. A closely related question, that of the effects of subcultural differences on language development, has been thoughtfully analyzed with a review of the literature on this topic by Cazden (1966).

Some specific differences between the language of the middle class and lower class child have been described by Bereiter and Engelmann (1966). One feature these writers have observed is the tendency of the disadvantaged child to fail to articulate distinct words, and to run whole strings of words together into a "giant word." Thus, for example, "That is a big dog" sounds like "Dabidaw," and "He is a big man" is turned into a giant word with indistinct parts: "Hebihmah."

The inefficiencies of such language forms from the standpoint of communication are readily apparent—the child is less well understood by others. But from the standpoint of language as a tool for thinking, there may be even more serious implications. Such failure of distinct word articulation may reflect an inability to form distinct and usable categories, well differentiated, in the child's thinking. In turn, this may mean a lessened ability to substitute those elements freely and flexibly in shifting contexts.

In the above examples, a child using the two giant words may not recognize the function of *is* in each sentence, since *is* does not stand out as a separately articulated word-meaning. The verbal concept *is* fails to emerge as a clear concept in such language habits, and thus is less available to a child in generalizing to new situations calling for use of that word.

Other language deficits of disadvantaged children have been observed, including (1) omission of articles, prepositions, conjunctions, and short verbs from statements, (2) failure to understand the meaning of *not*, (3) failure to produce correct plural forms or to perform the actions implied by plural forms, (4) failure to use simple tenses to describe past, present, and future action, (5) failure to use *it* correctly to describe inanimate objects, in distinction from correct use of *he* and *she* to describe male and female figures, (6) failure to understand many common prepositions and conjunctions, (7) inability to describe an action, even though he is able to perform it correctly when directed to do so, and (8) failure to understand that two or more words may describe a single object. In the latter instance, a simple example would be a child's failure to understand that the same block may be *big* and *red* simultaneously.

In some respects, this list resembles the characteristics of the language of all children in that these limitations may be found in middle class children, but perhaps are corrected earlier or more readily with the advantages of an environment that is geared to standard English forms.

It is true that the vocabulary of the disadvantaged child is smaller, speech seems to be more "telegraphic," with connecting words more likely to be omitted, and there is more limited use of modifiers and pronouns—all of which seem true of the younger middle class child. However, the disadvantaged child probably has a fairly rich language system pertaining to his own environment and life experiences, and he has probably engaged in a good bit of "rule-making" behavior, which governs his speech and which may be functional and adaptive for purposes of communication with family and peers. The primary handicap of such language patterns may be in their limited usefulness to the child as tools for thinking, preventing him from employing the full range of his intellectual capacity.

One possible reason for this consistent difference is suggested in the work of Hess and Shipman (1965), who observed the patterns of language employed by mothers in interactions with their own children. These researchers employed the notion of "restricted" and "elaborated" language forms, which they defined as follows:

> Restricted codes are stereotyped, limited, and condensed, lacking in specificity and the exactness needed for precise conceptualization and differentiation. Sentences are short, simple, often unfinished; there is little use of subordinate clauses for elaborating the content of the sentence; it is a language of implicit meaning, easily understood and commonly shared. . . . Elaborated codes are those in which communication is individualized and the message is specific to a particular situation, topic, and person. It is more particular, more differentiated, and more precise. It permits expression of a wider and more complex range of thought, tending toward discrimination among cognitive and affective content.
> (Hess and Shipman 1965, p. 871)

Hess and Shipman used a variety of strategies to analyze the language behavior of mothers of differing social classes in relation to or interaction with their own children. For example, one index of the degree of restricted vs. elaborated language was the amount of verbal output of mothers in response to such open-ended questions as "Let's imagine that (your child) is old enough to go to school for the first time. How do you think you would prepare him? What would you do or tell him?"

Lower class mothers produced significantly less verbal material in response to such questions. In addition, they tended to use "imperatives," or such statements as ". . . mind the teacher" relatively more than upper middle class mothers. At the same time, they used explanatory or "instructive" language relatively less. The implication is that economically disadvantaged children may be exposed to less elaborate verbal models, and that their language deficiencies may be in part a matter of such differences in the verbal behavior of their parents.

Language remediation for the economically disadvantaged child has been a central objective for many programs of education for young children, some of which will be described in later sections of the book. There is a wide range of variation in the approaches and strategies being employed to improve the language performance of children, but the general consensus on the part of program directors is that language is a central problem for the disadvantaged child. Some programs provide a rich environment to stimulate language development, along with warm and responsive adults to support and extend the language efforts of a child. Others provide explicit instruction in the use of language forms, with a heavy emphasis on drill and precise usage.

In the former case, teachers may make use of the daily events and circumstances that arise naturally in the course of a child's school day, using them to clarify and extend the child's language. In the latter case, teachers may have specific teaching objectives and drill the child in the use of certain words and verbal categories with the objective of making up for specific deficits in language behavior. Emphasis is on the development of useful verbal concepts in this case.

Other approaches to the remediation of language development show promise of providing some support for the language handicapped child. It is probably true that the effectiveness of particular strategies depends upon a large number of variables, including the age of the child, the level of competence and dedication of the teacher, enthusiasm, conviction, cooperation of parents as well as teachers, and so on.

An interesting experimental approach to remedial language instruction begins by defining the "standard English" forms as a second language for the child, on the assumption that instead of being merely deficient in language, the disadvantaged child is probably fluent in his own language forms, and therefore confronted with a task of second language learning as he broadens his social experiences into the school and community.

In this approach an analysis is made of the differences between the child's language and standard English. Then, through exercises, his own language is used as a basis for extending his language behavior to gradually approximate standard English, which will help him to succeed in the tasks confronting him both in the school and in the community.

Summary

Speech occurs whenever distinct vocal sounds are understood by a listener. Language is a broader category including all vehicles for human communication. The child is confronted with the task of learning many languages, including the language of facial expression, gestures, body posture, and pantomime, as well as spoken language. Language, the basic system for sharing experience with others, lies at the core of social interaction. It is also the basis for the development of human personality.

The early childhood years are the period of the most rapid progress in language acquisition, and there is much evidence that the child achieves his progress through the construction of language rules, or principles. Growth of language is orderly, progressing in a natural and predictable sequence but with a wide range of individual differences among normal children. Factors associated with these individual variations include intelligence, sex, birth order, mothering experiences, sensory factors, and socio-economic conditions. Many intervention programs for disadvantaged children place primary emphasis on improving language competencies.

References

Bellugi, U., and Brown, R. "The Acquisition of Language." *Monographs of the Society for Research in Child Development* 29 (1964).

Bereiter, C., and Engelmann, S. *Teaching Disadvantaged Children in the Preschool.* Englewood Cliffs, N.J.: Prentice-Hall, 1966.

Braine, M. D. S. "The Ontogeny of English Phrase Structure: The First Phase." *Language* 39 (1963) 1–13.

Brown, R., and Bellugi, U. "Three Processes in the Child's Acquisition of Syntax." In Lenneberg, E. H., ed. *New Directions in the Study of Language.* Cambridge, Mass.: Massachusetts Institute of Technology Press, 1964, pp. 131–161.

Brown, R., and Fraser, C. "The Acquisition of Syntax." In Bellugi, U., and Brown, R., eds. "The Acquisition of Language." *Monographs of the Society for Research in Child Development* 29 (1964) 43–79.

Bruner, J. S., Olver, R., and Greenfield, P. M., eds. *Studies in Cognitive Growth.* New York: Wiley, 1966.

Cazden, C. "Subcultural Differences in Child Language: An Interdisciplinary Review." *Merrill-Palmer Quarterly* 12 (1966) 185–219.

Davis, E. A. "The Development of Linguistic Skill in Twins, Singletons with Siblings, and Only Children from Age Five to Ten Years." *Institute of Child Welfare Monograph Series.* Minneapolis: University of Minnesota Press, 1937.

Day, E. J. "The Development of Language in Twins: I. A Comparison of Twins and Single Children." *Child Development* 3 (1932) 179–199.

Ervin, S. M. "Imitation and Structural Change in Children's Language." In Lenneberg, E. H., ed. *New Directions in the Study of Language.* Cambridge, Mass.: Massachusetts Institute of Technology Press, 1964, pp. 163–189.

Gesell, A., and Amatruda, C. S. *Developmental Diagnosis.* 2nd ed. New York: Hoeber-Harper, 1947.

Goldfarb, W. "Effects of Psychological Deprivation in Infancy and Subsequent Stimulation." *American Journal of Psychiatry* 102 (1945) 18–33.

———. "Emotional and Intellectual Consequences of Psychologic Deprivation in Infancy: A Revaluation." In Hoch, P. H., and Zubin, J., eds. *Psychopathology of Childhood.* New York: Grune and Stratton, 1955, pp. 105–119.

Hess, R. D., and Shipman, V. "Early Experience and the Socialization of Cognitive Modes in Children." *Child Development* 36 (1965) 869–886.

Jersild, A. T. *Child Psychology.* 4th ed. New York: Prentice-Hall, 1954.

Lenneberg, E. H. "The Biological Foundations of Language." *Hospital Practice* (December 1967) 59–67. Reprinted in Spencer, T. D., and Kass, N., eds. *Perspectives in Child Psychology.* New York: McGraw-Hill, 1970, pp. 165–176.

Maxfield, K. E. "The Spoken Language of the Blind Preschool Child: A Study of Method," *Archives of Psychology,* no. 201 (1936).

McCarthy, D. "Language Development in Children." In Carmichael, L., ed. *Manual of Child Psychology.* 2nd ed. New York: Wiley, 1954, pp. 492–630.

Minuchin, P., and Biber, B. "A Child Development Approach to Language in the Preschool Disadvantaged Child." *Monographs of the Society for Research in Child Development* 33 (1968), no. 3, 10–18.

Mowrer, O. H. "Speech Development in the Young Child: The Autism Theory of Speech and Some Clinical Applications." *Journal of Speech and Hearing Disorders* 17 (1952) 263–268.

Piaget, J. *The Language and Thought of the Child.* New York: Harcourt, Brace, 1926.

Rheingold, H. L., and Bayley, N. "The Later Effects of an Experimental Modification of Mothering." *Child Development* 30 (1959) 363–372.

Skinner, B. F. *Verbal Behavior.* New York: Appleton-Century-Crofts, 1957.

Spitz, R. A. "The Importance of Mother-Child Relationship During the First Year of Life." *Mental Health Today* 7 (1948) 7–13.

Vygotsky, L. S. *Thought and Language.* Cambridge, Mass.: Massachusetts Institute of Technology Press, 1962.

Werner, H. *Comparative Psychology of Mental Development.* New York: Science Editions, 1961.

Whorf, B. L. *Language, Thought, and Reality.* Edited and with an introduction by J. B. Carroll. Cambridge, Mass.: Massachusetts Institute of Technology Press, 1956.

CHAPTER EIGHT
The development of intelligence

Why is intelligence difficult to define?

How is intelligence measured in children?

What are the components of intellectual functioning, and how do they interact with each other?

How can we account for individual differences in mental abilities?

What are the stages of intellectual development?

How do early experiences affect growth through these stages?

Ever since the appearance of the first intelligence tests early in the present century, there has been increased interest in this more or less mysterious aspect of personality. There has also been much misunderstanding about the nature of intelligence, its growth during childhood, the significance of individual differences from one child to another, and the techniques for estimating the level of mental ability of a child. In this chapter we shall attempt to portray the meaning of intellectual functioning and the nature of its growth during early childhood.

The meaning of mental ability

In popular thinking, intelligence has frequently been defined as the ability to learn. It has been closely identified, for the school-age child, with the ability to perform well in school subjects. Certainly it is true that the more intelligent child is able to learn more efficiently than the less intelligent child, other things being equal. But learning ability and scholastic achievement, while affected by intelligence, should not be thought of as synonymous with intelligence.

Alfred Binet, one of the first psychologists to experiment with intelligence tests, and probably the most important single influence in the development of the mental age scale for testing mental ability, defined intelligence in terms of the child's ability to act in relation to goals and to revise his behavior if need be to reach a goal.

Other psychologists have provided varying definitions, stressing such qualities as abstract thinking, comprehension, creativity and originality, and the ability to make use of past experience in the solution of problems. Some have tended to view intelligence as a more or less unitary quality, a general level of efficiency of mental functioning. Others, in contrast, have viewed it not as a unitary trait, but as a series of relatively independent qualities (factors), which may exist in markedly different degrees within the same child.

There is no one right definition of intelligence, but these considerations give some impression of the breadth of the area to be covered. It is the gradual elaboration of the processes and characteristics included in such definitions that constitutes mental development.

Verbal and nonverbal intelligence

One major consideration in mental development is the distinction often made between verbal intelligence and nonverbal mental ability. The first of these consists of all of those mental functions that rely heavily for their operation on the ability of a child to organize a problem or task into words, and to deal effectively with that problem through the use of words, which may or may not be spoken. This aspect of mental behavior is closely linked with language development. Nonverbal intelligent behavior, on the other hand, presumably relies on the capacity for organizing problems and dealing with those problems without necessarily resorting to the use of formal language symbols.

These two aspects of mental behavior are not independent, of course, and the child who is advanced in one will probably be advanced in the others. However, as a basis for understanding his behavior, the relative strengths of a child in each aspect may be more significant than the level of his IQ. Particularly for children who have special circumstances that place them at a disadvantage in one or the other of these aspects of functioning, it may be important to be aware of discrepancies between these two kinds of abilities.

One example would be the deaf child, who is at a disadvantage with respect to language development and whose mental growth may be slowed in some respects in the achievement and use of verbal concepts. On the other hand, such a child may have a well-developed central nervous system, so that his capacity for intelligent behavior, particularly of the nonverbal variety, may be markedly superior to his score on a test of verbal intelligence.

Social definitions of intelligence

In the final analysis, the most important definitions of intelligence are not those ordinarily given in textbooks or manuals for

the testing of mental ability. The basic criterion of intelligent behavior is a social criterion: to what degree is the child capable of
reacting constructively to the countless problems presented by
living in his physical and social environment? In this sense the
only real test of intelligence is the test of life itself, which
measures the child's capacity for living effectively in a complex
world. In recent years, we have become increasingly aware that
this social test places some children at a severe disadvantage, for
reasons of economic handicaps, minority group membership, emotional or social deprivation, or environmental failure to provide
appropriate stimulation for normal mental growth.

In the following section, we shall attempt to understand how
psychologists estimate children's ability to adapt to their physical
and social environments. The use of tests of intelligence is merely
an attempt to make predictions about the child's personal resources for coping with and adapting effectively to his world.

The measurement of intelligence
in young children

In any attempt to understand the intellectual development of a
child, we must be concerned with two questions: (1) what is the
child's *present status* with respect to performance of intellectual
tasks, and (2) what is the *trend* of his growing and expanding
capacity for task performance?

The use of standardized tests or scales of intelligence provides
us with the basic information we may use to answer these questions. The intelligence test is merely a device that allows the
examiner to compare the performance of one child with that of
many other children in response to a series of standard tasks or
problems which demand a variety of mental activities and operations. The test is given under carefully controlled conditions,
and the examiner follows a rather elaborate set of instructions
in presenting the tasks to the child. Otherwise there would be no
basis for comparing one child with all the others. The comparison
is made by checking the child's performance on the tasks with
the norms, or standards, provided in the manual for the test.

These norms have been derived by examination of large numbers of children, and they represent the average performance of children in the population for each age level.

The concept of mental age

One of the most significant developments in the history of mental testing was Binet's concept of mental age. While there are certain limitations and disadvantages to its use, it paved the way for the establishment of useful testing procedures. The mental age concept is a fairly simple, straightforward notion in its basic features: *mental age is the average performance, on a standardized set of intellectual tasks, of children of a given chronological age.*

Thus if we had a set of tasks known to require intellectual ability for their performance, we might theoretically present the tasks to all children of a given age, say 4 years. By scoring the performance of every 4-year-old and averaging the scores, we could determine what the "typical" 4-year-old behavior is with respect to these tasks. It is this typical behavior of children of a given chronological age which then becomes the definition of that mental age (in this example, mental age 4). Presumably, if we gave the same tasks to all 5-year-olds, their average performance would be somewhat higher, and the difference between the two performance levels represents the distance between mental age 4 and mental age 5. From this procedure then, age scales have been derived, which define the performance levels for each chronological age.

It follows from this that mental age will mean somewhat different things, depending upon which specific set of tasks is used. This is important to keep in mind, since it means that a child's mental age, as measured by one test, may not be identical with his mental age on another test. There are many tests currently in use.

When we wish to know the level of mental ability of a given child, we present him with the same tasks as those employed in the standardization sample. We determine from his test performance how he compares with the norms. If his performance equals that of the average 4-year-old, we say he has a mental age of 4, regardless of his actual age.

A child who is actually 5 years old may perform at the 4-year-level; we would say his mental development is significantly below average. A child of 4 whose performance is equal to the 4-year-average would be described as having normal mental development. A child who is actually 3 years old, but whose performance equals that of the average 4-year-old, would be described as having accelerated mental development.

The IQ

Another device that has been used to draw comparisons among children is the *intelligence quotient,* commonly abbreviated as IQ. In earlier forms of individual tests of intelligence, it was common to compute the IQ by the following formula:

$$IQ = \frac{MA}{CA} \, (\times \, 100).$$

Thus if a child's mental age (MA) and chronological age (CA) were identical, the resulting ratio (1.00) when multiplied by 100 would yield an IQ score of 100. MA scores higher than CA would yield IQ scores higher than 100, and if the MA were not as large as the CA, the resulting IQ score would be below 100. The extent to which a child's IQ score varied above or below 100, then, would depend on the amount of discrepancy between his chronological and mental ages.

In later versions of individual tests of intelligence it became unnecessary to compute IQ from the above formula; instead, the IQ was obtained for a given child by comparing his MA score with published norms, based on the mean and standard deviation of MA scores for the norm group of children of his age. In some cases, a point score is obtained, which can be converted to an IQ figure without the intermediate step of obtaining an MA score.

Historically it has been assumed that a child's IQ should remain relatively constant, or stable, from one age to another. Thus, for example, the bright child whose MA is 4 when he is only 3 years of age should continue to make rapid progress in mental development so that, by CA 6, his MA will approximate the average for 8-year-olds, and at both age levels, such a child would have an IQ score of about 133.

There are a number of reasons why a child's IQ score will not be exactly the same from one age to another, however. Many things can affect the actual performance of a child in an intelligence test: the nature of the examination; the competence of the examiner; the degree of rapport (agreement or harmony) between child and examiner; freedom from distractions, fatigue, or boredom; and so on. Thus, any score obtained with an intelligence test is, at best, an *estimate* of mental ability, based on the child's performance under the conditions at the time of the test. A different examiner, using a different test, in a different room, at a different time in the child's life, with a different level of rapport, would undoubtedly arrive at a somewhat different estimate of the child's intelligence.

In addition to these effects on test performance, it is also important to note that individual children may not progress in their mental development in the same manner as others. Figure 8.1 shows the rather marked changes in intelligence test scores of five male subjects, tested repeatedly from infancy through the adult years in the longitudinal Berkeley Growth Study. The "standard score" used in that figure is based on the means and standard deviations of mental ages for the subjects in the Berkeley Growth Study. In that scoring system, the mean would be a score of 50, rather than 100, and changes in scores for a particular child from one age to another represent changes in his ability relative to the other subjects of the same study.

The data in Figure 8.1 are typical of the findings of other research also in the fact that there is relatively greater fluctuation in test performance during the early years than later. The relative instability of tests given to children younger than 4 or 5 years of age cannot be accounted for merely by unreliability of the tests, however. It appears that there are important differences in the "timing" of intellectual development from one child to another.

The practical implication of this, as Bayley (1970) notes, is

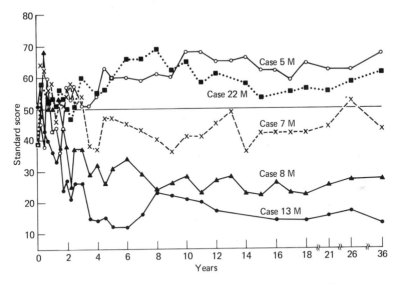

FIGURE 8.1 Individual curves of relative intelligence (standard deviation scores) of five boys, birth to 36 years, Berkeley Growth Study. Note significant changes occurring prior to age 6. (From Nancy Bayley, "Development of Mental Abilities," in P. Mussen, ed., *Carmichael's Manual of Child Psychology*, 3rd edition, Vol. I, Chapter 16.

that a test score may be a reliable and valid index of a child's level of functioning at the time the test is administered, yet not yield a reliable estimate of what the child's intellectual level will be in later years.

In individual cases, there may be important reasons for obtaining as much information as possible about a child's intellectual development. Frequently, such test information can provide important clues for understanding other aspects of a child's behavior. The experienced examiner, in an effort to get the most reliable indication of mental ability, will make use of the most appropriate scale available, since one test is not the equivalent of another.

Some tests are designed specially to measure performance (nonverbal) intelligence. Others are explicitly verbal in content. In some instances it may be inappropriate to use a test that requires instructions be given in the English language. When it is desirable for any reason to administer a test of intelligence to a young child, it should be done only by a qualified psychological examiner with special training in the administration and interpretation of psychological tests.

It is particularly important that a child not be "labeled" with his IQ, since the score he obtains on any given test depends upon many variables, and errors may occur if adults treat a child's score on a test as if it were a fixed trait, such as body build or eye color. Needless to say, any given score can be only as meaningful as the competence of the person administering the examination.

But there are additional limitations of tests, including these: (1) the tests are not equally applicable to all children, and (2) they do not measure all aspects of intelligence, but rather, a limited set of the total range of intellectual processes. In some ways, the use of tests may even limit or obscure our understanding of a child's mental operations, as Sigel (1963) has pointed out.

With respect to the applicability of tests to all children, we should be aware that test reliability and validity depends upon the age of the child (tests are less meaningful for infants and very young children than for school age children). Perhaps even more critical is the element of cultural differences among children. Most tests are based on the assumption that a child will be compared with other children (the norm group) having a similar cultural background. Such an assumption is rarely warranted for a child whose experiences have been severely limited, for example, in a remote Indian reservation or an urban ghetto. Attempts to develop "culture free" or "culture fair" tests have been made, but with limited success.

In other sections of this chapter, we will have occasion to consider intellectual processes, which appear to be important to a child's social competence, but which are not well measured by the present standard tests of intelligence. In doing so, we should keep in mind the positive contributions of tests, at their best, while recognizing their limitations. The complexity of the problem is illustrated by the work of Guilford (1959), whose research has led him to theorize that there are perhaps 120 distinct (although not necessarily independent) intellectual "factors," or abilities. If any given child is a unique combination of such a rich set of abilities, it is reasonable to suppose that there are many differences between children having the same IQ score.

Of particular interest in Guilford's work is his distinction between *divergent* and *convergent* thinking. Where the latter is concerned with the best, or most appropriate solution to a problem (doing a thing the "right" way), *divergent* thinking is concerned with variation in ideas, with finding new or different solutions, and with thinking of things in novel ways. Both are aspects of intelligence, but *divergent* thinking, thought to be associated with creativity, is less well measured by current tests of intelligence.

Individual differences
in mental abilities

Individual differences in intelligence must be accounted for either by genetic factors or by environmental forces, or some combination of the two. The problem of the relative role of each has been investigated in numerous studies, which have led us to the general conclusion that hereditary factors are of fundamental significance in determining the rate of intellectual development, or "brightness," of the individual child. At the same time, we have become increasingly aware of ways in which the environment must support and enhance the child's intellectual development if his genetic potential is to be achieved.

Attempts to sort out single, specific factors that account for wide variations in mental abilities from one child to another have met with many difficulties, and have yielded less than satisfactory conclusions. Such variables as sex, race, ordinal position in the family, and diet have been investigated, generally resulting in the conclusion that factors in intellectual abilities do not operate independently, but rather in interaction with each other.

Sex, an inherited characteristic, provides an example. Girls seem to mature more rapidly and perform at a higher level on verbal tests than boys, but it is difficult to determine how much of this superiority is a matter of inherited sex differences and how much is a matter of differential treatment of girls by parents. The traditional research strategy for examining hereditary influences is to compare sets of identical twins, since each twin pair has identical heredity. However, this procedure cannot tell us about possible sex differences, since identical twins are always of like sex.

Studies of identical twins have been useful, however, in shedding light on the relative contributions of heredity and environment in mental abilities. In one such study of identical twins who were reared separately, Burt (1969) reported a correlation coefficient of .87 for the intelligence test scores of 53 pairs of twins. This is a very powerful relationship, in spite of the environmental differences. By comparison, fraternal twins, not sharing identical heredity, even when reared together, obtained scores that yielded a correlation coefficient of only .53. Burt does not argue that environment has *no* effect; and he notes that identical twins reared in the same families show the strongest resemblance of all ($r = .92$). However, his results clearly indicate the primary role of genetic forces in the determination of general intelligence level.

Other studies, notably that of Newman, Freeman, and Holzinger (1937), have also reported high relationships between test scores for identical twins reared apart, and slightly higher relationships for those reared together. In cases of extreme environmental differences, these researchers observed rather wide variations between test scores of certain pairs of twins. This suggests that unusual degrees of environmental distortion may have more powerful effects on mental growth, even though the major component of the forces affecting mental ability remains that of genetic endowment.

After reviewing a number of twin studies, Jensen (1969) concluded that approximately 80 percent of the variation among individuals in the distribution of intelligence in the population can be accounted for by hereditary factors, and a relatively small remaining proportion by environmental forces. Jensen's research stirred great controversy, because he inferred from it that differences in mental ability are also associated with race. Superior performance on standard intelligence tests for white children, compared with black and Indian children, was interpreted as evidence that these differences, too, are primarily a matter of inheritance. Again, however, the difficulty of separating one factor from another becomes quickly apparent.

If one is to conclude that children of a given ethnic group perform at a higher or lower level or with a different quality on tests as a result of *inherited* differences, then he must deal with the question of *what other conditions in the lives of those children are also different,* and to what extent those other, environmental, differences may affect test performance. Any realistic assessment of this question must lead us, at present, to conclude that, on the average, many conditions are different for black children in America than for white children, and many conditions other than heredity operate in the lives of Indian children, Spanish-speaking children, or children of any other ethnic minority. We have not yet succeeded, for purposes of adequate scientific strategy, in holding all these other conditions constant in order to examine the precise effects of ethnicity on the development of mental abilities. Furthermore, since no test in current use has been shown to be precisely equivalent for all ethnic groups, it would seem premature to conclude that we have a clear answer to such a complex question.

In the years since the large-scale development of intervention and enrichment programs for young children (for example, Head Start, begun in 1965), many investigations have shown that children's performance on standard tests of intelligence improves as a function of their participation in quality educational programs. One outstanding example of this is a report by Weikart (1970), showing initial increases as great as 27 to 30 IQ points as a result of program attendance by 3- and 4-year-olds.

Other researchers have reported IQ gains also, although generally not as large as in the Weikart report. Follow-up studies of the same children at later stages, however, have led to discouraging results in that children whose IQs were apparently raised in the early years tended to return to a level in keeping with their preintervention test scores. The interpretation of such findings is again complicated by the fact that events other than those under consideration (in this case, effects of early enrichment) might account for the failure to maintain the higher level of test performance.

The child development student should be aware of some of the issues involved, and should be hesitant to draw conclusions prematurely, for we have much yet to learn about the role of early experiences in the formation of mental abilities. In the above example, we would need to know to what extent the schools and families continued to provide the incentive, encouragement, stimulation, intellectual challenge, and support for mental development as the children moved into the elementary school years. We would need to consider the degree to which parents and teachers were able to provide for a continuity of experiences and stimulation in keeping with the new, higher level of functioning, which seemed to arise from the initial intervention.

If we are really to understand the cumulative effects of environmental conditions on children's mental abilities, we must be aware also that 2 to 6 hours a day, 5 days a week for, say, 30 weeks (representing a year of Head Start) is a small proportion of the living and learning time of a child and may in fact represent only a small fraction of the amount of time a child has spent, by age 5, in such activities as, for example, watching television.

Whether this failure to maintain the higher level of mental functioning is a result of inadequate stimulation as the child ages, or a reflection of having initiated the enrichment too late in the child's life (some authorities argue that the most effective programs, so far as intellectual stimulation is concerned, are those for infants and toddlers), or because the higher test performance reflects factors other than true intellectual change, remains a rather large issue, which can only be answered through extensive research over a period of years.

The work of Gray and Klaus (1969), however, argues strongly that there is a progressive retardation effect of environmental poverty and that programs of planned enrichment, particularly when these involve the child's family, can indeed offset the negative environmental effects if begun early and carried through consistently.

In a later report, Gray (1970) compared the effectiveness of a children's program with one that taught mothers to provide continuing stimulation for their children. The latter program was equally effective, less costly, and reached more children than the former, more traditional approach to intervention and enrichment.

Equipment and resources for intelligent behavior

Intelligent behavior is coordinated by the central nervous system, especially the higher brain centers, which are essential to thinking and concept-formation, reasoning, and problem solving. In addition, vital roles in intellectual development are played by the sensory mechanisms, such as those of seeing, hearing, and touching, and by the motor mechanisms concerned with the control of body action. Intelligent behavior, then, is not merely a matter of the efficiency of the brain itself. Instead, it involves coordination of sensory stimulation, with memory of past experiences, and with action. Mental development involves the increasing competence of all systems of the body involved in intelligent behavior.

Sensory equipment

The child's first explorations of his environment have a strong sensory component. The infant explores with his mouth as well as with his eyes and hands. The sensory capacities of the mouth are well developed at birth, and the sensations they provide encourage the continuation of this oral effort to examine the world. In the process of these explorations, there are many opportunities to learn a great deal about the texture, size, shape, and weight of objects.

Auditory sensations also participate in intellectual development from the beginning, particularly in the sensory feedback they represent when, for example, an infant hears his own vocal efforts and is encouraged to expand and improve his vocalizing, which may be viewed as a stimulus to mental growth.

Sensations arising from touch play an important role in stimulating mental development. As with tactual sensations of the mouth, touch sensitivity of fingers, toes, face, and body can also convey to the child numerous fundamental impressions of the nature of his environment. These are essential to his gradual understanding of and effective dealings with his world—one way of defining the essence of intelligent behavior.

Vision and hearing play major roles in allowing the child to achieve understanding and mastery of his world. The most dramatic evidence of the importance of these sensory avenues is provided by the case histories of individuals who have been deprived of normal vision or hearing during the early years. The long, arduous, and specialized training required for such children to achieve the basic intellectual concepts that are taken for granted with nonhandicapped children bespeaks the vital role played by the sensory processes.

The story of Helen Keller makes us aware of their importance, not only in learning to speak, but in formulating ideas about the nature of the world, which can then be used to represent the world and to deal effectively with it. Miss Keller recounts, in her moving autobiography, a critical turning point in her life, at the age of 6, when her teacher (Anne Sullivan) finally succeeded in getting her to make the mental association of objects or events with "words," which Miss Sullivan would "spell" into the palm of the blind and deaf child's hand:

> We walked down the path to the well-house, attracted by the fragrance of the honeysuckle with which it was covered. Someone was drawing water and my teacher placed my hand under the spout. As the cool stream gushed over one hand she spelled into the other the word *water*, first slowly, then rapidly. I stood still, my whole attention fixed upon the motions of her fingers. Suddenly I felt a misty consciousness as of something forgotten—a thrill of returning thought; and somehow the mystery of language was revealed to me. I knew then that "w-a-t-e-r" meant the wonderful cool something that was flowing over my hand. That living word

awakened my soul, gave it light, hope, joy, set it free! There were barriers still, it is true, but barriers that could in time be swept away.

I left the well-house eager to learn. Everything had a name, and each name gave birth to a new thought. As we returned to the house every object which I touched seemed to quiver with life. That was because I saw everything with the strange, new sight that had come to me. . . .

I learned a great many new words that day. I do not remember what they all were, but I do know that mother, father, sister, and teacher were among them—words that were to make the world blossom for me, "like Aaron's rod, with flowers." It would have been difficult to find a happier child than I was as I lay in my crib at the close of that eventful day and lived over the joys it had brought me, and for the first time longed for a new day to come. (From *The Story of My Life* by Helen Keller. Reprinted by permission of Doubleday and Company, Incorporated.)

Motor equipment

In Chapter Six we noted that the child's achievement of body control plays an important part in his coming to deal effectively with his world. Intellectual behavior frequently expresses itself in motor action of one kind or another, particularly in the early years. In addition, it is often through motor action that the child engages in trial-and-error processes in the solution of problems.

The *meaning* of any particular cue or stimulus in the environment is often a matter of what he *does* about that stimulus. Just as it is reasonable to assume that for the infant the bottle is "to suck," it is reasonable that for the 2-year-old the crayon is "to scribble," for the 3-year-old the tricycle is "to pedal and ride," and for the 4-year-old the big boxes are "to climb on and jump from." The child's repertory of motor responses is both a resource and a limitation for his imaginativeness, his inventiveness, and his degree of variability in coping with his world.

A simple laboratory investigation of children's learning (Gardner and Judisch 1963) will serve to illustrate the interacting roles of sensory and motor processes in intellectual behavior. In this study children were taken individually into a testing room and seated in front of a "discrimination box," which could be arranged with varying combinations of colored lights and different shaped pushbuttons. The child's task was to learn which button to push when a given light came on. If he pushed the correct one he was rewarded with a marble, delivered through a small opening at the bottom of the box; if he pushed a wrong button, he received no marble.

Three- and 4-year-old children learned the task very quickly, and not only were they eager to push the appropriate button when the light was turned on, but they actively inhibited a motor response of any kind until the light came on. Their behavior could be described as not only pushing the correct button, but actively avoiding the incorrect ones. Such remarks as "Oh, no! I almost pushed the wrong one!" were not infrequent. It was apparent that solving the problem meant coordinating a particular pattern of sensory stimulation with a well-defined motor act. In nonlaboratory settings, intellectual behavior is frequently of this sort also. *The meaning of a given stimulus is, in many instances, what one does about that stimulus with his muscles.*

The central nervous system

It may appear obvious that the brain and the rest of the central nervous system play the central role in the conduct of intellectual behavior, but the manner in which that role is played is, in fact, far from obvious. We may describe the role, in very general terms, as one of integration, and illustrate that role in the integration of sensory and motor events.

Figure 8.2 shows a highly schematic representation of intelligent behavior in which some of the major intellectual processes are depicted. The "sensory intake" component, A, represents the process of taking in sensory stimulation from the environment. The "filter" component, B, represents the process of selecting, or "weighting," the sensory stimuli, giving higher priority to some sensory features and lower priority to others.

Mothers, as well as teachers of young children, will testify that not all children are equally attentive to the same set of sounds, sights, and so on and further, that any given child is not constant in his attentiveness to particular sensory stimuli available to him.

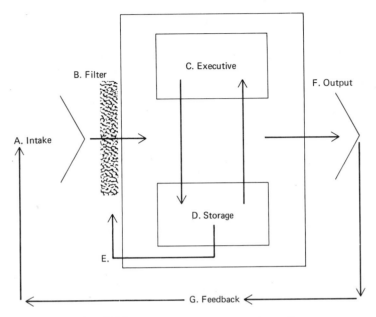

FIGURE 8.2 The child as an open system—a schematic
representation of intelligent behavior.

Thus the "filter" component reminds us that the child actively
selects from the stimulus array available to him certain elements
or features to which to attend, and others to which lower priority
is assigned.

The basis for assignment of priorities to sensory events becomes one of the intriguing questions for scientist and layman
alike. "Why does a child hear what I am saying at one time and
not at another?" "Why does he tune me out sometimes when I
try to explain something important to him, and why does he tune
me in sometimes when I am talking to someone else about things
that are none of his business?"

In these examples, the perceptive student may find a hint of
the answer embedded in the questions themselves, for there is a

suggestion that the motives of the speaker enter into the issue. If a child "tunes me out," one might speculate that "My motive to manipulate the child may be showing in my voice again, and perhaps he has learned to tune me out in those circumstances when I am trying too hard, or too obviously, to make him different from what he is!" And similarly, perhaps he "tunes me in, whether I wish it or not, in those circumstances when my behavior implies that things are not for his ears, precisely because I am conveying a message of such mystery and intrigue!"

But that, of course, is speculation. What matters is that we understand the child is not merely a passive, unselective receiver of all sensory stimulation available in his world. He plays an active role in filtering that world through a process which changes dynamically from one time of day to another (he is not equally sensitive to the sight and sound of food at all times during the day), from one time of year to another (he is not equally sensitive to the sight of a Santa Claus mask at all times during the year), and from one period in life to another (he is not equally sensitive to the appearance of a strange adult at the door at all ages in his life).

The "executive" component of intelligent behavior, C, refers to the prime coordinating role of the central nervous system. It implies a "decision" of some kind, although not necessarily at a conscious level of thought. The decision may be at a very primitive, reflexive level, illustrated by the "decision" to show a startle response to an unexpected loud sound. The executive component also implies more abstract, symbolic decisions illustrated by a child's choice of finger painting over playing with blocks, when given a free choice. On another occasion, he decides in favor of the blocks.

The exercise of this executive function may appear to be arbitrary and capricious as it manifests itself in the daily behavior of a child, but the student must understand a child's decisions are based upon a kind of psychological orderliness. In any given instance, a decision occurs as the product of a mixture of signals penetrating the filter system, with signals coming from the "storage component," D, and it is the combined effect of these two sources of information that yields the decision. We might think of the storage component as being analogous to memory, since it represents the residue of previous experiences, still existing in the child. However, we are speaking of a very *active* kind of process, in which our emphasis is perhaps less on the ability of a child to *store* bits of information than it is on his ability to *recover*, in usable form, the effects of prior experiences and integrate them with incoming sensory events for the purpose of making immediate decisions.

A seemingly minor, but perhaps crucial, component of the intellectual system is depicted by E, a "filter revision" process arising from the storage function, implying that one of the effects of storing information is to revise one's filter. Another way of saying this is that "priorities" attached to various sensory events become altered with experience as the child becomes increasingly sensitized to certain classes of sensory stimulation and possibly desensitized to others. All of our experience with children suggests that their memory of previous events helps define their degree of "openness" to similar events in the future.

What we have said up to this point is that the child is continuously filtering his sensory world, integrating the incoming information with what is there in the presently existing storage system, and making decisions, on the basis of this mixed set of signals as to a course of action (F). The course of action, however, is one of the lines of action available to him *in his repertory* —within his capability, and also within the set of possibilities allowed by the physical and social environment.

Later, we will attempt to relate this point to matters of child guidance in home and school settings. For the present, we will merely note that our schematic description of the intellectual process implies a major role for the child himself as a decision maker, choosing from among an increasingly complex array of possible courses of action. To the extent that this emphasis is warranted, we might speculate further that intellectual development consists, in part, of the achievement of an increasingly sophisticated "decider." This position implies further that the child's task of intellectual development is facilitated by his experience with *true choice situations,* and that the task is less likely to be achieved if he has fewer opportunities to experience alternatives.

However, the experience of alternatives is not complete in the act of making a decision. The completeness of the experience is contingent on being informed of the outcomes of one's decision. Intellectual behavior, then, is constantly guided by "feedback," G, which informs the child of the outcomes of his acts, and therefore the outcomes of his decisions to employ given lines of actions. Feedback, like decisions themselves, operates at varying levels of abstraction.

The infant hearing his own babbling is getting auditory feedback in the process, but he is also getting feedback from within his own body—what it feels like in the chest, the larynx, the palate, the tongue, the jaws, and the lips to make sounds, and furthermore, to make sounds which sound a certain way in the ears, and so on. A child could not learn to walk in the absence of feedback from his body informing him of body position, balance, and muscular action.

While it may seem like a big "jump" from these examples to thinking and reasoning and problem solving, the implication is that a child could not learn to think, or engage in any complex intellectual activities, without getting feedback informing him of the effects of his cognitive decisions.

The pattern
of cognitive development

The schematic portrayal of intellectual processes outlined in the previous section provides a basis for discussing the growth of mental behavior in a somewhat broader and more inclusive sense than the notion of the "brightness" or intelligence of a child. When we speak of cognitive processes, we are referring to the manner in which a child represents the world around him, the ways in which he makes decisions about it, and the courses of action he may follow in dealing with that world. When we speak of the *development* of cognitive processes, we are speaking of the changes that occur as a child's system for intellectual processes becomes increasingly sophisticated and elaborate in its capability for representing and dealing with the world.

In this section we will draw heavily from two sources of information on this process of cognitive development: (1) the Swiss developmental psychologist, Jean Piaget and his colleagues and students, and (2) the American psychologist Jerome Bruner and his colleagues and students. Both have provided, through years of investigation and experimentation, valuable insights for the child development student. In both cases, also, the student's appreciation and comprehension of the course of cognitive development will depend on his grasp of the *vocabulary* of cognitive processes as employed by Piaget and Bruner.

The primary feature of cognitive development according to Piaget (1970) is the process of *adaptation*—both adaptation of the child to his environment, and adaptation of the cognitive system to a set of internal demands. These adaptation requirements may be seen as analogous to the incoming sensory signals and the stored information of the system we have already described.

However, Piaget is referring to the *coordination of internal cognitive structures* when he speaks of this second type of adaptation, and not limiting the idea to that of "storage" or "memory" as most of us would employ such terms. When he talks of cognitive structures and their adaptation, he is talking about a mental system with certain features and provisions for handling information, and the fact that this system is *constructed* actively by the child, not merely by copying the external world nor merely through a process of biological maturation, but rather through the continuous interaction between the presently existing structure and the demands made on that structure by both internal and external events. Knowledge (in the Piagetian sense of "knowing" or cognizing) is not derived directly from an object, or directly from within the person dealing with that object; it is, rather, the product of an interaction between person and object:

> From the most elementary sensorimotor actions (such as pushing and pulling) to the most sophisticated intellectual operations, which are interiorized actions, carried out mentally (e.g., joining together, putting in order, putting into one-to-one correspondence),

knowledge is constantly linked with actions or operations, that is, with *transformations*. (Piaget 1970, p. 704)

The preceding is consistent with what has been pointed out previously, that the *meaning* of an object or event arises from the *activity* of a person who involves himself with that object or event. But in the course of that involvement, demands may be made on the presently existing cognitive structures. The child's cognitive structure at any point in time provides a set of *schema*, or capacities to respond in given ways. Adaptation, the essential process in cognitive growth, consists of a continuous interplay between two subprocesses: (1) *assimilation*, which is the integration of external events (we have said it begins with sensory intake) into the present structures, and (2) *accommodation*, which is the modification of those present schema or structures by the events which are assimilated.

Adaptation, in Piaget's view, is analogous to biological processes of adaptation, and is indeed used in much the same sense as in biological adaptation. The processes of digestion (assimilation) of nutrients by the biological system provide for the growth of an increasingly complex structure capable of assimilating a wider array of nutrients through the process of accommodation or revision of the biological structures. The interaction of these two processes in cognitive development is illustrated with an example provided by Sigel (1964): A child who has learned to attribute the word *animal* to four-legged creatures then learns that two-legged creatures can also be defined as animals. As this new information is assimilated, he alters his concept of animal to include a wider variety of cases.

Cognitive development involves the balance, or equilibrium, between these two complementary processes of assimilation and accommodation as the child moves to progressively higher levels of adaptation. Each stage involves more complex structures and a wider range of schema for responding to the world. Piaget has outlined the overall process of cognitive development in a series of stages from infancy through adolescence. It is an elaborate and complex theory of intellectual development, and the student should appreciate the fact that the highly condensed summary of stages of cognitive growth presented here can only provide the general flavor and trend of the total theory.

The sensorimotor period

As we noted in Chapter Four, this stage of cognitive functioning extends from birth through the first 1½ to 2 years. The term "sensorimotor" is used to denote a period in which language and symbolic processes are absent, or nearly so. This lack of ability to deal with the world symbolically means that the infant's intellectual action is expressed relatively more at the body surface, in his sensory contacts and motor responses to his environment, than through central symbolic representation of the world.

Late in the second year there are the beginnings of primitive symbolic representation, revealed in the child's invention of "mental" solutions to problems, not directly observable in his overt body action.

The period of representative intelligence

This stage extends from 1½ or 2 years to about 11 years of age, and is subdivided into two major phases. In the first subperiod, lasting until 7 or 8 years of age, the central task is the development of internal cognitive structures and the organization of means of representing the external world with its laws and relationships. It is a period marked by unstable logic, inconsistencies, and contradictions. It is a time when adult logic does not "fit" the mental action of the child.

Initially in this subperiod (which Piaget labels "preoperational"), the child's thinking is egocentric, and he has little ability to assume the point of view of another person, to comprehend any position he is not directly experiencing, or even to recognize that there *is* any position other than his own. Things are judged on face value, and thought is not reflective.

The child's categorization of his world is "single-classification," which means he is unable to deal simultaneously with two or more dimensions. He might respond to objects in terms of their color, for example, *or* their shape, but could not be expected to deal with a set of objects in terms of color *and* shape characteristics simultaneously. Neither is the child able to reverse a mental operation, which means that he cannot mentally "undo" his thought processes to return to a prior state of thought.

Furthermore, the child cannot "conserve" the physical properties of objects in his world during this period. He is overwhelmed still by the perceptual qualities of objects and events and has not yet achieved the essential cognitive structures that allow him to hold a stable representation of things by their invariant qualities. Changing the shape of a ball of clay, for example, does not change the mass or amount of the material, which in this instance remains invariant. However, the shift in the shape, if the ball is flattened into a pancake or sausage-shape, is a compelling distortion to the young child, who treats the transformed material as if the amount had changed. Similarly, such a nonconserving approach leads the young child to act as if the *number* of beads changes when a row of, say, seven beads is extended or contracted merely by changing the spacing between beads but leaving the number constant.

A classic example of the nonconserving approach by the young child is his response to the amount of liquid in different shaped containers. The young child's lack of stable cognitive structures for dealing with volume and quantity allow him to be overwhelmed by irrelevant changes when, for example, a given quantity of water is poured from a short, "fat" cylindrical beaker into a tall, "skinny" beaker before the child's eyes, and he responds to the visual transformation in shape of the liquid as if it were a change in the amount or volume of liquid.

During the "concrete operations" substage of this period of representative intelligence, which begins at about age 7 or 8, reasoning begins to take on the formal appearance of logic. The child begins to engage in mental processes such as classifying objects into hierarchical sets, with larger classes of things comprising smaller classes of things. Thus "dogs," "horses," and "cows" all become members of the class "animals." In turn, "animals" shares with "plants" membership in the still larger class, "living things."

It is also during this subperiod that the child comes to deal with certain invariant, or changeless, properties of things in a realistic fashion. Piaget has labeled this capability with the term *conservation,* since the child is now able, for the first time, to "conserve" the invariant properties of things regardless of changes in the perceptual field of the child. Using the examples cited previously, the child now recognizes that the amount does not change when a ball of clay is flattened into a pancake or sausage-shape. Neither does the number change when a row of beads is expanded by spacing a given set with greater distances between beads. The amount of liquid in a glass beaker is not changed by pouring the liquid into a different shaped beaker.

Along with conservation the child becomes capable of *transitivity,* which is illustrated by simple logic: If A is greater than B, and B is greater than C, then A is greater than C. The fact that the child of 4 cannot engage reliably in such logic helps us to understand why some adults find young children frustrating and "impossible," because mentally, they are not bound by the same rules of logic as the older child and adult.

The period of formal operations

Beginning about age 11, there are the first evidences of truly abstract thought, with the capability of following the logical form of propositions and inferences which may be derived from those propositions. For the first time, the child is able to follow the *form* of an argument without regard to its *content,* and thus is able to deal with hypothetical questions which he has never experienced directly.

The distinction between having and not having this capability is illustrated in children's responses to hypothetical questions, as, for example, "Suppose all the air were taken out of the room but there is a fan running in the room. Would there be a breeze?" The child who has achieved the capability of formal operations follows the form of the premise, recognizes its implications, and responds to the hypothetical situation by inferring correctly that there would be no breeze where there is no air. The younger children in Piaget's experiments, who were not yet operating with formal structures, responded to the question by insisting that there would still be a breeze, even though they might have recognized that air is essential to a breeze, because they could not adopt the proposition of "no air in the room," nor could they reason from this hypothetical premise to an abstract inference. One child, for example, insisted that the reason there would still be a breeze was because there would still be "a little air" in the room. When pressed further and told "Yes, but suppose this time we took *all* the air out of the room, would there still be a breeze?" the child still insisted there would be, because, he said "there would *still* be a *little* air" in the room!

Piaget's theory has many implications for the development and guidance of intellectual processes in children. Americans have been slow to accept the theory and its implications in part because Piaget's approach to the study of the child has not always conformed to our criteria for scientific research. But in recent years, more American scientists have paid serious attention to Piaget's ideas and have found substantial evidence in support of the general theory. While Piaget himself has not stressed the practical implications of his theory, either for parents or for teachers of young children, acceptance of his theoretical position does suggest, among other things, the importance of both experience and biological maturation, in continuous interaction with each other, in the child's construction of his own cognitive system. It also suggests a natural "sequencing" of mental operations in a child, with given structures and schema being viewed as the orderly products of preceding stages and, in turn, as essential prerequisites for stages to follow.

The scientific discipline of child development, and the applied aspects of this discipline such as child guidance and early childhood education, in all probability will be engaged for many years to come in assessing the implications of this vital theory of human cognitive growth.

Jerome Bruner (1964, 1965, 1966), too, has given us an insightful description of the course of cognitive development. Like Piaget, Bruner envisions the course of cognitive growth in a series of stages, each of which provides for more sophisticated and flexible ways for the child to "represent" his world cognitively. The key stages, in Bruner's description, are as follows:

Enactive representation

This stage implies the representation of past events through motor action. It is a mode of functioning analogous to Piaget's sensorimotor period and, in fact, Bruner employs examples used by Piaget to illustrate this mode of functioning. One such example is that of the infant playing with a rattle in his crib:

> The rattle drops over the side. The child moves his clenched hand before his face, opens it, looks for the rattle. Not finding it there, he moves his hand, closed again, back to the edge of the crib, shakes it with movements like those he uses in shaking the rattle. Thereupon he moves his closed hand back toward his face, opens it, and looks. Again no rattle; and so he tries again. In several months, the child has benefited from experience to the degree that the rattle and action become separated. Whereas earlier he would not show signs of missing the rattle when it was removed unless he had begun reaching for it, now he cries and searches when the rattle is presented for a moment and hidden by a cover. He no longer repeats a movement to restore the rattle. In place of representation by action alone—where "existence" is defined by . . . present action—it is now defined by an image that persists autonomously. (Bruner 1964, pp. 2–3)

Bruner also illustrates the enactive mode of representing and dealing with the world by citing certain adults who have suffered brain injury and who are unable to define an object or derive a meaning from a common object unless they can perform actions with it. Such a patient, for example, might be unable to say the actual word to label a boiled egg until he has taken the egg in hand and begun to crack the shell and peel it. At this level of functioning, the meaning or identity of the object is discoverable only in the actions one can perform with it. Definitions given by young children, even well beyond the infancy stage, tend to support this idea in that their verbalizations emphasize action, as in the well-known example of the child who defines a hole as "to dig."

Iconic representation

This mode of cognitive functioning involves representing the external world through imagery. Visual images are the most obvious example, and Bruner argues that such "imaging" is the dominant mode of cognizing in the young child. It is a more flexible mode of operating than the enactive mode, since it does permit dealing with objects and events in terms of an internalized copy, in the form of an image, without the necessity of a direct engagement of sensory and motor processes.

But it is nevertheless a restricted mode of functioning compared with the next stage, in that it does not provide the highly fluid and flexible means of separating the *signs* and *symbols* of objects and events and recombining these in infinite variations. Instead, the meaning of events and objects, even though it may now be dealt with in the absence of the events and objects (the child can "image" his mother and deal with that image as a more or less constant aspect of his cognizing of the world, regardless of whether or not his mother is physically present and available for him to participate in a reciprocal set of *actions;* the actions, too, can now be imagined), can now be discovered in the quality of the imagery of the child associated with those events or objects.

Symbolic representation

This highest level of cognitive functioning allows the child to represent his world with a very flexible, functional set of signs and symbols, which can be manipulated internally in very abstract ways in the child's efforts to deal with his world. Language, the clearest manifestation of this mode of cognizing, is nevertheless viewed by Bruner as only an example. However, as we have seen in the preceding chapter, it is a crucial example in that it affords the child a tool by which to engage in thought, free from the constraints of bodily action or of mental images, which have limited flexibility.

The achievement of this highest mode of cognitive representation is illustrated by an experiment carried out by Bruner and Kenney (1966) dealing with a task of double classification. Children of ages 3 to 7 were presented with an array of plastic

Scale in inches

0 2 4 6

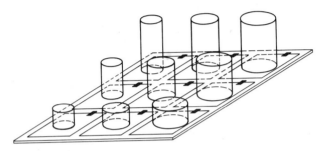

FIGURE 8.3 The Matrix Problem, employed by Bruner and Kenney.
(From J. S. Bruner and Helen J. Kenney, "On Multiple Ordering,"
in J. S. Bruner, Rose Olver, and Patricia M. Greenfield, eds.,
Studies in Cognitive Growth, New York: Wiley, 1966, pp. 154–
167.

glasses (Figure 8.3) arranged in a matrix, with height varying in
one dimension and width varying in the other dimension. Each
child was asked to replace the glasses in their correct position
when first one, then two, and then three glasses were removed.
The children were asked to describe the ways in which the
glasses were alike and how they differed, then the glasses were
scrambled and the children asked to reconstruct the matrix
"something like what was there before." Finally, the glasses were
scrambled once more, but this time the glass that had originally
been in the near-left corner (the shortest, thinnest glass) was
placed in the near-right position, and the child was again asked
to make something like what was there before. The three tasks
were described as *replacement, reproduction,* and *transposition,*
respectively. The youngest children (3 and 4) could replace one
glass correctly, but many of them failed when two glasses were
removed, and the majority of them failed with three glasses removed. All of the older children (5, 6, and 7) succeeded in the
replacement task, but not until age 7 did the majority of children

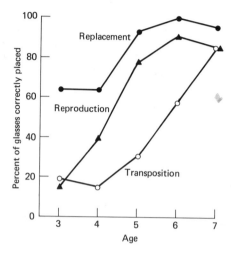

FIGURE 8.4 Results of children's performance on the Matrix Problem, presented by Bruner and Kenney. (From J. S. Bruner and Helen J. Kenney, "On Multiple Ordering," in J. S. Bruner, Rose Olver, and Patricia M. Greenfield, eds., *Studies in Cognitive Growth*, New York: Wiley, 1966, pp. 154–167.)

succeed in the final task with the transposed glass. Figure 8.4 shows the results, with improvement over age for all three tasks, but a sharply different trend for each task. The authors explain this difference partly in terms of the young child's tendency to be very "perceptual," being guided by the immediate and tangible perceptual field and being able to deal with only one dimension at a time (height *or* width, but not both simultaneously).

In the reproduction task, the visual matrix is no longer present as a perceptual guide, and most children below 5 fail it. It is a task the authors view as one of copying a memory image of the original matrix, and thus employs an iconic strategy for its solution. But in the final task (transposition), it is not imagery that is called for, but rather the ability to organize the problem, with its size-space relationships, into a symbolic system of some kind which can be understood in terms of rules. It requires, in the authors' words, ". . . reckoning, not simply copying."

It is this distinction between reckoning and copying that helps one to understand the difference between the iconic and the symbolic ways of representing the world. In the first case, an image, or copy, of the external world, vivid and useful as it may be, is nevertheless too rigid a system to allow the child to engage freely in truly abstract thought. When confronted with a task in which one's image of previous experiences is inadequate as a means of task representation, the child has no reliable tools for coping with the task unless he begins to engage in the more abstract manipulation of the signs and symbols of the world.

Bruner's and Piaget's descriptions of the course of cognitive growth have many points in common. Both stress the general beginnings in the sensorimotor action systems of the child, and the movement toward abstract and symbolic modes of dealing with the world. An important distinction in the underlying philosophy, however, is that Bruner appears to give more weight, relatively, to cultural and social events (experiences) in defining the course of cognitive growth, and Piaget appears to give relatively more weight to the genetic factors which define the course of mental development.

These are relative matters, of course, rather than absolutes; most child development specialists seem to agree, as do both Piaget and Bruner, that important aspects of development, such as cognitive operations, rely on the interaction of biological and social events for their emergence.

Cognitive style

One of the most significant trends in the child's mental development is implied in the preceding discussion in this chapter. We have moved beyond some of the limiting assumptions about intelligence being a fixed genetic trait which, in the course of intellectual development, "unfolds" through maturation of the child. We are making an effort to understand the qualities of mental organization as well as the various "styles" of cognitive functioning which characterize the child, not only as a function of his chronological age, but as a reflection of his experiences and cultural conditioning. It is not that we have lost interest in the question of why some children may be brighter than others, but rather that we are seeing additional issues, some of which may have greater bearing on a child's adaptation to his world than does his score on a standard intelligence test.

Sigel (1963), for example, has made a strong case for understanding the ways in which a child approaches an intellectual task, suggesting that even the types of *errors* he makes while taking an intelligence test may be more revealing about his individual style of mental functioning than is his IQ score.

Hunt (1961) also has argued that the assumptions made previously about the nature of mental functioning may, in fact, be invalid, and that we will learn more about the nature of intellectual functioning if we incorporate the experiences of a child into the formulas used to account for mental growth.

Kagan, Moss, and Sigel (1963), among others, have explored a number of aspects of cognitive functioning in children, and have sorted out some significant dimensions of "cognitive style" that persist in individual children. One such dimension that holds implications for understanding individual children is that of *impulsivity-reflectivity.*

Impulsivity appears to be a relatively stable individual characteristic of certain children to respond to a wide range of tasks without delay and without allowing sufficient time to evaluate one's responses or consider their probable implications. Reflectivity, by contrast, is characterized as the tendency to delay response to a task until internal processes have been employed to assess the implications of a response, implicitly, before it is made.

The child's degree of impulsivity vs. reflectivity is measured primarily by the length of time a child delays, after being presented with a task, before giving his response. The implication is that the highly impulsive child has not developed a set of internal cognitive controls, which allow him to monitor successfully his own mental operations, and which ensure successful "reflection" on a task. The reflective child, by contrast, has learned to monitor his own cognitive processes, and has also learned that his success in coping with tasks is more likely ensured by implicit "trying out" of potential responses. The child prefers this way of functioning over the impulsive style, which places relatively less emphasis on correctness of response than it does on speed of response.

Other aspects of cognitive style are also being studied. We are in the process of broadening our approach to the problem of children's intellectual functioning to include such considerations, some of which relate to creativity as an aspect of mental operation somewhat independent of brightness. These additional aspects of mental functioning may prove, in the long run, to hold vital implications for the conduct of child guidance, and for the education of young children in our society.

Summary

Intelligence has been defined in many ways. As used here, it refers to the efficiency with which a child processes the sensory events of his world and organizes those events for the purpose of solving problems. Some aspects of intelligence are primarily verbal, while others are nonverbal. The ultimate criterion for intelligence is a social one: the ability of a child to adapt successfully to his world. Aspects of intelligence have been measured traditionally with standardized tests, some of which provide a mental age (MA) score, from which the IQ may be derived. Such scores are useful as indicators of the child's level of functioning in comparison with the average, but must be interpreted with caution when dealing with young children. For economically deprived children, who have had markedly different experiences from those of the middle class child, such tests have not been as useful.

Resources for intelligent behavior include the sensory and motor systems as well as the central nervous system. The major factor that determines intellectual growth is genetic, although unusual or extreme distortions and deprivations in early childhood can have significant effects.

Current approaches to understanding intellectual development stress the nature of mental operations and the *quality* of a child's comprehension of his world, in addition to his IQ or level of brightness. In this chapter we have stressed the child's active role in organizing and processing the events of his environment, and utilizing feedback, which informs him of the effects of his own behavior; we have examined the theories of Piaget and Bruner in relation to this notion of the child as an intellectual being.

References

Bayley, N. "Development of Mental Abilities." In Mussen, P. H., ed. *Carmichael's Manual of Child Psychology.* 3rd ed., vol. 1. New York: Wiley, 1970, pp. 1163–1210.

Bruner, J. S. "The Course of Cognitive Growth." *American Psychologist* 19 (1964) 1–15.

———. "The Growth of Mind." *American Psychologist* 20 (1965) 1007–1017.

Bruner, J. S., and Kenney, H. J. "On Multiple Ordering." In Bruner, J. S., et al., eds. *Studies in Cognitive Growth.* New York: Wiley, 1966, pp. 154–167.

Bruner, J. S., Olver, R., and Greenfield, P. M., eds. *Studies in Cognitive Growth.* New York: Wiley, 1966.

Burt, C. "The Genetic Determination of Differences in Intelligence: A Study of Monozygotic Twins Reared Together and Apart." In Rogers, D., ed. *Issues in Child Psychology.* Belmont, Calif.: Brooks/Cole Publishing, 1969, pp. 56–69.

Gardner, D. B., and Judisch, J. M. "Transfer of Discrimination Learning Across Sensory Modalities in Preschool Children." Unpublished paper presented at the 1963 Biennial Conference of the Society for Research in Child Development, Berkeley, Calif.

Gray, S. "Home Visiting Programs for Parents of Young Children." Paper presented at the meeting of the National Association for the Education of Young Children, Boston, 1970.

Gray, S., and Klaus, R. "The Early Training Project: A Seventh Year Report." John F. Kennedy Center for Research on Education and Human Development. Nashville: Peabody College, 1969.

Guilford, J. P. "Three Faces of Intellect," *American Psychologist* 14 (1959) 469–479.

Hunt, J. McV. *Intelligence and Experience.* New York: Ronald Press, 1961.

Jensen, A. R. "How Much Can We Boost IQ and Scholastic Achievement?" *Harvard Educational Review* 39 (1969) 1–123.

Kagan, J., Moss, H. A., and Sigel, I. "Psychological Significance of Styles of Conceptualization." In Wright, J. C., and Kagan, J., eds. "Basic Cognitive Processes in Children." *Monographs of the Society for Research in Child Development* 28 (1963) 73–118.

Keller, H. *The Story of My Life.* New York: Grosset and Dunlap, 1904.

Newman, H. F., Freeman, F. N., and Holzinger, K. J. *Twins: A Study of Heredity and Environment.* Chicago, University of Chicago Press, 1937.

Piaget, J. "Piaget's Theory." In Mussen, P. H., ed. *Carmichael's Manual of Child Psychology.* 3rd ed., vol. 1. New York: Wiley, 1970, pp. 703–732.

Sigel, I. "How Intelligence Tests Limit Understanding of Intelligence." *Merrill-Palmer Quarterly* 9 (1963) 39–56.

———. "The Attainment of Concepts." In Hoffman, M. L., and Hoffman, L. W., eds. *Review of Child Development Research*. Vol. 1. New York: Russell Sage Foundation, 1964, pp. 209–248.

Weikart, D. P. "A Comparative Study of Three Preschool Curricula." In Frost, J. L., and Hawkes, G. R., eds. *The Disadvantaged Child*. 2nd ed. Boston: Houghton Mifflin, 1970.

CHAPTER NINE

Achieving selfhood: the personality of the young child

What kinds of behavior should be included under the heading of personality?

How does a child's definition of himself become a basis for his behavior?

What are the fundamental tasks of human development?

What crises and conflicts normally occur during the course of healthy personality development?

What role do emotions play in the growth of personality?

Such words as *personality* and *self* represent useful ideas—
what we might call *constructs*—which are not intended to be
"proven" or "disproven" scientifically, but which can serve as
useful ways of organizing our understanding of particular topics.
The construct of the self, for example, is useful to the extent that
it offers a helpful frame of reference in understanding the behavior of a child. It offers a basis for characterizing the uniquely
organized features of a child, and also for grasping an orderliness
to children's behavior, which would otherwise appear mysterious,
capricious, or meaningless.

The notion of personality implies the child's emotional life, his
intelligent behavior, his muscular coordination, and his social
interaction with family and friends. At the same time, we are
accustomed to think of personality as somehow going beyond the
limits of emotional, muscular, intellectual, and social behavior.
Personality seems to be more than just these things added together. Whatever else it may be, it seems to represent the peculiar
orientation of a child toward himself and toward the world
around him. In that orientation, he seems to act as a unified
whole, not merely as a muscular, a mental, a social, or an emotional system.

The meaning
of personality

When we use the term personality here, we include such traits
and characteristics as honesty, aggressiveness, tenacity, and dependence, since these are important qualities that vary from one
child to another. However, we also include the processes by
which a child comes to organize his unique orientation to himself
and to his world of people and things. It is this aspect, rather
than the emergence of specific traits, which forms the central
issue of this chapter.

The word *persona* as used in ancient Rome referred to a
theatrical mask, from which was derived the notion of one's *appearance* as the central aspect of personality. This implies more
than "looks" and "clothes" of course, and includes the notion that

a person adopts a mask of behavior in order to present a view of himself to the world, or to present himself in a certain light.

Another key element in historical definitions of personality includes the concept of the *role* played by the individual or, more correctly, the complex of many roles a child learns to play in relation to the objects and people which form his world. Finally, personality has sometimes been conceptualized not as the mask or the role, but as the *actor himself*—the individual who wears the mask and plays the roles.

As analyzed by Bronfenbrenner and Ricciuti (1960), child personality includes three major elements: (1) the ways in which a child responds, (2) his motives, and (3) the way he stimulates other people. The first two aspects, response tendencies and motives, refer to dispositions toward action on the part of the child himself. The third, stimulus characteristics, refers to tendencies to bring out responses in others. John is physically competitive and combative, and elicits defensive reactions in other children. Sally is dependent: she clings to mother or teacher; avoids other children; and brings out nurturant, supportive responses from adults. Susan is task-oriented, and seems to need other people only to assist her in dealing with the physical world when problems arise; but her autonomous, somewhat aloof attitude does not elicit warm personal responses from children or adults.

This suggests rather well, in broad outline, the scope of our problem. If we are to understand personality development in the early years, we must consider how a child achieves his unique ways of responding, his peculiar system of motives, and his characteristic ways of affecting other people. We must also understand that these three features interact with each other and reinforce the development of a unique pattern or combination of features, which is the total child.

In the Midcentury White House Conference on Children and Youth, the concept of personality was employed to include ideas derived from psychology, sociology, physiology and psychiatry: "We mean by personality the thinking, feeling, acting human being who, for the most part, conceives of himself as an individual separate from other individuals and objects. This human being does not *have* a personality; he *is* a personality" (Witmer and Kotinsky 1952, p. 3). This statement makes an important distinction. The popular notion of a person as having, or acquiring, or losing, or strengthening something called personality, misses the central point in its confusion of personality with likableness, popularity, or attractiveness. Rather than thinking of an individual as "having" such characteristics and equating these with personality, we must focus on the self—the organic and psychological individual who *is* a personality.

The White House Conference definition also stresses the self-awareness aspect of personality, noting as it does the individual's consciousness of self as a separate being. The self-concept, a subject of much interest to child development specialists, might be thought of as including the elements of awareness of one's own identity and, at the same time, a set of value judgments about the worth of that person. Thus the self-concept has intellectual components, including one's understanding of who he is; it has affective or feeling components, such as feelings of pride or shame in who one is; and it includes motivational components, such as striving to become competent in a skill in order to identify oneself as one who can perform certain valued tasks. As a child achieves a clearer notion of self, that notion, or self-concept, becomes an important determiner of his level of aspiration, and of the quality of his interaction with the objects and people in his world.

The course of development of selfhood

The achievement of selfhood is not a simple, direct growth process. It involves continuous movement between assertions and questioning, between thrusting ahead and retreating, between pushing and hauling on the environment, and being pushed and driven by the forces of one's world. Jersild describes the overall process in powerful language that brings out the complexity and paradoxical qualities of self-development:

Each child strives to be himself, to realize his own resources, to come into his own. In other words he strives for selfhood. But while the self shows a powerful impetus to grow, it also, as part of its essential character, has a strong resistance to change.

This is the paradox of the self: It is a changing, growing phenomenon, and it comes into existence by a process of learning, yet it also is strongly geared to prevent change. It is both flexible and rigid. From the time when the child begins to become aware of himself, and to take thought of who and what he is and begins to have attitudes regarding himself, he is constantly in the process of expanding his perception of who and what he is, and he is constantly involved in experiences that might help to revise or redefine his conception of who he is or might be. Yet from an early age he also is eager to preserve whatever concept of himself he then may have, and he may strongly resist anything that might threaten to change it. (Jersild 1954b, p. 32)

This point of view on self development is parallel with the philosophy expressed by Lecky (1956) in his description of the development of personality. For Lecky there is one major drive, or goal, of all human striving. This objective is the achievement and maintenance of self-consistency. It is an internal self condition in which the various self operations are harmoniously allied one with another, without serious discrepancies or conflicts among them. Personality disturbance, or poor psychological health, in this point of view, is essentially an inability to maintain harmony and consistency among the components of one's self.

Growth, according to Jersild (1954b), is not just a pleasant series of steps forward. Every step ahead is accompanied by certain threats, risks, and inherent dangers. When the infant learns to walk, he achieves not only the grand possibility of getting himself around on his own two feet under his own power, but also a higher level of capacity for getting into trouble. With each new achievement there are new threats blended with the advantages, and new hazards combined with new powers. This means that each step in growth carries a double implication: it is significant in its own right as an accomplishment by a child, but in addition it is significant for the manner in which a child resolves the balance of forces between the "good feelings of achievement" and the "fear of the hazards." There is a constantly shifting balance between the positive forces striving for growth, achievement, increase in productivity, creativity, and positive action on the one hand, and the conservative forces demanding safety, security, and satisfaction with the status quo on the other.

Normally, the net effect of these two general forces is a balance in favor of growth, or forward progress. But there is, in normal growth, an irregularity in the speed of forward progress. The whole pattern of the achievement of selfhood is marked by spurts ahead, then slower periods of doubt and questioning and consolidation of one's resources in preparation for the next movement ahead.

One of the effects of this balancing of forces in the child's total effort to achieve selfhood is the development of ambivalence about his own growth. It is as if, in every normal child, there are really two "selves." There is one that wants to be big, strong, independent, achieving, productive, expansive, and self-actualizing. And there is the other that wants to be small, protected, dependent, secure, and nurtured by the strength of others. The first seeks responsibility, the second seeks security. The first joyously enters into relationships with the world of people and things; the second seeks to protect itself against threats from people and things. The first demands new experiences and novelty; the second demands the assurance of sameness and predictability.

The distinction is well illustrated in the following two incidents, which occurred in the normal routines of two children in the process of adjusting to school. Both were girls, 3 years of age. The first, Christine, was being taken to school one morning by her father. She was riding in the back seat of the car, when suddenly her father realized that she had gotten down off the seat and was crouched low on the floor of the car. "Where's my girl?" he teased. "Doesn't she want to look outside and see all the pretty things?" The child's muffled answer was not forceful in volume, but it carried a powerful insight: "Sometimes the pretty world is too big to look at."

Christine had made an excellent adjustment to school; she was never reluctant to go or to stay, or to let her mother or father leave her there. The balance of positive, outgoing, self-developmental forces in her life was favorable and she involved herself with apparent enthusiasm in the activities of the school. Nevertheless, even for this girl there were times when the whole world looked too big, and the wish to shut some of it out and protect oneself from the bigness of it all asserted itself.

The other incident involved Anita, who had also made a reasonably positive adjustment to school as a 3-year-old. After getting into the car after a busy, strenuous morning in school, Anita and her father started toward home. The teacher had mentioned to Anita's father before they left that the girl had been taking a more mature social role in school of late, and that this morning in particular she had been working and playing very productively with the other children. But as they drove home, Anita, who was riding on the front seat next to her father, leaned her head over onto his knee and sighed "I want to go home and be Mommy's baby." Then she put her thumb in her mouth and closed her eyes. She had been a grown-up school girl for about as long as she could manage that day.

Both of these incidents reveal the dual nature of the striving for selfhood during the early years. It is the desire to be big and the desire to be little at the same time. It demands that reasonable adults understand both of these wishes and provide an accepting environment in which the balance of forces will be generally favorable for growth. But this favorable balance is achieved, in part, through full acceptance of the reality of the conflict within the child, and the normality of the immature behavior that results at times from the wish to be secure, protected, nurtured by others, and free of the responsibilities of being big.

Such behaviors as crying, whining, clinging, throwing tantrums, showing jealous reactions, engaging in aggressive and hostile behavior, being unwilling to share, and even losing established controls such as sphincter control might be viewed as manifestations of this conflict. Adults who recognize the source of such behaviors, and can understand them without being disturbed or overly concerned by their presence, are likely to place them in proper perspective and not give them undue attention. The fortunate child who is not punished for the existence of his wish to be little, but whose efforts to be big are met with positive support and reinforcement, seems more likely to achieve a healthy balance between the two forces operating within himself.

The writings of Erikson (1950, 1953) stimulated an important approach to the understanding of self-development. Erikson's point of view, which is based on psychoanalytic theory, attempts to outline stages in the development of personality beginning with infancy and extending through the adult years. At each of the eight major stages in personal development there is a kind of crisis in which the balance of positive, growth-producing forces and negative, handicapping forces is for a time in question. The successful accomplishment of certain psychological objectives at any stage is essential to smooth progress through that stage and provides a foundation for further personality development.

Like most of the current approaches to personality development, this approach has strong implications for the role of early childhood in the achievement of adult personality. In Chapter Four we noted Erikson's emphasis on the importance of infancy as a time of establishing a firm sense of trust as a foundation for all further personality growth. The issue, or crisis, of the infantile stage is in the balance of trust vs. basic mistrust, the latter represented by excessive doubts that the world is safe and nurturant. A sense of trust, for Erikson, is based on the ability to predict the continuity and regularity of satisfaction of basic needs. It grows out of regular experiences with the everyday routines of infancy—sleeping, eating, eliminating, being warm and comfortable, and being in close bodily contact with a loving mother. The accumulation of successful, need-satisfying experiences around these everyday routines builds in the infant an assumption that such experiences will continue, and can be depended upon.

Figure 9.1 helps to explain the nature of the relationship envisioned by Erikson between trust and later stages in the development of selfhood. "Trust" is not a stage that is fully accomplished at any particular point in development. In one sense it persists as an issue right on through childhood and into the adult years.

First stage (about first year)	BASIC TRUST	Earlier form of AUTONOMY	Earlier form of INITIATIVE
Second stage (about second and third years)	Later form of BASIC TRUST	AUTONOMY	Earlier form of INITIATIVE
Third stage (about fourth and fifth years)	Later form of BASIC TRUST	Later form of AUTONOMY	INITIATIVE

FIGURE 9.1 A diagrammatic representation of the interaction among stages in healthy personality development in infancy and the preschool years. (From E. H. Erikson, "Growth and Crises of the Healthy Personality," in M. Senn, ed., *The Healthy Personality; Supplement II: Problems of Infancy and Childhood,* Transactions of the Fourth Conference on Infancy and Childhood, New York: Josiah Macy, Jr., Foundation, 1950, pp. 91–146.)

But the diagram is intended to show that the sharp features of the crisis of trust vs. basic mistrust will have been resolved and the issues decided, with the balance relatively stabilized and the child's personal balance in the issue established as he moves out of infancy into the early years of childhood.

The sense of autonomy

By the time a child gets up on his own feet and begins to take physical steps in the exploration of his world, he enters a crisis stage described by Erikson under the heading of *autonomy vs. shame and doubt.* As children progress through their second year what seems to matter most is to try out their own capabilities, their personal resources, and to see how far these resources will take them in their expanding world of people and things. Parents of toddlers describe a wide (and sometimes wild!) array of behavior and misbehavior with seemingly countless variations —but these are variations on one central theme: the discovery of the possibilities and limits of his control of himself and his world. What he seems to be doing and saying suggests that he wants complete freedom and independence. It is more likely that what he is after is freedom (and a resulting sense of personal autonomy) within reasonable and consistent limits.

To be a real person at this stage seems to require a sphere or domain within which a child has personal control of himself and his body, and where his decisions count for something. Saying "No!" is, of course, one of the characteristics of this stage, and expresses his concern over the issue of who is in charge of his life.

There is a risk, according to Erikson, in shaming a child into being good in order to avoid the inevitable conflicts of this stage, many of which revolve around basic routines of eating, sleeping, and eliminating (especially the establishment of bowel and bladder control). In the case of toilet training, for example, rigid demands that the toddler conform to adult expectations about time, place, facilities, clothing, cleanliness, and so on fail to consider the child's emerging sense of management of his own body functions. Such natural human functions as elimination can, in those circumstances, become an artificial source of a prolonged power struggle between parent and child, with all parties losing in the process. But the chief loser is the child, whose experiences during this critical period lead to an overwhelming sense of shame, whose attitudes toward such normal functions become confounded with doubts about himself as a worthy human being and as a person whose essential integrity is respected.

But the young child is still very much under the influence of the earlier crisis of trust vs. basic mistrust. Freedom to make decisions, then, must be tempered with reasonable limits, which let a child know where he stands. Limits to autonomy appear to be not only compatible with, but are also essential to, complete development of trust.

One way to understand this is to consider the child who is given too much freedom on the assumption that if a little freedom is good then a lot must be that much better! Such a child finds himself confronted with a world too large, too complex, and too threatening to handle, and this includes the handling of the impulses that arise from within, as well as the threats from the outside world. Too much freedom may threaten his confidence both in his world and in his ability to cope with it and make good decisions about it.

The sense of initiative

If the crisis in autonomy is a chief issue with the child between ages 1 and 3, the crisis in *initiative vs. guilt* characterizes the life of the 3-, 4-, and 5-year-old. As the term *initiative* implies, this stage is concerned with plans, ideas, imagination, and action. Sometimes the action is a bit uncontrolled and may tend to go out of bounds. But a child feels good about the person he is to the extent that his plans and ideas count for something. He has already established himself as a person with some autonomy, and now he is working hard to discover *what kind of person* that self can be.

This is also a time of questioning: "What can I do? What can I make of this self I have discovered and established as a separate identity? What can I be? What can I become?" All this means that there is a good deal of fantasy and imagination mixed up with the real world of people and things. By the time a child is 4 he has mental maturity to discern great possibilities in the world—for doing, for being and becoming—and some of these can be frightening to the child himself.

The 4-year-old has such a fluid imagination that he can "be," within a very short space of time, a tiger; a bunny; a wild, charging horse; and a big strong man brave enough to tame the tiger, skillful enough to ride the horse, and nurturant enough to protect the bunny. In the incredibly fluid imagery of the 4-year-old there is more happening than merely pretending or playing a part. He is living through the intense feelings associated with discovering, in his own fantasy, the kind of person he can be. By making all these feelings a part of himself, he is discovering modes of operation by which he can incorporate them into a total, growing self.

One key to the nature of the child's strivings at this stage is his creative action of all kinds. Through drawing; dancing and other rhythmic activities; dressing up and playing parts; through creating roles with other children and living them out in tea-parties, doll-play, and so forth; and through all manner of building, constructing, and reconstructing, the child is exploring the world of possibilities as to what he can do and be. At the same time, he is integrating his feelings about all the exciting things that are opening up to him.

The failure to achieve some semblance of a sense of initiative results, in its most tragic form, in an overwhelming sense of guilt. Again, we should stress that these are not "all or none" matters; there are undoubtedly signs of guilty feelings in every healthy child. But what Erikson is describing is a healthy balance between the freedom to explore one's world and the crippling, inhibiting effects of extreme guilt.

This is an age when conscience is developing, and the child is vulnerable to adult efforts to organize his conscience too soon and too completely. The child can be made to feel guilty about too many things with all too little effort on the part of well-meaning adults. Guidance and discipline techniques that rely primarily on shaming, or forcing, the child to think less well of himself on account of his behavior, imagination, or productions work against the achievement of a positive sense of self.

Erikson (1953) suggests that such adult behaviors as over-doing, overcompensating, overachieving, and never feeling satisfied with oneself as a person may stem from the guilty feelings arising during this period that conscience is developing. Ideally, the child's fantasies and productions are understood and accepted, and need not result in an excessive burden of guilt.

For Erikson, these initial stages of personality development form the foundation for the later emergence, during the school years, of a *sense of industry,* in which the chief concern is the development of tangible, working competencies. Subsequently, during adolescence one achieves a more or less integrated definition of who he is and what he believes in and stands for—a true *sense of identity.*

The critical stages per se, in this view, are defined by the very nature of man in his genetic potential; but the manner in which an individual child works through the crises is based on his special experiences, what he learns about himself, and how he defines himself at each point along the way. In the next section we will take a closer look at three areas, or types of tasks, in relation to which these learnings must occur.

Tasks in the achievement of selfhood

In the development of personality, or selfhood as we have chosen to call it, there are three fundamental types of tasks the child must master. They are not independent, of course, and the accomplishment of any one of these rests heavily on progress in the other two. Neither are they achieved in chronological sequence; they progress simultaneously.

The task of tool mastery

One essential task in the construction of a healthy sense of self may be described as mastery of the world of tools. In this task, the child's problem is to acquire skills that promote independence and allow him to function effectively and successfully in meeting his own needs, of whatever kind.

Tools come in all shapes, sizes, and varieties. Some of them are very tangible, such as, for example, play equipment, blocks, puzzles, dolls, climbing frames, swings, and slides. Such items as shovels, rakes, and hammers obviously fit this category. But other kinds of tools are far less tangible, such as the social customs that people use to enable them to make and maintain successful relationships with others—the folkways and mores described by sociologists and anthropologists. Language is such a tool, and a highly significant one. In fact, it might be argued that of all the tools a young child learns to use, none is more essential to his personality growth than that of language.

Tools may be thought of as implements for achieving essential control over the environment, and it is this ability to control or cope with the environment which represents the major challenge. Mastery of tools implies more than the immediate satisfaction gained by successful operation of some particular implement; it extends into one's attitudes toward self as more or less able to cope with whatever situations and circumstances arise.

The feeling of competence in use of the typical tools of both the home and school setting yields a further benefit of confident entry into and willingness to try to cope with each new challenge as it arises. Thus it relates both to the sense of autonomy and the sense of initiative previously described.

The task of interpersonal competence

The second central task of the growing personality is that of learning to live successfully in a world of other people. It is, in essence, the task of social adjustment. For the young child, this involves a rapidly expanding awareness of the individuality of others, both children and adults, and an acceptance of the reality of the needs of others. It involves a wide range of skills in interaction, including the language skills and nonverbal communication skills, which allow the child to deal with the feelings, attitudes, and needs of others as well as the intellectual content of things said or implied by others. It includes the development of a degree of sympathy and feeling for others, the ability to wait one's turn, and the readiness to postpone one's own immediate satisfaction for the greater satisfaction of being socially valued (liked) by others.

But living successfully in a world of others implies more than just yielding to them or being self-effacing with respect to one's personal interests. It implies learning to use one's resources and the resources of a social group for the sake of cooperative effort of all kinds. It implies awareness of the values of team action, or cooperative behavior, and the recognition that there are certain satisfactions to be gained from successful articulation of one's personal concerns with the well-being of others. The notion of social competence, and the key settings, institutions, and resources which support its development in the young child, will be the central theme of Part IV of the book.

The combined tasks of self-acceptance and self-regulation

The third major task of self-development involves learning to live productively with the impulses that arise from within oneself. There are two main features to this task: (1) acceptance of the reality and validity of all aspects of oneself, and (2) acceptance of the primary responsibility for one's own actions.

There are powerful feelings, intense drives, conflicts, doubts, and questions that stem from within the child. There are barriers and constraints as well as goads to action in the external environment. Numerous child development specialists have stressed the importance of helping a child live with himself by helping him accept the normality of his own feelings and impulses and responses to external events.

Learning to live with self includes the realistic understanding that one's feelings and impulses do exist, along with the realities of the external world, and that the experience of frustration is normal and inevitable. Learning to live with self also implies the expanding awareness of one's resources for coping with reality—the recognition of one's strengths and capabilities as well as the more or less negative feelings and impulses, which require direction and control.

Because the task of living harmoniously and productively with self is really the central challenge to the emerging personality, we will examine some of its features in greater detail. In addition to defining oneself with a balance of *big* and *little* self characteristics, these include incorporating emotional behavior into the self-concept, constructing an integrated motivational system, and defining oneself acceptably as male or female.

In all of these aspects of learning to live with oneself, the psychological process of *identification* seems to be at work in the young child. Some authorities hold that this is nothing more than imitation learning; others regard it more dynamically as the process of taking into one's own personality certain qualities or characteristics of the personality of another person. In its most obvious form it has the appearance of simple imitation: the 2-year-old who walks the way his father walks; the 4-year-old who dresses up like her mother in high-heeled shoes, long skirt, fur piece, and hat and carries an impressive handbag; the young child bathing a doll and putting it to bed with a bottle in obvious imitation of maternal behaviors; the use of certain words and certain voice inflections by a child in evident imitation of speech mannerisms of important adults—all reveal imitative behavior of young children. It was such imitative behavior, no doubt, that gave rise to the despairing comment of one father who observed "My son is becoming so much like me that it's . . . well, it's *frightening!*"

But to some authorities, the notion of identification implies a process somewhat more complicated than the merely external behaviors which take on the appearance of the behavior of others. It also implies incorporating aspects of the personality of the "model" into one's own personality, thereby absorbing the values, the concerns, the attitudes, and the general orientation of the model into oneself, and making them his own values, concerns, and general orientation. It is an idea, for example, that has been used to explain the development of conscience, which might be thought of as the child's internalization of the values of others through identification with them. Conscience development appears to be heightened through identification with powerful persons, or with persons who control rewards and punishments in the child's life—usually the parents. We will examine this notion more carefully in a later chapter on the child and his family.

Emotional aspects of self-development

When we speak of affective, or emotional behavior, we are referring to (1) the physiological changes in the body that accompany emotion (changes in circulation, respiration, glandular activity, and so on), (2) changes in observable behavior (laughing, crying, fighting, running away, being "silly" or "moody," and so on), and (3) changes in the conscious experience of emotion (feeling sad or feeling elated, for example). Any given emotional experience involves all three levels.

The distinction among the three can be kept in mind by noting that the first level can be measured with sensitive electronic instruments, while the second can be observed simply by watching a child. The third level is available only to the individual experiencing the emotion. Our understanding of the development of personality must include an understanding of the ways a child learns to deal with all three of these levels of emotional behavior.

The infant is born with the capacity for emotional behavior, which, although limited, vague, and general at first, gradually becomes more specific and definite. The senses, muscles, glands, and nervous system are the resources necessary for emotional behavior. Part of understanding the individual child is a matter of understanding what events and circumstances are likely to activate these resources.

Anger, for example, is a normal human response to frustration. However, not all children respond in the same angry way to the same frustrating external situation. Some of the differences in children's responses to being blocked, or thwarted, might reflect differences in self-concept, in the form of differing numbers of alternatives available to a child. That is, the child who is frustrated by a parent who prevents him from scribbling on the walls may be less angry if he perceives other alternatives, such as scribbling on a cardboard carton, thus defining himself as one who is capable of substituting acceptable behaviors for unacceptable ones. The child who does not perceive such substitute behaviors as being accessible to him, or within his competencies, may be more likely to express strong anger in the same situation.

Anger can also serve to illustrate another dimension of relatedness between the self-concept and emotional behavior. The child who repeatedly wins concessions from adults or other children as a result of angry behavior is more likely to "learn to be angry" as his typical mode of interaction with others. Conversely, the child who is not rewarded for angry behavior is less likely to resort to anger as his standard means of attempting to influence the behavior of others or to deal with frustrating events.

Anger reactions typically change with age, as was revealed in a classic research study conducted by Goodenough (1931). Incidents involving anger were recorded in detail by parents. Among children under 1 year of age, one-fourth of the incidents developed in connection with some child care routine such as dressing or bathing. Another fourth related to minor physical discomforts. Only 6 percent were based on a direct restriction of bodily movement. With 2-year-olds, the establishment of routine physical habits was the basis for a large proportion of anger responses, and a second major cause of anger was conflict with persons in authority. Social relationships were becoming the source of angry responses by age 2. By age 4, much anger was observed to be directed toward specific objects that became the target of the child's frustration.

Some anger responses may be thought of as essentially defensive—designed to protect a somewhat fragile self-image. In children as well as adults, the person who is most certain of who he is and most confident of his own personal resources, is less likely to have to defend his self-image through angry retaliation against perceived threats.

An important feature of anger is that the angry child (or adult!) may be unaware of the reasons for his feelings, and may even have learned that it is "not nice" to be angry. This latter bit of learning can be critical, because a child may be forced to regard himself as a "not nice" person to the extent that he has angry feelings. His task of achieving an integrated, accepting, positive view of himself is thus made more difficult. One of the challenges to adults is to deal with a child's angry behavior, accepting it as natural, without encouraging him to develop anger as a standard habit, or making him feel unworthy or inferior for having these feelings.

Fear and anxiety are also normal emotional responses of early childhood, representing the child's "emergency response system." Anxiety is defined by Berger (1971) as ". . . the effect or feeling that follows upon the perception of danger, be it real or imagined." Berger notes that fear and anxiety involve the same physiological changes and feelings; hence distinctions between the two are not really important.

Any situation that can be conceived as a potential source of danger may serve as a fear stimulus to a child. In infancy, responses that have all the earmarks of fear have been noted frequently. The conditions that cause them include sudden changes of physical position; loss of support; or sudden, intense stimulation of most any sensory modality.

Fear of strange persons, objects, and situations often appear in the latter half of the first year. Valentine (1930) observed many years ago that things which may not ordinarily arouse fear may do so in the presence of unusual, novel, or strange situations. Fears of the strange and unfamiliar may be explained partly on the grounds that an individual has no prepared way of responding, thus creating uncertainty and anxiety. Seen in relation to the self-concept, this implies that one's definition of self as competent to respond in the face of new stimuli may reduce the anxiety level. Healthy emotional development includes the gradual, orderly expansion of the child's sphere of living, with sufficient support from familiar outside resources (parents, siblings, friends, and teachers) to carry a child through in the face of immediate threats and, more importantly, to reinforce in the child the notion that he can respond in a positive way when such threats arise.

Certain kinds of fear reactions in children have long held special interest for parents, teachers, and researchers alike. Among these are fears of the dark, of pain or injury, of animals, and of imaginary creatures. These fears show developmental trends in that they are more likely to be found in children of one age than another. From birth to about 6 years, fears of noise and of strange objects, situations and persons ordinarily decline in frequency, while fears of imaginary creatures, being alone and/ or in the dark, animals, and threat or danger of harm, traffic, and so on tend to increase in frequency (Jersild 1954a).

Some of these developmental changes seem to be related to intellectual development, that is, to a child's increasing awareness of the threat potentials of some situations while at the same time awareness of lack of danger in other situations previously perceived as threatening.

It is never easy to determine just where the line is between the normal fears of childhood and the abnormal, pathological fears of the seriously disturbed child. Dreams and nightmares, for example, are common and do not, by themselves, indicate serious disturbance. However, if a child's health is being impaired through loss of sleep resulting from fear of his own dreams, we may be dealing with a problem serious enough to warrant professional treatment.

More frequently, however, parental acceptance and understanding of the normality of fear in children's lives is the only treatment required. Such acceptance and understanding makes it less likely that parents will resort to punishing a child who shows fearfulness, or ridiculing him for expressing fear. Such negative approaches to a child's emotional behavior complicate his personal growth task, making it difficult for him to think well of himself.

Other emotions, too, enter into the process of building the self-concept, including emotions of joy, love, affection, and jealousy. The continuously fluctuating evaluation of self in which the child engages is much less a conscious intellectual activity than it is a set of feelings, often mixed and ambivalent, about himself and his status in the world.

Motivational aspects of selfhood

The question of motivation is the "why?" question of human behavior. For the serious student, it is more than a matter of "What makes ——— behave the way he does?" and includes the very fundamental issues of why a child "behaves" at all, and why his behavior undergoes revisions over time. For the psychologist, an understanding of the causes of behavior has long been a central issue.

Traditionally, we have believed that behavior is motivated by the need to reduce tension associated with some drive. One eats when hungry, for example, to reduce the tension associated with the hunger drive. We also thought of these drives as being innate, as in the case of hunger and other biological drives, or acquired through association with these innate drives. Thus we thought of the social drives as secondary motives, learned by association with the processes of meeting biological needs. In either case, we assumed that drives function to increase tension, and action (behavior) is the response of the person aimed at reducing the tension.

But as Hunt (1960) and White (1959) have shown, there is ample evidence that we are also motivated toward excitement and novelty, and not merely toward freedom from tension. White observes, for example, "We may seek rest and minimal stimulation at the end of the day, but that is not what we are looking for the next morning. Even when its primary needs are satisfied and its homeostatic chores done, an organism is alive, active, and up to something" (White 1959, p. 302).

The newer concepts of motivation, as described by Hunt, White, and others suggests an interesting circular relationship between experience and motivation, which might lead to some such hypothesis as this: *A rich variety of experiences in an approving, reinforcing context leads to the emergence of a richer set of motives to undertake further new experiences.* We might hypothesize further the existence of some sort of intervening variable, the self-concept, as the quality that is enhanced by successful experiences, and which in turn mediates efforts toward new experiences.

Thus, if the initial motivation for novelty is reinforced, the resulting increased probability of involvement with new experiences might be accounted for by the enhanced image of himself, which a child derives as an accompaniment to the satisfaction of the curiosity motive. Such a hypothesis, if supported, would have strong implications for the role of early experience in the development of achievement motivation. This would be particularly true for children whose experiences may not be accompanied by consistent positive reinforcement in the normal course of events.

Defining oneself as male or female

The emergence of a masculine or feminine personality is a complex issue, itself the topic of numerous books and research articles. It cannot be accounted for solely by the biological differences between the sexes, nor simply by the differences in treatment of girls and boys in a society. It illustrates, once again, the interaction of biological with cultural forces in shaping one of the central features of personality—one's notion of self as masculine or feminine.

This personality feature has begun to emerge very strongly by the age of 4 or 5 years. As Brown (1956) has pointed out, young children respond differently to standardized tests of sex-appropriate behaviors, depending on their sex. More subjectively, teachers of young children frequently observe different types of activity characteristic of boys and girls, when children are given a free choice. Their distinctive choices of free play activities appear, in part, to reflect differences in the models they employ in the identification process. That is, girls' greater frequency of domestic play activities and boys' preoccupation with games representing the world of work outside the home are undoubtedly a reflection of the tendency of girls and boys to identify with their mothers and fathers, respectively.

One kind of behavior thought to be learned at least partially through the process of identification is that of aggression. Hartup and Himeno (1959) found that among nursery age children, following brief periods of social isolation, boys exhibit more aggressiveness than girls in doll play. Furthermore, research findings support the common observation that boys differ from girls with respect to overtly aggressive behavior. This difference between the sexes has been corroborated in many investigations. Even older children themselves regard boys as being more aggressive than girls (Gill and Spilka 1962). In controlled studies of the imitative behavior of young children, boys were found to imitate physically aggressive behavior of adults more than girls (Bandura, Ross, and Ross 1961).

From a very early age, children appear to recognize aggressiveness as being "appropriate" for males and "inappropriate" for females. Bandura (1967) employed adult models of both sexes, both "live" and on film, to portray aggressive acts to young children. Boys, especially, made comments about the behavior of the aggressive female model, such as "That's no way for a lady to behave. Ladies are supposed to act like ladies."

Bandura noted further that the sex differences in aggressive behavior resulting from imitation appear to depend on the differential rewards which children perceive to be associated with aggressiveness. When these rewards were experimentally manipulated in such a way that both boys and girls recognized a "payoff" for aggressiveness, then both boys and girls, to the same degree, acquired aggressive behaviors through imitation.

This suggests that it is a pervasive characteristic of our society to reward boys for aggressive behavior to a much greater degree than girls. The implications of such a conclusion are far-reaching, indeed, for a theory of personality development. It would seem, for example, that the self-concept of a girl who adapts herself to our kind of society would incorporate such "statements" as "I respond to frustration with behaviors other than direct, overt aggression," while the self-concept of the boy is much more likely to incorporate such "statements" as "I respond to frustration with directly aggressive acts." If one of these statements is "appropriate" for girls, and the other for boys, the further question arises as to the adjustment problems of the individual child who is unable to incorporate the appropriate statement. The boy, for example, who is nonaggressive may, in effect, be punished by a society that defines his behaviors as "effeminate"! The girl, however, is more likely to be punished for assertiveness.

Aggression, of course, is not the only kind of behavior assumed to differentiate males and females in our society. The traditional cluster of behaviors deemed appropriate for the two sexes has been summarized by Kagan as follows:

> . . . females are supposed to inhibit aggression and open display of sexual urges, to be passive with men, to be nurturant of others, to cultivate attractiveness, and to maintain an affective, socially poised, and friendly posture with others. Males are urged to be aggressive in face of attack, independent in problem situations, sexually aggressive, in control of regressive urges, and suppressive of strong emotions, especially anxiety. (Kagan 1964, p. 143)

There are signs that such traditionally stereotyped definitions of sex-appropriate behaviors and attitudes may be undergoing challenge and revision in today's society, which verbalizes another value partly in conflict with tradition: *freedom from the constraints of sexual inequality.* The long-term implications of such cultural change for the personality development of individual children can only be surmised, but among the potential benefits there might be mentioned the increased social awareness that aggressiveness appears to be a learned behavior, and that it is learned in part as a function of the child's efforts to cope with society's stress of sex-appropriate behaviors. A weakening of such a stereotype could conceivably lead to less "payoff" for aggressiveness on the part of the male child.

Stability and self-consistency of personality

One of the perennial questions of interest in child development is that of the relationship betwen personality in infancy and early childhood with that of later childhood and the adult years. To what extent is it safe to assume that fundamental personality changes may occur after the early years? To what extent is it correct to assume that the personality is so well established by age 5 or 6 that no significant changes may be brought about later?

The common belief that personality characteristics are well established by age 6 was given considerable support in the conclusion by Bloom (1964) that the "half-developed age" (when 50 percent of the variance for individual differences is fixed, or stabilized) is about age 3 for males in aggressive tendencies, about age 4 for females in dependency behavior, and about age 4 for intellectuality for both sexes.

Other authorities (for example, Emmerich 1967) are more cautiously optimistic that basic personality attributes might remain "open" to significant changes over much longer, extended periods of development. Emmerich notes, for example, that a trait that has stabilized in early childhood does not necessarily remain stable into the adult years, or even into the years of later childhood. Some well-designed investigations support the notion that even though early personality formation certainly is critical, it would be unwarranted to conclude that personality is so fixed by a given age, say 6, as to preclude further basic revision of the self.

In the Berkeley Growth Study, for example, Schaefer and

Bayley (1963) concluded that emotional adjustment during the first two years (for example, happy, calm, positive behavior) was not always the forerunner of comparably positive emotional adjustment in later childhood. In that study, extensive ratings of such behaviors as responsiveness to persons, positive behaviors, and calmness were rated frequently for the same children from ages 10 months to 18 years. The usefulness of ratings at any age to predict behavior at a later age decreased significantly as the time between ratings increased.

Moss and Kagan (1964) have summarized an extensive amount of longitudinal data on children with respect to this question of stability of personality over time. Their subjects were 36 males and 35 females of the Fels Longitudinal Study, in which ratings were made for aggression, achievement, and passive-dependent behavior during four childhood periods. The subjects were also rated independently as adults. There was a significant correlation between aggressive behavior in childhood and adult years for males, but not for females. By contrast, passive-dependent behavior in childhood and adult years correlated significantly for females but not for males. Childhood achievement behaviors were predictive of analogous behaviors in adults for both sexes.

Specifically, in that study, "aggression toward mother" between ages 3 and 6 correlated with "adult anger arousal" at a level of $r = .39$ for males, and $r = .10$ for females. "Behavioral disorganization" (that is, loss of control when frustrated) correlated with adult anger arousal at a level of $r = .35$ for males 0 to 3 years, and $r = .30$ for males 3 to 6 years. By comparison, the correlation coefficients for females at ages 0 through 3 and 3 through 6, respectively, were $r = .04$ and $r = .06$.

The authors concluded that the popular notion that personality characteristics are established in early childhood is a valid notion, although the specific areas of early stabilization of personality depend on the sex of the child.

Summary

The organization of personality in the early years involves meeting and resolving central crises. The early stages of life appear to be critical in the formation of the adult personality, in part because these early years result in the achievement of a concept of oneself as a unique person. This self-concept becomes a basis for defining appropriate behaviors and roles in relation to others in subsequent years, as the child strives to maintain a sense of continuity and self-consistency.

The basic tasks essential to healthy growth include mastery of the tool world; learning to live with others; and learning to accept one's own limitations, drives, impulses, and capabilities. Defining oneself requires a healthy acceptance of one's sex. Much of the development of personality occurs through the process of identification with significant adults. This central process is responsible for the development of conscience, a major variable in individual personality.

References

Bandura, A. "The Role of Modeling Processes in Personality Development." In Hartup, W., and Smothergill, N., eds. *The Young Child: Reviews of Research.* Washington, D.C.: National Association for the Education of Young Children, 1967, pp. 42–58.

Bandura, A., Ross, D., and Ross, S. A. "Transmission of Aggression Through Imitation of Aggressive Models." *Journal of Abnormal and Social Psychology* 63 (1961) 575–582.

Berger, A. S. "Anxiety in Young Children." *Young Children* 27 (1971) 5–11.

Bloom, B. S. *Stability and Change in Human Characteristics.* New York: Wiley, 1964.

Bronfenbrenner, U., and Ricciuti, H. N. "The Appraisal of Personality Characteristics in Children." In Mussen, P. H., ed. *Handbook of Research Methods in Child Development.* New York: Wiley, 1960, pp. 770–817.

Brown, D. G. "Sex-Role Preference in Young Children." *Psychological Monographs* 70 (1956).

Emmerich, W. "Stability and Change in Early Personality Development." In Hartup, W., and Smothergill, N., eds. *The Young Child: Reviews of Research.* Washington, D.C.: National Association for the Education of Young Children, 1967, pp. 248–261.

Erikson, E. H. *Childhood and Society.* New York: Norton, 1950.

———. "Growth and Crises of the Healthy Personality." In Kluckhohn, C., and Murray, H. A., eds. *Personality in Nature, Society, and Culture.* 2nd ed. New York, Knopf, 1953, pp. 185–225.

Gill, L. J., and Spilka, B. "Some Nonintellectual Correlates of Academic Achievement Among Mexican-American Secondary School Students." *Journal of Educational Psychology* 53 (1962) 144–149.

Goodenough, F. L. *Anger in Young Children.* Minneapolis: University of Minnesota Press, 1931.

Hartup, W., and Himeno, Y. "Social Isolation vs. Interaction with Adults in Relation to Aggression in Preschool Children." *Journal of Abnormal and Social Psychology* 59 (1959) 17–22.

Hunt, J. McV. "Experience and the Development of Motivation: Some Reinterpretations." *Child Development* 31 (1960) 489–504.

Jersild, A. T. "Emotional Development." In Carmichael, L., ed. *Manual of Child Psychology.* 2nd ed. New York: Wiley, 1954a.

———. *Child Psychology.* 4th ed. New York: Prentice-Hall, 1954b.

Kagan, J. "Acquisition and Significance of Sex Typing and Sex Role Identity." In Hoffman, M. L., and Hoffman, L. W., eds. *Review of Child Development Research.* Vol. 1. New York: Russell Sage Foundation, 1964, pp. 137–167.

Lecky, P. "The Personality." In Moustakas, C. E., ed. *The Self.* New York: Harper, 1956, pp. 86–97.

Moss, H., and Kagan, J. "Report on Personality Consistency and Change from the Fels Longitudinal Study." *Vita Humana* 7 (1964) 127–138.

Schaefer, E., and Bayley, N. "Maternal Behavior, Child Behavior, and their Intercorrelations from Infancy Through Adolescence." *Monographs Society for Research in Child Development* 28 (1963).

Valentine, C. W. "The Innate Bases of Fears." *Journal of Genetic Psychology* 37 (1930) 394–420.

White, R. W. "Motivation Reconsidered: The Concept of Competence." *Psychological Review* 66 (1959) 297–323.

Witmer, H. L., and Kotinsky, R., eds. *Personality in the Making.* New York: Harper, 1952.

PART IV
Agents
of
socialization

The previous parts of this book were intended to give a general introduction to the field of child development, to describe the nature and patterning of child growth, and to explore the various facets of development through infancy and the early years.

The primary objective of the remaining section is to examine the processes of child socialization; that is, the processes by which a child comes to use whatever resources lie at his command to relate himself effectively and productively to the world of people and things.

Many institutions and agencies of society participate in socializing the child by making contributions of varying degrees of significance. The child does not develop in a cultural or social vacuum, of course, but in a society rich with stimulating and inhibiting influences. It is the shaping forces of the child's society— particularly the cultural, familial, and educational forces—to which we now turn in an effort to understand the complex task confronting the child in his efforts to achieve selfhood.

CHAPTER TEN
The child's cultural heritage

What is meant by the term "culture"?

How does the concept of culture help us understand the development of personality?

How does child-rearing differ from one culture to another?

What important cultural differences exist *within* the United States?

How can conflicts and adjustment problems arise as a result of cultural inconsistencies?

$\mathbb{D}$uring 1971 the first official contacts were made between the Tasaday people and the outside world. The Tasaday tribe are a small group of people living in the interior of Southern Mindanao in the Philippine Islands and are believed to have been isolated from the rest of the world until June of 1971. They were "Stone Age" people in that their most advanced tools were a knife with a bamboo blade and a hammer of chipped stone bound with rattan to a wooden handle (National Geographic Magazine 1971).

When first contacted, the Tasadays knew nothing of the existence of other nations such as "The Philippines," and had no words in their primitive language for such concepts as "sea" or "boat." One can only speculate on the initial reaction of a Tasaday tribe member on being exposed to such complex cultural artifacts as watches, cameras, radios, television sets, plumbing, automobiles, flashlights, and firearms. One might speculate, also, that whatever a child needed in order to become a competent member of the Tasaday tribe could readily be learned through direct imitation of the adults, without the intervention of books, teachers, and classrooms.

The Tasaday people serve as a reminder of the comparative complexity of the cultural milieu of the typical American child. Such a tribe stands almost as a primitive baseline against which one might ponder the complexities of technological society, and consider the vast gulf separating the experiences of children who do not share the same culture. However, we should not make the mistake of confusing *culture* with *technology*, for they are not identical.

The meaning of culture

It is easier in some respects to say what culture *is not* than what it *is*. It is *not*, for example, something that some individuals possess or that some people or families *have* to a greater degree than others. And it is *not* something that can be transmitted biologically from one generation to the next. Sometimes culture has been defined as the *learned behavior of a people*. However, this is an abstract concept which refers only indirectly to the specific learnings of a given individual. Thus, while particular modes and themes pervade the art forms of a given society in the twentieth century, it would not be appropriate to say that a particular artist has more culture than someone with little or no interest in art. Each of these individuals is living and functioning in a society that holds cultural values and cultural techniques, including the values and techniques relating to art forms. Each is affected by the existence of these values and techniques.

Further, it can be demonstrated that a specific culture determines not only the variety of gadgets, modes of transportation, communication, economic matters, assorted customs, folkways and mores, not only style of dress and manner of speech, not only systems of expressing emotional involvement or lack of involvement, but also the most fundamental internal processes of the central nervous system: the content of one's thought, and the manner or style of one's thinking process.

Anthropologists, in making detailed observations of various societies, have noted that different groups living in different parts of the world have quite different ways of categorizing their experiences and of viewing their world. It has been observed, for example, that certain Alaskan Indian groups have in their language many nouns that represent the thing we label "snow." Because their economy and life-activities are so thoroughly and inevitably intertwined with snow in its various forms, their language in reference to snow is richer and more elaborate than ours. Thus, there is a noun that stands for each of many kinds of snow, and many nouns for conditions in which snow might be encountered. Similarly, the Arabian camel-driver has a large and rich vocabulary pertaining to the types of camels and the accessories and strategies associated with the care and use of camels. By contrast, the vocabulary of the Alaskan Indian and Arabian camel-driver concerning automobiles is probably quite limited compared with that of the typical American teen-age male.

The latter has been acculturated within a society which makes fine distinctions among sedans, wagons, convertibles, and hard-tops, which have either automatic or "stick" transmissions, with V-8 or six-cylinder engines mounted in the front or rear, and with or without air conditioning, which may or may not have been installed in the factory! Such fine distinctions would seem to offer little help or usefulness to either the Arabian camel-driver or the Alaskan Indian.

These differences in ways of categorizing experiences are the result not simply of difference in place, but of deeply differing points of view about the world. As Dorothy Lee (1956) has observed, there are fundamental differences in ways of thinking, which the languages of different societies provide for. Some societies are time-oriented, with events having significance in relation to past, present, or future. The language of such societies provides for this time orientation.

Other societies are much less time oriented and tend to value things and events in terms of present existence only. Events which we would regard as historical are viewed as a part of the existing state of affairs, or else they are not viewed as having any significance. When events are recounted, they are told without reference to chronological sequence, thus deemphasizing the element of time or history. Even events anticipated in the future have significance only insofar as they can be incorporated into the existing reality. The language of such a society is consistent with this kind of thinking.

Of greatest importance is the fact that every society defines ways of cataloguing experience, which must be learned by a child if he is to achieve competence for living in that society. The learning is part of his experience from cradle to grave—that is, if it happens that his culture uses cradles and graves! The learning becomes part of the child, and a vital force in shaping his personality, as stressed by the Fact-Finding Committee of the Mid-century White House Conference on Children and Youth:

> Culture is powerful and pervasive, changing the character of our biological drives, affecting our thinking, our emotions, and our perceptions. For example, there are distinct patterns of aggression, sibling rivalry, jealousy, loving, frustration, play, participation in

the different cultures. What was there before culture entered the picture? Are human beings jealous by nature? There are some polygynous societies where co-wives exhibit so much jealousy that a man has to apportion himself with care and tact. There are other polygynous societies where an only wife will taunt and nag her husband until he brings her a co-wife, with whom she then lives amicably. Is jealousy an inborn trait, which some cultures suppress effectively? Or is it a potentiality, fostered by some, atrophied by other cultures? (Witmer and Kotinsky 1952, p. 167)

Current thinking on the question raised by this quotation is that such traits of personality are primarily the products of social living, rather than innate human characteristics transmitted through biological inheritance. To the extent that this is true, our task becomes one of understanding the cultural forces and pressures that result in the development of certain traits and dispositions under some circumstances, and other traits and dispositions under differing circumstances.

To achieve a clearer perspective on the role of culture in the development of the child, a student may need to overcome two related tendencies: (1) to evaluate a society's culture in absolute terms, and (2) to assume that there is such a thing as "cultural neutrality." Failure in the first instance leads one to easy generalizations containing some truth but at the same time much error. The argument, for example, that our society is too competitive, and that we teach our children too insistently to become competitive, may have validity; but we should not overlook the fact that we have no absolute scale of the optimum, or "best" amount of competitiveness, which any society should instill in its children.

Depending on the values of a given society, competitiveness as a personal characteristic may be both very useful or very handicapping in one's ability to cope with the realities of that society. For example, it may require very different amounts and kinds of competitiveness to become a "success" in Middle Class America than in a traditional Hopi village in Arizona, but it is futile to argue that one of these societies is right and the other wrong in any absolute sense.

It is more helpful then to ask, not whether a given cultural practice is a good one in an absolute sense, but how one feature of the culture of a society is integrated with the total network of customs, practices, and values of the society. Even in instances in which cultural change would be a clear advantage to a primitive group—as, for example, learning to use more nutritious foods in children's diets, or learning to inoculate children against certain diseases—the validity of such changes must be measured also in relation to the emotional and religious significance of present customs.

Failure in the second instance may lead to another kind of error, that of assuming that it is possible to examine a given society, with whatever cultural characteristics it may possess, from some objective frame of reference which has no a priori value system, and which is therefore completely objective and scientifically dispassionate with respect to the cultural phenomena one is observing. The pitfalls of such an assumption are recognized when one understands that even the motivation to study a culture is, itself, a cultural artifact!

Even the language one might employ to aid his understanding of a culture is a cultural phenomenon. Such *ideas* as *culture,* and *cultural relativity,* are cultural phenomena. Again, we are better advised not to aspire to complete cultural "objectivity" or "neutrality" so much as to a deeper insight into the ways in which a culture is both cause and effect in the lives of members of a society.

One might conceptualize culture both as the outcome of the experience of a people, and at the same time, as the complex of forces representing the learned behavior of a people. These forces shape the specific behaviors and learnings of the individuals of a society.

Some central questions on the effects of culture on the child

Just how does culture influence the child's development? This general question can be answered, in part, with reference to somewhat more specific questions. Who is responsible for the care of the child? What is the place of a child in relation to family and to adults in the community? What behaviors are valued, and therefore reinforced, in children? What other behaviors are merely tolerated, and what behaviors are actively forbidden? What methods are typically employed, and by what members of a society, to reinforce desired child behaviors and to suppress forbidden behaviors?

What institutions are provided by a society, charged specifically with inducting a child into approved social roles, or with developing the competencies regarded as essential for successful adoption of approved social roles? In what manner does a society express and teach to its children such fundamental values and competencies as *concern with time, appropriate behaviors associated with maleness and femaleness, appropriate behaviors associated with older and younger ages, relative importance of logical thought and reasoning vs. affect, ritual, magic, taboo, and so on?*

Our assumption is that all societies, in order to survive, must have developed ways of dealing with basic realities of human existence: need for food, clothing, and shelter; provision for reproduction and care of dependent persons; some system of communication and provisions for exchange of goods and services; and so on. But that at the same time each of these aspects of human experience has a near-infinite variety of ways of more or less successful adaptation to the geography, climate, and resources available to a people.

Such questions as these could be used to illustrate wide ranges of cultural diversity, and the fact that there is no "one right way" of organizing the forces that participate in the socialization of a child. In each case, extensive documentation from many different societies could be brought to bear on the question, but brief examples only will be given here for illustrative purposes.

Who is responsible for care of child?

We tend to assume that the mother will be the primary caretaker and probably the primary socializing agent in the life of the infant and young child. There are societies, however, in which servants or nurses not biologically related to the child are retained for this purpose. The Trobriand Islanders assume that the child's maternal uncles will have a closer tie to the child, and more responsibility for his upbringing, than his father. In the Israeli kibbutz the child encounters many specialists who have more immediate concern for his care, upbringing, and socialization than his biological parents.

It is quite apparent that responsibility for care of the child is a cultural *variable,* and that assumptions made in a given society about the correctness of its assignment of this responsibility are not necessarily shared by other groups.

Position of child in relation to family and community

We tend to cherish childhood and value it for its own sake as a period of life having validity of itself, independent of what it may portend for the child's future. In some societies, however, a child may not even be regarded as essentially human until he ages beyond early childhood—say 5, 6, or 7 years.

Some societies place inordinately high value on an individual child because of his sex or family position (oldest, youngest, for example), at the expense of other features. In some societies, large families may still represent a cultural value, while in others large numbers of children are viewed with perhaps social disapproval. In any event, children are not viewed by adults in the same way in all societies.

Which behaviors are valued, which are tolerated, and which are forbidden?

Child behavior that is accepted and even encouraged in one society may be sharply curtailed or severely punished in another. One example of this is the varying attitudes of different social groups toward sexual curiosity and sex play on the part of children. In our own society sex play is severely curtailed and perhaps punished. In some societies it is humorously indulged by adults.

Numerous other examples of cultural variation on acceptable and unacceptable behaviors could be cited pertaining, for example, to manner of expressing aggressiveness, ways of showing deference to one's elders, respect for property of other persons, amount and kind of dependency behavior, etc. In some cases, what is acceptable behavior depends clearly on the age or sex of the child. In other cases the society takes little note of age or sex in prescribing appropriate behavior.

What methods are employed
to shape the behaviors of children?

Is desirable behavior given tangible rewards? Is undesirable behavior punished? If punishment is used, is it physical, such as spanking, or more "psychological," as in withdrawal of signs of love for the child? If verbal criticism or scolding is used, is it accompanied by verbal statements which define positive alternatives for undesirable behavior? Is the child given reasons or explanations for whatever discipline is used? Is the child's *status as a person* vulnerable if he fails to conform, or does his society make a sharp distinction between the acceptability of certain behaviors and his essential worthiness as a person? Are fear, shame, threats of dire consequences such as magical or supernatural events, and so forth regularly employed as a means of controlling behavior? All of these illustrate ways in which the means and strategies for socializing and regulating child behavior vary from one society to another.

To what extent is the socialization process institutionalized?

What are the specific experiences that teach a child what he must do, what he must not do, and what he must value if he is to be an acceptable member of his group? Are these experiences ritualized and attended with great ceremony and public recognition? Or are they almost unnoticed incidents along the way—experiences that blend into a total pattern of living, which gradually provide the child with a definition of acceptable and unacceptable behavior? Are they formalized, institutional training programs as in the American schools and churches and the Israeli kibbutzim? Or are they retained exclusively or primarily as the province of the immediate family?

In the preceding discussion, no attempt is made to evaluate practices or to show any relationship between a given practice and specific personality characteristics of children. Scientists who study culture are properly cautious about attributing personality characteristics to isolated practices. Intsead, they stress the total cultural context within which a given practice occurs, viewing cultural effects on the child as a more or less unbroken network of experiences, with a single practice being significant only in relation to this total set of practices, customs, and values.

Nevertheless, a keener insight into the nature of the child, and into the complex task of growing into a competent member of his society, may be achieved through examination of cultural practices of different groups. As we turn our attention to such an examination, we should again remind ourselves of the need for caution. It is a mistake to evaluate a culture (especially, perhaps, one's own culture!) in absolute terms.

It is also a mistake to assume that there is such a thing as cultural neutrality. Of necessity, we start from the position of human beings who are already socialized, with the terms and conditions of that socialization process having been determined by cultural events, values and expectations, and artifacts. We experienced these without participating in the decisions as to whether or not they would be part of our socialization process. Maturity of thinking about culture does not call for abandoning the effects of that socialization process; it calls for awareness of and sensitivity to its impact.

Major findings
from cross-cultural investigations

The student is also well-advised at the outset of this section to remember that comparisons of various cultures can result in a keener understanding of similarities, common themes, and "cultural constants" as well as cultural variation from one society to another. This point is well made in the following statement by two authorities, Whiting and Child:

> . . . Child training the world over is in certain respects identical
> . . . in that it is found always to be concerned with certain
> universal problems of behavior. Parents everywhere have similar
> problems to solve in bringing up their children. In all societies the

helpless infant, getting his food by nursing at his mother's breast
and having digested it, freely evacuating the waste products,
exploring his genitals, biting and kicking at will, must be changed
into a responsible adult obeying the rules of his society. . . . There
is no clear evidence in any case that any of these basic problems are
in fact absent from the life of any people. Child training everywhere
seems to be in considerable part concerned with problems which
arise from universal characteristics of the human infant and from
universal characteristics of adult culture which are incompatible
with the continuation of infantile behavior. (Whiting and Child
1953, pp. 63–64)

But even the primary group within which these universal problems are dealt with vary greatly from one society to another. For
example, Whiting (1966) presents data from the Six Cultures
Study, summarized in Table 10.1, giving a comparison of household and courtyard composition in six widely differing communities. In that study, "courtyard" refers to a domestic unit of
close interaction among members, but larger than the individual
household. It is clear from that data that the experiences of the
New England child in close contact with an average of five other
persons would have to differ from those of a Tarong child in
close contact with over 15 persons, on the average, just on the
basis of the sheer differences in the numbers of people involved.

It will also be seen that Khalapur has the largest number of
adults in each household, and Nyansongo has the largest number
of children. However, the Kenya community is polygynous, with
each wife having her own house for her children, but with child
socialization occurring primarily in the courtyard of the extended
family. The Orchard Town community not only has the smallest
number of children per household, but also the smallest number
of persons closely involved in the socialization of the child.

Such gross variations in family and household composition are
of more than "academic" interest. As LeVine observes:

. . . It is not only the number of persons and the age and sex
composition of units that varies, but the kinship, authority, and
functional relations in the units, producing variations in the
standards of behavior children must learn to conform to and
variations in the models for behavior they are exposed to. (LeVine
1970, p. 593)

TABLE 10.1. Composition of Households and Courtyards in Six Communities.

	Taira (Okinawa)	Tarong (Philippines)	Khalapur (India)	Juxtlahuaca (Mexico)	Orchard Town (New England)	Nyansongo (Kenya)
Household						
Average No. of adult males	1.3	1.4	2.6	1.3	1.0	.87
Average No. of adult females	1.8	1.7	2.4	1.2	1.0	1.0
Average No. of children	3.5	3.5	5.7	4.0	2.8	5.8
Courtyard						
Average No. of adult males	1.4	3.2	2.9	2.9	1.1	2.1
Average No. of adult females	1.8	4.3	2.6	3.0	1.2	3.2
Average No. of children	3.9	7.9	5.9	6.7	2.8	7.1
Total	7.1	15.4	11.4	12.6	5.1	12.4

SOURCE: B. B. Whiting, ed., *Six Culture Series,* vols. I–VII, New York: Wiley, 1966, as reproduced by R. A. LeVine, "Cross Cultural Study in Child Psychology," in P. Mussen, ed., Carmichael's Manual of Child Psychology, 3rd ed., vol. 2, New York: Wiley, 1970.

An especially tangible example of variation in living conditions which might have a bearing on the socialization process for children has to do with the sleeping arrangements of family members from one society to another. The intensive survey of sleeping arrangements in Japanese households by Caudill and Plath (1966) yielded a picture of sleeping patterns far different from the norm for Western societies. These investigators found that from birth to age 15, a child typically slept either with a parent or with a sibling, but rarely alone. The striking contrast with the American middle class pattern, which separates the infant from others early and maintains sleeping isolation as the ideal during childhood and adolescence, is seen by the investigators as symptomatic of the larger emphasis on independence in our society.

Differences among cultures with respect to amount and duration of breast-feeding, extensiveness of direct skin contact between child and other family members, and the nature of training for cooperative and independent action also seem to be part of this larger pattern. Where other societies foster interdependence and interrelatedness, we appear to foster increasing independence and separateness.

In some studies of cultural variation, the comparison groups are geographically remote from each other as well as being culturally distinctive. It is quite possible, of course, for distinctive societies to share a common geographical region, allowing comparison of the ways in which different groups adapt to similar external conditions.

Such is the case with three groups included in the Harvard Values Study reported by Whiting, et al. (1966). These were the Zuni Indians, the Mormons, and the Texans—all living in separate communities but in the same part of New Mexico at the time of the study. The authors reported an average of three persons per room for the Zuni, two for the Mormons, and one for the Texans. Interesting differences in child-rearing patterns emerged from the study of these communities, including the fact that the Texans used breast-feeding least frequently (44 percent as compared with 68 percent for the Mormons and 86 percent for the Zuni), they weaned the infants earlier (9 months average, as compared with 11 months for the Mormons and 24 months for the Zuni), and they initiated toilet training earlier (9 months as compared with 12 months for the Mormons and 18 months for the Zuni).

Another interesting variation was with respect to parental tolerance of aggressive behavior of children. Whiting, et al. (1966) reported that 77 percent of the Zuni mothers could be rated as "high on intolerance of aggression among peers," while the corresponding figures for Mormons was 69 percent, and for Texans, 6 percent. The tolerance or encouragement of fighting among children has been shown in other investigations, also, to vary sharply from one group to another.

In the Six Cultures Study mentioned earlier, Minturn and Lambert (1964) reported on the "Percent of cases with positive factor scores on maternal restriction of peer-directed aggression," and observed that the percentages for the non-United States groups varied from a low of 57 for the Tarong villagers to a high of 91 for the Juxtlahuaca villagers. In other words, the mothers of the Mexican children studied were far more restrictive and punitive in handling aggressive behavior of their children toward peers than were the Philippine mothers.

It was the New England mothers, however, who represented the clearest contrast; only 8 percent of these showed "positive" factor scores in comparison with the relatively high percentages for the other five cultures, indicating that the New England sample, like the Texan sample in the Harvard Values Study, were quite lenient with respect to allowing aggressiveness on the part of their children.

Such wide differences in aggression training, we might speculate, could have a strong bearing on the development of personal and social behavior of children in different societies. LeVine, after noting the existence of such extremes in a rather significant aspect of socialization, suggests that they could also account for some of the differences in intellectual (cognitive) functioning which have been observed among different cultural groups as well:

It does not seem too far-fetched to propose that these differences (in aggression training) might be related to the differences in compliance and active mastery noted (among children of different cultures). . . . In other words, the severe aggression training of some traditional African, Latin American, and other peoples may be part of a larger tendency to make children orderly, obedient, and pacific, producing an inhibitedness that manifests itself in performance on cognitive tasks. (LeVine 1970, p. 594)

The contrasting ideologies of the American society and that of Soviet Russia, viewed by some as competitors for world supremacy on a grand scale, make the question of child socialization in these two societies one of special interest. In each case, it could be argued that there exists, openly or covertly, a "national policy" with respect to inculcation of a set of ideals into its children—ideals that are consistent with, and calculated to maintain and enhance the viability of, the society itself. One might expect, then, to find some sort of parallel between the values of the society, in general, and the particular types of child-rearing practices followed within the society.

Bronfenbrenner (1970) studied the child-rearing patterns characteristic of the United States and of the Soviet Union, contrasting and comparing especially the collective-centered system of Russia with the family-centered system of the United States. His study was based on observations and interviews made in Russia between 1960 and 1967. He found that Russian babies are given more physical handling than American infants, not merely because of the high incidence of breast-feeding in Russia, but because hugging, cuddling, and kissing seemed to be more characteristic of adult treatment of children in Russia. He also observed that Russian adults were very solicitous of their children, and conscientious in protecting children from discomfort, illness, or injury.

Nurturance of children by Russian adults, even apart from the collectivist institutions for child-rearing, appeared to be more diffuse—that is, not only relatives but complete strangers are more likely to be perceived as appropriate caretakers and to step into what we would regard as a maternal role very easily and be identified by a child as "uncle" or "auntie." This nurturant role of adults is also seen in older children of both sexes, who show strong interest and well-developed competencies for caring for the very young.

One effect of this pattern, which Bronfenbrenner sees in sharp contrast to the typical Western practices, is to avoid anxiety on the part of the Russian child when left by his mother in the care of another person or in a nursery. Bronfenbrenner also notes that the Russian parents place great emphasis on character development, and strive to achieve obedience and self-discipline in their children. Self-discipline is regarded as internalized obedience, and is not seen by professionals or parents in Russia as being inconsistent with the development of normal independence. Obedience is fostered by explanations to the child, by persuasion, by judicious use of praise and encouragement, and by withdrawal of love.

Physical punishment is reported by Bronfenbrenner to be regarded as extremely undesirable—not merely ineffective, but clearly harmful to the child—by the Russians. He notes that there is a very intense affective relationship between parents and their children, and that the relationship is a more demonstrative one. Such devices as withdrawal of signs of affection in response to disobedience appear to be a most effective means of control of child behavior under these circumstances. They would perhaps be less effective under conditions in which the "normal" psychological distance between adult and child is greater.

Experience in collective living is reported by Bronfenbrenner to be relatively common from the very earliest years in Russia. (Even there, however, while over 10 percent of all children were reported to be enrolled in public nurseries, and 20 percent of children between ages 3 and 6 to be in preschool institutions, it should not be assumed that the large majority of children are being reared primarily in collective arrangements.) In the case of infants, groups of six to eight babies are placed in raised playpens permitting face-to-face interaction between adult caretakers and infants. The caretakers, or "upbringers," provide sensory-motor stimulation and attempt to instill self-reliance under a prescribed regime. The upbringer is taught to encourage speech development, which in turn is seen as the vehicle for developing social behavior. Emphasis is placed on the development of cooperative behavior, with the group becoming the basis for regulation of individual behavior.

Cultural variation
within the American society

If America is indeed the great melting pot it was envisioned to be historically, it is obvious that there remain numerous "lumps" of varying sizes and textures within the society which have not lost their separate identity as special groups, or subcultures. What constitutes a true subculture is a matter of definition, and various scholars may disagree on this issue. Nevertheless, there are special groups, some of which are identifiable by geographical location, while others are defined primarily by religious affiliation, by skin color, by social class, by a special set of values which have emerged in opposition to the prevailing values of the larger society, or, more frequently, by some combination of these variables.

To the extent that such subgroups foster the development of behavior and values in children which are in some way different from those of the larger society, they have special significance for our understanding of child development. The Midcentury White House Conference on Children and Youth stressed this in its report:

> There is no such thing as *the* environment of *the* American child. We all know that, broadly speaking, a Southerner has a pattern of family relationships, an attitude toward a settled existence, toward the land, toward the stranger, toward efficiency that is different from the patterns of a person from the North or the Midwest. Again, the functioning farm provides a different background of experience from that of the suburb or the city street. Within the city, there is difference occasioned by the income bracket of the family; and within the income bracket, there is the pattern that is affected by the occupation of the father. Miners and sanitation workers and college instructors have approximately the same income but, as a rule, they provide different designs of living for their children. (Witmer and Kotinsky 1952, p. 165)

The significance of culture to child behavior, and to our reactions to children with different backgrounds, is brought out in this further quotation from the same report:

> We cannot treat children as if they all felt and evaluated and interpreted and reacted to experience in the same way. Neither can we treat great differences in reaction and attitude as if they were always due to individual peculiarity. When a Navajo boy calls a robin's egg "green," he is not color blind or ignorant; he is classifying colors as his culture classifies them. When a Mexican boy said he had an angel whispering in one ear and a devil in another, he was neither peculiar nor emotionally disturbed or even poetic; he was voicing his culture's expression of minor conflict. (Witmer and Kotinsky 1952, p. 166)

The cultural pluralism of our society represents a major interest for child development. Whatever values, attitudes, and competencies a child develops through interaction with his subcultural milieu become the basis for his interaction with people throughout his life cycle. In earlier generations it was not uncommon for a child to live out this life cycle in the community of his birth, marrying someone known to his family and raising children who themselves saw the family home as a "permanent" thing. Today, it is far more common for a person to move, perhaps many times into widely varying types of communities, during a lifetime. In so doing, he carries with him the impact of his early socialization.

One implication of this is that socialization conditions in all parts and segments of the society have increasingly direct effects on all other members of the society. Conditions of economic poverty, for example, affect not only the children who are directly deprived, but all of society, if they limit the potentials or distort the motives of the individual child.

In one sense, whatever is happening to a child in Appalachia, or on an Indian reservation, or in an urban ghetto, is happening to *all* children, for all will eventually be affected by each other's attitudes, values, and personal resources for coping with life.

The culture of poverty

Since the early 1960s a large number of investigations and reports have been made which have stressed the different and sometimes extreme conditions that characterize the lives of economically disadvantaged people in our society. The implications of poverty for child development are indeed compelling.

No simplistic solutions to overwhelming social problems are suggested in this discussion, and we should recognize that no "solution" is to be found through the single avenue of giving money to people who have not had money in the past. Whatever solutions are devised by the society to cope with the social disease of poverty must include provisions for developing the competencies of individuals and groups—for supporting their resourcefulness at the same time as providing additional resources.

That we have been less than successful in our efforts to do this in the past is evident from the most recent statistics available. The economic poverty of families residing in urban slums, of large numbers of American Indian families, and of rural families in economically depressed regions of the country remains a visible fact of modern life.

In 1970 there were 22.5 million persons in the United States living in technical poverty, as defined by the U.S. Department of Labor. In general, this meant living in a family whose annual income was below $3800 (for a four-member, nonfarm family) or $3200 (for a four-member farm family). The corresponding nonfarm and farm poverty levels, according to this definition, for five-member families was $4400 and $3700. During 1970, the median family income in the United States was $9867 (Source: U.S. Bureau of the Census).

The proportion of persons living below the poverty level varied considerably from one ethnic minority group to another. About one-third of the black population, compared with 10 percent of the white population, were classified as "poor" in 1970. Mexican-American family income is generally reported as lower than that of non-Spanish-speaking whites, but higher than that of Negroes (Harth 1971). The economic and social plight of some 792,000 American Indians is revealed in the following excerpt from the New York Times Encyclopedic Almanac for 1972:

> Fifty thousand Indian families live in unsanitary, dilapidated dwellings: many in huts, shanties, even abandoned automobiles. The unemployment rate among Indians is nearly 40 percent—more

than 10 times the national average. Forty-two percent of Indian school-children—almost double the national average—drop out before completing high school. Indian literacy rates are among the lowest in the nation; the rates of sickness and poverty are among the highest. Thousands of Indians who have migrated into the cities find themselves untrained for jobs and unprepared for urban life. The average life expectancy of an American Indian today is 64 years; for all other Americans, it is 70.5. The problems of Indian education are legion: Ten percent of American Indians over age 14 have had no schooling at all. Nearly 60 percent have less than an eighth grade education. Even those Indians attending school are plagued by language barriers, by isolation in remote areas, by lack of a tradition of academic achievement. . . . The infant mortality rate is 30.9 for 1,000 live births for Indians and Alaskan natives as contrasted with 21.8 for all other races in the United States. The incidence of new active cases of tuberculosis among Indians and Alaskan natives outstrips the national average seven times. Twenty-nine percent of Indian homes rely on unsatisfactory sources of water and more than 50 percent of all Indian homes have inadequate facilities for sanitary waste disposal. . . . Fifty percent of Indian families have cash incomes below $2,000 a year, 75 percent below $3,000. (Harth 1971)

In our society, the variables of social class, ethnic group membership, geographical location, and poverty are all interwoven in such a way as to make it extremely difficult to sort out the effects of any one of them, independent of the others, as a factor in child development. However, Hess (1970) has argued that poverty conditions are associated with a failure to develop any sense of power or efficacy in shaping one's own destiny. There is a resulting feeling of helplessness and dependence on "luck" rather than one's own initiative for any economic improvement.

According to Hess there is also an associated vulnerability to disaster among the poor, who have no financial reserves, little or no borrowing power, low job security, and less likelihood of having friends with reserve economic resources. Life under such circumstances is ". . . lived on the edge of incipient tragedy which they are powerless to avert" (Hess 1970, p. 465).

While we have not yet sorted out with precision the exact effects on the motivation system of children, or on other aspects of social development, it is reasonable to speculate that the costs to society are indeed heavy if we continue to allow children to be socialized in poverty. Hess has noted further that the combined effects of poverty conditions restrict the range of alternatives of action available to the individual, both through the direct effects of poverty on children (for example, nutritional and educational effects, medical services, and so on) and indirect effects operating through the socializing behavior of parents as a function of their poverty status.

Socialization processes among the poor

Differences in parent-child relationships according to socio-economic status have been observed by a number of investigators, although the firsthand reports of such studies generally imply a great deal of overlapping between practices of different class levels. Sometimes relatively minor differences in parent behavior between class levels have been found to be statistically significant and have been used to magnify disproportionately a class difference in some behavior pattern (for example, if 50 percent of lower class mothers in one study employ a given discipline procedure, while only 40 percent of middle class mothers employ the same procedure, the difference may be statistically reliable without providing a clear basis for distinguishing between the two class levels). Nevertheless, there is evidence of important differences in child-rearing behaviors of parents in different social class groupings.

One of the more interesting examples of class differences in socialization was reported by Hess, et al. (1971), who compared the interaction of lower class mothers and their children with that of middle class mothers and children. In standardized situations requiring a mother to instruct her child in the performance of a series of cognitive tasks, striking differences in the patterns of communication were observed between middle class mothers and working class mothers. The middle class mothers used a more elaborate language system to explain the tasks and to teach principles underlying task completion, while the lower class mothers tended to operate on a "power" dimension, using a limited language system to give more or less arbitrary commands to the child. Hess, et al. elsewhere interpret this general difference as a fundamental one in the child socialization process:

> Although her intentions may be quite the opposite, a mother may unwittingly structure the situation so that the child not only fails to learn the intended lesson or skill, but also acquires undesirable attitudes or habits in the process. In achievement and mastery situations, for example, exposure to such experiences can cause the child to develop negative attitudes characterized by expectation of failure and by reliance upon punishment avoidance coping techniques rather than upon active attempts to understand the material presented. In discipline and control situations, imposition of demands without adequate specification of rationales may cause the child to become responsive only to power and status differences, external sources of reinforcement, and immediate goals, rather than developing internalized self-guidance based on application of a complex system of perceptions, standards, values, and goals to individual situations. (Hess, et al. 1971, pp. 195–196)

The pervasive effects of language, as a function of social class, on parent-child behavior was first suggested by Bernstein (1961), who was concerned with the interaction of language with other forms of social behavior, and who provided the theoretical rationale for the Hess, et al. investigations.

A general conclusion from research in this area is that lower class is associated with restricted language systems, which fail to provide the child with an adequate basis for generalizing principles leading to social competence in a wide range of skill areas. The general hypothesis, with which much research work remains to be done in sorting out the precise ways in which the variables operate, is that the lower class child is not provided with an adequate language model which affords a basis for developing the essential skills and social competencies that lead to success in the middle class social economy. Thus the cycle of poverty is repeated for such individuals in their own family patterns as they establish families of their own.

Much work remains to be done in sorting out the precise ways in which poverty relates to child-rearing practices, and in turn, to the personal-social characteristics of children; but there is general agreement that the child reared in poverty is, on the average, significantly handicapped by his circumstances, and that his relative success in the academic world and the world of work cannot be accounted for on the basis of his native intelligence.

Ethnicity

As we have noted, membership in a particular ethnic minority group in America may have its own special significance for the socialization process, but it is extremely difficult to sort out effects of ethnicity apart from regional and social class variables. In theory, one might predict that the child would normally generalize whatever level of prestige or status is attached by society to a given group to himself through a process of identification as he comes to define himself as a member of that group. Hence, a child's self-evaluation or sense of self-esteem might come to reflect the general stereotypes that prevail in a society regarding a minority group. Some studies of race awareness and self-concept in minority group children tend to support this general notion, although they must be interpreted cautiously.

According to Hess (1970), studies of racial awareness in young children consistently show that by the age of 4, children attending either interracial or segregated schools have become aware of race, and the awareness increases consistently with age, regardless of the kind of school the child attends.

Some studies report an early preference for the white race on the part of Negro children, accompanied by some ambivalence toward their own race; but the latter finding depends upon many related variables such as age of child, place of residence, and the research techniques employed. In general, the studies that report depreciation by the Negro child of his own race also report a decrease in this tendency with increasing age. Nevertheless, Hess reports that "Rejection and depreciation of his own racial group have been found to be accompanied in the young Negro child by self-doubt, self-rejection, anxiety, insecurity, fearfulness, and passivity" (Hess 1970, p. 483).

We still have a great deal to learn about the ways in which minority group membership influences the development of self-attitudes and personal adjustment. However, the extensive report by Coleman, et al. (1966) revealed significant differences in school achievement in the first grade among children of different ethnic groups in low income communities. These differences in performance for different racial groups persisted on through the school years, and implied a heavy involvement of motivational factors in the differential performance of the various groups.

Cultural inconsistencies and conflicts

In discussions of the effects of culture on the development of the child it would be easy, but erroneous, to conclude that a given society, or a given subculture, exerts consistent and systematic shaping forces on the child to become a particular kind of personality. As we have seen in the preceding sections, there certainly are powerful cultural forces in operation, but a given society may be far from consistent or systematic in the manner in which such forces are applied. Particularly in cultures as complex as those of Western Europe and America there are inevitably cultural forces that are inconsistent with each other, which lead to cultural conflict for the child.

Such cultural conflicts are illustrated whenever a given society places high positive value on two more or less mutually exclusive patterns of behavior. If a given society, for example, values personal modesty and tends to reward behavior that is somewhat self-effacing and not overly forward or presumptuous in relations with others, while at the same time it places a strong positive value on self-assertiveness, strong leadership, and personally aggressive initiative in dealing with others, there is certainly the potential for cultural conflict on the part of a child who experiences difficulty in finding a reasonable balance between these two value positions.

In a sense, the example represents our society to the extent that we value those behaviors that lead to "being liked by others" but at the same time value behaviors that are associated with "success" in an individualistic society. Somewhat opposing sets of values that exist as parts of the basic fabric of a society do not, in

themselves, prevent the achievement of balanced self-development. However, our understanding of the socialization task of the
individual child is enhanced by our awareness that such contradictions do exist, and that individual children may experience
conflict because of them.

Another kind of cultural inconsistency should also be noted. In
addition to the simultaneous operation of two or more contra-
dictory forces in the life of a child, there may be inconsistencies
in the form of discontinuities over time in the life of an individual
child. These are illustrated by changes in expectations, demands,
and privileges from one time to another. Expectations about control of body elimination represent a simple example in which the
society asserts its right to expect different levels and types of behavior in keeping with different age and maturity levels of the
child. In the normal course of events such changes in expectation
are adapted to by most all children; however, therapists who deal
with the maladjustments of older children and adults can find,
even in such a relatively simple social requirement as control of
body elimination, the roots of sometimes severe conflict and pain-
ful maladjustment.

A significant type of cultural discontinuity would be illustrated
if the society actively demands a pattern of behavior at one age
level that it later insists must be destroyed and replaced by com-
peting forms of behavior. Such discontinuity may occur for
children whose early instruction in matters of sex and reproduction is deliberately inaccurate or misleading. But whether in the
realm of sex or any aspect of human experience (e.g. politics,
ethics, religion, etc.), the important consideration is the degree of
internal consistency of a society in its demands on a growing
child. Internal consistency need not imply an absolute sameness
in behavior or belief systems demanded of a child, however; it
may include the notion of "open-endedness" in instruction. Such
an approach allows for concepts to be gradually elaborated, clari-
fied, modified, and revised without the necessity for destroying
and replacing them at some point when the child will inevitably
question his earlier understandings.

It should not be assumed that the simpler, nonliterate societies invariably provide a consistent, conflict-free set of socializing forces for their children. Some conflicts, however, may be inherent as a function of social and technological change, and thus occur more frequently and with greater impact in societies that are undergoing rapid transition, as is true currently in the Western world. For a perceptive analysis of the impact of change on a society and on personal adjustment, the reader is encouraged to examine such writings as *Future Shock*, by Toffler (1970).

Summary

Culture refers to the learned behavior of a people. It includes such diverse elements of one's social world as language, technology, finance, politics, religious values, art, music, and patterns of family living and child-rearing. Even the manner in which children learn to categorize their experiences is a reflection of cultural conditioning.

Each society develops unique ways of dealing with its environment and of using personal, social, and environmental resources to meet common human needs. Each society also defines acceptable and unacceptable behavior, formulates and maintains a value system, and provides rewards for children in terms of that system.

Markedly different techniques of caring for children and training them in the ways of the society are found from one subcultural group to another. However, the effect of any particular cultural practice in the formation of the child's personality must be seen in the context of the full network of cultural values, practices, and artifacts. Within a given society, healthy child development is fostered in part through the existence of cultural consistency and the avoidance of cultural contradictions.

References

Bernstein, B. "Social Class and Linguistic Development: A Theory of Social Learning." In Halsey, A. H., Floud, J., and Anderson, C. A., eds. *Education, Economy, and Society.* Glencoe, Ill.: Free Press, 1961.

Bronfenbrenner, U. *Two Worlds of Childhood.* New York: Russell Sage Foundation, 1970.

Caudill, W., and Plath, D. W. "Who Sleeps by Whom? Parent-Child Involvement in Urban Japanese Families." *Psychiatry* 29 (1966) 344–366.

Coleman, J. S., et al. *Equality of Educational Opportunity.* Washington, D.C., United States Government Printing Office, 1966.

Harth, M., ed. *Family Almanac '72.* New York: The New York Times, 1971.

Hess, R. D. "Class and Ethnic Influences upon Socialization." In Mussen, P., ed. *Carmichael's Manual of Child Psychology.* 3rd ed., vol. 2. New York: Wiley, 1970, pp. 457–557.

Hess, R. D., Shipman, V., Brophy, J. E., and Bear, R. M. "Mother-Child Interaction." In Gordon, I., ed. *Readings in Research in Developmental Psychology.* Glenview, Ill.: Scott, Foresman, 1971, pp. 177–197.

Lee, D. "Being and Value in a Primitive Culture." In Moustakas, C. L., ed. *The Self.* New York: Harper, 1956, pp. 120–139.

LeVine, R. A. "Cross-Cultural Study in Child Psychology." In Mussen, P., ed. *Carmichael's Manual of Child Psychology.* 3rd ed., vol. 2. New York: Wiley, 1970, pp. 559–612.

Minturn, L., and Lambert, W. W. *Mothers of Six Cultures: Antecedents of Child Rearing.* New York: Wiley, 1964.

National Geographic Magazine. "First Glimpse of a Stone Age Tribe." Vol. 140 (December 1971) 880–884.

Toffler, A. *Future Shock.* New York: Bantam Books, 1970.

Whiting, B. B., ed. *Six Culture Series, Vols. I–VII.* New York: Wiley, 1966.

Whiting, J. W. M., et al. "The Learning of Values." In Vogt, E. Z., and Albert, E. M., eds. *People of Rimrock: A Study of Values in Five Cultures.* Cambridge, Mass.: Harvard University Press, 1966.

Whiting, J. W. M., and Child, I. L. *Child Training and Personality.* New Haven, Conn.: Yale University Press, 1953.

Witmer, H., and Kotinsky, R., eds. *Personality in the Making.* New York: Harper, 1952.

CHAPTER ELEVEN
The child and his family

What are the traditional functions of the family?

How are these functions being modified?

How does the family create needs, as well as satisfy needs, for its members?

How are cognitive and personality processes in children influenced by their families?

What implications are there for child development in the current experimentation with alternatives to the traditional family?

In what sense does a child shape the personality of parents and other family members, just as he is shaped by them?

The American child's culture is mediated for him first by his family. It is within the family setting that he ordinarily experiences the first impact of his cultural world. The organization of the family and the nature and quality of interaction among family members become not only the primary interpreters of culture to the child but at the same time primary shapers of the child's personal attributes. An understanding of the child requires an understanding of the nature of family relationships as well as the forces that come to bear upon the quality of interpersonal behavior within the family setting.

The nature of the family

Some definitions of the family place emphasis on structure, membership, and organization. Others stress the functions of the family as a social institution. Still others emphasize the roles of family members and the relational qualities among members as a basis for definition of the term. One widely accepted definition includes some elements of all these different emphases:

> (The family is) a group of persons united by ties of marriage, blood, or adoption; constituting a single household; interacting and communicating with each other in their respective roles of husband and wife, mother and father, son and daughter, brother and sister; and creating and maintaining a common culture. (Burgess and Locke 1953, p. 8)

Such a definition conveys well a general, abstract meaning of the concept "family." In its emphasis on creating and maintaining a common culture, it also implies another level of definition of the term. That is, the functional, operating definition each of us carries with us, which is based on our own special experiences and responses to family life as we have participated in it, becomes a profound influence of the family in its role of creating and maintaining a common culture.

One example, then, of the role of families in the lives of children is the functional definitions of family life they provide: what it means to be a brother; what it means to be a father; what it means to be a husband or wife or mother—these and other basic familial roles are defined for the child as he witnesses their performance in day-by-day interaction among family members.

Family functions

The family of which we are speaking at this point should be further defined as the *nuclear group* comprising a single household in our society. That is, we do not ordinarily include cousins, uncles, aunts, nieces, nephews, and in-laws. While there are variations that may sometimes include a grandparent in this nuclear group, we are speaking now of the more typical household consisting of husband and wife and their children.* This is in contrast to the *extended* family, common to some other societies, which may include a larger kinship group within the single household.

Students of family life have provided us with classifications of family functions. While there is not perfect agreement among these specialists, the list provided by Winch covers the primary areas of basic family functioning rather well:

1. *The economic function:* concerned with the family's production and consumption of goods and services, provisions for domestic division of labor, and handling of economic dependency needs.
2. *The status-conferring function:* concerned with the family's role in determining the status of its individual members by establishing subcultural attributes which define family status and by providing a status orientation for its members.
3. *The reproductive function:* concerned with the family's right and responsibility to have children.
4. *The functions of socialization and security-giving:* concerned with the family's role in providing the child with a foundation of psychological security for becoming a productive member of the larger social group. (Winch 1952)

---

* There are other obvious variations: adopted child, step-relationships, foster parent-child relationships, missing parent, and so on.

Changes
in family functions

From a historical perspective, there have been significant changes in family functions as well as in family structure over the years. Families are smaller; they are more mobile; they do not produce as high a proportion of the goods and services used in the home as was formerly true. From an economic standpoint they are primarily purchasers of consumer goods and services. The status-conferring function still exists, but with possibly less influence than in earlier generations.

For example, with increased mobility, both socially and geographically, there is less concern about the status of one's father and relatively more concern about one's personal attributes independent of his family's status. The child comes to stand more on his own merit as he enters the world of social, educational, and economic action. The family's status-conferring role functions relatively more through its fostering of a motivational system, a level of aspiration, and a set of social competencies in a child, which become the bases for his later social status.

The reproductive function remains the right and responsibility of the nuclear family in our society, but there is evidence of striking change in the manner of carrying out this primary function. Decreases in average size of family, increased acceptance by large segments of society of the idea of family planning as well as emphasis on the prevention of conception, some significant beginnings of the practice of artificial insemination, and changing social and legal positions with respect to abortion—all represent aspects of these qualitative changes in the family's reproductive function.

The functions of security-giving and socialization have taken on increased significance in some respects. Along with the decrease in family size and the relative separation of the small nuclear group from its extended kinship ties has developed a somewhat intensified emotional investment in their children on the part of parents.

Nuclear families are more likely to be established in new locations, apart from grandparents and other kin, and are more likely to be moved with greater frequency than ever before in history, which suggests that some traditional sources of psychological support for the child may be less available, and that indeed the modern child cannot depend on the kind of geographical and social stability in his life as has been true in previous generations. Toffler (1970) even argues that as the rate of change increases in our society, children will need increasing emotional preparation for kinds of interpersonal relationships which are more transitory and less enduring, if they are to cope effectively with the kind of society now emerging. During the early years, larger numbers of children than ever before adapt to frequent changes of residence, acquisition of new friends and new living circumstances—all of which argue for the significance of the role of the small nuclear group in supporting the psychological needs of its members for continuity and security in the face of external change. At the same time, to the extent that these trends occur, the family plays a major role in shaping the social competence of all its members, including especially its young children.

The family as a unit of interacting personalities

One might view the family as a set of individuals, each with a special combination of motives, competencies, resources, habitual ways of responding, styles of thought, attitudes, and values. With this perspective in mind, the family can be viewed as a kind of arena within which its members interact, making use of their resources in an effort to satisfy their motives in an ongoing, changing relational process with each other.

Implicitly, within each family unit there is an unspoken (indeed, it may be poorly understood by the family members!) system of rewards and punishments which have the effect of shaping the behavior of its members. As used here, a "reward" may be something as fleeting, unplanned, and spontaneous as a smile; a "punishment" something as innocuous as a failure to respond to a question, or a turning away of one's face while another family member is speaking.

Although we still have much to learn about just how rewards and punishments operate to shape the behavior of children, we have much evidence that behavior that is followed by a reward will have a higher probability of occurring again.

It seems paradoxical to some parents that behavior that is followed by punishment may also have a heightened probability of occurring again. However, there are important reasons why this may be the case. First, "punishment" is frequently an interpersonal event, just as is often true of "rewards." Being a social event, of sorts, punishment should be seen as having some things in common with other social events, many of which *are* rewarding and which tend to *reinforce* the behaviors they follow. The social attention given a child, even in the negative form of active punishment, can be far more reinforcing than, for example, being merely ignored. At the very least, punitive social events can provide attention for a child who may be uncertain of ways to obtain attention and, in his search for attention, learns quickly to employ methods that will work even though they bring punishment with them.

Secondly, in addition to the fact that punishment is often "social" in nature, and thus carries a mixed message of pain and reinforcement, it is also often administered by a person with whom the child is developing an identification relationship. That is, the one who administers the punishment is usually a model serving to define and illustrate behavior patterns for the child to emulate and imitate. Thus, what a child *learns* from being punished is rarely as simple and direct as we might wish to believe. It could well include learning that the way to respond when frustrated is to be punitive.

While positive rewards for desired behavior have a clearly positive effect of increasing the likelihood of such behavior in the future, punishment cannot be said to have a clear-cut effect in decreasing the likelihood of the behavior for which a child is punished. Nevertheless, through the subtle, cumulative effects of the family's system of rewards and punishments, a child shapes his behavior in a way calculated to win rewards and reduce the probability of punishments.

Much of child socialization appears to result from this shaping process, with signs of adult approval serving both as cues and reinforcers of behaviors, which the child strives to master. The system of rewards and punishments functions in relation to the "modeling" role of family members for each other also.

Within the family matrix, the behavior of one member frequently serves as a guide or reference point for another member, illustrating the form of exemplary behavior and providing illustrations of rewards for such behavior as well. As a force in the socialization of children this is indeed powerful, and will be discussed in greater detail in the following section.

Family members
as behavior models

Research in the processes of socialization in children has placed emphasis on the imitative behavior of children. Much of children's social behavior is patterned after the actions and mannerisms of the adults in their lives. The powerful effect of imitation has been confirmed in numerous studies, illustrative of which is the work of Bandura (1967), who has shown that patterns of behavior can be acquired very rapidly, and in large segments or in their entirety, confirming the observation that children readily reproduce the behavior modeled by their parents. "The pervasiveness of this form of learning is also clearly evident in naturalistic observations of children's play in which they frequently reproduce the entire parental role, including the appropriate mannerisms, voice inflections, and attitudes, much to the parents' surprise and embarrassment" (Bandura 1967, p. 43).

Bandura has shown, further, that such personal behaviors as physical and verbal aggression are readily imitated by children, whether modeled by a "live" adult or in films or television portrayals of aggression. In general, there is compelling evidence that basic patterns of behavior—which, taken together, represent the personality of the child—result from exposure to the behavior by the significant adults in the child's life. It is such a powerful factor in shaping personality, in every aspect, that we should understand the reasons underlying its operation.

One explanation for the potency of the imitative process in the shaping of personality goes back to the fundamental state of dependency on the part of the human infant. He is literally incapable of sustaining his own life at birth without the intervention of others who provide nurturant care—food, warmth, shelter, protection from disease and injury, and so on. While he becomes less dependent with age, and relatively more able to provide for his own needs, the process of achieving this relative independence is facilitated by his doing for himself essentially the same things that he has observed others doing for him.

The learning to do the things for himself that his parents generally have done for him, like other forms of learning, may generalize in the sense that learning to do what his parents do is a satisfying and rewarding thing since it is so frequently a source of immediate satisfaction and gratification of his personal needs. Thus this learning becomes the basis for the development of a powerful, generalized motive to imitate the behavior of others.

The process is more readily understood when the child imitates the behavior of powerful models, or models who have the ability to regulate and control rewarding and punishing events in his life. However, it is also clear that the child typically generalizes imitative behavior to persons who do not necessarily have great power or who do not control vital rewards and punishments, as in the case of 2- and 3-year-olds who readily imitate one another in spontaneous behavior in play situations.

Other explanations of the development of imitative behavior do not place as much emphasis on the fact of the initial dependency state of the child. Gewirtz and Stingle (1968), for example, argue that the first imitative response must occur by chance, through direct physical assistance or through direct training, and is then strengthened and maintained by reinforcement from the environment.

One poorly understood aspect of the onset of imitative behavior is the role of *parental* imitation of *child* behavior as a stimulus to the emergence of imitative behavior on the part of the child. Many parents, for example, spontaneously engage their infants in play which includes forms of reciprocity—baby makes random vocalization, mother makes similar sounds in playful imitation; baby repeats, and once again the mother's vocalization in response reinforces the baby's vocal effort.

In such a sequence there is the possibility of significant learnings which extend, in their implications, far beyond the matter of learning to produce certain vocal sounds. Reinforcement, in this instance, takes the form of behavior that is designed to produce a "match" between the behaviors of the two persons involved in the parent-child dyad. All the reinforcing elements of the satisfying social occasion then are bound up with this matching effort.

To be sure, the initial effort at matching was made by the adult, but it must be borne in mind that the adult is "modeling" behaviors for the child, as well as reinforcing them. Thus it might be conjectured that the initial impetus to match, or imitate behavior of others, is derived in part from the imitative behavior of the adult. This possibility, if given adequate research support, could in turn lend support to the general admonition to parents that early and continued interaction with their infants is a major psychological support for the emergence of personality.

Some theorists (for example, Piaget 1951) argue that this early development of imitative processes is vital not only in the development of social responsiveness and such personality characteristics as conscience, but more generally to the emergence of intellectual functioning. Earlier research, which reported faulty intellectual growth as well as inadequate personal and social adjustment on the part of infants receiving limited "mothering" (for example, Spitz 1946, Ribble 1943, Bowlby 1961, Goldfarb 1945), might be accounted for, in part, by this failure to develop significant attachments to adult models and adequate motivation to emulate such models.

If the role of imitative behavior is truly as significant as this discussion implies, we should attempt to understand the breadth of implications for the overall emergence of personality. It is as if the *basic resource material* necessary for achieving selfhood is provided in the biological tissue the infant has at birth, but that the *motivation* to begin and maintain the struggle to achieve selfhood is constructed out of the interaction process, first between parent and child, and later between child and others.

Effects on cognitive development

The eminent development psychologist, Dr. Nancy Bayley, concludes her review of research on the growth of mental abilities in children with the following statement:

> In essence, given the undamaged genetic potential, mental growth is best facilitated by a supportive, "warm" emotional climate, together with ample opportunities for the positive reinforcement of specific cognitive efforts and successes. (Bayley 1970, p. 1203)

Depending on how one defines cognitive processes and what instruments one uses to measure them, they are relatively more under the control of genetics or relatively more under the influence of environmental effects. Regardless of the exact proportion of effects contributed respectively by heredity and environment, it is likely that Hunt (1961) is correct in his conclusion that environmental influences do make a difference. No more succinct statement of the nature of environmental nurturance of intelligence seems possible than that provided above by Bayley.

Sears, Maccoby, and Levin (1957) reported that warm, democratic parents had brighter children than those who were cold and nonindulgent. Recent research in this area stresses two kinds of contributions to cognitive growth which conceivably accrue to the child as a result of parental behavior. One of these is the potential benefits on mental growth resulting from living in a richly stimulating environment. Language behavior, concepts, reasoning, and problem-solving—all seem to reflect the amount and quality of early stimulation in the home for children under 6. The early steps in turning native intellectual endowment into functioning mental ability are supported, then, by environmental stimulation in the home and family setting.

If this first parental effect might be thought of as an influence on the *amount* or *level* of mental functioning, the second general way in which cognitive processes are influenced by parental behavior (and that of other family members) is in the *style* or *quality* of mental activity. As we noted earlier, the work of Hess and Shipman (1965) suggests a role of parents in providing language models for children. Language, in turn, becomes a tool for thinking. The richness or lack of richness of the language tool upon which the child can draw, or to which he can turn for dealing with his environment, interacts with the style of mental operations he can bring to bear on the solution of problems or even on thinking about his world.

There remains sharp theoretical disagreement on the place of language in the child's thinking, with some theorists giving language a first priority in placing constraints on a child's thought, and others seeing language largely as an accompaniment to thought, but not essential to its full development. Regardless of the merits of this theoretical debate, it seems safe to conclude that the child's ability to make manifest the mental operations of which he is capable *is* dependent on his language competency to an important degree.

We are also aware that to an important degree the intellectual development of children is influenced by the expectations that other people hold for them. In turn, it seems reasonable that the child of limited language ability will be treated by some adults (perhaps quite mistakenly!) as if the language level were a reflection of limited native endowment. It is the circular relationship between expectations held by others and the actual emergence of functioning intelligence that is of special interest here. Success in cognitive action leads to expectations and fulfillment of further successes; failures seem to lead to expectation of further failures and, too frequently, to the fulfillment of those expectations.

Although our general conclusion here seems to be favorable to the idea of intellectual stimulation, and the positive role of such stimulation from parents and other family members in the early development of the child, a word should be said about extreme views on this subject. Here, as in most every area of interest in the field of child development, there will be some who conclude that ". . . if a little is a good thing, then a lot must be that much better," and use this reasoning to justify a heavy and arduous regime of early stimulation with the expectation that one's child will only benefit and achieve superior mentality as a result.

Conscientious parents are often vulnerable to the high pressure tactics of those who would sell them gadgets, educational toys, and early learning programs and who are not constrained by ethical concerns or any well-established results which may reasonably be expected from such. We do not have any basis for assuming that a specific type of "gadget" at any particular age is an essential or even *important* adjunct to healthy mental development. Nor do we assume that it can take the place of some kind of experience contributing to mental development. This does not mean that well-designed toys are unimportant; it means merely that no one gadget, prescription, book, and so on seems to be irreplaceable in the life of a healthy child.

Effects on personality development

Radke (1946) reported on 43 children of nursery-kindergarten age who were observed in free play periods in a picture interpretation task and whose parents were given a standard parent questionnaire. Children from homes described as restrictive and autocratic showed less aggressiveness, less rivalry, more passivity, and were characterized as less colorful and less popular. Children from freer homes were more active, showed more rivalry, and were more popular. Parents who were more democratic in discipline and who showed respect for their children fostered the development of consideration for others on the part of the children.

Baldwin (1949) studied 64 4-year-olds and observed that parents who were strict and undemocratic in methods of control were likely to have children who were quiet, well-behaved, unaggressive, but restricted in curiosity, originality, and imagination.

Shoben (1949) found that parents of "problem children" (defined as children referred for help to a guidance clinic, or brought into juvenile custody at least twice) were more apt to agree with statements approving strict discipline and demand for obedience.

Watson (1957) studied 44 children from "good, loving but strictly disciplined" homes, compared with 34 from the same community whose parents were also described as equally "good, loving," but who differed from the first group in that they were unusually permissive. He compared the two groups of children on nine personality rating dimensions. On three of these dimensions (self-control, inner security, and happiness) he found no significant difference between the two groups. He reported that "factors making for anxiety, emotional disorganization, and unhappiness are found about equally often under either type of home discipline." He also found no differences in energy and activity level for the two groups of children.

With respect to the variable of persistence, an interesting finding was that permissiveness was associated with moderate degrees of persistence, while strict discipline was associated with extremes of unusually high or unusually low persistence as a personal quality in the children, and relatively poorer use of intellectual resources by the children from the strict homes.

Four additional variables showed significant differences favoring the permissively raised children: (1) they showed more initiative and independence, (2) they were better socialized and more cooperative, (3) they showed less hostility and more friendly feelings toward others, and (4) they had a higher level of spontaneity, originality and creativity.

The interesting thing was that on *none* of the nine dimensions was there any evidence in favor of the strict discipline, when both sets of children came from "good, loving homes." However, the student is cautioned to ask the question, which unfortunately remains unanswered in such research: What else is true of these parents, in addition to their being "good and loving" parents? Are they typical of the general population with respect to their intelligence level? Their family size and income level? The books they have read on child-rearing?

Results of such a research project are rarely directly translatable into a child-rearing formula, and the sophisticated student will recognize the dangers of attempting to make such a translation without first achieving a meaningful operational definition of what is meant by "strict" and what is meant by "permissive" for such families, rather than using such research as an excuse to promote a given kind of child-rearing pattern that one would *like* to believe in. Put simply, one family's *permissiveness* is another family's *license!*

The effects of parent behavior on child personality have been approached from more than one direction. Sometimes we have looked at families having known characteristics (authoritarian parents, missing father, and so on) and then asked "What seems to be true of the children of such families?" In other cases we have examined children and noted certain personal characteristics, and then asked "What kind of family was it that produced this kind of child?" A variation on this procedure has been to ask adults, such as college students with known personality characteristics (for example, competitiveness, leadership, underachievement in relation to ability, and so on), to recall, perhaps with the help of rating scales and interview techniques, their early experiences within the family setting as children.

None of these methods has proven as precise or unambiguous as would be desirable in establishing causative antecedent conditions in the family which produce clear-cut personality effects in children. This lack of precision has perhaps been one reason why recent research has stressed theoretical considerations and the testing of specific hypotheses about the effects of child-rearing practices on child personality.

One early study carried out by Goodenough and Leahy (1927), for example, well-done in its day, was an investigation of the effects of sibling position on personality development. In a sample of kindergarten children, these investigators reported that "oldest" children showed the greatest number of "extreme deviations" from the "ideal norm" on teacher rating scales for each of 14 traits. Traits included such things as aggressiveness, suggestibility, demonstrativeness, and so on, and the scales were built on the assumption that extreme deviation from some midpoint represented a less adequate adjustment than moderate ratings by the teachers. "Middle" children—those with both older and younger siblings—showed a slightly overdemonstrative rating, on the average, and a higher frequency of sex misconduct. The authors speculated that the more frequent extreme deviations for oldest children could have occurred as a result of these children having less experienced parents in the early years, combined with a larger number of responsibilities given them, and the adjustment of making the shift from being an only to the oldest child upon the arrival of the second child. They also speculated that the middle children, whose parents were preoccupied with both older and younger siblings, may have developed their personal-social behaviors in part as a response to unsatisfied desires for parental attention. But Goodenough and Leahy also concluded that "there is probably no position in the family which does not involve, as a consequence of its own peculiar nature, certain special tasks of adjustment." The general conclusion, in spite of the research done on that topic in the ensuing years, still appears to be valid.

Perhaps more important than any specific research finding on the effects of sibling position that we have developed over the years since 1927, however, is the firm conclusion that no one factor operates in isolation. We have asked many good questions, for example, about the effects of early vs. late weaning, effects of bottle vs. breast feeding, effects of early and severe toilet training, and so on.* We have similarly raised questions about the effects of democratic vs. authoritarian vs. permissive parents and warm and accepting vs. cold and rejecting parents, and our best conclusion still is that no one factor operates in isolation.

The frustrated mother of three active young children seeks, understandably, an intelligent answer from the "expert" as to what kinds of child-rearing practices she should use, and at present the only honest answer has to be "It all depends!" There are, of course, numerous helpful materials—books and pamphlets, motion pictures, and so on—that provide voluminous guidelines and suggestions for ways of relating productively to children. However, these do not guarantee that a given practice will lead to the development of a given kind of personality in the child, nor are they able to do so, since in truth it "all depends."

A good example of the interaction of child-rearing factors in the personality development of children has been drawn together by Becker (1964), who surveyed and reviewed the research

---

* Such research was well summarized in an excellent article by Harold Orlansky (1949), who concluded that for every argument raised on the precise effects of one kind of infant care on personality development, a counter argument could be raised and supported by research!

literature on the effects of different kinds of parental discipline on child personality. Becker showed, for example, that the effects of parental restrictiveness vs. permissiveness (perhaps the issue that most concerns parents in their practical, everyday roles as mother and father) depend on, among other things, whether we are dealing with a warm, accepting parent or a cold, rejecting one.

Table 11.1 summarizes this interaction effect, making use of the research findings from a variety of investigators. The student is encouraged to read that table carefully, not because it "prescribes" an ideal parent-child relationship, but because it illustrates so clearly that the personality outcomes in children depend not on one dimension of parent behavior alone, but on the organized complexity of the interaction process of a living, growing, pulsating pattern of interpersonal behavior. The illustration is indeed oversimplified, because no doubt the two factors of "warmth-hostility" and "restrictiveness-permissiveness" also interact additionally with a large number of *other* variables in producing their unique balance of effects in any given child.

One of the more interesting aspects of the relationship between parent behavior and children's personality has to do with discipline used and the amount and kind of aggressiveness on the part of children. Aggressiveness as a personal quality has mixed meaning for most Americans—it can be viewed as part of the "rugged individualism in which we have taken some pride as the quality that allowed us to settle and conquer this continent," and it can also be viewed as a quality that has given us a name and reputation around the world for "violence and lawlessness as a society." There is, no doubt, some truth in both points of view, but our ambivalence about aggressiveness makes us uneasy with respect to the child-rearing patterns we employ, and perhaps somewhat lacking in confidence and conviction that we are capable of producing children and socializing them to the point of being effectively independent—able to "stand on their own two feet" or defend themselves if the need calls for it—without at the same time producing large numbers of violence-prone individuals whose standard solution for problems employs a weapon of some kind.

TABLE 11.1.   Interactions in the Consequences of Warmth Vs. Hostility and Restrictiveness Vs. Permissiveness

	Restrictiveness	Permissiveness
Warmth	Submissive, dependent, polite, neat, obedient (Levy) Minimal aggression (Sears) Maximum rule enforcement, boys (Maccoby) Dependent, not friendly, not creative (Watson) Maximal compliance (Meyers)	Active, socially outgoing, creative, successfully aggressive (Baldwin) Minimal rule enforcement, boys (Maccoby) Facilitates adult role taking (Levin) Minimal self-aggression, boys (Sears) Independent, friendly, creative, low projective hostility (Watson)
Hostility	"Neurotic" problems (clinical studies) More quarreling and shyness with peers (Watson) Socially withdrawn (Baldwin) Low in adult role taking (Levin) Maximal self-aggression, boys (Sears)	Delinquency (Gluecks, Bandura and Walters) Noncompliance (Meyers) Maximal aggression (Sears)

SOURCE: Table from "Consequences of Different Kinds of Parental Discipline," by Wesley C. Becker in *Review of Child Development Research*, Vol. I, edited by Martin L. Hoffman and Lois Wladis Hoffman. Copyright © 1964 by Russell Sage Foundation, New York.

It is a complex issue we raise here, for we do not have simple answers nor should we be deceived into grasping for them. The question of parent behavior in relation to aggressiveness of children, for example, probably has a "simple answer" in the minds of those who see strict discipline, including physical punishment, as the "treatment" for the child who shows signs of aggression against his brother or his neighbor. One trouble with this superficiality is that at the same time as the strict parent is "inhibiting" the aggressive behavior of his child by spanking him, he is also *modeling* aggressive behavior for the child, and giving the child a prime example of the thing to do when one is angry! And what the child may be learning through the modeling experience may have stronger and more enduring effects than what he is learning about the inhibition of his aggressiveness. Besides, if he is at all alert, he can quickly come to discriminate between being punished for being aggressive, on the one hand, and being punished for getting caught, on the other!

Gordon and Smith (1965) made an incidental observation as a part of a larger research project with young children: (1) the stricter a girl's mother, the more aggressive was the daughter, if the mother *used* physical punishment, and (2) the stricter the boy's mother, the less aggressive the son, especially if physical punishment was *not* used.

General findings of relationships between aggression on the part of children and child-rearing patterns have been noted by other researchers, especially by Sears, et al. (1957). The conclusion is also clearly supported by the extensive work of Bandura (1967) and his colleagues, which showed that children respond to aggressive models and exhibit rather striking patterns of aggressive behavior, which in some instances reproduces clearly the aggressive actions of the adult model.

Traditional and experimental family forms

It is probably true that for most of us there is a typical American nuclear family, consisting of a husband and wife and their children, living in a household separate from other families or individuals. Historically, the variations on this pattern in our society have been regarded as social experiments (for example, the Oneida Community, early Mormon polygyny, and so on) outside the mainstream of society and have been treated as "abnormal" in many respects.

At all times, however, our complex society has produced reactions to the "standard" more or less stereotyped family form, and these variations have been regarded by their participants as embodying enduring values and expressing a kind of faith that alternate family forms can provide more effectively for the needs of their members than the traditional, restricted nuclear group. The experimentation that characterizes the present society is no exception, and an analysis of the variety of family forms in existence today could occupy the pages of many volumes.

Without attempting to account for or explain the emergence of the wide range of alternative life styles, we should nevertheless note their existence and some of their implications for the processes of child development. For one thing, some students of this phenomenon see the family presently undergoing major revision—with the more radical experimentation representing perhaps extreme reactions against the traditional family forms— so that the family of the future will inevitably shift its form and style from the traditional to a less conservative position, incorporating some features of the experimental versions that have been developed.

Today's student of child development and family relationships has access to a far greater range of information on the existence of "alternative" and "deviant" life styles than ever before in history. There are nearly infinite variations on heterosexual and homosexual arrangements; nuclear and communal family arrangements; marital and extramarital sexual behavior, including "mate-swapping"; and seemingly endless variations on provisions for child care and socialization.

Some of these variations are formally organized in planned communities, such as the commune; others exist in a marginal "underworld" shrouded in secrecy, with participants living in two worlds: the "straight" world of work and family life and citizen participation, and the covert world of, for example, nights and weekends of homosexuality, mate-swapping, or informal communal living, and so on. The challenge for the student, as for the scientist, is to understand the reality that such arrangements do exist, and that their existence may hold some implications for the processes of child socialization.

The Israeli kibbutz, described briefly in the preceding chapter, serves as a graphic illustration of variations on living styles since, according to some scholars—and depending upon how one defines the family—it (the family) does not exist in the kibbutz.

the hospital, following delivery. Parents may feed the infant there, and may visit the baby after working hours. Only after the baby is 6 months old is it taken to its parents' room for short visits of an hour at a time. With increasing age the length of the visit may be extended. As a young child he may visit his parents' room whenever he wishes during the day, but is expected to return to the children's house before bedtime. In practice, this turns out to be an evening visit, typically of 2 hours or so, since the child is in school and the parents are working during the day. They may also spend weekends together, however.

In effect, socialization is the responsibility of a succession of nurses and teachers to whom the child relates as he moves through his childhood in a series of children's houses. The attitudes and values and specific competencies of the child are the direct responsibility of these teachers. Spiro notes that parents have important psychological functions for their children, providing key identification models and forms of emotional security, so that the child does typically become as attached to his own parents as is true in other societies. In this sense, the "socialization" and "security-giving" functions of the family are somewhat separated in the kibbutzim example, with the parents participating in one (security-giving) much more than in the other (socialization).

Research findings by Rabin (1958, 1965) indicate that children reared in kibbutzim, while they may appear slightly retarded in some aspects of development in the early months, do not appear in any way retarded intellectually, or hampered in their personality development as they grow older. The hints of possible early retardation is attributed by Rabin to less stimulation than would ordinarily be provided the infant in ordinary family living; but if anything, the findings on older children suggest a higher degree of emotional maturity and superior ego strength, compared with family-reared children.

Questions on the depth of the emotional life of kibbutz-reared children remain an issue, and some scholars argue that a more or less intense emotional relationship with a specific mother figure

The children of the kibbutz do not share a common res
with their parents, nor do parents have special responsibilit
the economic well-being of their children any more than tl
for all children of the kibbutz. As we noted previously, ch
live in special children's homes, where they are cared fc
educated by nurses and teachers with special training for
duties.

As described by Spiro (1971), a kibbutz couple lives
single room that serves as a combination bedroom and !
area. Meals are eaten in the communal dining room. Botl
man and the woman have work responsibilities in the kib
which might include a variety of service occupations (fo
ample, clerical, food preparation, educational, laundry, an
on) as well as agricultural work. The couple relationship typi
develops after graduation from high school, at which time
butz members are living in small private rooms.

If two young people decide they love each other (and !
sexual activities are not closely regulated while this decisio
being made) they ask for permission to move to a larger, j
room. Upon moving into the joint room, and by virtue of
move, they are recognized by the kibbutz community as a cou
No other formal marriage ceremony occurs until, usually, at
the time their first child is born, which marriage is in accorda
with the laws of the state and for the protection of the right:
the child, since children born out of wedlock have no legal rig
In this couple arrangement the woman retains her maiden na
and an equal status legally and socially with the man. Marria
in such a system, is essentially an institutionalized provision
sexual and intimacy needs, and the relatively clear-cut distincti
between "single" and "married" which characterizes our socie
does not seem to prevail in the kibbutz.

Similarly, the rather sharply defined categorization of peop
as "parents" or "childless" seems less significant for the kibbu
couple, since their role in the socializing of their children is n
much greater than that of other adults, and certainly less tha
that of the nurses and teachers in the children's houses. The ii
fant is placed in an infant's house when the mother returns fro

must be experienced if a child is to become capable of developing a strong emotional relationship later with other people.

Some research studies in this country have been carried out on children whose experience in infancy subjected them to the care of "multiple" mothers, for example, in a university home management house. Since some theories of personality development have implied the necessity of a one-to-one mother-infant relationship to ensure healthy growth, the hypothesis was tested empirically in a series of investigations with Iowa children (Gardner, et al. 1961).

In the physical, mental, emotional, and personality development of children who had resided in home management houses and been cared for by large numbers of "mothers" over a period of months, no discernible ill effects could be found at any age up to the preadolescent period, the latest age at which data were obtained. Traditional beliefs that an infant must be mothered by one consistent "mother figure," and more especially, that the person providing the mothering must be the biological parent of the child, seem not to be supported by these research findings.

The question of the social and psychological well-being of infants and children in American communes, however, is somewhat different and more difficult to answer. In the first place, the modern American experiences with communes reflect a multitude of variables not to be found in, for example, the Israeli kibbutz.

American communes, as they have developed in the middle and latter part of the present century, do not represent a coherent life style which can be described readily with certain common features, but rather a welter of "styles" having in common mostly the single feature of rejection (at least at the superficial level) of the mainstream, "establishment" style of living. In most instances the modern commune is more readily described by what it rejects than by what it aspires to.

Child-rearing practices of communal families in America have been investigated by Berger, et al. (1971), mostly as they have been established in Northern California. These investigators have lived as participant-observers in the communes with the knowledge and acceptance of commune dwellers. They report that much of the child-rearing in such settlements is deliberate and quite self-conscious, which reflects the fact that the basic motivation to "drop out" of the mainstream of society and establish an alternate life style was their rejection of their own personal child-rearing experiences.

There is generally an attempt to create a kinship spirit among children that extends beyond immediate nuclear family ties, and to use this spirit as a basis for appeal to the child in an effort to provide social regulation of behavior (for example, "Janey is your sister; don't abuse her"). The nuclear family (man and woman and their child or children) is visible in such communes, however, in many variations, as expressed by Berger, et al.: ". . . everything from legally married spouses-plus-their-children, to unmarried couples with and without children, to couples in which the male partner is not the father of the female's child, and even to one case in which the female partner is not the mother of the male's child" (Berger, et al. 1971, p. 512–513).

These investigators have found, thus far, an informal understanding among commune dwellers that biological mothers have primary responsibility for the care of their nursing infants, but that not only older children, but infants as well, left around the communal house will be cared for by whatever adults or older children are around, without the need for any formal "babysitting" arrangements. Some ambiguity has been observed with respect to adult responsibilities for older children, and apparently a good deal of variation on that score exists from one settlement to another.

There is an emphasis on natural childbirth, and sometimes a ritual celebration of life on the occasion of a birth in the community. Fathers are often encouraged to participate in the birth of the child. Children are seen as needing essential freedom from the constraints that limit creativity and individuality, which of course presents the age-old problem of finding a reasonable balance between conformity, on the one hand, and freedom to destroy the social group within which one exists, on the other.

The following excerpt from Berger, et al. seems to convey this issue and the general stance typical of commune dwellers in response to the issue:

> . . . life has a habit of resolving everything, even dilemmas, and the communards cope with their problem in *ad hoc* ways every day, sometimes preferring to impale themselves on their dilemma rather than applying severe sanctions to recalcitrant children as a matter of principle, and sometimes making efforts toward creating a model of child rearing which encourages the child's desire to "do his own thing," even if such socialization undermines the sources of recruitment to the commune's next generation. Most communes, it seems at this point, if faced with a choice between training the next generation of communards and training children to be free, would opt for the latter. In the terminology of the communes, there are strong pressures on adults not "to lay their own heavy trip" on the children, and only light pressures toward conformity are exercised, as exemplified by the appeal to kinship in settling aggression among children, or by refusal of a father to forcibly take an adult's smoking pipe away from his sixteen-month-old son, who insisted upon smoking it, and would not give it up even after he was coughing on the smoke. The father applied only the gentlest pressure, under the apparent assumption that the child would willingly give it up after a little while (an assumption that turned out to be correct). (Berger, et al. 1971, p. 515)

The main contrast in child-rearing experiences which we have drawn thus far between the child in the nuclear family and the child in one or another variation on living styles is the relative focus of child-rearing responsibilities on the part of parents vs. a more diffuse set of responsibilities distributed among adult members of a community. Our best conclusion to date is that greater diffusion of child-rearing experiences does not, per se, result in social or psychological harm to the child.

In many of the experimental styles in existence in America, however, the factor of diffusion of child-rearing responsibilities is mixed with a variety of other variables which make it difficult to sort out specific sources of effects on children. Many of the communes in operation, for example, are drug cultures, and the long-term effects on a child of exposure to a drug culture are yet to be determined in any objective manner. Because of the legal issues surrounding drug use, and the difficulty in acquiring objective reports for use in scientific investigations, there will remain many unanswered questions pertaining to the effects on children for some time to come.

While the devastating effects of drug usage in the lives of individuals can readily be documented in the files of medical clinics, jails, and hospitals, the matter of the effects on a child reared in a community in which hallucinogenic drugs, for example, are openly used by adults remains unanswered. The analogy to being reared in a society in which alcohol is openly used by adults is not entirely accurate, since in the case of drug use, the drugs are more likely to be regarded as an integral expression of rejection of "straight" life, and used by individuals with full awareness of the illegality of their use in the larger society.

Other variables, too, may be inextricably mixed with the obvious differences between "standard" child-rearing experiences and the experimental variations on these. Massive rejection of industrial-technical values; of values pertaining to private ownership of property; of values pertaining to use of time; of the traditional economic base of the mainstream of society; and of the educational, social, and other institutions of the larger society make it difficult again to trace specific effects on children to any single source. Attitudes toward food, clothing, shelter, body cleanliness, work, and forms of interpersonal behavior all may be assumed to vary with such subcultural experimental arrangements, and we might speculate that the child experiencing the socialization process in a given experimental community would, initially, absorb fully the values that find expression in that group.

We could also speculate that the child, as he grows, would experience a desire to discover the larger society. With this would come a potential for rejecting the values of the community that socialized him just as surely as his parents rejected the values that socialized them.

We appear to be presently in the midst of rapid transition, and we lack solid answers to questions as to how effective one's early socialization has been in preparing him for social settings *other* than the milieu of his early experiences. Given the probability of continued rapid change and social evolution, the problem of raising and socializing children to live constructively with rapid change becomes a most pressing and intriguing one for the scholar and student of child development.

The child's response to crisis

In the normal course of events, all children and adults experience stress situations that demand major adjustments. Serious illness, injury, death of a family member, separation or divorce of parents, a move from one part of the country to another or merely from one home to another, loss of income on the part of a father, and so on—all these and many other situations represent events to which people must respond. It is the role of the family in providing (1) support for the child in times of crisis, and (2) preparation for handling crises that will occur later in the child's life that is our immediate concern.

Separation from one's parents can be, for the young child, a stressful situation, understandable as a loss of the familiar, trustworthy source of nurturance. Gewirtz (1961) describes the process in terms of learning theory: Maternal separation involves an abrupt and continuing change in what was earlier a satisfactory pattern of availability of cues and reinforcing stimuli. Freud and Burlingham (1944) reported that in London during World War II, children who were separated from their families and placed in residential nurseries outside the city suffered more disturbance from this event than those who remained and were subject to the stress of the Nazi aerial bombardment.

Such findings suggest an important underlying principle: *a child can learn to tolerate and live productively with a wide range of stressful or threatening events provided he has the proper psychological support from the important people in his life.*

Perhaps more important than any specific disturbance or trauma in the life of a child is the gradual accumulation of learning (1) what constitutes "crises" in life, and (2) what resources and strategies are available to cope with crisis situations. In both of these kinds of learning, the family plays a key role for the child.

Parents, through example and through communication of their own attitudes, can define the inevitable stressful events of life as being "too much to cope with," on the one hand, or as "problems to be solved," on the other. They exhibit varying degrees of confidence in the child's gradually increasing ability to solve his own problems.

There is a kind of self-fulfilling prophecy operating in some families where parents treat young children as if they were incapable of coping with any problems, large or small, and in the process of protecting them against any and all threats, succeed in preventing their children from developing a reasonable degree of autonomy and confidence in their own ability to deal with stress.

The gradual accumulation of experience in coping with increasingly difficult situations has been thought of by some authorities as analogous to the development of immunity, in that the process reduces the child's vulnerability to the overwhelming effects of major crises when they do occur—as they inevitably will.

Summary

The family may be viewed as a unit of interacting personalities striving to use their varied resources to satisfy individual and group needs. The traditional functions of the family—economic, reproductive, status-conferring, socializing, and security-giving—are gradually being modified. There is relatively greater emphasis on the family as a unit that plays the major role in meeting the personal needs of all its members, but especially its dependent children. The family not only satisfies children's needs and thus provides a basis for healthy personality development but also operates to create and modify needs.

Home atmosphere and the degree of psychological maturity of parents seem to be primary factors in child behavior and development. Much of the child's behavior is learned from parents through the vital process of identification. We are beginning to view the family in terms of interaction processes, in which the impact of children on their parents is as vital a consideration as the effects of parents on children. In this view, a child may play a role in determining the kind of mothering he receives, for example, because of the special combination of qualities that he brings to the mother-child interaction process.

Current experimentation with nontraditional family forms has implications for child-rearing and the development of personality, some of which can only be speculated on until adequate research investigations have been carried out. However, the form or structure of the family can vary greatly within rather broad limits, evidently, without necessarily bringing psychological damage to a child.

References

Baldwin, A. L. "The Effects of Home Environment on Nursery School Behavior." *Child Development* 20 (1949) 49–61.

Bandura, A. "The Role of Modeling Processes in Personality Development." In Hartup, W., and Smothergill, N., eds. *The Young Child: Reviews of Research*. Washington, D.C.: National Association for the Education of Young Children, 1967, pp. 42–58.

Bayley, N. "Development of Mental Abilities." In Mussen, P., ed. *Carmichael's Manual of Child Psychology*. 3rd ed., vol. 1. New York: Wiley, 1970, pp. 1163–1209.

Becker, W. C. "Consequences of Different Kinds of Parental Discipline." In Hoffman, M. L., and Hoffman, L. W., eds. *Review of Child Development Research*. Vol. 1. New York: Russell Sage Foundation, 1964, pp. 169–208.

Berger, B., et al. "Child-Rearing Practices of the Communal Family." In Skolnick, A. S., and Skolnick, J. H., eds. *Family in Transition*. Boston: Little, Brown, 1971, pp. 509–523.

Bowlby, J. *Child Care and the Growth of Love*. London: Penguin Books, 1961.

Burgess, E. W., and Locke, H. J. *The Family*. 2nd ed. New York: American Book, 1953.

Freud, A., and Burlingham, D. T. *Infants Without Families*. New York: International Universities Press, 1944.

Gardner, D. B., Hawkes, G. R., and Burchinal, L. G. "Noncontinuous Mothering in Infancy and Development in Later Childhood." *Child Development* 32 (1961) 225–234.

Gewirtz, J. L. "A Learning Analysis of the Effects of Normal Stimulation, Privation and Deprivation on the Acquisition of Social Motivation and Attachment." In Foss, B. M., ed. *Determinants of Infant Behavior*. New York: Wiley, 1961, pp. 213–303.

Gewirtz, J. L., and Stingle, K. G. "The Learning of Generalized-Imitation as the Basis for Identification." *Psychological Review* 75 (1968) 374–397.

Goldfarb, W. "Psychological Privation in Infancy and Subsequent Adjustment." *American Journal of Orthopsychiatry* 15 (1945) 247–255.

Goodenough, F. L., and Leahy, A. M. "The Effect of Certain Family Relationships on the Development of Personality." *Journal of Genetic Psychology* 34 (1927) 45–72.

Gordon, J. E., and Smith, E. "Children's Aggression, Parental Attitudes, and the Effects of an Affiliation-Arousing Story." *Journal of Personality and Social Psychology* 1 (1965) 654–659.

Hartup, W. W., and Coates, B. "The Role of Imitation in Childhood Socialization." In Hoppe, R. A., Milton, G. A., and Simmel, E. C., eds. *Early Experiences and the Processes of Socialization.* New York: Academic Press, 1971, pp. 109–142.

Hess, R. D., and Shipman, V. "Early Experience and the Socialization of Cognitive Modes in Children." *Child Development* 36 (1965) 869–886.

Hunt, J. McV. *Intelligence and Experience.* New York: Ronald Press, 1961.

Orlansky, H. "Infant Care and Personality." *Psychological Bulletin* 46 (1949) 1–48.

Piaget, J. *Play, Dreams, and Imitation in Childhood.* New York: Norton, 1951.

Rabin, A. I. "Some Psychosexual Differences Between Kibbutz and Non-Kibbutz Israeli Boys." *Journal of Projective Techniques* 22 (1958) 328–332.

———. *Growing up in the Kibbutz.* New York: Springer, 1965.

Radke, M. "Relation of Parental Authority to Children's Behavior and Attitudes." *University of Minnesota Institute of Child Welfare Monographs,* no. 22 (1946).

Ribble, M. *The Rights of Infants.* New York: Columbia University Press, 1943.

Sears, R. R., Maccoby, E. H., and Levin, H. *Patterns of Child Rearing.* White Plains, N.Y.: Row, Peterson, 1957.

Shoben, E. J. "The Assessment of Parental Attitudes in Relation to Child Adjustment." *Genetic Psychology Monographs* 39 (1949) 103–148.

Spiro, M. "The Israeli Kibbutz." In Skelnick, A. S., and Skelnick, J. H., eds. *Family in Transition.* Boston: Little, Brown, 1971, pp. 501–508.

Spitz, R. "Anaclitic Depression." *Psychoanalytic Studies of the Child* 2 (1946) 313–342.

Toffler, A. *Future Shock.* New York: Bantam Books, 1970.

Watson, G. "Some Personality Differences in Children Related to Strict or Permissive Parental Discipline." *Journal of Psychology* 44 (1957) 227–249.

Winch, R. F. *The Modern Family.* New York: Holt, 1952.

CHAPTER TWELVE
Schools
for
young children

What current trends are there in enrollment of young children in
  school?

What are the major kinds of school programs?

What are the objectives and strategies of these programs?

What theoretical and practical issues exist among modern philosophies
  of early education?

How are parents involved in school programs?

What are the qualifications of the teacher?

It has been traditional in our society to refer to children of ages 2, 3, and 4 as "preschool children." The term has been avoided in this book, because it is misleading. Its use reinforces a misconception that can interfere with the quality of our thinking about both children and school. "Preschool" suggests that we are dealing with a child too young for appropriate involvement in a school experience. It suggests, further, a narrow and anachronistic view of "school" as an institution concerned with competencies unrelated to the child under 6 years of age.

Education can have a deeper meaning, based on the idea that a child's total relationship with people and things can become more productive through organized learning experiences. In this light, a school is an institution for facilitating the child's emerging competence as a human person. In this sense, it would be misleading to think of the child of, say, age 3 as a "preschooler." Indeed it would be more appropriate to say of any society that, to the degree it denies access to the best it knows how to provide its young children in the way of school experience, then it could fairly be labeled a "post-early-childhood society"!

The central purpose of this chapter is to describe some current trends in the emergence of early childhood education, and to introduce certain issues that enter into the planning of school programs for children under age 6.

The need
for school experience

Early education at its best can indeed bring about significant change in the lives of young children. Potentially, these positive changes endure and contribute to later school success and healthy personality development. Regrettably, the progress of schools in the achievement of these positive changes may be impeded by the false issue of schools vs. family life. The sanctity of the home and the rights and responsibilities of parents are not threatened by the emergence of quality educational programs for young children. Nor is it necessary to "choose sides," and declare oneself to be against one institution in order to be in favor of the other. Arguments that have been raised against sending young children to school, based on the false notion that it removes children from the healthy influence of parents at too tender an age, are gradually being replaced by more positive views of the contributions of a school experience. These latter views are based on an understanding of the mutual support of home and school for the healthy development of the child.

The major argument in favor of schools is that they can provide growth experiences that are not otherwise available. There is a substance and strategy to early education along with a special physical setting equipped with particular objects and materials, which are not generally available in ordinary homes. In addition, there is a planned social environment, supervised by a teacher trained in child growth and development. The availability of such a resource represents, potentially at least, a significant psychological support to parents who normally wish to provide their children with an environment conducive to healthy growth.

Trends in the enrollment of children

One measure of the increasingly favorable attitude toward school programs for 3-, 4-, and 5-year-old children is the statistical trend on enrollment. There were 4.1 million children in the 3- to 5-year age range enrolled in school in 1970, which represented 37.5 percent of the population of that age group (10.9 million). Significant increases in the percentage of children enrolled have been reported each year, as shown in Table 12.1. These figures do not include enrollment in day care programs if the objectives were primarily custodial.

Less than a third of the 3- and 4-year-olds were enrolled in programs of public education, whereas the 5-year-olds were predominantly in public education. In 1970, Western states led the rest of the nation by enrolling 44 percent of their young children in preprimary programs. In addition to factors of geography, attendance in schools is influenced by family income level, ethnic group membership, and educational level of parents. For example,

TABLE 12.1.   U.S. Enrollment of 3- to 5-year-old children in Preprimary Programs, 1964–1970 (Numbers in Thousands)

	Total 3-to-5 population	Number enrolled	Percentage enrolled
1964	12,496	3,187	25.5
1965	12,549	3,407	27.1
1966	12,486	3,674	29.4
1967	12,242	3,868	31.6
1968	11,905	3,928	33.0
1969	11,424	3,949	34.6
1970	10,949	4,104	37.5

SOURCE: U.S. Office of Education. Reprinted from *Report on Preschool Education*, published by Capitol Publications, 2430 Pennsylvania Avenue, N.W., Washington, D.C., 20037, 20 October 1971, p. 9.

71.2 percent of white 5-year-olds were in school, while the corresponding figure for black children was 57.8 percent. At the younger ages, however, the figures were different, with slightly higher percentages for black than for white children (14.4 vs. 12.6 for 3-year-olds, and 30.9 vs. 27.1 for 4-year-olds).

While these figures do not seem large in relation to the total number of children in the population, the trend is a striking one. It appears to reflect both the increasing availability and visibility of schools for young children, and increasingly favorable attitudes toward early education on the part of the public.

Growth trends in enrollment are shown graphically in Figure 12.1, using the years 1964, 1967, and 1970 as reference points, and comparing the trends for the three age groups. In this comparison, it is evident that the enrollment of 3's, while still a small figure compared with that for older children, doubled in the years between 1967 and 1970.

Perhaps a major reason for the growing enthusiasm for early education is the increasing public awareness of the effects of early experiences on cognitive as well as emotional and social behavior. Awareness has been aroused, in part, by the high degree of visibility of intervention programs—educational programs for preprimary school disadvantaged children, aimed at improving their chances for later school success.

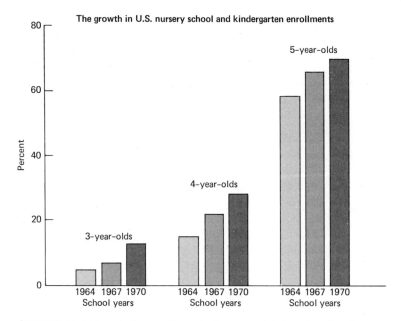

FIGURE 12.1 Trends in enrollment of young children in school. (From U.S. Office of Education, reprinted from *Report on Preschool Education*, published by Capitol Publications, 2430 Pennsylvania Avenue, N.W., Washington, D.C., 20037, October 20, 1971, p. 9.)

Such programs began on a relatively large scale with the advent of Project Head Start in 1965. That program, which has served millions of children and families in the ensuing years, was established as an integral part of the Nation's "War on Poverty," in an attempt to interrupt the poverty cycle, which tends to perpetuate itself across generations. Its central thrust was directed at increasing the likelihood of a successful school experience for disadvantaged children, thus increasing the probability of vocational and economic success for children whose impoverished circumstances too often lead to failure.

Historically, early education, because of its costs, had been available only to high income families. In recent years, more emphasis has been placed on efforts to enroll children from all socioeconomic levels. Instead of viewing such education as merely remedial for impoverished children, or a special benefit for children of high income families, we have gradually come to view it in a more positive sense, as a generally desirable experience that supports the cognitive, social, and personal development of all children. In the words of the Educational Policies Commission:

> The development of the intellectual ability and of intellectual interest is fundamental to the achievement of all the goals of American education. Yet these qualities are greatly affected by what happens to children before they reach (primary) school. A growing body of research and experience demonstrates that by the age of six most children have already developed a considerable part of the intellectual ability they will possess as adults. Six is now generally accepted as the normal age of entrance to school. We believe this practice is obsolete. All children should have the opportunity to go to school at public expense beginning at the age of four. (Educational Policies Commission 1966, p. 1)

More recently, the Education Commission of the States (1971) published a related document that stressed the need and justification for the involvement of the states in a range of educational programs for children under 6, not limited to children of given income levels.

In addition to such public statements by nationally recognized bodies, there has been a general accumulation of information on the effects of early school experiences on children, and high visibility in the public media for programs serving young children and their families. Such visibility contributes to the demand for educational programs, and it appears that the demand will continue to increase for the foreseeable future.

Our changing views of the nature of human intelligence have also heightened our awareness of the need for early education. Hunt (1961) has been an effective spokesman for a revised view of intellectual development, and has documented his criticisms of the traditional views of mental growth as a fixed, static, genetically determined process. Hunt argues that social and cultural factors inevitably participate in the child's cognitive development, and that our failure to provide adequate stimulation to some of our children has resulted in performance and achievement levels significantly below their potential level.

There is limited justification, however, for enrolling children with the sole or major motive of increasing their performance level on tests of intelligence. While substantial initial gains in IQ have been reported for some groups of children, it remains less clear as to what kinds of early stimulation—provided for what kinds of children under which set of conditions by what kinds of teachers—can yield enduring changes.

However, early childhood educators have decried the use of a single criterion, such as the IQ score, as the only or principal measure of the effectiveness of a program. Most programs have a much more inclusive set of objectives for the child. These include a range of subtle and intangible potential benefits, some of them difficult to measure, such as the development of attentiveness, the growth of achievement motivation, the acquisition of more positive attitudes toward self and others, the achievement of a constructive attitude toward school as a satisfying experience, the learning to delay need gratification, and the learning to use a wider range of adult and peer models as bases for one's emerging social competence.

Such qualities are indeed difficult to measure. Furthermore, their functioning in a child is extremely complex; they are affected by many variables in his life. Thus it becomes extremely difficult to show a direct cause and effect relationship between school attendance and the emergence of such qualities.

A somewhat more tangible, if indirect, benefit of early education programs has to do with the discovery and treatment of individual problems of development that might otherwise go undetected. Project Head Start, for example, has been responsible for large numbers of physical, dental, and psychological examinations that would never have occurred in the absence of the program. These examinations have led to specialized treatment in thousands of cases. Early diagnosis and treatment is essential in many kinds of developmental problems, and even if no other arguments could be advanced for early educational programs, certainly this is a substantial justification, particularly in the lives of disadvantaged children.

The nutrition emphasis, which has been a central feature of many educational programs, might also be cited as a positive influence in the healthy development of children and families, both in its direct effect on the diet of young children and in its indirect influence on development of positive attitudes toward foods, involvement of parents in meal planning at home and school, and so on.

Types
of educational programs

The varieties of educational programs for young children which have emerged in recent years is so great as to defy complete description in the limited space of one chapter. There are now excellent source materials available to the student who wishes to understand these many kinds of programs in detail.

These programs vary greatly not only in objectives and strategies, but in quality as well. In comparison with elementary schools, programs for young children range from among the poorest of educational experiences to among the very highest quality to be found anywhere in our society.

The wide range in quality can be attributed partly to the diverse origins of these schools. Many were developed initially as custodial day care services with only marginal educational objectives but it must also be noted that some such institutions have progressed remarkably in incorporating educational components with the custodial services; others have done so to a very limited degree.

Another source of variation in quality is the somewhat haphazard development of guidelines, standards for licensing, and related legislation in the various states dealing with minimum and desirable features of early education programs. Many states have recently moved toward establishing constructive guidelines and standards for schools, and either have codified such standards into state laws or are moving in this direction.

Unfortunately, it is often difficult for the nonprofessional to distinguish among levels of quality in early education programs, and there may be a tendency for parents to identify program quality with such visible features as physical plant, amount or orderliness of equipment, and so on. While equipment, materials, and indoor and outdoor space management are important in the operation of a program, these factors should not be used to evaluate a program independent of the philosophy, objectives, teacher competencies, and degree of parental involvement.

Trends in day care services

In many communities, particularly in large urban areas, there is an increasing number of programs of day care for children of working mothers. Such centers may be supported by combinations of funds from parent fees, gifts and grants, and state and community aid. A few receive federal government support as training and demonstration centers. Some are operated by private industry as, for example, a large corporation which establishes a day care center for children of its employees.

A most important trend, along with the steadily increasing number of such centers nationwide, is the incorporation of child development and educational objectives along with the traditional custodial services. One common variation on the day care theme is a full-day program for children, who may range in age from infancy into the elementary school years. Some of these children may be enrolled in public schools during school hours, and cared for in the day care facility before and after school hours. Others, from as young as toddler age through 5 or 6, may have educational experiences built into their day at the facility. During the day there is usually provision for meals, either prepared in an on-site kitchen or catered.

It has been estimated that the population of children under age 5 in America will increase from the 1970 figure of 20 million to a 1975 figure of 25 million and a 1980 figure of 28 million. If this trend is borne out, along with the parallel trend of increase in the proportion of mothers in the labor force, the statistical demand for day care provisions can only be expected to increase.

This brings with it additional demands for facilities and trained personnel. It is reasonable to expect that the demand for an educational component of day care will also continue as parents become increasingly sophisticated and knowledgeable about the role of early experience in the formation of cognitive and personality processes. Thus, we may assume that developmental day care centers will become an increasingly common feature of our society, and that larger numbers of men and women will find careers in this field.

A related trend which has arisen in response to the demand for child care services is the franchised center which provides for a combination of custodial and educational services for young children. Such centers are operated as private businesses, for profit, and are based on the assumption that adequate social services for young children can be provided by private enterprise as well as by governmental or other public arrangements. Again, the criterion for evaluation of programs should not be primarily the source of financial support so much as the quality of interaction between the child and people and objects in his environment. Only when the sponsorship of a program can be seen to function against the best interests of children and families would we be justified in arguing that program sponsorship should be limited to one or another segment of the society.

In this regard, however, one must learn to be properly cautious in evaluating claims of any sponsoring agent who may have other interests at stake apart from the well-being of children and families. When the profit motive leads to making claims of radical improvement of children's competencies or personalities, one should be properly skeptical.

We might note, further, that the commercial child care center, like the traditional private nursery school, may be limited with respect to accessibility by large segments of the population at the lower end of the income curve. Parents with marginal family income can rarely afford the high expense of fees which must be charged to operate such centers if they are supported exclusively by parent fees.

University-based laboratory schools

Most state-supported institutions of higher education, and many private universities and colleges as well, operate schools for young children as an integral part of their total educational effort. The general objectives of such laboratory programs are at least fourfold: (1) to provide for the total development of the child, usually beginning at age 3 or younger; (2) to provide a training facility for students in education, psychology, home economics, social welfare, and related areas; (3) to provide for parent education; and (4) to provide a setting for conducting research on child development and educational processes.

The relative balance among these objectives varies, of course, from one institution to another. Some, in addition, have day care as one of their functions. In most cases, however, these programs have been supported primarily as research and teacher-training facilities, and in these capacities they have provided a setting within which major portions of our supply of teachers of young children have been trained. Significant contributions to our understanding of developmental processes have also been made through the research conducted in such centers.

These laboratory schools are usually equipped with observation booths, laboratory rooms for research with individual children or small groups, facilities for conferring with parents and, in some cases, fairly elaborate research apparatus and recording equipment, including such features as closed-circuit television capabilities.

Private nursery schools

In many communities it is common to find privately operated programs which declare their primary objective to be the educational development of the young child. Such programs may or may not have a well-developed and highly visible philosophy, which is identified with a particular point of view about the nature of the child and a clearly defined set of educational strategies.

The Montessori school, operated as a private program for

young children, would be an example of such a clearly defined philosophy. Again, the quality of such private programs may vary from the very best to the very poorest in our educational services to children, and the quality appears to be related to the standards established in a given state for maintaining schools.

Such standards vary greatly, but an encouraging trend is the gradual establishment of clearer and more meaningful regulations for the licensing of schools. Such regulations generally cover the professional qualifications of staff, especially of the director, as well as teacher-child ratio, amount of space per child, safety, health, and fire regulations. Clearly the qualifications of the staff become an important criterion for evaluating a given private school.

Cooperative schools for young children

The movement toward the establishment of cooperative schools has gained impetus in many communities partly because of their feature of economy of operation, and partly because of increased parent involvement, which many parents find stimulating and challenging. The unique feature of the parent-cooperative school is that while there is a professional staff employed to direct the overall program and provide for continuity in work with the children, it is the parents themselves—often mothers *and* fathers—who provide many of the services including those of assisting the teacher. Building maintenance, record keeping, preparation of snacks, organization of parent education programs, and many other tasks of the school can become parts of the contributions of parents whose children are enrolled in the school.

Usually a schedule is worked out so that staff duties are shared by all cooperating parents on an equitable basis. By reducing the high costs which may otherwise prohibit a child's obtaining a school experience, and by ensuring a continuing close relationship between parent and school, such cooperative ventures have much to be said in their favor. One special contribution is the continuing opportunity for parents to observe their own and other children functioning in a school setting.

The Head Start and Parent-Child Center

Project Head Start was inaugurated with the Economic Opportunity Act of 1964 as one of a variety of community action programs aimed at alleviating poverty in America. It was activated in the summer of 1965, and almost immediately involved 562,000 children in over 2,500 centers in every American state and territory (Osborn 1966). The program soon came to involve large numbers of teachers and nonprofessional aides drawn from the economically disadvantaged populations.

As Osborn notes, "Head Start had programs as far North as the Arctic Circle, as far South as American Samoa, as far East as the Virgin Islands, as far West as Guam. Children came from rural and urban areas, from Indian reservations and Eskimo villages, from migrant groups and 'the Hollows' of West Virginia. In some counties one out of three children who entered kindergarten or first grade (in Fall 1965) were in Head Start programs during the summer" (Osborn 1966, p. 6). From its inception, the project was guided by a philosophy of the comprehensive child development center, providing not merely educational services, but a range of components concerned with the physical, social, and mental health of children and families:

> The Child Development Center is both a concept and a community facility. In concept it represents drawing together all the resources—family, community, and professional—which can contribute to the child's total development. It draws heavily on the professional skills of persons in education, health, nutrition, and social services. It recognizes that professional and nonprofessional can make a meaningful contribution. It emphasizes the family as fundamental to the child's total development and the role of parents in developing policies and participating in the program of the Center. As a community facility the Child Development Center is organized around the classroom and the play area. It provides a program for health services, parent interviews, feeding of children, and meetings of parents and other residents in the community. (Osborn 1966, p. 8)

According to some authorities (for example, Jensen 1969), intervention programs of the Head Start variety failed when, after a few years of tabulating the results of intelligence tests of the children who had been enrolled, it was discovered that initial gains in performance on these tests did not hold up after the children went into the elementary grades. However, the final evaluation of Head Start is yet to be written; much controversy exists in the interpretation of the statistical data available. Apart from the matter of changing the performance of children on tests of intelligence, we should consider points such as the following:

> Most children involved in Head Start (in the Summer of 1965) received a physical examination and a dental checkup. . . . for many children this represented their first visit to a physician or dentist. Approximately two-thirds of the children examined needed medical treatment, and in the majority of cases referrals were made and the necessary treatment given. The children averaged three dental caries per person.
>
> Approximately 5 percent of the children studied displayed severe behavior problems . . .
>
> In Boston 1,442 Head Start children who were examined revealed thirty-one percent had major physical defects or emotional problems. . . . (including cases of) congenital heart disease and active tuberculosis . . . twenty children had umbilical hernia requiring correction . . . two out of every three required a significant degree of dental treatment . . . ten percent had (severe) psychological difficulties. (Osborn 1966, p. 10)

The role of intervention programs such as Head Start in revealing and publicizing cases of malnutrition in America is, by itself, sufficient justification for many people to have concluded that it has been a positive investment in the nation's children. The large-scale involvement of parents and communities in efforts to support the healthy development of children has become one of the additional benefits of Head Start, the implications of which are perhaps not possible to evaluate objectively, but are most meaningful in the lives of individuals, which have been changed through their involvement.

In 1967, pilot programs of parent and child centers were established, also with federal funding. The aim of these centers, as described by Weber (1970), is to give parents the necessary help in child-rearing and family development so that their children may move effectively into the mainstream of American life. Such centers involve parents and infants and toddlers, although the children are not necessarily served in group situations or "classrooms."

The impetus for such efforts has arisen from the awareness that significant aspects of development occur prior to entry into early childhood education programs, and that there is a need to provide support to parents during the earliest periods of child growth. Similarly, we have become aware of the need to integrate the programs for early childhood with the later efforts in the elementary grades in order to achieve a truly comprehensive approach to the support of child development in America. Follow Through and related federal programs represent one approach to such integration efforts. Begun in 1967, Follow Through attempts to provide for continuity of stimulation for disadvantaged children, which was initiated with Head Start, and carry it on through the primary grades of the elementary school.

Schools for exceptional children

The establishment of school programs in hospitals and clinics for handicapped, disturbed, or otherwise exceptional children has become an increasingly common practice, in part because of the recognized benefits of early stimulation and the feeling that such benefits should not be withheld from a child by virtue of his having a special problem. In some instances the schools are essentially therapeutic and have treatment as their primary objective. The therapeutic nursery for emotionally disturbed children is an example.

In other cases, school programs within larger residential treatment centers provide education and social stimulation for children whose mental or physical condition does not allow them to attend regular schools. Such programs generally provide for teams of medical, psychological, and educational specialists who cooperatively establish a plan for the kinds of experiences appropriate to further the individual growth of a child through use of the classroom, outdoor space, or in some instances bed-based activity programs to carry out this individually prescribed program.

Providing for social development

Most American schools for young children—even those that include a heavy academic orientation—also make provisions for social development, either through planned activities or through free play in a setting rich with possibilities for social interaction. In many instances, materials and equipment are specifically designed to foster social participation. One sees telephones, dress-up clothes to foster role taking, dolls and hand puppets to encourage socio-dramatic play, and even large muscle equipment such as teeter-boards which involve two or more children in an activity.

The child's social development is probably the aspect of growth traditionally most taken for granted as the central objective of schools for the very young. The opportunity to play with others and the stimulation involved in responding to others of approximately the same stage of development is indeed no small matter. The child's increasing ability to wait his turn, to share materials, to consider the needs and interests of others—all represent aspects of this developmental process. The increasing ability to use language as the basic tool for interpersonal behavior is also fostered by the school. Along with this is the general broadening of the child's frame of social reference, that is, the range of people to whom he can relate with a degree of competence and assurance.

The natural flow of interpersonal exchange around the objects and situations of the classroom and play yard provide an infinite number of ways in which social problems can be worked out. The process of working them out becomes an integral part of the daily experience of the young child. It does not necessarily involve serious conflict, although it is a rare day in the life of the teacher if there are no conflicts to resolve! The following excerpt from the record of a child development student, taken almost at random, is illustrative of this ongoing flow of social interaction:

. . . Christie is putting water in and out of a pan by the sink. She takes the pan over to a table. Laura is also playing there. Christie tells Laura not to splash water. Christie goes into the bathroom and returns with paper towels. She dries plates, cups, glasses, and pots. She dries while she walks back and forth to the table. The doll is on the table and she takes it and puts it to bed. While she is doing this, she is talking to Laura. There are some doll clothes lying around. Christie picks them up and puts them in the dresser. She runs over to the teacher and says, "Knock on the door when you come." Christie goes back to the house and sweeps. The teacher comes and knocks on the wall, but Christie says, "That's the wrong door." She adds, "Be quiet; the baby is sleeping." The teacher comes in and Christie tells her to sit down by the table. They all sit down at the table, drinking from glasses and using the salt and pepper shakers. Christie says, "The baby is crying." She gets the baby and gives it to the teacher. Christie begins taking the dishes off the table, and puts them in the sink. She washes them and puts them on the drain board. She gets the soap bottle out and turns it upside down at the sink. Laura helps Christie. They talk between each other. They put the dishes away, then go into the bathroom. They come out of the bathroom and Christie runs up to the teacher and puts her arm around her. Laura and Christie then go over to a slide. . .

The anecdote illustrates a number of things about the role of the school in stimulating social interaction. First, much of the social behavior occurs in the spontaneous, free play that children initiate themselves; it is not dependent on specific "programming" by adults. We should note, however, that a well-planned environment and a skillful teacher make a difference in the amount and quality of social play.

Second, this anecdote illustrates the rather tenuous nature of social involvements and commitments on the part of 3- and 4-year-olds. While there may be lasting friendships in this age group, it is typical to observe transitory and fragmented episodes of social interaction. There is much learning, however, about the ways in which other people respond and ways of entering into and departing from episodes easily, with little anxiety. Sometimes among 3-year-olds, social episodes terminate as easily and as casually as they develop, with no apparent need to "complete" the scene with the formal social niceties observed by older children and adults. The 3-year-old does not seem threatened if his friend departs for another activity without saying goodbye or making plans for the "next time." Other times, however, social episodes on the part of young children terminate more violently in physical explosions of major or minor noise level. One of the features of the school, however, is that any one of such conflicts, constructively resolved or not, is tempered by the effects of many other social situations in which a child learns from the experiences of others, whether he is a direct participant or an observer.

One of the advantages of this early school experience is that the young child reacts so honestly to the behavior of the other children. There is little in the way of pretense or social sophistication in the behavior of 3-year-olds toward one another. Feelings are expressed directly and openly, serving as effective feedback to each other on the impact of one's own behavior. The anecdote further illustrates the important role played by equipment in stimulating social play. In the midst of such settings, social play takes on a delightful spontaneity that tends to produce keen satisfactions. It is good to be one with others in such a setting.

The special competencies of the teacher come to bear on the quality of social play and the learnings to be derived from it. The teacher is alert to the prevention of situations in which a child's social status is placed in serious jeopardy by his own actions or those of others. She is equally sensitive to the special social needs of children of all degrees of social competence, assurance, and skill. She is aware of the risks both of overprotecting the timid child against the active and sometimes boisterous events of her group, or of pushing a child too vigorously in the direction of social participation.

The teacher is aware, also, that she provides both a powerful social model herself, and a potent source of reinforcement for positive social behaviors through the attention she directs toward individual children as they make tentative approaches toward social involvement. Attention, timed properly, gives the child positive feedback that his tentative initiation of a social contact is appropriate and valued. We might note in passing, also, that the reverse seems to be true: the experienced teacher learns when *not* to "see" certain kinds of behavior, as she is sensitive to the fact that her attention to a child frequently reinforces the behavior that is occurring at that moment, and that behavior that is ignored is less likely to be repeated than behavior that is attended to.

Curriculum and teaching strategies in early education

When a child is enrolled in school, often about the age of 3, he brings with him all of his habits of reacting to people; all of his likes and dislikes; all of his fears and anxieties; all of his intellectual concepts and processes; all of his competencies in body control; all of his speech facility; and all of his physical strength, nutritional status, and resistance to illness.

Traditionally it has been easy to think of the school for young children as a place for the development of social competencies which, in truth, it can be. However, the trend of thinking and practice in America has clearly been toward the comprehensive child development center, which attempts to foster and stimulate the child's growth in all aspects of his total self. In one sense, then, the curriculum of the modern school for young children is a set of ideas and strategies aimed at fostering psychological, social, and physical well-being of young children.

Physical well-being is encouraged through a planned environment with ready access to attractive and safe equipment, which encourages the use of large muscle systems and develops strength, skill, body balance, and control. In many centers there are planned health and nutrition programs with provisions for medical, dental, hearing, speech, and vision examinations, with arrangements for referrals for treatment when indicated.

Social well-being is facilitated not only through specific activities and arrangements within the classroom—particularly the natural interaction of children and the socio-dramatic play which characterizes young children—but also through home-school cooperation in fostering and maintaining a healthful social environment for the child out of school.

The psychological well-being of the child implies a variety of considerations, including mental health, positive attitudes toward self, healthy motivation including the capacity to delay gratification, and emerging ability to use one's intellectual resources. The latter includes, in turn, the development of cognitive processes and skills relevant to academic progress. It is in this connection that perhaps the most sharp divergence of opinion exists among professional educators as to the proper curriculum for young children.

Expressed very simply, the difference in view becomes essentially a difference in sequencing of experiences. There is concensus, of course, that when the total sweep of child development is considered from birth to adolescence, every child must develop basic academic competencies, including reading, proficiency in mathematics, handwriting, and so on. In one view, the child becomes ready for the acquisition of such skills through a gradual interaction between maturation and wide experience, development of a large store of intellectual concepts with which to deal with these specific skills, and a generally unhurried, pressure-free atmosphere in which there are few demands from adults for specific performance in any one of the skills at any particular time. Of special importance in this view is the notion that the development of sound personality has priority over the acquisition of specific skills, such as those of reading and writing.

Some professionals, however, equally concerned about the development of competencies and of the ultimate achievement of sound personality are in fundamental disagreement about the sequencing of events and about the manner in which readiness for particular skills is acquired. Their argument, briefly, is that the development of tangible skills, including concept formation, reading, arithmetic skills, and so on, is brought about through specific instruction, first with the simplest elements of such skills, and then gradual movement from the simpler to the more complex through a sequence of stages based on the nature of the tasks to be learned.

This view holds that it is the function of the school to order man's knowledge in meaningful sequences so that the simplest elements become the foundation for the next level. It is held that the proper exposure of children to this sequence builds in them the readiness for each new level. Furthermore, the proponents of this view argue that it is the achievement of tangible skills that provides the essential basis for healthy personality development, allowing the child to experience success, to become aware of his own progress and confident of his ability, and, in general, to achieve a healthy view of himself.

Although there does not appear to be basic disagreement between these two extreme views as to the goals of the total socialization and education process, there is disagreement about the methods and sequencing of experiences to reach those goals. In one instance, the teaching of reading has no place in the initial school program except insofar as teachers respond appropriately to the rare individual child who begins to read on his own. In the other case, not surprisingly, we find teachers actively instructing 3- and 4-year-olds in not only reading, but typewriting, handwriting, arithmetic, and exercises in concept development. Thus the program day of the two types of schools takes on markedly different appearances in the two instances.

But the two points of view described above are just that— points of view. The preceding discussion does not directly describe any particular program. In the following section, however, we will examine three specific "models" of early childhood education, chosen not because they are "best" but rather because they provide vivid illustrations of the variations in the manner of conducting the program.

The Bank Street model

One general approach to teaching the young child has become identified with the Bank Street College of Education in New York City. The approach has been employed in many laboratory schools, private schools, and Head Start centers.

This approach focuses on the personal development of the individual child, stressing the achievement of healthy personality as being fundamental to subsequent success in academic and technical competencies. The teaching strategies involve the child heavily in directing his own learning activities. In an enriched environment, there is much freedom for a child to explore and exercise his options in selecting from among a wide range of activities available to him. A child is encouraged to investigate and organize the materials of the classroom, to establish his own spheres of interest, and to utilize both the objects and the social aspects of the school to facilitate his personal development.

Teachers and parents are vital elements in this model, and the resources of both are seen as supports for the child's efforts to organize his own personality. The teacher not only provides for a wide range of sensory, motor, and language experiences, but serves as a consistent adult model to whom the child relates. It is assumed that the child should be able to invest a good deal of psychological trust in his teacher, and that the most fundamental role of the teacher is to serve this psychological purpose.

At first, because of the relative emphasis on personal-social development, one's impression of the Bank Street model is that it does not give high priority to academic competencies in young children. A more careful analysis of this model, however, leads one to the conclusion that its proponents are indeed concerned with academic development, but that they believe this is best facilitated by introducing new tasks only as the child indicates his readiness and interest in them. Higher priority, however, in the initial school experience of the young child is placed on healthy growth of personality.

The behavior analysis model

This approach, also employed in a variety of laboratory and experimental situations and in certain Head Start and related programs, is aimed at teaching the child specific skills by means of systematic reinforcement procedures. Learning tasks are organized in finely graded sequences, progressing from the simple to the complex. The teacher's role is that of a behavior modifier who is trained to reinforce those behaviors that are consistent with the sequenced learning tasks, while not reinforcing behaviors that are inconsistent with or incompatible with those tasks.

Reinforcement may be social in nature (attention, verbal praise, and so on) or of a tangible variety, such as plastic tokens. The latter are employed as a convenient and unobtrusive (when used properly) means to reinforce specific ongoing behaviors without interrupting them, and are later exchanged for "backup" reinforcers, such as a special privilege or enjoyable activity when the instruction period has ended.

Instruction in such a program is highly individualized, allowing a child to progress through a programmed sequence of material in reading, handwriting, or mathematics, for example, at his own rate. A teacher works closely with a small group of children (four or five) for periods of 20 to 40 minutes at a time, consistently reinforcing each child's efforts to master the material. When a token is used, it is accompanied by verbal reinforcement. At the end of the prescribed instruction period, children may be allowed to exchange their tokens for a choice of activities available to them in the classroom or outdoor play area.

There is nothing inherent in the token economy which limits its use to academic curricula. It has, in fact, been employed with marked success in modifying the social, emotional, and motor behavior of individual children. However, its recent application to the education of young children in planned programs has been in an effort to provide maximum impetus to the early achievement of basic skills on the part of disadvantaged children in particular. In this application, the objective has been to foster not only the specific competencies necessary for school success, but a generally positive attitude toward the school situation and toward oneself as an able learner, prior to entry into the first grade.

The cognitive-developmental model

This approach to early education has been formulated by Weikart, et al. (1971) and is based on the cognitive-developmental theory of Piaget. Language training and development of the self-concept are recognized ingredients, but the key feature is that learning objectives, stated as behavioral goals to be achieved through learning activities, are derived explicitly from Piagetian concepts.

The curriculum is essentially intellectual, that is, grounded in concept formation processes. A child's level of performance must be determined so that materials and experiences can be arranged for him in a sequential fashion, supporting his progress from the simple to the complex and from the concrete to the abstract. Again, the teacher has a vital role in understanding the mental processes of the individual child and providing the essential next experiences to further this development. It is assumed that new experiences, to provide the essential impetus for cognitive development, must have a good deal in common with the present intellectual processes of the child, yet be sufficiently new and different to require accommodation on the child's part.

Theoretical comparison of educational models

The models we have described here were selected in part because they illustrate the application of quite distinct theoretical and philosophical foundations which have had powerful influences on the emerging field of child development. The Bank Street model, for example, comes nearest to illustrating a historical convergence of normative and psychoanalytic philosophies, as described in Chapter One. Both of these laid great stress on the epigenetic development of the individual from an inherited "ground plan." Both stressed the timing of stages of personal development and the heavy contribution of maturational factors in the movement into and through each stage.

The normative approach did so in the fluctuating spiral-shaped movement toward maturity through interlocking stages of equilibrium and disequilibrium. The neo-Freudian approach did so in the progressive, dynamic movement of the human person through a preprogrammed sequence of encounters with significant crises, in his efforts to achieve the fruits of maturity—the integrated self. The notion of readiness for new experience, based on the present stage of maturity which is genetically controlled and merely given shape by experience, is fundamental to these theoretical orientations. It is also fundamental to the Bank Street approach to early education.

The behavior analysis model, in sharp contrast, arises from the work of the behavioristic learning psychologists, particularly

B. F. Skinner (1953). Skinner's emphasis on environmental forces and his elaboration of the role of reinforcement contingencies in shaping the behavior of living organisms has become well known.

The behavior analysis model has emerged from intensive and scholarly investigation of the use of reinforcement strategies with young children in relation to a wide range of kinds of behavior (Harris, et al. 1967; Horowitz 1967). But it has been particularly the work of Bushell (1969) in integrating the strategy of reinforcement control with specified content of an academic educational program for young children that has produced what has been described here as the behavior analysis model.

Understandably, this approach is less concerned with hereditary limitations to behavior than it is with the strategies for shaping the behavior of individual children in relation to carefully defined educational objectives. The approach is heavily dependent on quantitative measures; it employs the strategy of counting or tallying the frequency with which a child exhibits given bits of behavior, emphasizing precision, objectivity, and reliability of records of the actual behavior of children.

With the exception of the use of tokens, which may be gradually "faded out" of the program as the child progresses, it does not require the teacher to relate to the child in a different *manner* than she would normally use; that is, she need not refrain from being the warm and responsive adult that led her to becoming a teacher in the first place! However, this system demands that the teacher regulate the *timing* of interactions with children. Since it presupposes that attention to a child reinforces the behavior in which the child is immediately engaged, this system organizes those reinforcement occasions deliberately to maximize the probability that desirable behaviors will occur in the future and minimize the probability that undesirable behaviors will occur.

The gulf between the Bank Street approach and the behavior analysis approach seems vast and impossible to bridge at first glance. Some students see the behavior analysis approach as a manipulation of nurturant, loving behavior toward the child, whereas traditional ways of relating to the child, embodied in the Bank Street model, stress unconditional love for the child. Misbehavior, for example, is often viewed as a sign that the child needs more love, and it is offered freely without reservation. The behavior analyst, however, would reject any implication that he loves children less, but would argue that it is a mistake to reinforce those behaviors that one does not value in a child. In the latter view, one helps the child more by shaping in him the behaviors that will likely elicit nurturant, loving responses from other people—both children and adults—in the long run.

One criticism which has been raised with respect to the use of deliberate behavior-shaping techniques with children is that such techniques seem to work against the development of creativity in a child. If a child's pattern of behavior is to be prescribed by adults, some have argued, it leaves little or no room for inventiveness on the part of a child, and no incentive to employ his creative abilities in exercising options, organizing new alternatives, and so on. This argument has been considered carefully and subjected to research investigations by behavior analysts themselves. Goetz and Baer (1971), for example,* used social reinforcement to *train* creativity in children's block-building activities. They defined creativity as behavior previously not displayed by the child in a specific play setting, then provided specific social reinforcement (favorable verbal comments) whenever a child showed diversity in block construction.

As can be seen from Figure 12.2, the 3- and 4-year-old children in that study did show increasing diversity (creating more new forms) during the periods of reinforcement, and decreased levels of creativity during nonreinforcement periods. Thus the powerful technique of consistent reinforcement of given classes of behavior is not inherently limiting and need not restrict creative action.

The cognitive-developmental model stands apart from many of the issues raised by this comparison of Bank Street with behavior analysis. One of these issues, of course, is the age-old

---

* In a subsequent study, these investigators found that children not only increased the amount of form diversity, but also the frequency of creation of new forms not previously constructed, as a function of social reinforcement. (Personal communication, Donald M. Baer.) See E. M. Goetz and D. M. Baer, "Social Control of Form Diversity and the Emergence of New Forms in Children's Blockbuilding," *Journal of Applied Behavior Analysis,* 1973, vol. 6, no. 2, 73–81.

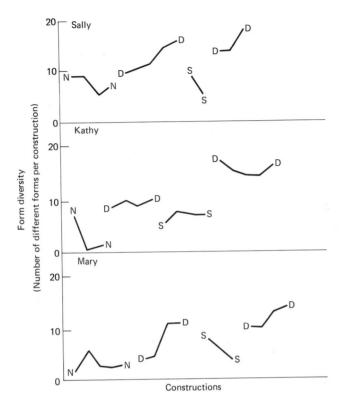

FIGURE 12.2 Effects of positive reinforcement on creativity in
block constructions of three girls. N, no reinforcement; D, reinforce
only different forms; S, reinforce only same forms. (From
Elizabeth M. Goetz and D. M. Baer, "Descriptive Social Reinforcement of 'Creative' Blockbuilding by Young Children," in A. E. Ramp
and B. L. Hopkins, eds., A New Direction for Education: Behavior
Analysis 1971, Lawrence, Kansas: University of Kansas Support
and Development Center for Follow Through, 1971, pp. 72–79.)

controversy between heredity and environment as factors in
human development: the nature-nurture issue. If Bank Street
leans more on the *nature* of the child, and behavior analysis more
on the *nurture* (that is, stressing the role of experience in the

shaping of behavior), then it might fairly be said that the cognitive-developmental view denies the importance of the issue. For the latter approach, there is no question but that heredity and environment both participate in the child's behavior and development. However, it is never a question of which is more important; it is always a matter of interactional processes between present functioning and environmental stimulation.

In the implementation of the cognitive-developmental approach, particularly with disadvantaged children in certain Head Start centers, much emphasis has been placed on the planning of activities that foster the development of logical concepts and understanding the laws of relationships among physical objects. In addition to planning activities for direct work with children on such concepts, which form an integral part of the orderly development of the intellect in the Piagetian system, the teacher also works closely with parents in helping them to support the cognitive development of their children.

Comparison of these three educational models also raises another central issue in educational strategy. That is the issue of whether it is appropriate to employ external incentives, such as candy, tokens, or social approval, as a deliberate strategy in modifying child behavior. One school of thought is that such strategies represent a kind of bribery, and that the inevitable result is to focus the child's attention on the reward rather than on the intrinsic satisfactions in desirable behavior.

In contrast, another position is that for many children the intrinsic satisfactions can be obtained only after the child has developed basic competencies. After a productive level of skill development has been reached there is much greater likelihood, in this view, that a child will find enjoyment in the desired behaviors, but he may need considerable support in the initial stages of skill development. The suggestion in this argument is that when extrinsic rewards are employed as systematic "starters" to involve the child in a valued activity, the sustaining effect of these extrinsic reinforcements may gradually be replaced through the construction of an internal system which enjoys and maintains the activities.

It is clear that each of the three models described here assumes fundamentally different things about the nature and sources of human development. The Bank Street model assumes that development is initiated from within and regulated by internal mechanisms established genetically. The behavior analysis model assumes that development of the significant individual differences in children is regulated by environmental contingencies which reinforce, and thus shape, the emergence of patterns of individuality. As these become established they form the life style of the person. The cognitive-developmental model defines development as the product of an interactional process, in which the presently existing mental structures of the child interact with the environment in an ongoing series of adaptive processes. Development, for Piaget, is essentially an equilibration process which does not rely on the nature-nurture dichotomy. Instead, growth is triggered by disequilibrium, or imperfect "matching" between the complementary processes of accommodation and assimilation, described in Chapter Eight. It is the child's use of energy to accommodate himself to new demands, and the assimilation of the new material to the presently existing mental structures, that results in psychological growth. These brief descriptions illustrate the emergence of educational models and strategies based on significant streams of theory about the nature of human growth. Other educational models might well have been used to illustrate this idea.

It has not been our purpose here to recommend one approach over others. At this stage in the emergence of the science and art of teaching young children, it would be premature to conclude that any one model is "correct" and that the others are in error! Rather, the thoughtful student will wish to understand the principles on which educational models are constructed, and will seek to develop competencies as a professional teacher with full awareness of the existence of these rich alternatives in approaches to the overall task of educating the young child.

At the same time, serious evaluation efforts are under way, the most ambitious of which is the "Planned Variation" research project, sponsored by the U.S. Office of Child Development. This is a long-term follow up study, initiated in 1969, designed to provide information about the impact of various curricula on

Head Start children, and also to follow these Head Start children for a number of years into elementary school and continue to observe their progress. As described by Dr. Jenny Klein (1971a, 1971b), Project Director, it is coordinated with Project Follow Through, a program designed to continue in elementary schools the particular educational approaches, as well as the comprehensive objectives, of Head Start.

While this long-term evaluation effort, now comparing 15 somewhat distinct curricular approaches in over 35 different centers around the country, was intended primarily as a comparative evaluation of strategies for educating the young disadvantaged child, it promises to offer significant insights into the relative validity of these alternative approaches for all children. It is of special interest that the project has selected centers in all regions of the country, in both urban and rural areas, and involves white, black, Spanish-speaking, and American Indian populations.

Thus it is a potential of the project to discover that given approaches are relatively more effective with certain subcultural groups than with others. As an example of this, the behavior analysis model is being evaluated in classrooms in Illinois, Missouri, and Arizona. The Arizona centers are located on the Hopi Indian Reservation, and the other centers include both white and black children. One of the features that characterizes all of the models in this Planned Variation project is their emphasis on parent involvement. This has become an increasingly significant aspect of early education, and will be discussed more fully in the next section.

The central role of parents

The link between home and school has always been closer in early childhood education than in other phases of education in this country. Traditionally, many programs have included parent education as a major objective and have attempted to consolidate the efforts of school and home to provide a coherent set of stimuli and motivational forces in the life of the young child. Realistically, however, even in the child's first school experiences, the cooperation of home and school has often occurred more as a "necessary" thing, based on the school's need to understand the factors operating in the life of the child in order to maximize its effectiveness with that child.

The other aspect of the relationship—actual involvement of parents in the operations of the educational program—has been slowly emerging and is now being seen as a highly desirable feature of early educational efforts. This emerging process has sometimes been hastened in communities where the schools have become isolated from the homes and families of the children they have served.

As Hess, et al. (1971) have observed, there have been increasing demands on the part of parents themselves for active involvement, including having a major voice in the decisions that affect the education of their children. Hess and Croft (1972) regard this as a reassertion of parental rights in counteraction against the historical trend of increasing isolation of the school from the home, which has accompanied the increasing specialization and professionalization of the educator in America.

These authorities along with other specialists in early education regard it as one of the central competencies of today's teacher to work effectively with parents and to organize programs in such a way as to maximize direct involvement of parents in all aspects of the program. These levels of involvement include decision making, parent-developed educational and community activities, and direct participation in the classroom; they are not limited to the traditional periodic home visits by teachers. Hess and Croft (1972) present a number of practical suggestions for involving parents, including fathers as well as mothers, and low- as well as middle-income families.

The physical setting

There is no one right way to construct a building or an outdoor area to be used for an early childhood education program. Weather and climate considerations, and the natural surroundings which offer special features for outdoor activities, represent major considerations. The size and complexity of the building will be determined in part by considerations of economy, the number of children and staff members to be involved, the provisions for auxiliary services including food preparation, and the degree to which the center is operated as an integral part of a larger system—an elementary school, a community service agency such as a neighborhood house, or a church.

Characteristics of the children become a paramount consideration. Safety factors are critically important inasmuch as young children are not sufficiently aware of or able to control the potential hazards of their world to assume responsibility for automobile traffic, heating and electrical hazards, and so on. The center for young children is designed to protect the child from ordinary hazards and to provide a safe environment in which exploration and freedom of movement may occur without serious threat.

Outdoor play areas are generally separated from adjacent space by sturdy fencing material, which eliminates the necessity for "herding" children or restricting their movements with imperatives based on authority and power. The latter point is a key principle, since it sets realistic and absolute limits on a child's wandering, and removes from both child and teacher the preoccupation with setting and maintaining limits. Movement in and out of the fenced areas should be under adult supervision; hence gates are usually equipped with latches above the reach of 3- and 4-year-olds.

The outdoor play area provides for a variety of quiet and active functions. Slides, swings, climbing apparatus, sand boxes, boards, barrels, and facilities for water play are standard equipment. But with imagination and sensitivity to the characteristics of children, excellent use can be made of natural features of the playground area. Trees, rocks, small streams and pools, natural sand, rolling, hilly terrain, and many other natural features have all been incorporated into the plans for attractive and well-used outdoor areas without destroying essential safety features or aesthetic considerations.

Indoor playrooms are designed to take hard wear from active children daily. A tough floor covering which can be kept clean without resorting to a hard wax finish is desirable. Ideally, there is adequate light from both natural and artificial sources. Ventilation and air transfer within the classroom are important. Heating equipment should not present burn hazards. The playroom is designed for flexibility of use and it is helpful to be able to rearrange equipment and furnishings with minimal effort and disruption to the rest of the building. One large playroom which can be partitioned in a variety of ways with low, child-high screens is generally preferable to a series of small, fully partitioned rooms. Even toileting facilities for children need not be completely partitioned off into a separate room; there is no essential reason for making toileting behavior a secretive function in young children.

In evaluating the physical facilities and arrangements, it is essential, of course, to consider the requirements of the licensing agency in the state where one conducts a program. Requirements covering minimum space, sanitary facilities, fire protection, and so on, will vary somewhat, and can usually be obtained from state regulatory agency offices (for example, state department of social welfare).

In addition, consideration should be given to the following questions: Do the facilities promote smooth operation of the program? Do they encourage constructive contacts between children and adults and minimize the need for direct adult control? Do they provide for adequate storage, yet accessibility, of equipment and materials? Do they eliminate or minimize safety hazards? Do they encourage social interaction and eliminate needless frustration for both children and teachers? Do they provide for a reasonable balance of sensory stimulation, physical activity, and quiet contemplation? Are there possibilities for dramatic play, musical and artistic endeavors, books and stories, and so on? Do these arrangements allow a child access to a range of animal and plant life? (If a guinea pig or gerbil in the classroom would throw everything into chaos, perhaps the teacher should examine her priorities on physical arrangements or her program values or both!)

In the well-planned program for young children, careful thought is taken for the kinds of indoor and outdoor equipment to be provided. Sturdy, long-wearing, and dependable equipment which is adaptable to a variety of uses is preferable to "gimmicky" items which sometimes appeal to adults but may have limited versatility and durability.

Aside from safety considerations, the basic criterion for equipment selection relates to program objectives: to what degree does a given piece of equipment support the achievement of the purposes for which the program exists? For most modern programs, these objectives are more or less synonymous with long-standing child development objectives in the social, cognitive, perceptual-motor, aesthetic, and linguistic areas. Decisions about the purchase (or construction) and use of any particular item are best made with such child development objectives in mind.

Qualifications and preparation of the teacher

The teacher training program normally includes considerable emphasis on human growth, psychology, and sociology. It should also include work in biology, physiology, and human nutrition. Ideally, it includes work in the fields of family relationships, housing, and human resources. There should also be academic experiences which can help the teacher provide challenging experiences in the natural and biological sciences for her children.

Because of the wide range of developmental rates in children, it is not unusual to find children of 4 who have made rapid strides on their own in the direction of reading. Thus, even though the program may not be one in which reading is a planned part of the normal curriculum, it is most desirable that teachers have an understanding of the reading process.

It is axiomatic that the teacher have a degree of self-understanding, including an understanding of her reasons for teaching young children. It is not enough to be an affectionate and warm person with children; teachers must be motivated by an essential wish to participate in the development of psychological, educational, and social processes of the child. They must be able to grasp the significance of play in the lives of children, recognizing, as Erikson has pointed out, "Play is to the child what thinking, planning, and blueprinting are to the adult, a trial universe in which conditions are simplified and methods are exploratory" (Erikson 1964, p. 120).

These comments should not imply that the young child must have a teacher who is a paragon of perfection in education and personal adjustment. Aside from the fact that there is no such thing as a perfect teacher, it is probably true that what children require for their healthy development is, in the final analysis, not models of *perfection* so much as models of *humanity*. The goal of teacher training is not to take from a teacher the natural spontaneity and human responsiveness to children, but rather to integrate these natural qualities with an additional set of skills in relating to and fostering the development of children.

In recent years we have become aware of the increasing need to prepare larger numbers of persons who want to work with young children. The U.S. Department of Labor Statistics has estimated that until 1980 we will need to prepare annually 23,000 new teachers of young children in order to meet the rapidly increasing demand. That figure should be compared with the 4,400 new teachers who were prepared in the academic year ending in 1968, for example. One response to this discrepancy, which is being supported by the U.S. Office of Child Development, is the preparation of large numbers of persons at the 2-year "Associate" level of college work, and the encouragement of states to recognize the qualifications of such personnel with regular certification programs (Zigler 1971).

Whether in 2-year, 4-year, or graduate programs, it is generally agreed that the qualified teacher will have had a considerable portion of her (or his, hopefully!) preparation in supervised work with children, as well as the academic course work of the kind referred to above. We are also seeing a number of other interesting variations, which may hold promise for the future, including such things as the development of strong paraprofessional programs and the preparation of secondary school pupils to work with young children. It is perhaps in early childhood education, as in no other aspect of American society, that we are seeing possibilities for new alternatives to facilitate the development of human beings.

One essential quality of effective teachers has to do with personal security, which includes self-confidence and freedom from excessive anxiety about oneself. In part, this is a quality that allows a teacher to maintain a relaxed and spontaneous form of interaction with children, sometimes in the face of severe tests of patience and self-control.

Challenges to authority, verbal abuse and insults, and trials of physical and psychological endurance occur in the life of a teacher of young children. While they may not be the standard events of every day for most teachers, they occur often enough to represent a potential psychological hazard for the teacher who is personally not well-integrated or emotionally mature.

One learns a great deal about himself or herself by being a teacher of young children. One also makes a wiser decision about entering the field by being very realistic as to what the profession holds. It holds these personal challenges: hard work, frustration, endless problems to solve, and countless questions as to whether things could or should be done differently since there is never anyone around to provide all the answers to questions posed by children's behavior. It also holds rewards in personal satisfaction, which would be difficult to find in any other endeavor, including a feeling of partnership with parents in a rather fundamental life task—being there to help a child as he goes about the business of constructing a unique personality.

Summary

There is a trend in enrollment of larger proportions of the population of young children in school programs based on increasing public recognition of the importance of the early years in cognitive and personality development. Education components are frequently an integral part of day care services. Early education programs are also found in the form of laboratory schools, private and cooperative nursery schools, Head Start and parent-child centers, and schools for exceptional children.

The traditional assumption that schools for young children have a limited objective in training the child in personal-social competence has been questioned in recent years. Many schools have explicit cognitive and academic objectives as features of their programs today. However, major issues in philosophy and strategy of early education remain unresolved, including those of the timing and sequencing of specific academic tasks and the use of explicit reinforcement procedures in modifying child behavior. A matter in which there is considerable consensus is the importance of parental involvement in the schools—an increasingly common feature.

The teacher represents a significant behavior model for young children. It appears that the demand for well-qualified teachers, both men and women, will continue to increase. In addition to basic competence in human growth and development, and teaching proficiency, it is essential for teachers to have a high degree of self-understanding and psychological maturity in order to relate productively to the young child.

References

Bushell, D. "The Behavior Analysis Program for Follow Through." Lawrence, Kan.: University of Kansas Support and Development Center for Follow Through, 1969.

Education Commission of the States. *Early Childhood Development: Alternatives for Program Implementation in the States.* Denver: Education Commission of the States, 1971.

Educational Policies Commission. *Universal Opportunities for Early Childhood Education.* Washington, D.C.: National Education Association, 1966.

Engstrom, G., ed. *Play: The Child Strives Toward Self-Realization.* Washington, D.C.: National Association for the Education of Young Children, 1971.

Erikson, E. H. *Insight and Responsibility.* New York: Norton, 1964.

Goetz, E., and Baer, D. M. "Descriptive Social Reinforcement of 'Creative' Block Building by Young Children." In Ramp, E. A., and Hopkins, B. L., eds. *A New Direction for Education: Behavior Analysis 1971*. Lawrence, Kan.: University of Kansas Support and Development Center for Follow Through, 1971, pp. 72–79.

Harris, F., Wolf, M., and Baer, D. M. "Effects of Adult Social Reinforcement on Child Behavior." In Hartup, W., and Smothergill, N., eds. *The Young Child: Reviews of Research*. Vol. I. Washington, D.C.: National Association for the Education of Young Children, 1967, pp. 13–26.

Hess, R. D., et al. "Parent Training Programs and Community Involvement in Day Care." In Grotberg, E. H., ed. *Day Care: Resources for Decision*. Office of Economic Opportunity, Washington, D.C.: U.S. Government Printing Office, 1971, chap. 10.

Hess, R. D., and Croft, D. J. *Teachers of Young Children*. Boston: Houghton Mifflin, 1972.

Horowitz, F. D. "Social Reinforcement Effects on Child Behavior." In Hartup, W. W., and Smothergill, N., eds. *The Young Child: Reviews of Research*. Vol. I. Washington, D.C.: National Association for the Education of Young Children, 1967, pp. 27–41.

Hunt, J. McV. *Intelligence and Experience*. New York: Ronald Press, 1961.

Jensen, A. R. "How Much Can We Boost IQ and Scholastic Achievement?" *Harvard Educational Review* 39 (Winter 1969) 1–123.

Klein, J. W. "Planned Variation in Head Start Programs." *Children* 18 (January–February 1971a) 8–12.

———. *Implementation of Planned Variation in Head Start, First Year Report, I. Review and Summary*. Washington, D.C.: Office of Child Development, DHEW, 1971b.

Osborn, D. K. *Head Start: Past, Present, and Future*. Bevier Lecture Series, 1966.

Report on Preschool Education. Washington, D.C.: Capitol Publications, Inc., 16 June 1971, and 20 October 1971.

Skinner, B. F. *Science and Human Behavior*. New York: Macmillan, 1953.

Weber, E. *Early Childhood Education: Perspectives on Change*. Worthington, Ohio: Charles A. Jones, 1970.

Weikart, D. P., Rogers, L., Adcock, C., and McClelland, D. *The Cognitively Oriented Curriculum*. Washington, D.C.: ERIC-National Association for the Education of Young Children, 1971.

Zigler, E. "A New Child Care Profession: The Child Development Associate." *Young Children* 27 (December 1971) 71–74.

INDEX

Abuse of children, 4, 166
Accidents, childhood, 164–166
Accommodation, 116–118, 250
Adaptation, 116–118, 249
Adcock, C., 386
Adoption, 126, 341
Age norms, 11–15
Aggression, 285–286, 306–307, 336–337
Albert, E. M., 319
Almy, M., 41, 60
Amatruda, C. S., 13, 31, 122, 123, 132, 179, 191, 205, 226
Ambivalence, 269–270
Anderson, C. A., 318
Anderson, J. E., 6, 31
Anecdotal record, 45–47
Anger, 280–281
Anthropology and child development, 24
Anthropometric measurements, 149
Anxiety, 281–282
Appetite, 156
Aries, P., 4, 31
Articulation, 204
Assimilation, 116–117, 250
Attitudes, development of, 76, 344
Autonomy, sense of, 272–274

Babbling, 121, 204
Baer, D. M., 50, 52, 60, 374, 375, 386
Baldwin, A., 20, 31, 118, 131, 331, 347
Bandura, A., 285, 289, 326, 337, 347
Bank Street model, 369–370, 372–378
Bayley, N., 85, 93, 111, 131, 146, 147, 148, 149, 167, 179, 191,

219, 226, 234, 235, 262, 288, 290, 329, 347
Bear, R. M., 319
Becker, W. C., 334, 335, 336, 347
Behavior analysis, 51–53, 370–371, 372–378
Bellugi, U., 208, 209, 211, 225
Bereiter, C., 221, 225
Berger, A. S., 281, 289
Berger, B., 341, 342, 343, 347
Bernstein, B., 314, 318
Bertalanffy, L., 21, 31
Biber, B., 221, 226
Bijou, S., 50, 60
Biological sciences and child development, 23
Binet, A., 7, 229
Birth, 96
Birth order, effects of, 218, 334
Blindness, 220
Bloom, B. S., 287, 289
Body proportions, 147–149
Bone. See Skeleton
Bowlby, J., 128, 132, 328, 347
Brain development, 103
Braine, M. D. S., 207, 225
Brazelton, T. B., 98, 132
Breast feeding, 128, 334
Bridges, K. M. B., 124, 125, 132
Bronfenbrenner, U., 266, 289, 307, 308, 319
Brophy, J., 319
Brown, D. G., 285, 289
Brown, R., 203, 208, 209, 211, 214, 225
Bruner, J., 69, 74, 93, 118, 132, 199, 225, 249, 254, 255, 256, 257, 258, 259, 262
Buhler, K., 65

Burchinal, L. G., 75, 93, 128, 132, 347
Burgess, E. W., 321, 347
Burke, B. S., 81, 82, 93, 154, 156, 157, 158, 167
Burlingham, D. T., 345, 347
Buros, O. K., 54, 60
Burt, C., 238, 262
Bushell, D., 373, 385

Capacities
  acquisition of new, 67–68
  loss of, 68–70
Carbonara, N. T., 41, 60
Caudill, W., 305, 319
Cazden, C., 221, 226
Central nervous system, 244
Central tendency, measures of, 55
Cephalo-caudal development, 84
Child, I., 302, 303, 319
Child
  historical views of, 4–8
  modern concept of, 20–22
Child development
  associate, 28–29
  fields related to, 22–28
  laboratory, 46, 359
  professional field of, 28–30
Child rearing patterns, 298–316, 329–337, 341–345
Child study
  behavioristic, 9–11
  cognitive-developmental, 18–20
  experimental, 50–53
  normative-descriptive, 11–15
  psychoanalytic, 17–18
  scientific, 47–49
  statistics in, 55–58
Chromosomes, 71–74
Coates, B., 348
Cognitive development, pattern of, 248–259
Cognitive-developmental model, 371–378
Cognitive style, 259–261

Cohen, D. H., 41, 60
Coleman, J. S., 316, 319
Communes, 338–345
Competitiveness, 297
Complexity, changes in, 66–67
Conception, 71
Concrete operations, 252
Conditioning
  classical, 77
  instrumental, 79–80
Conflict, 16–17, 316–318
Conservation, 252–253
Convergent thinking, 237
Cooper, A. A., 5
Cooperative schools, 360
Correlation, coefficient of, 57–58
Creativity, 332, 336, 374–375
Creeping, 112
Crisis, response to, 345–346
Critical periods, 67–68
Croft, D. J., 379, 386
Culture
  definition, 294–298
  intelligence tests and, 236
  role in development, 296–297
Curriculum in early education, 367–378

Darwin, C., 6
Davis, E. A., 218, 226
Day, E. J., 218, 226
Day care, 357–358
Dennis, W., 6, 7, 31
Dependency, 75
Deprivation, maternal, 128, 341
Development
  cephalo-caudal, 84
  definition of, 70, 138
  goals of, 90–92
  inconstancy in rate of, 85–86
  individual patterns of, 86, 235
  principles of, 83–90
  proximo-distal, 84
  sources of, 70–83
Diary record, 43–45

Differentiation, 21, 86–90, 124–126
Discipline, 335–337
Diseases, childhood, 160–163
Divergent thinking, 237
DNA, 72–73
Dreams, 282–283
Drugs, use of, 344

Early childhood education
    curriculum for, 367–378
    enrollment of children in, 351–355
    need for, 350–351
    parent involvement in, 378–379
    physical facilities for, 379–382
    professional field of, 383–384
    teacher qualifications for, 382–384
Eating behavior, 155–158
Education and child development, 26
Egg cell, 71
Ego integrity, 90
Eichorn, M. M., 163, 167
Embryo, 74
Emerson, P. E., 76, 94
Emmerich, W., 287, 289
Emotions, development of, 124–126
Englemann, S., 221, 225
English, H. F., 126
Engstrom, G., 385
Equifinality, 21
Equilibration, 83
Equipment for motor activities, 184–185
Erikson, E. H., 90, 93, 126, 132, 271, 272, 273, 274, 275, 289, 383, 385
Ervin, S., 209, 211, 226
Ethics, in child study, 58–59
Ethnic groups, 239, 315–316
Event sampling, 49
Exceptional child, 363–364
Exercise, 158–159

Experimental methods in child study, 50–53
Eyre, M. B., 184, 191

Falkner, F., 96, 97, 100, 132
Family
    functions of, 322–324
    nuclear, 342
    traditional vs. experimental, 337–345
Fear, 281–282
Feedback, 248
Fetus, 72
Field theory, 15–17
Flavell, J., 83, 93, 118, 132
Floud, J., 318
Foss, B. M., 347
Fraser, C., 203, 214, 225
Freedman, D. G., 73, 93
Freeman, F. N., 238, 262
Freud, A., 345, 347
Freud, S., 17, 18, 20, 31
Frost, J., 263

Gardner, D. B., 75, 93, 128, 132, 176, 191, 243, 262, 341, 347
Garn, S. M., 152, 167
Gesell, A., 11, 12, 13, 14, 15, 20, 31, 69, 86, 93, 102, 122, 123, 132, 179, 191, 205, 226
Gewirtz, J., 75, 93, 327, 345, 347
Gill, L. J., 285, 290
Goetz, E., 374, 375, 386
Goldfarb, W., 219, 226, 328, 348
Goodenough, F. L., 84, 280, 290, 333, 334, 348
Gordon, J. E., 337, 348
Gray, S., 82, 93, 240, 241, 262
Greenfield, P. M., 93, 225, 257, 258, 262
Greulich, W. W., 151, 152, 167
Grotberg, E. H., 386
Growth
    channels, 109–110

Growth (*Continued*)
   defined, 138
   requirements, 155–167
Guilford, J. P., 237, 262
Guilt, 274

Haith, M. M., 132
Hall, G. S., 7
Halsey, A. H., 318
Halverson, H. M., 113, 114, 115, 132
Handedness, 180–184
Harlow, H. F., 127, 132
Harris, F. R., 52, 60, 189, 191, 373, 386
Harris, J. A., 87
Harth, M., 311, 312, 319
Hartup, W. W., 75, 93, 285, 290, 347, 348, 386
Hathaway, M. L., 142, 168
Hawkes, G. R., 75, 93, 128, 132, 263, 347
Head Start, 361–363
Health, 155–166
Hearing, 220
Height, growth in, 139–147
Helfer, R. E., 166, 168
Heredity, 71–74, 81
Hess, R. D., 223, 226, 312, 313, 314, 315, 319, 329, 348, 379, 386
Hierarchization, 86–90
Hildreth, G., 182, 183, 184, 191
Himeno, Y., 285, 290
Hoffman, L. W., 336, 347
Hoffman, M. L., 336, 347
Holophrastic speech, 205
Holzinger, K. J., 238, 262
Home economics and child development, 27–28
Hopkins, B. L., 375, 386
Hoppe, R. A., 348
Horowitz, F., 373, 386

Hostility, 332, 336
Hunt, J. McV., 260, 262, 284, 290, 329, 348, 354, 386
Hurley, J. R., 166, 168
Hurlock, E. B., 154, 168
Hutt, C., 41, 60
Hutt, S. J., 41, 60

Identification and imitation, 205, 278–279, 326–329
Ilg, F., 31, 69, 86, 93, 102, 132
Illness. *See* Diseases
Imagination, 274
Immunization, 162
Infant
   accomplishments of, 109–129
   definition of, 108
   programs, 129–131
Infants of low birth weight, 100
Inhelder, B., 53, 60, 74, 83, 93
Initiative, sense of, 274–276
Integration, 86–90, 244
Intellectual processes, outline of, 244–248
Intelligence
   environmental effects, 239–241
   individual differences in, 235–240
   quotient, 233–234
   tests of, 231–236
   verbal and nonverbal, 230
Intentional behavior, 118

Jackson, C. M., 87
James, W., 102, 132
Jensen, A. R., 238, 239, 262, 361, 386
Jersild, A. T., 202, 226, 267, 268, 282, 290
Johnston, M. K., 188, 189, 191
Judisch, J. M., 243, 262

Kagan, J., 260, 262, 286, 288, 290
Keister, M. E., 130, 132

Keller, B., 73, 93
Keller, H., 242, 243, 262
Kelley, C. S., 189, 191
Kempe, C. H., 166, 168
Kennedy, W. A., 51, 60
Kenney, H. J., 256, 257, 258, 262
Kessen, W., 5, 31, 104, 106, 132
Kibbutz, 300, 338–341
Kimura, D., 180, 191
Klaus, R., 82, 93, 240, 262
Klein, J. W., 378, 386
Kluckhohn, C., 132, 289
Kotinsky, R., 267, 290, 297, 309,
    310, 319

Lambert, W. W., 306, 319
Landreth, C., 184, 191
Language
    beginnings of, 119–124
    comprehension, 202, 211–213
    elaborated, 223
    factors in development of, 215–
        224
    functions of, 195–202
    restricted, 223
    self definition and, 201–202
    social interaction and, 200–201
    thinking and, 197–200, 296
Leahy, A. M., 333, 334, 348
Learning, processes of, 77–80
Lecky, P., 268, 290
Lee, D., 296, 319
Lenneberg, E. H., 124, 132, 199,
    204, 205, 206, 215, 216, 226
Levin, H., 329, 348
LeVine, R. A., 303, 304, 306, 307,
    319
Lewin, K., 15, 16, 17, 20, 31
Lewis, M. M., 119, 120, 122, 132
Locke H. J., 321, 347
Locke, J., 6
Locomotion, upright, 110–113
Love, maternal, 127–128

Lowrey, G. H., 55, 60, 103, 105,
    133, 139, 168

Maccoby, E. H., 329, 348
Martin, E. A., 156, 168
Maslow, A. H., 90, 91, 93
Maxfield, K. E., 220, 226
McCarthy, D., 208, 209, 216, 218,
    219, 226
McClearn, G., 72, 93
McClelland, D., 386
McGraw, M., 111, 132, 186, 191
McNeill, D., 122, 132
Mean, mathematical, 55–56
Median, 55–56
Medicine and child development,
    25–26
Melnick, B., 166, 168
Mental age, 232–233
Meredith, H. V., 138, 142, 144, 145,
    168
Milton, G. A., 348
Minturn, L., 306, 319
Minuchin, P., 221, 226
Montessori schools, 359
Moriarty, R., 165
Moss, H. A., 260, 262, 288, 290
Mothering
    effects of, 219
    multiple, 75–76, 128, 341
Motivation, 17, 266, 283–284
Motor action, components of, 169
Motor development
    guidance of, 184–190
    principles of, 173–178
Movement education, 186
Mowrer, O. H., 215, 226
Murray, H. A., 132, 289
Muscles, development of, 153–155,
    177
Mussen, P., 132, 235, 262, 304, 319,
    347

Needs, 90–91, 299
Negativism, 273
Neonate, 98–108
    characteristics of, 99
    individual differences in, 98
Newman, H. F., 238, 262
Nightmares, 282–283
Normative approach, 11–15
    limitations of, 15
Nossal, G. J. V., 69, 93, 162
Nursery schools, 359
Nutrition, 81–82, 155–158, 356

Observation
    booth, 46
    records, 40–48
    experimental, 50–53
    informal, 33–39
    scientific, 47–54
Olver, R. R., 93, 225, 257, 258, 262
One-word sentence, 205
Open system, 21
Orlansky, H., 334, 348
Orton, S. T., 181, 192
Osborn, D. K., 361, 362, 386

Parent-child centers, 361–363
Parent involvement in schools, 378–379
Pattison, M., 41, 60
Pavlov, I., 9, 10
Payne, G. H., 4, 31
Pease, D., 40, 41, 60, 176, 191
Permissiveness, 332, 336
Personality
    definitions of, 265–267
    development of, 267–287
    infant resources for, 106–108
    stability of, 287–288
    tasks, 276–278
Peterson, D. G., 87
Phillips, J. L., 118, 133
Piaget, J., 18, 19, 20, 31, 53, 60,
    74, 83, 93, 116, 117, 118, 133,
    199, 200, 226, 249, 250, 251,
    253, 254, 255, 259, 262, 328,
    348
Picharello, J., 163
Plath, D. W., 305, 319
Plato, 5
Poisoning, 163–165
Polygyny, 303, 337
Poverty, effects of, 82, 221–223,
    240–241, 310, 315
Prehension, 113–116
Premature infant. See Infants of low
    birth weight
Preyer, W., 6
Proportions, changes in body, 64–66
Proximo-distal development, 84
Psychoanalytic child study, 17–18
Psychology and child development,
    23
Punishment, 324–325, 337
Pyle, S. I., 151, 152, 167

Rabin, A. I., 340, 348
Radke, M., 331, 348
Ramp, E. A., 375, 386
Rayner, R., 77, 94
Reflective behavior, 103–104, 173–174
Reinforcement, 75, 324–325, 370–371, 373–376
Relationship, measures of, 57–58
Representation, cognitive, 251–259
Rest and sleep, 159–160
Restrictiveness, 335–337
Rheingold, H., 75, 93, 219, 226
Ribble, M., 128, 133, 328, 348
Ricciuti, H., 266, 289
RNA, 72–73
Rogers, L., 386
Ross, D., 285, 289
Ross, H. W., 75, 93
Ross, S. A., 285, 289
Rousseau, J. J., 6

Rubella, 68, 82, 163
Rudolph, N. 185, 192

Salapatek, P. H., 132
Sanford, F. H., 71, 94
Scammon, R. E., 87
Schaefer, E., 290
Schaffer, H. R., 76, 94
Schmeekle, M. M., 184, 191
Schneider, D. M., 132
Scientific method, in child study, 47
Sears, R. R., 329, 337, 348
Self
  acceptance, 278
  concept of, 267, 277, 283
  consistency, 268, 287–288
  maintenance, 21
  understanding, teachers, 384
Senn, M., 272
Sensorimotor period, 117–118, 251
Sensory processes, 74, 110, 127, 220–
    221, 241–243
  neonatal, 105–106
Sentence length, 209–210
Separation, 345
Sex
  determination, 71
  differences, 218, 238, 286
  play, 300
  role definition, 284–286
Shamir, Z., 167
Shaw, G. B., 211
Sherman, M., 124, 133
Shipman, V., 223, 226, 319, 330,
    348
Shirley, M., 111, 112, 133
Shoben, E. J., 331, 348
Sibling position, 334
Siegel, I., 236, 250, 259, 260, 262,
    263
Simmel, E. C., 348
Size, changes in, 64
Skeleton, development of, 149–152

Skinner, B. F., 11, 31, 215, 226,
    373, 386
Skolnick, A. S., 347
Skolnick, J. H., 347
Smith, E., 337, 348
Smothergill, N., 289, 347, 386
Social work and child development,
    27
Sociology and child development, 24
Socrates, 5
Solberg, P. A., 154
Speech, 122–124, 171, 202, 204–210
Sperm cell, 71
Spilka, B., 285, 290
Spiro, M., 339, 348
Spitz, R., 128, 133, 219, 227, 328,
    348
Standard deviation, 56
Statistical tools, 55–58
Stingle, K. G., 327, 347
Stitt, P. G., 102, 133
Stone, J. G., 185, 192
Stone Age. *See* Tasaday tribe
Stress, 345–346
Stuart, H. C., 165, 168
Suchman, J. R., 41, 60
Sullivan, A., 242
Sweeney, R. T., 186, 192
Symbolism, 21, 256
Syntax, 213–215

Tanner, J. M., 109, 133, 138, 168
Tasaday tribe, 294
Teeth, 153
Terrell, G., 51, 60
Tests and measurements, 53–54
Thompson, G. G., 184, 192
Thompson, H., 150
Time sampling, 48–49
Toffler, A., 318, 319, 324, 348
Toilet training, 273
Tools, child's use of, 276–277
Trait rating, 49–50
Trust, sense of, 126, 271–272

Twins, 73, 238
Tyler, L. E., 84

Valadian, I., 160, 161
Valentine, C. W., 282, 290
Values, 299
Vandenberg, S. G., 71, 94
Variability, measures of, 55–57
Vision, 220
Vocabulary, 205
Vocalizing, infant, 121–122
Vogt, E. Z., 319
Vygotsky, L. S., 198, 227

Warmth, 335–337
Watson, E. H., 55, 60, 103, 105, 133, 138, 168
Watson, G., 331, 348
Watson, J. B., 9, 10, 20, 31, 77, 94
Weber, E., 362, 386

Weight, 100–101, 139–147
Weikart, D. P., 239, 263, 371, 386
Werner, H. 205, 227
Wetzel, N. C., 109, 133
White, R. W., 284, 290
Whiting, B. B., 303, 304, 319
Whiting, J. W. M., 302, 303, 305, 306, 319
Whorf, B., 198, 227
Winch, R. F., 322, 348
Witmer, H. L., 267, 290, 297, 309, 310, 319
Wolf, M. M., 52, 60, 189, 191, 386
Wright, H. F., 48, 49, 60

X-ray photography, 150–153

Zigler, E., 28, 31, 383, 386
Zubek, J. P., 154
Zygote, 71